LONE WOLF AND CUB

story
KAZUO KOIKE

art
GOSEKI KOJIMA

DARK HORSE COMICS

translation
DANA LEWIS

lettering & retouch
DIGITAL CHAMELEON

cover illustration
MATT WAGNER

publisher
MIKE RICHARDSON

editor
TIM ERVIN-GORE

assistant editor
JEREMY BARLOW

consulting editor
TOREN SMITH for **STUDIO PROTEUS**

book design
DARIN FABRICK

art director
MARK COX

Published by Dark Horse Comics, Inc., in association
with MegaHouse and Koike Shoin Publishing Company.

Dark Horse Comics, Inc.
10956 SE Main Street, Milwaukie, OR 97222
www.darkhorse.com

First edition: June 2002
ISBN: 1-56971-594-7

1 3 5 7 9 10 8 6 4 2

Printed in Canada

To find a comics shop in your area, call the
Comic Shop Locator Service toll-free at 1-888-266-4226.

HEAVEN AND EARTH

子連れ狼

By KAZUO KOIKE
& GOSEKI KOJIMA

VOLUME

22

A NOTE TO READERS

Lone Wolf and Cub is famous for its carefully researched re-creation of Edo-Period Japan. To preserve the flavor of the work, we have chosen to retain many Edo-Period terms that have no direct equivalents in English. Japanese is written in a mix of Chinese ideograms and a syllabic writing system, resulting in numerous synonyms. In the glossary, you may encounter words with multiple meanings. These are words written with Chinese ideograms that are pronounced the same but carry different meanings. A Japanese reader seeing the different ideograms would know instantly which meaning it is, but these synonyms can cause confusion when Japanese is spelled out in our alphabet. *O-yurushi o* (please forgive us)!

LONE WOLF AND CUB

TABLE OF CONTENTS

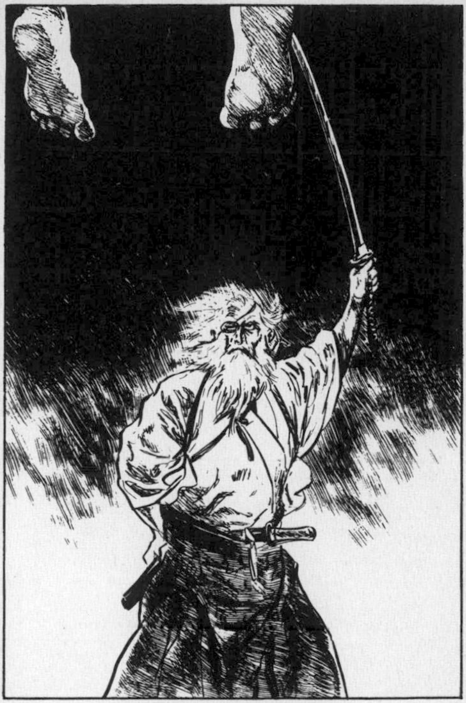

the hundred and eighth

The Last Fistful

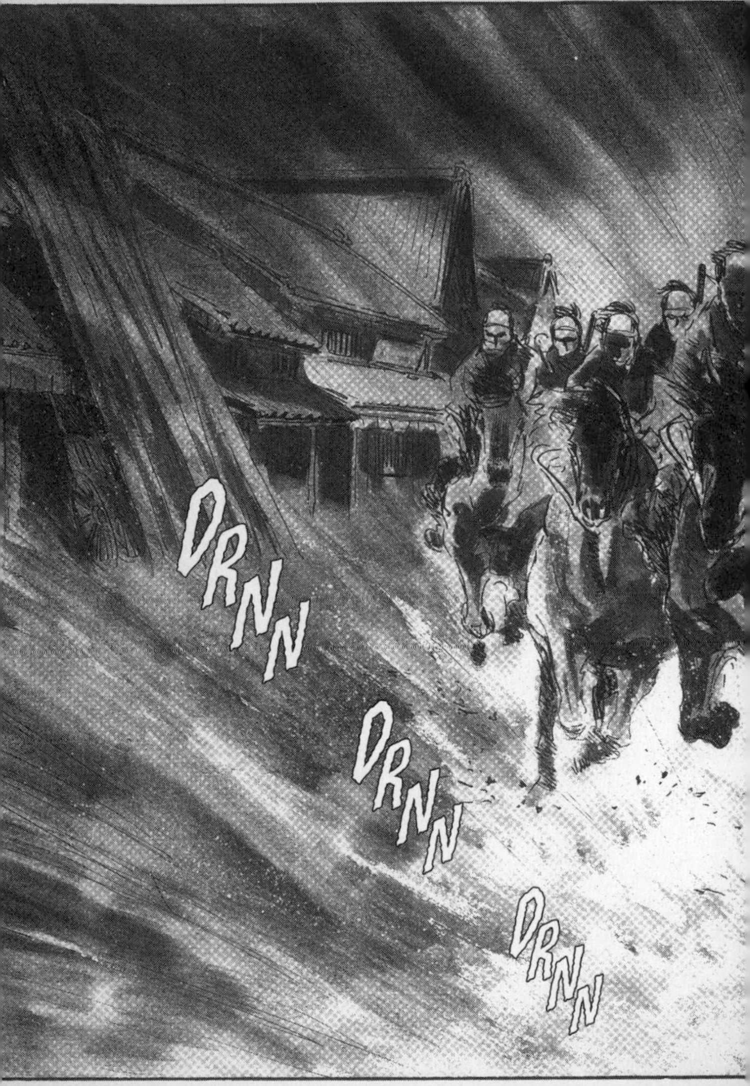
DRNN
DRNN
DRNN

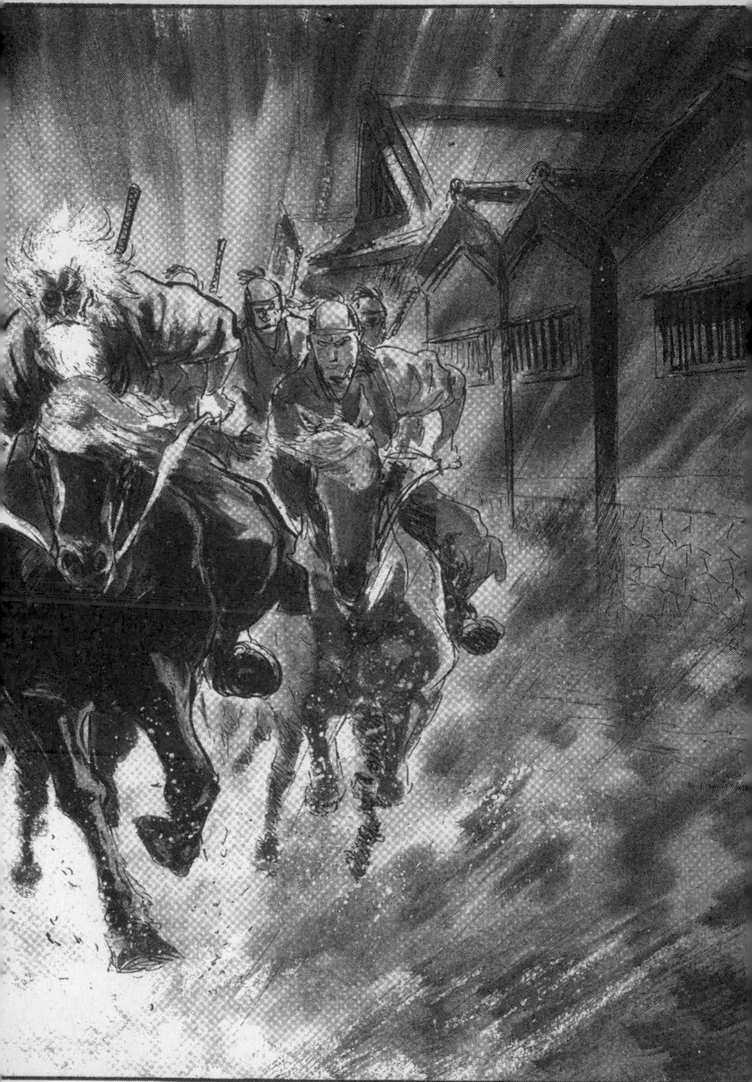

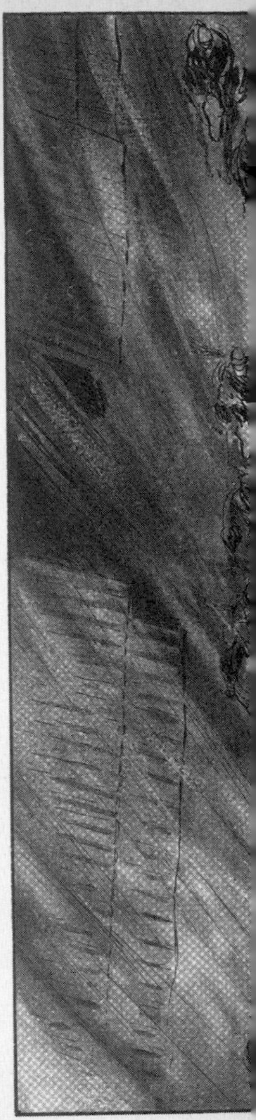
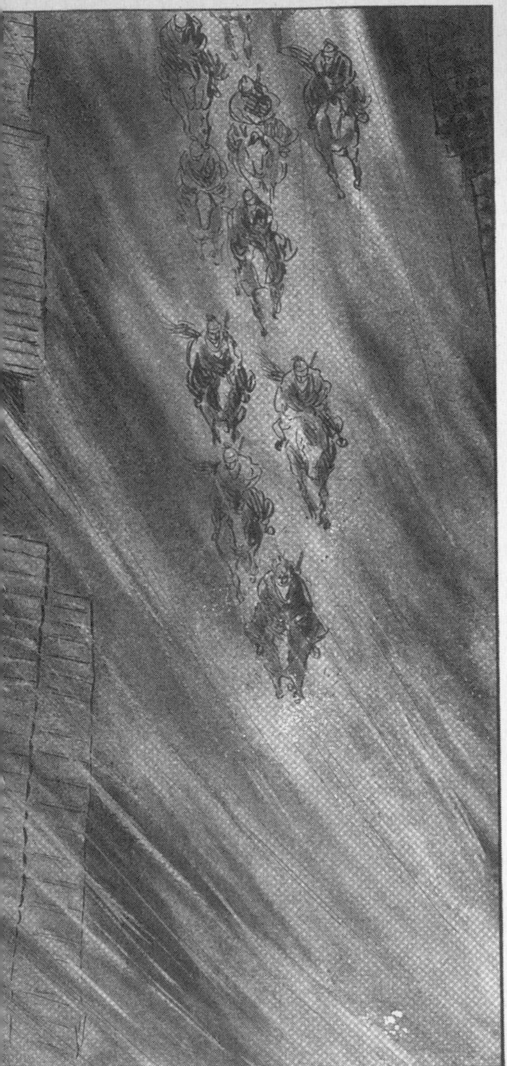

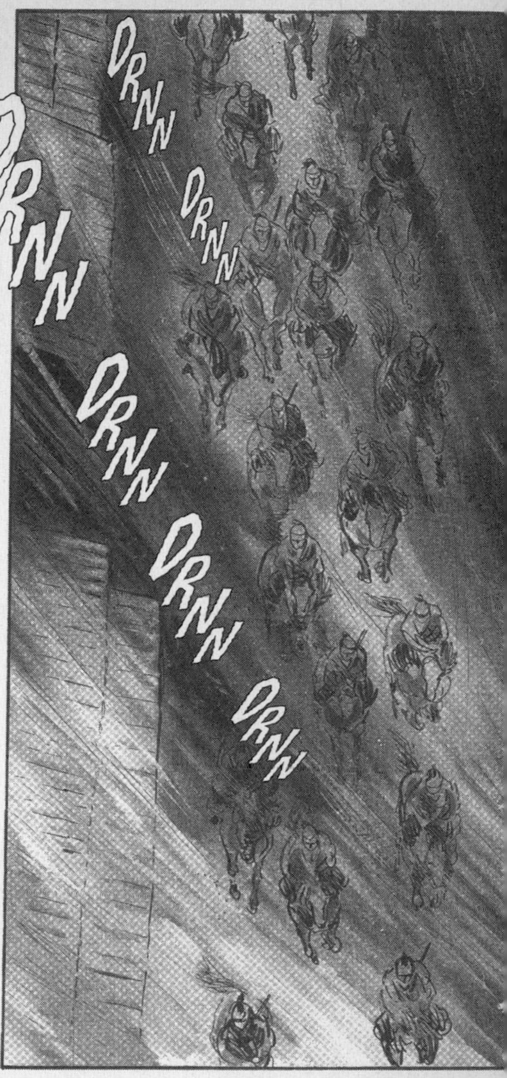
DRNN
DRNN
DRNN
DRNN
DRNN
DRNN
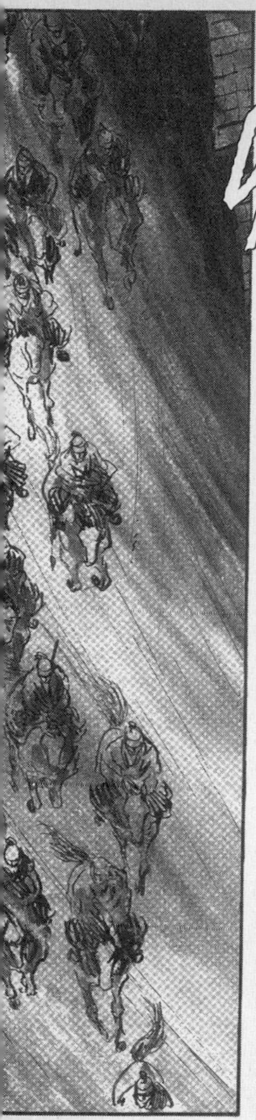

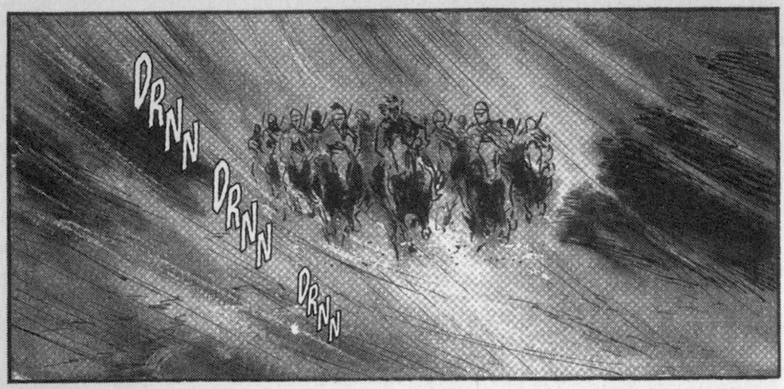
DRNN
DRNN
DRNN
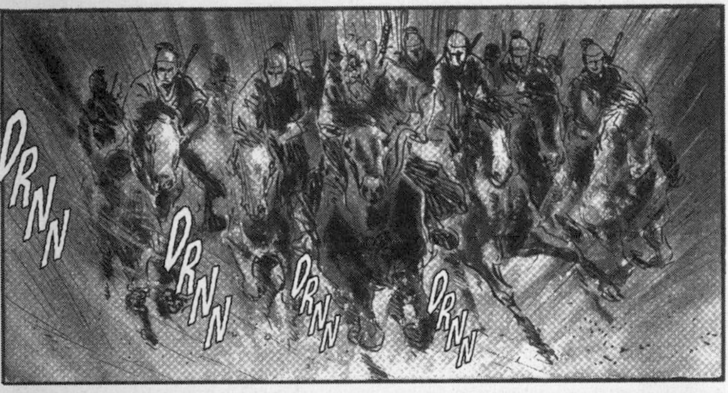
DRNN
DRNN
DRNN
DRNN
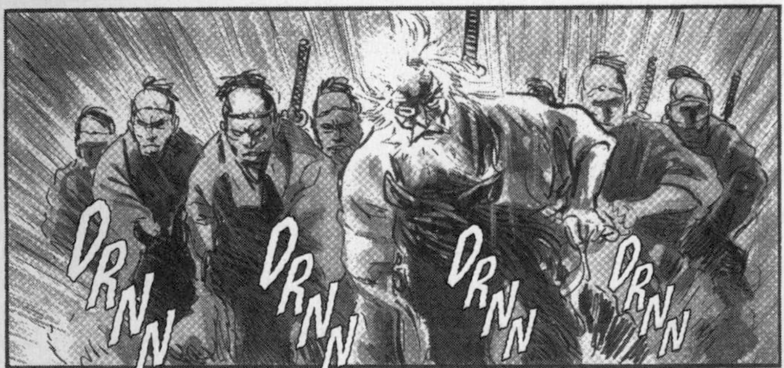
DRNN
DRNN
DRNN
DRNN

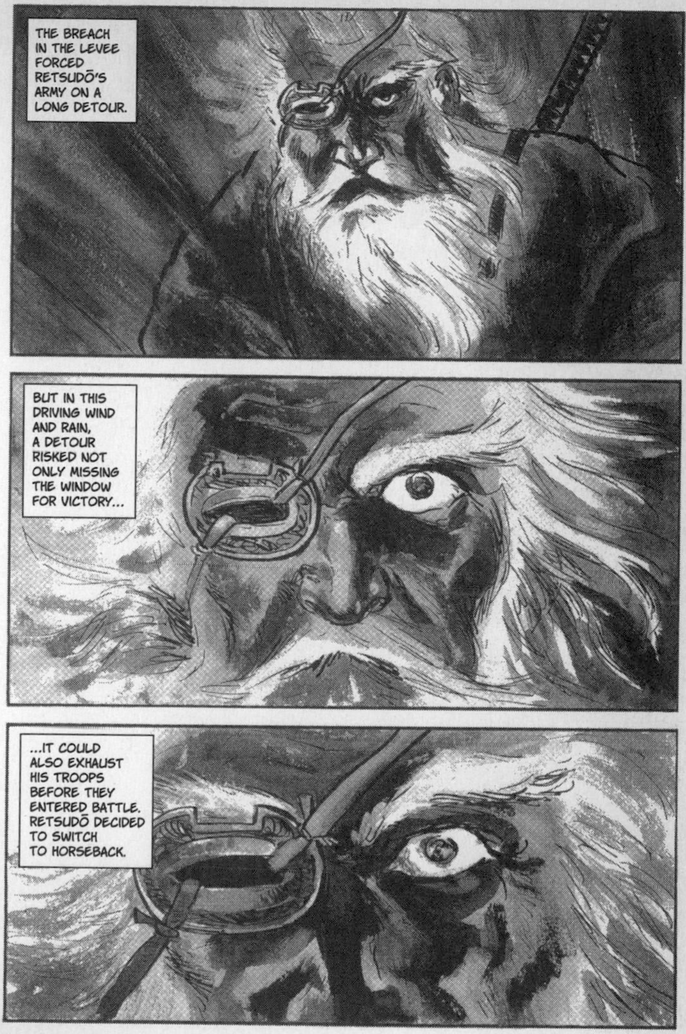
THE BREACH IN THE LEVEE FORCED RETSUDŌ'S ARMY ON A LONG DETOUR.
BUT IN THIS DRIVING WIND AND RAIN, A DETOUR RISKED NOT ONLY MISSING THE WINDOW FOR VICTORY...
...IT COULD ALSO EXHAUST HIS TROOPS BEFORE THEY ENTERED BATTLE. RETSUDŌ DECIDED TO SWITCH TO HORSEBACK.

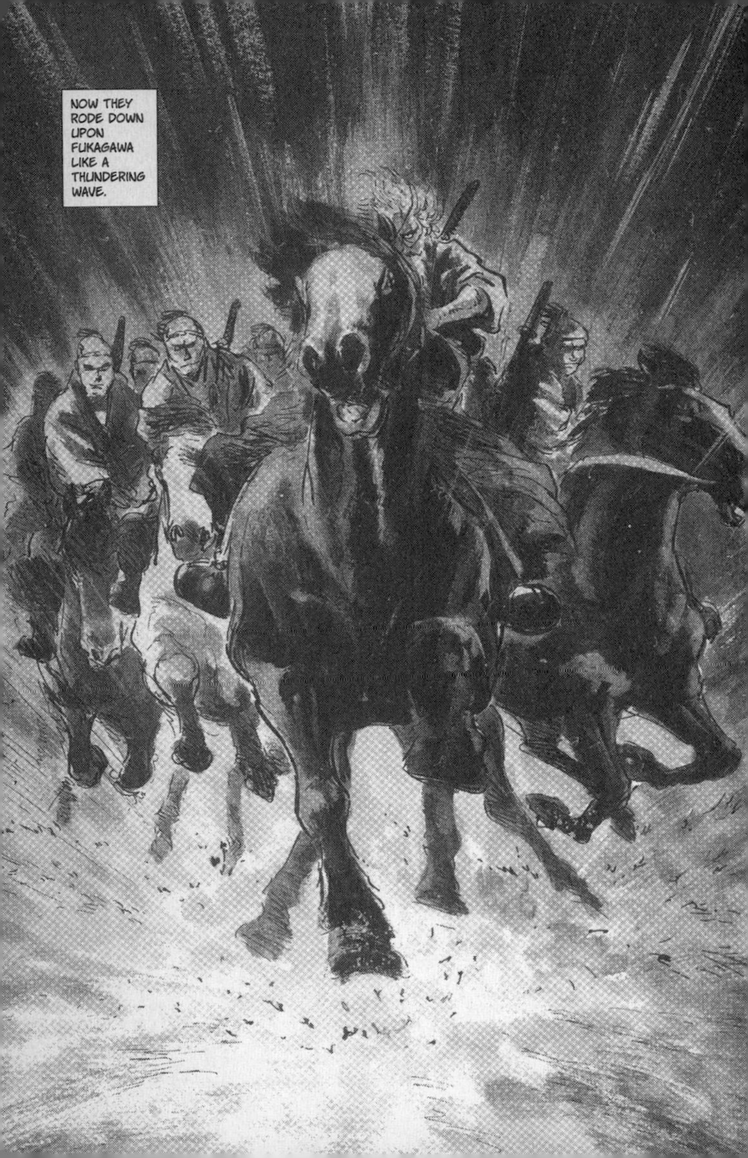
NOW THEY RODE DOWN UPON FUKAGAWA LIKE A THUNDERING WAVE.

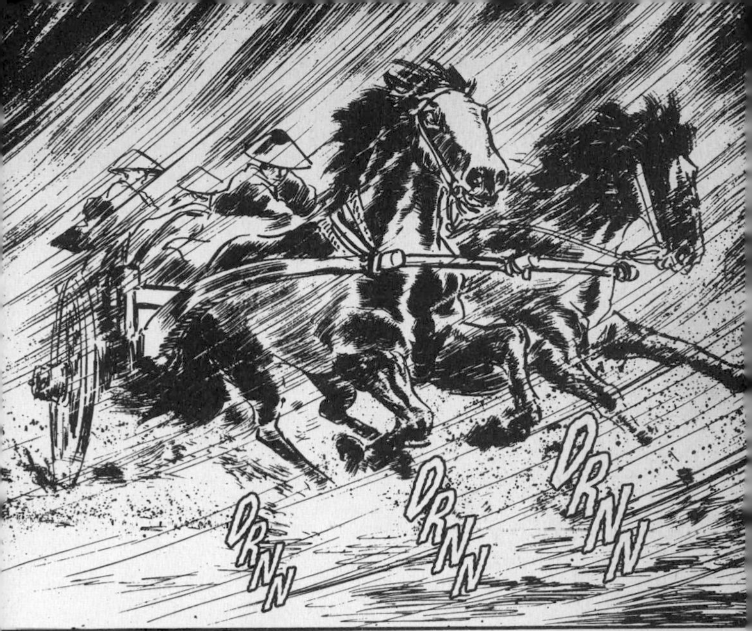
DRNN
DRNN
DRNN

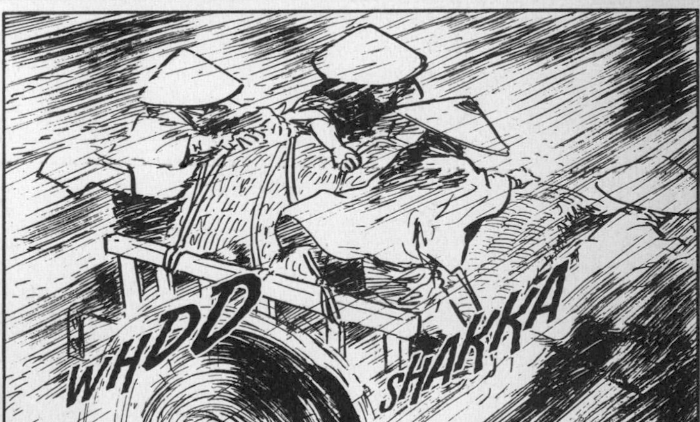
SHAKKA
WHDD

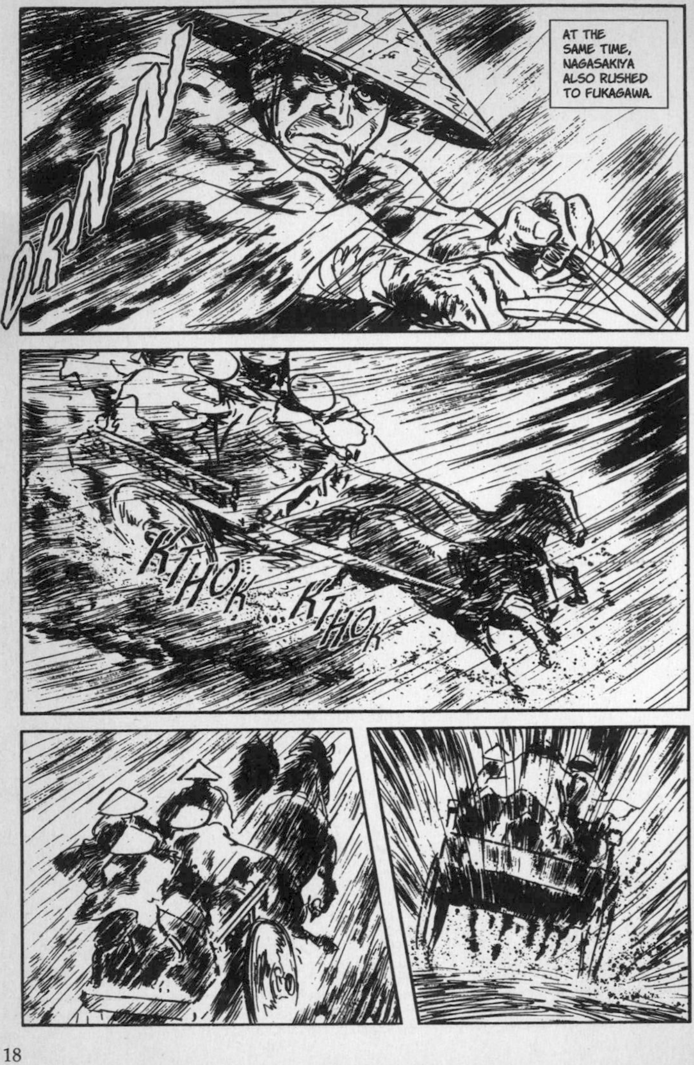
AT THE SAME TIME, NAGASAKIYA ALSO RUSHED TO FUKAGAWA.
ORNIN
KTHOK... KTHOK

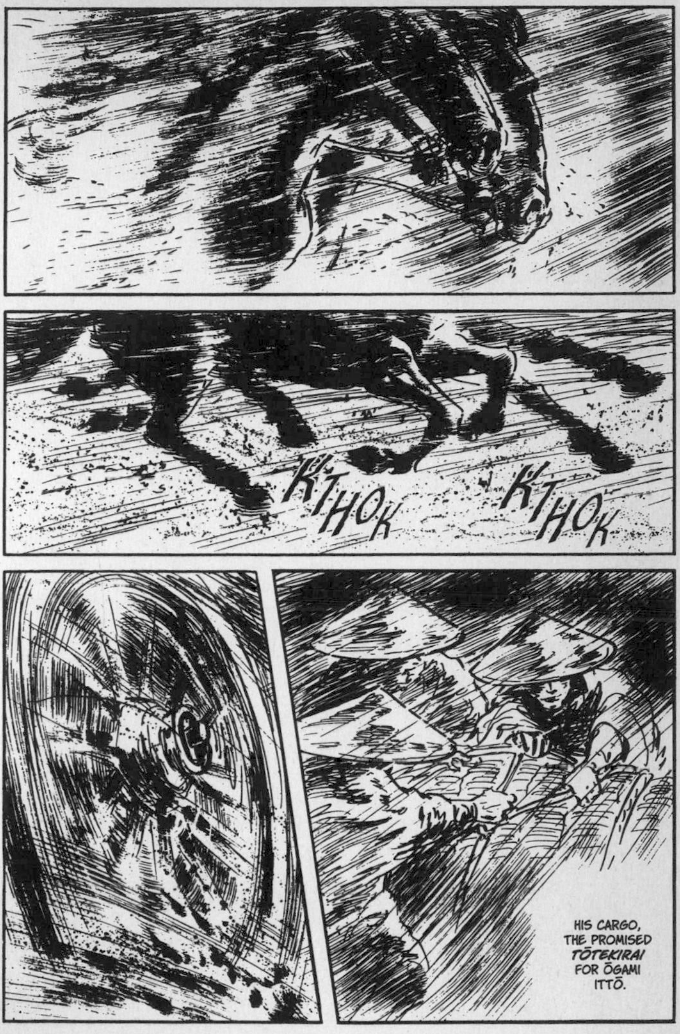
KTHOK
KTHOK
HIS CARGO, THE PROMISED *TŌTEKIRAI* FOR ŌGAMI ITTŌ.

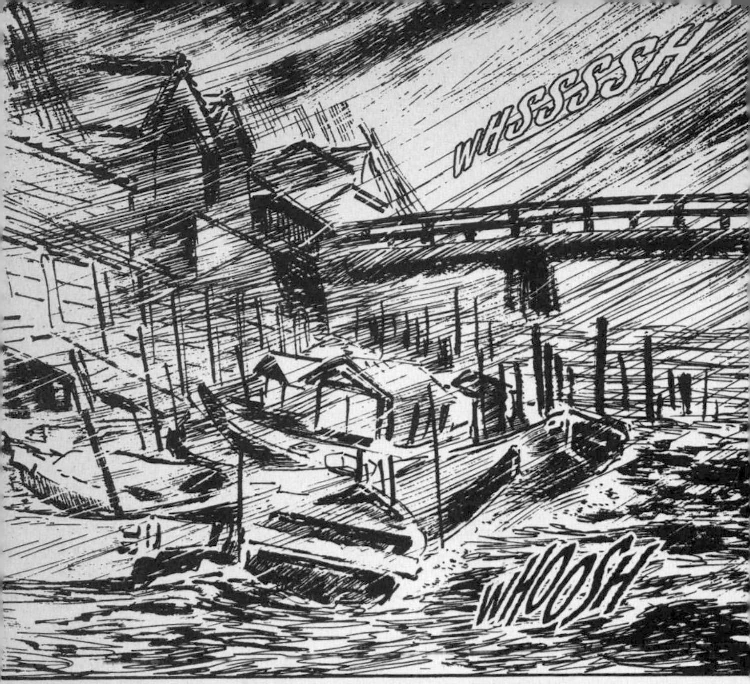
WHSSSSSH
WHOOSH
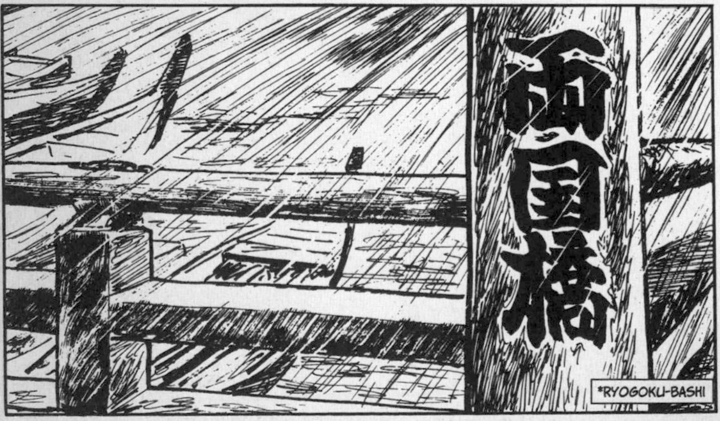
両国橋
*RYOGOKU-BASHI

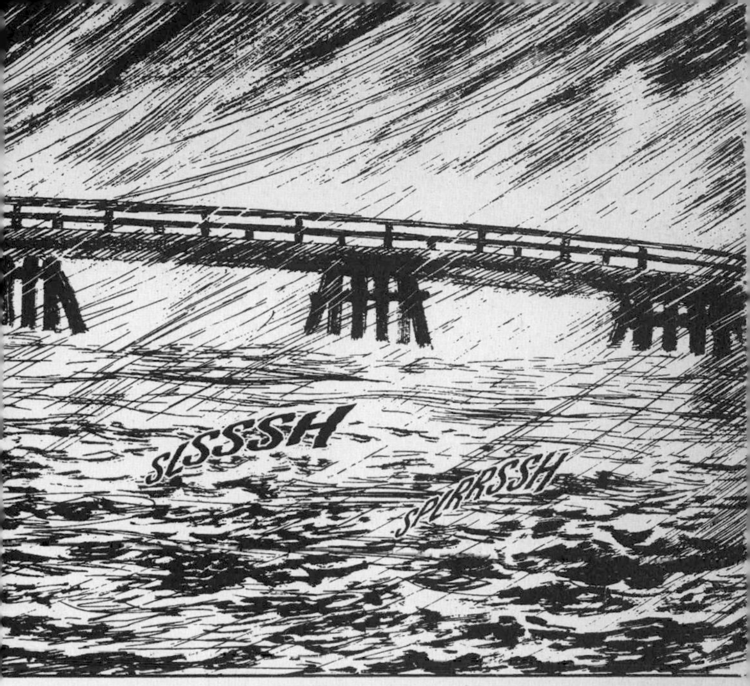
SLSSSH
SPLRRSSH
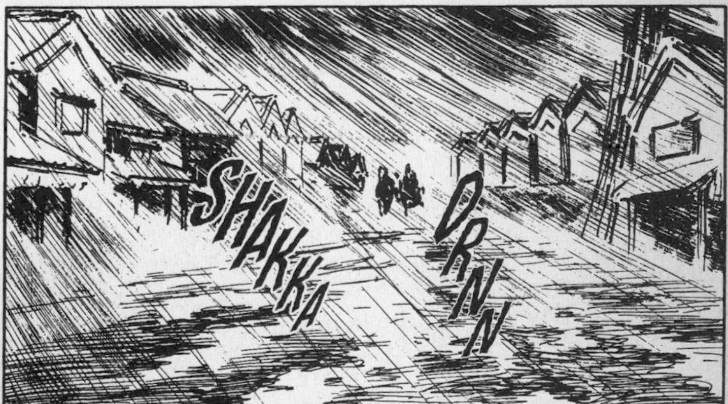
SHAKKA
DRNN

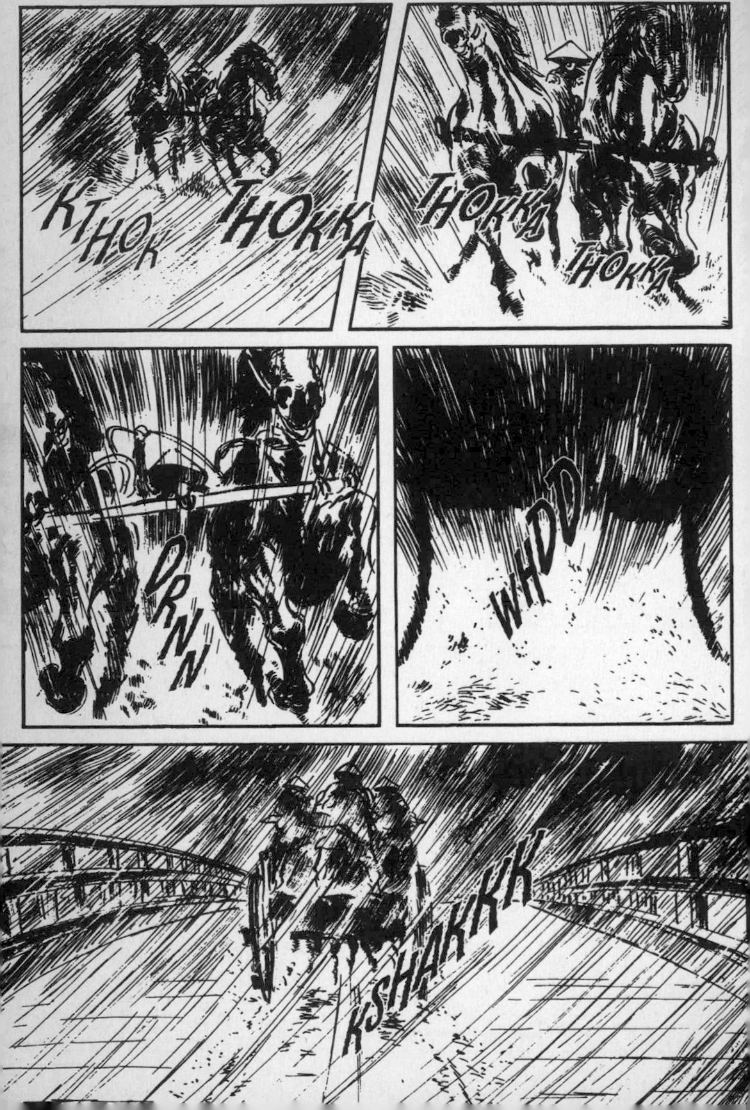
THOKKA
THOKKA
KTHOK
THOKKA
WHDD
DRNN
KSHAKKK

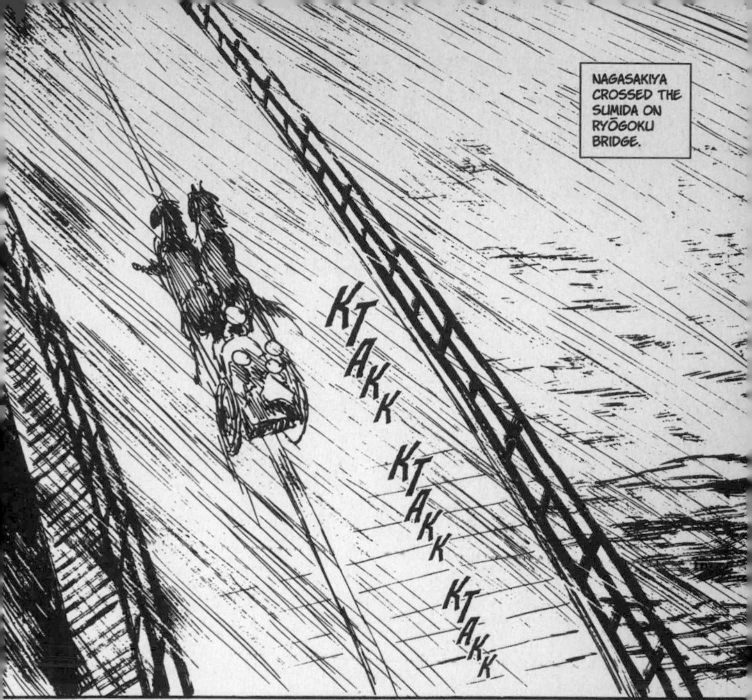
NAGASAKIYA CROSSED THE SUMIDA ON RYŌGOKU BRIDGE.
KTAKK KTAKK KTAKK

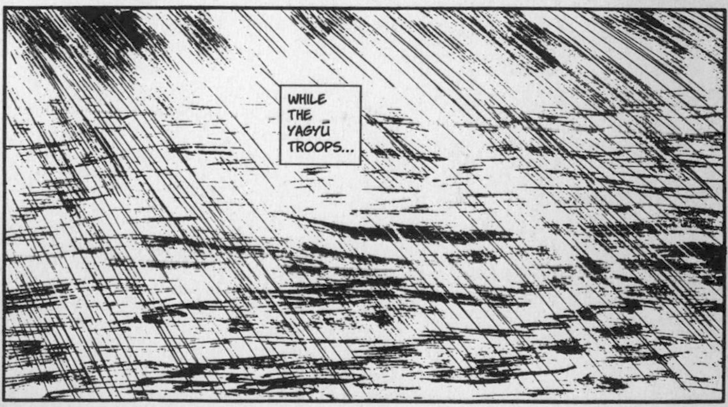
WHILE THE YAGYŪ TROOPS...

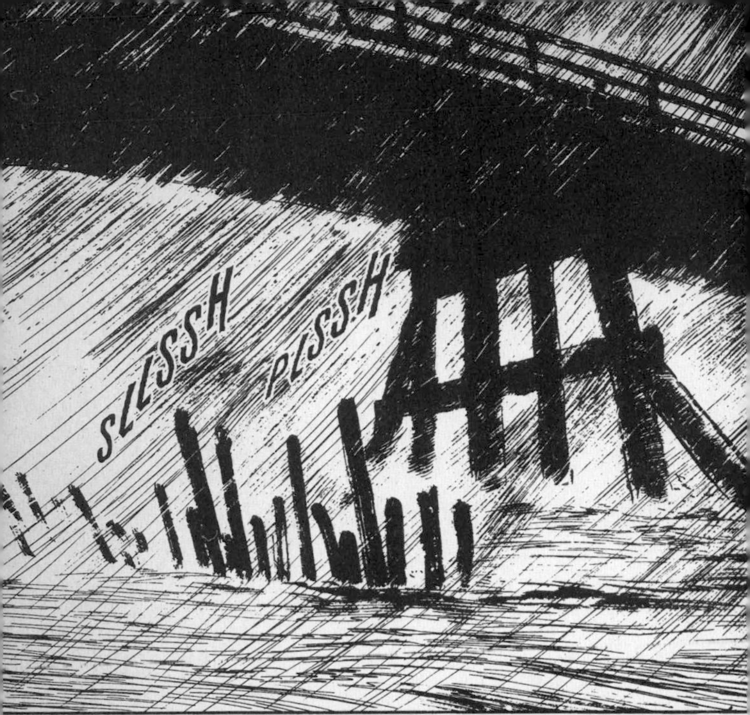
PLSSH
SLLSSH
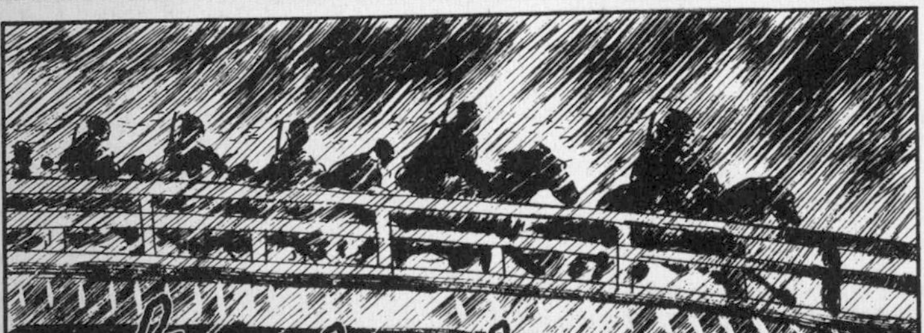
DRNN
DRNN
DRNN

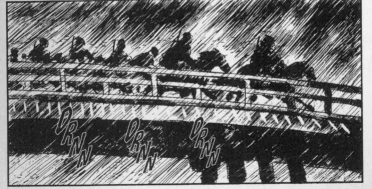

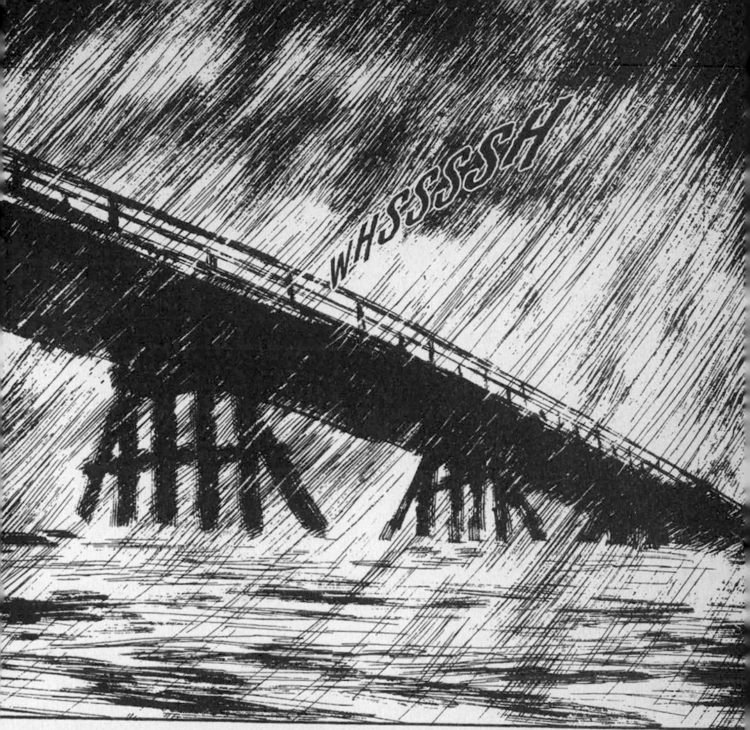
WHSSSSSH
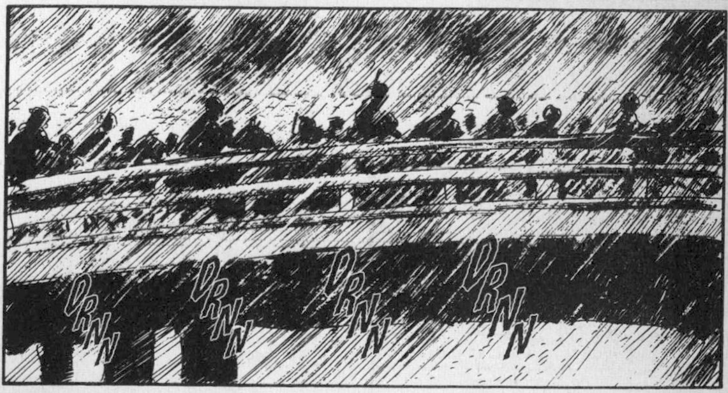
DRNN
DRNN
DRNN
DRNN

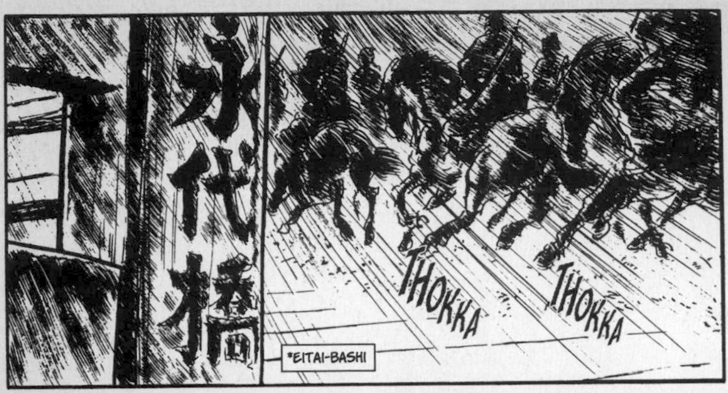
THOKKA
THOKKA
*EITAI-BASHI

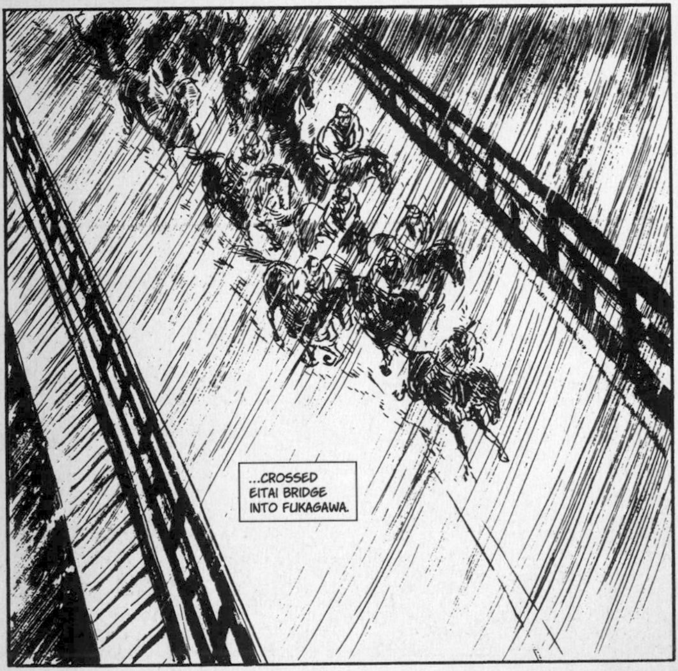
...CROSSED EITAI BRIDGE INTO FUKAGAWA.

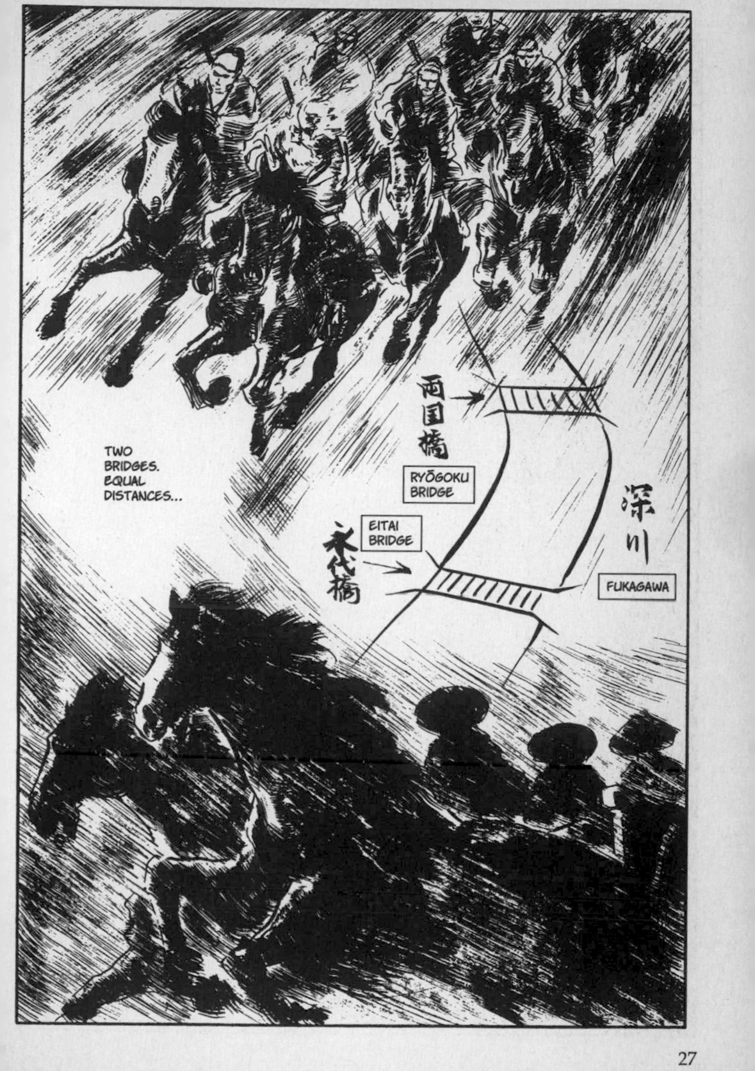
両国橋
RYŌGOKU BRIDGE
深川
FUKAGAWA
TWO BRIDGES. EQUAL DISTANCES...
永代橋
EITAI BRIDGE

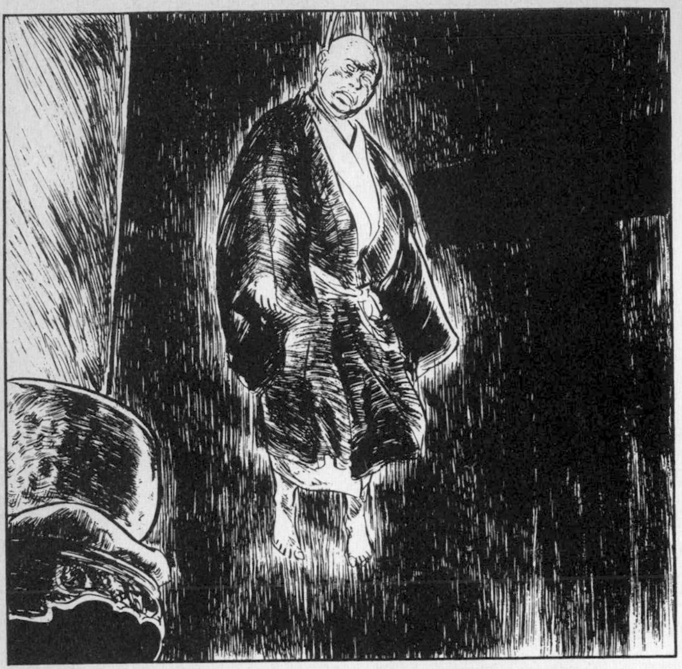

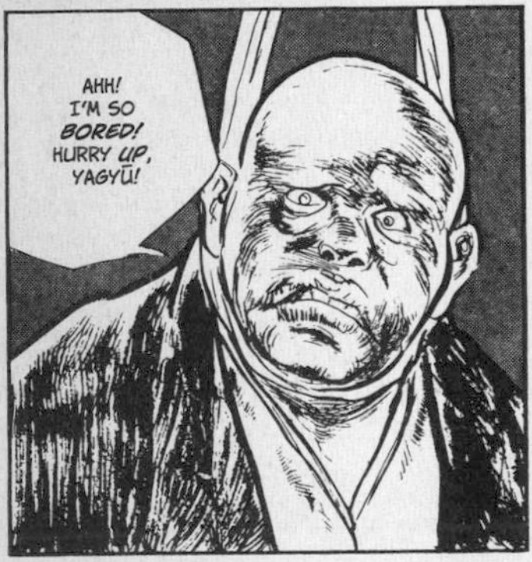
AHH! I'M SO *BORED!* HURRY *UP,* YAGYŪ!

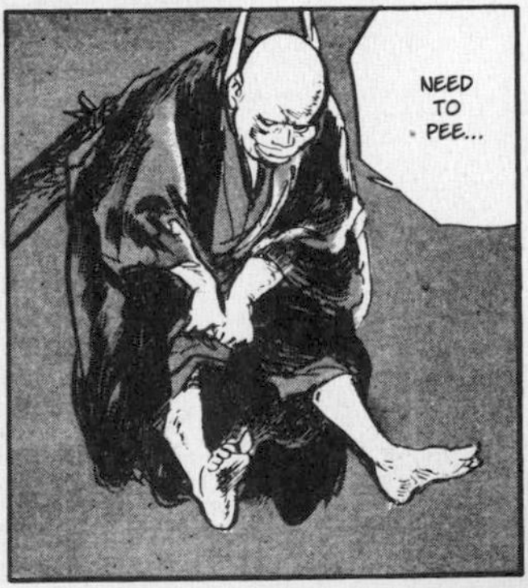
NEED TO PEE...

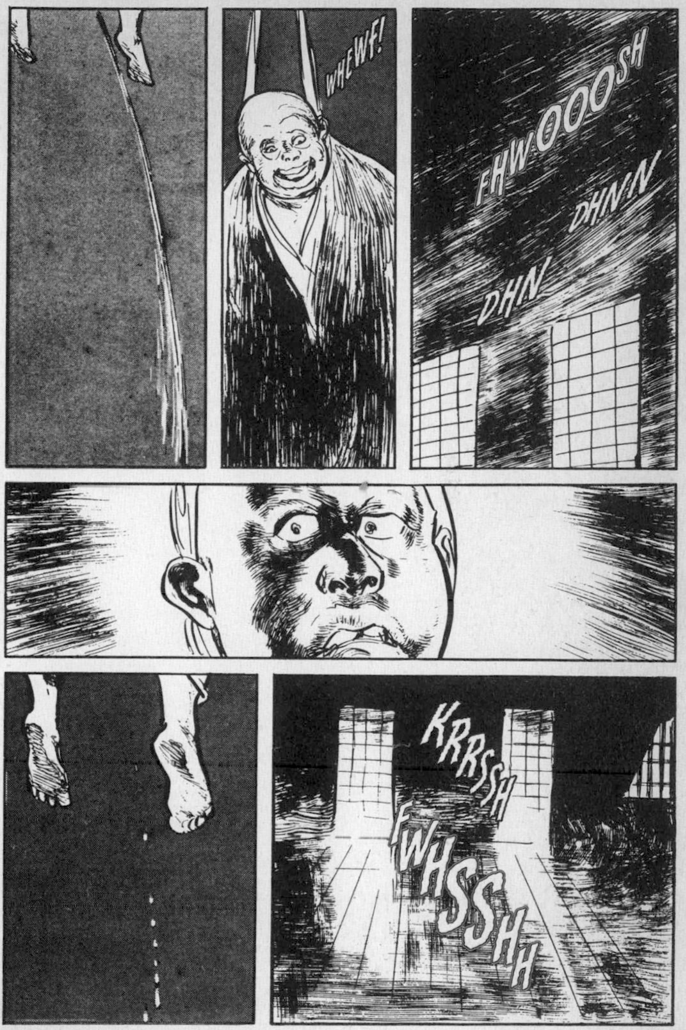
FHWOOOSH
DHIN
DHIN
WHEWF!
KRRSSH
FWHSSSHH

JUST THE WIND ...?

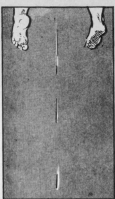

NOW I'M *HUNGRY*...

BUT, I DON'T *GET* IT...

THEY'RE *LATE*. DON'T TELL ME MY LADIES *BEAT* THEM..?

EVEN IF THEY SLOWED THEM DOWN, THEY'D BE HERE BY *NOW*... UNLESS...?!

RIGHT!

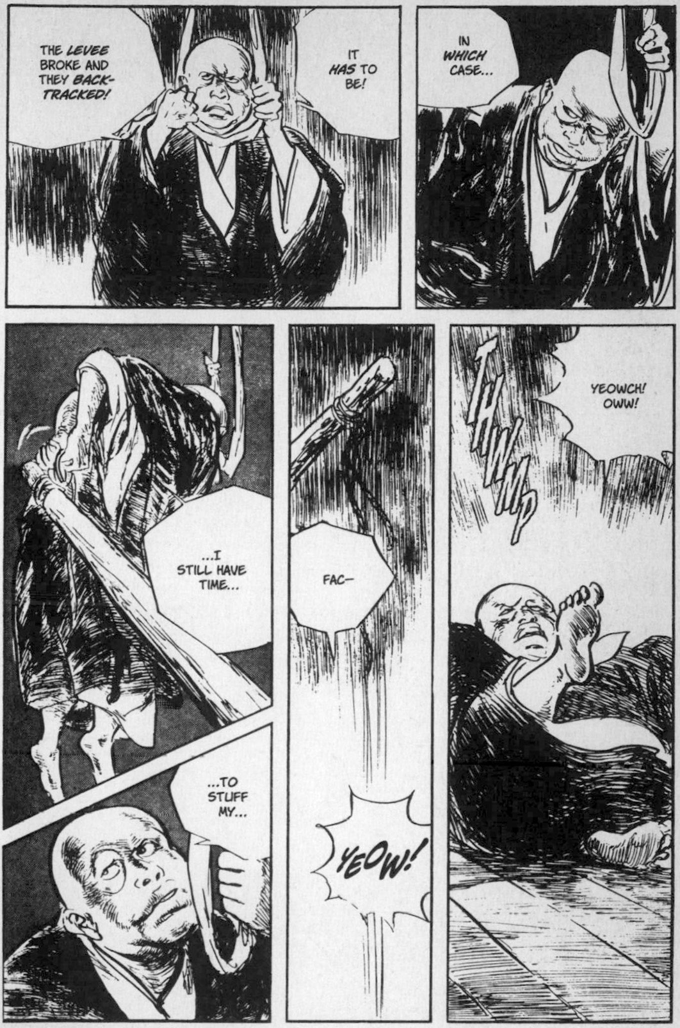
THE LEVEE BROKE AND THEY BACK-TRACKED!
IT HAS TO BE!
IN WHICH CASE...
...I STILL HAVE TIME...
...TO STUFF MY...
FAC—
YEOW!
THWUMP
YEOWCH! OWW!

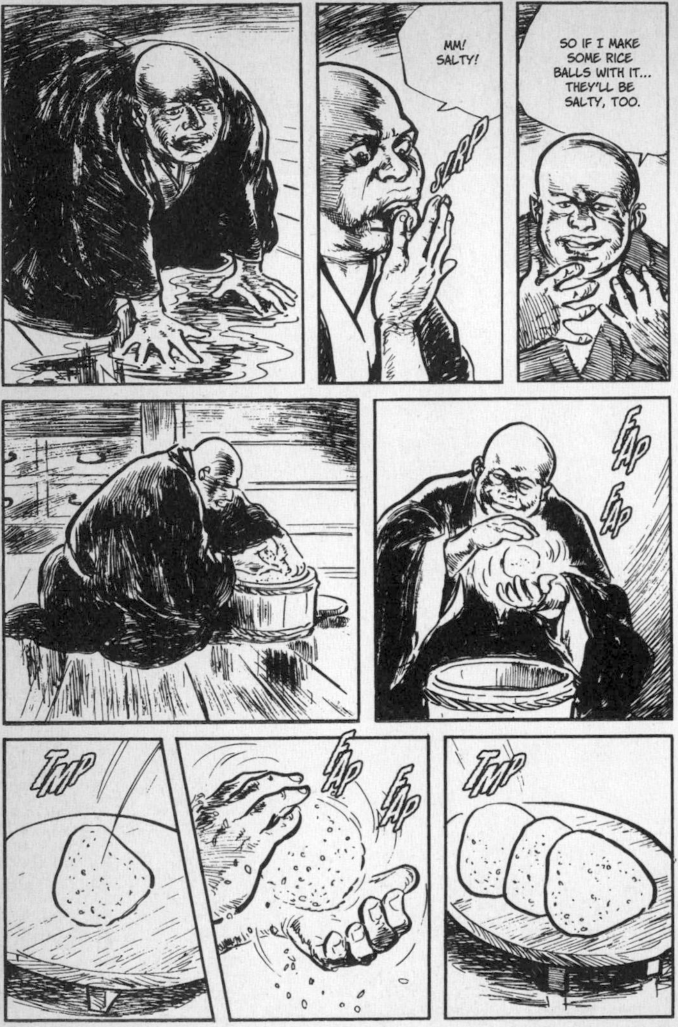
MM! SALTY!
SLRP
SO IF I MAKE SOME RICE BALLS WITH IT... THEY'LL BE SALTY, TOO.
FAP
FAP
TMP
FAP
FAP
TMP

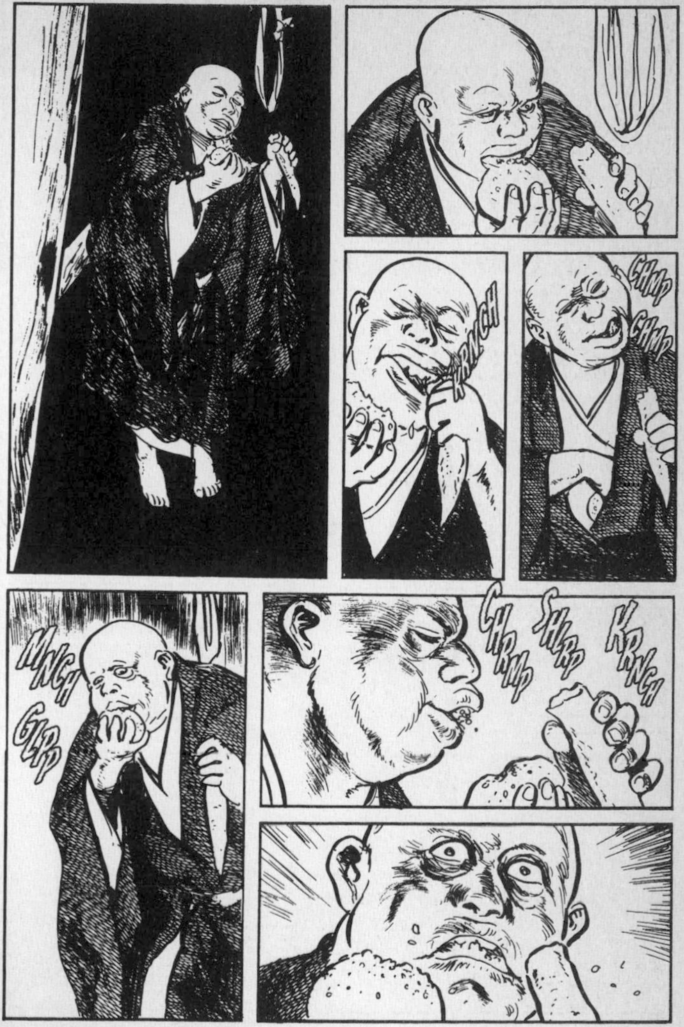
CHMP
CHMP
KRNCH
CHRMP
SHRP
KRNCH
MNCH
GLPP

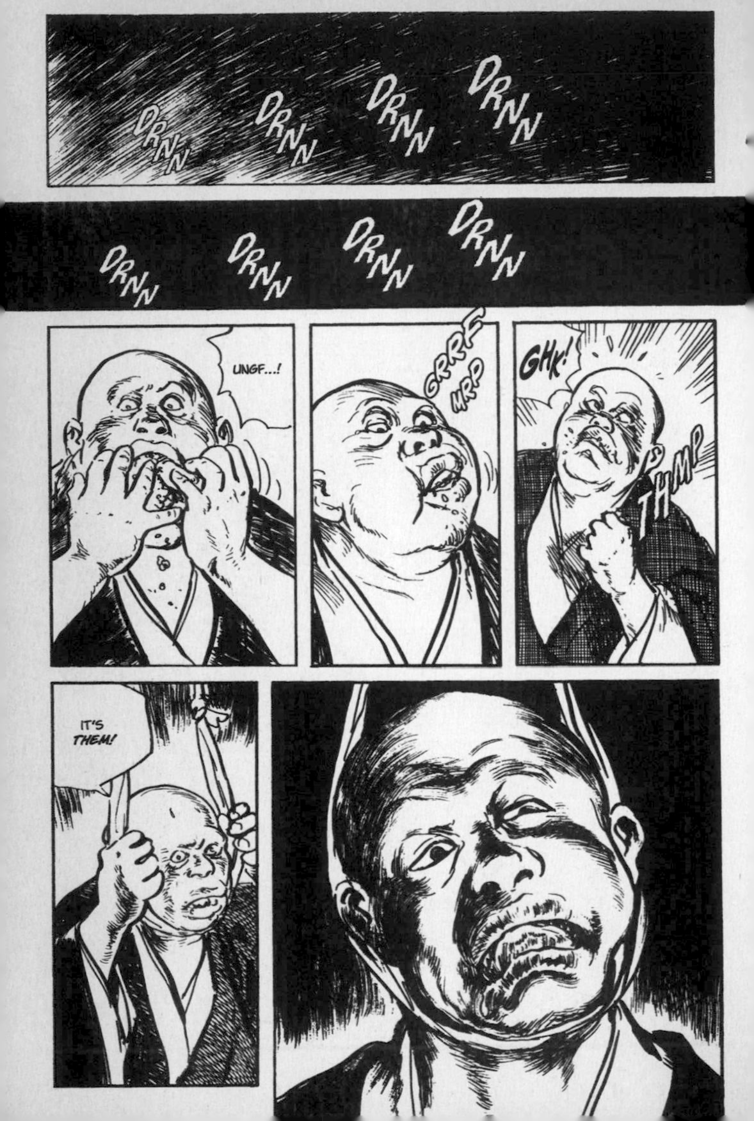
DRNN DRNN DRNN DRNN
DRNN DRNN DRNN DRNN
GHK!
THMP
GRRF
MRP
UNGF...!
IT'S *THEM!*

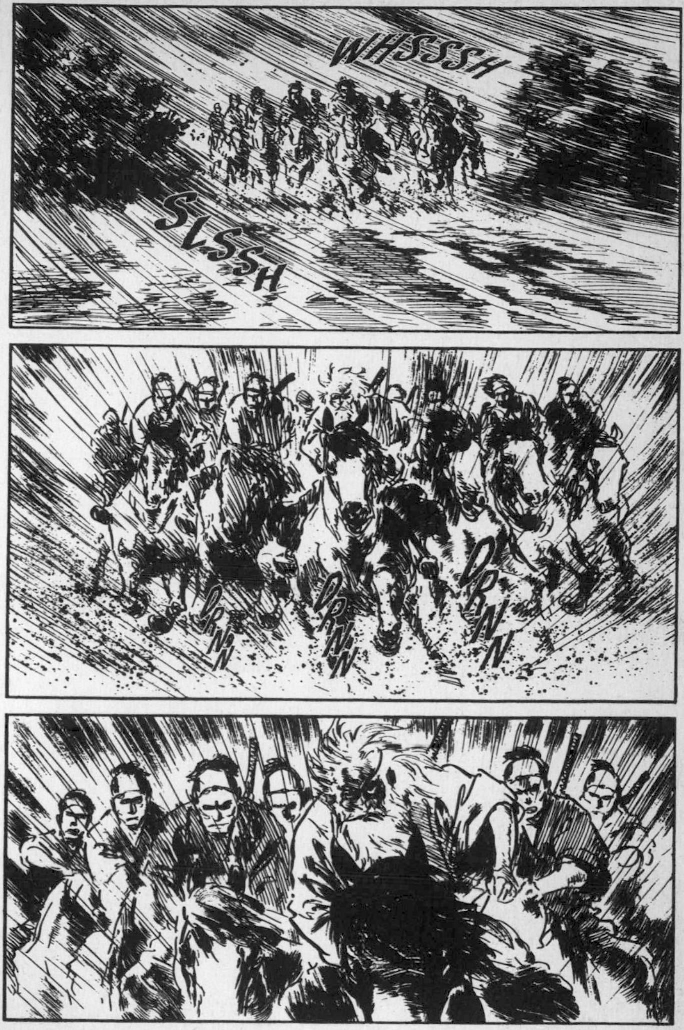
WHSSSH
SLSSSH
DRNN
DRNN
DRNN

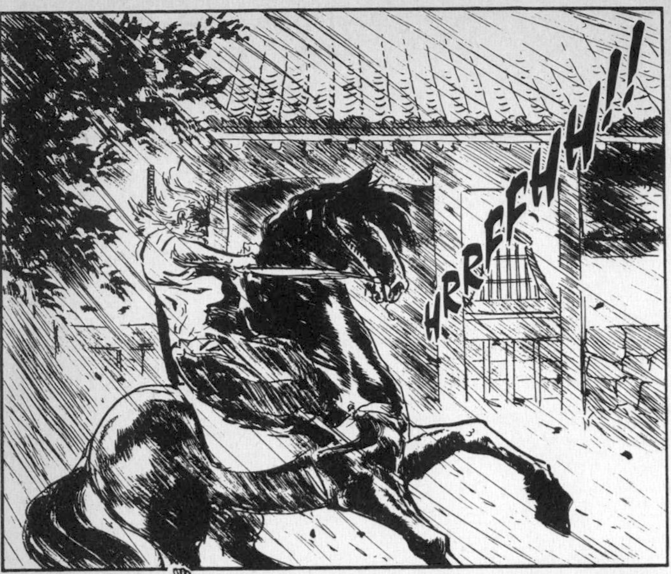
HRRFFHH!!

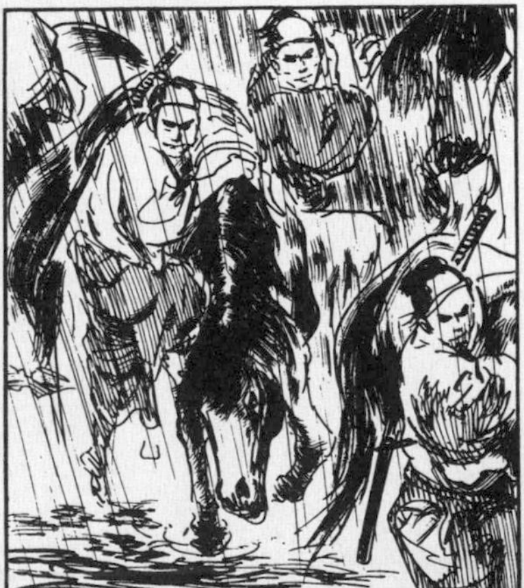

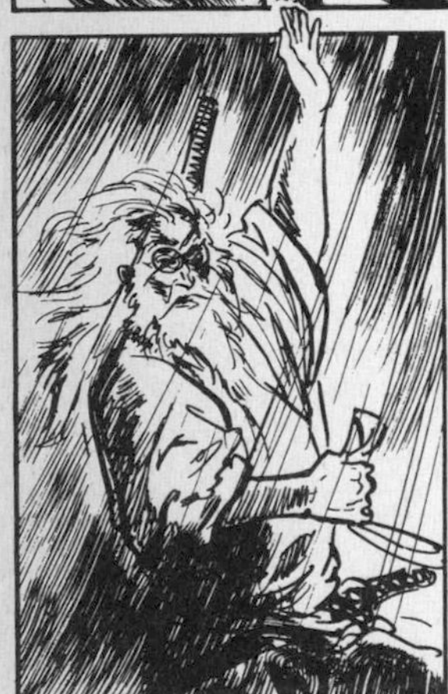

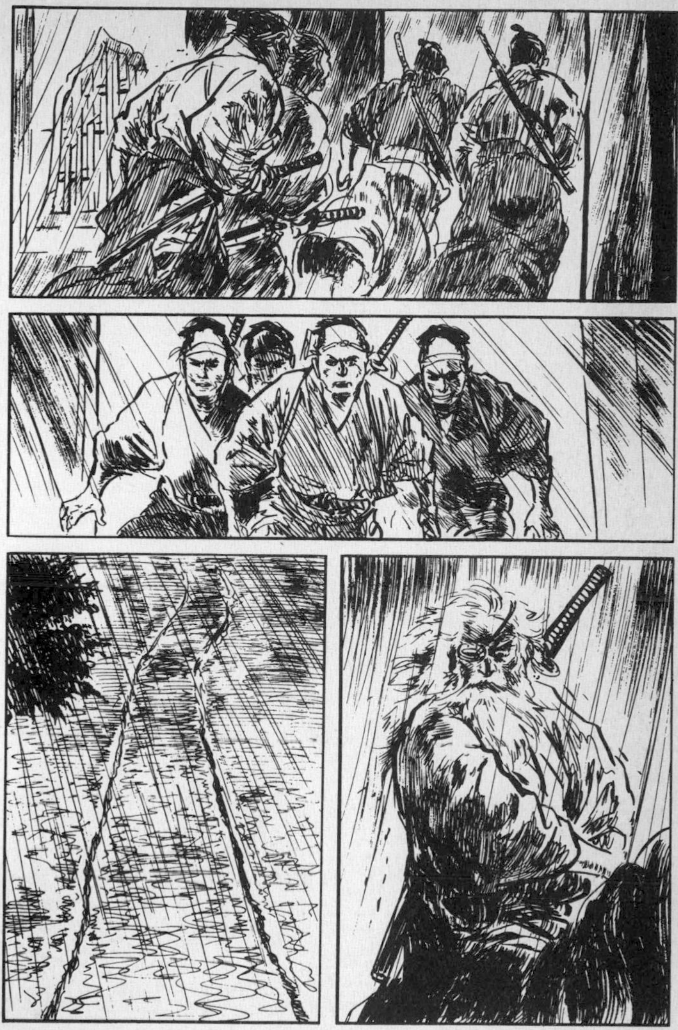

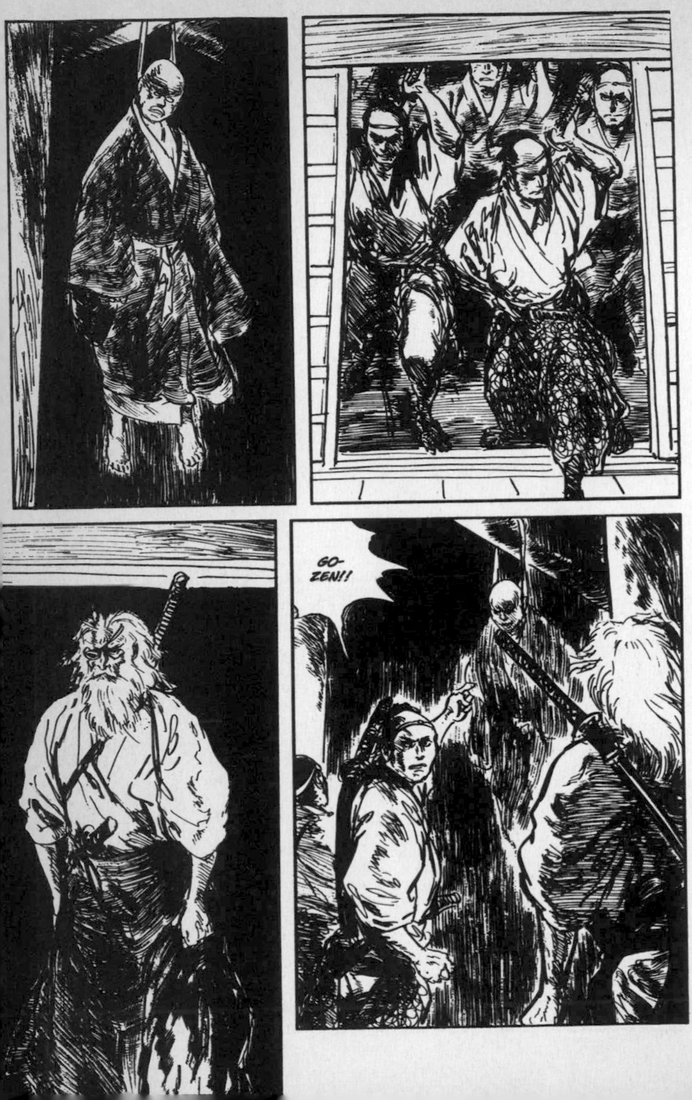
GO-
ZEN!!

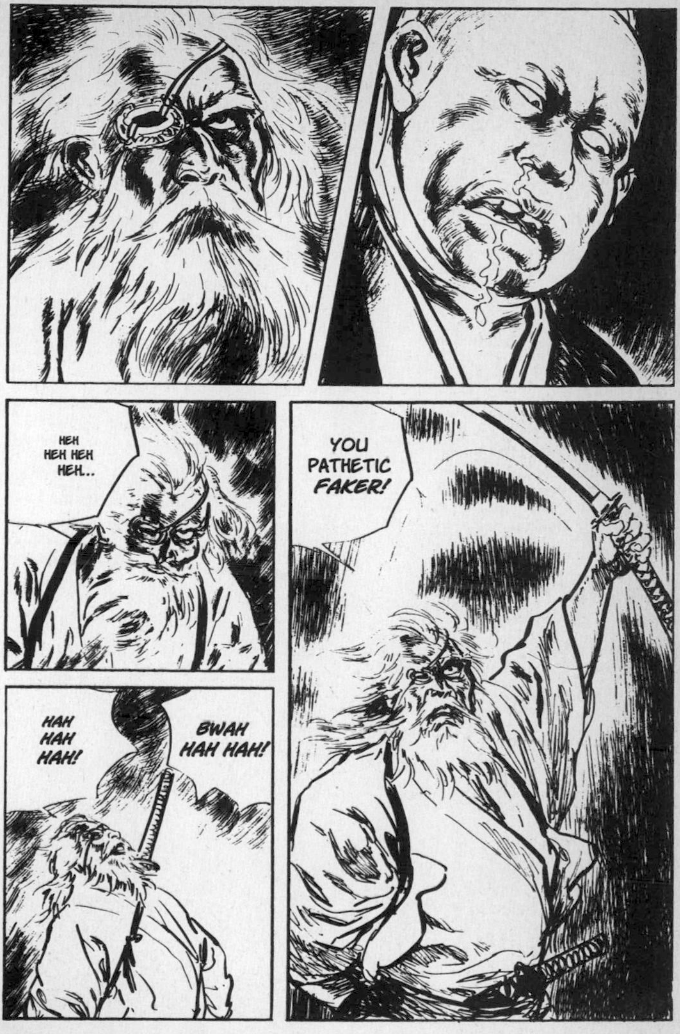
YOU PATHETIC FAKER!
HEH HEH HEH HEH...
BWAH HAH HAH!
HAH HAH HAH!

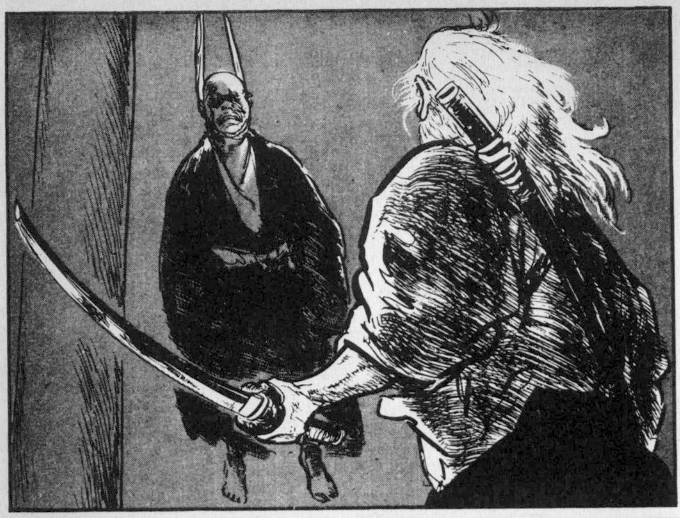
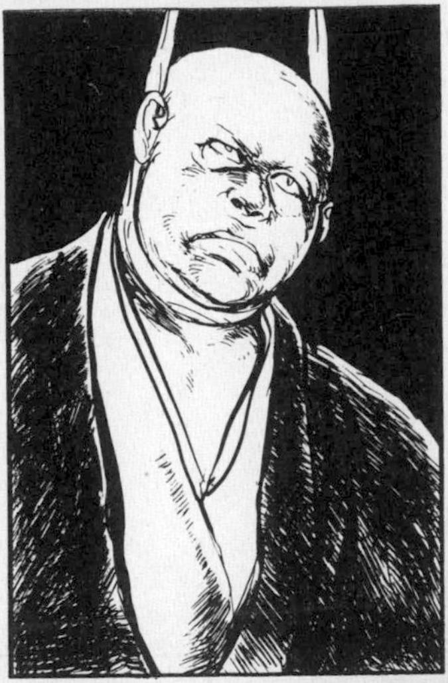
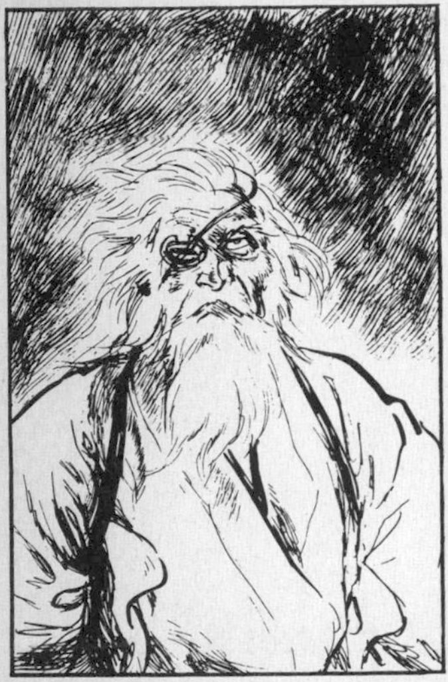

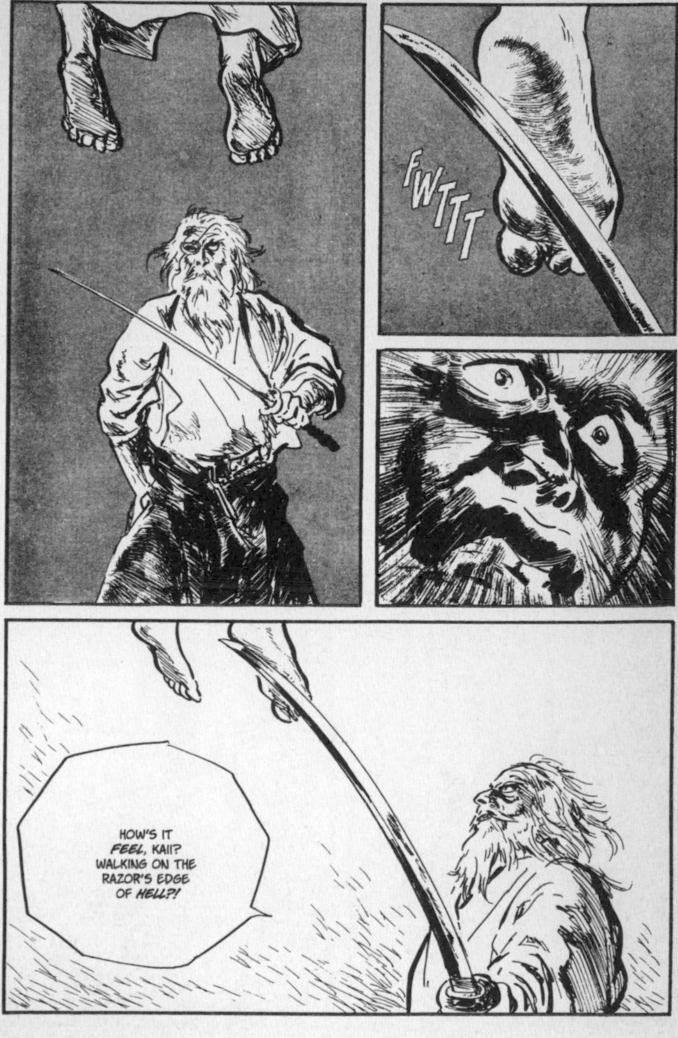
FWTTT
HOW'S IT FEEL, KAII? WALKING ON THE RAZOR'S EDGE OF HELL?!

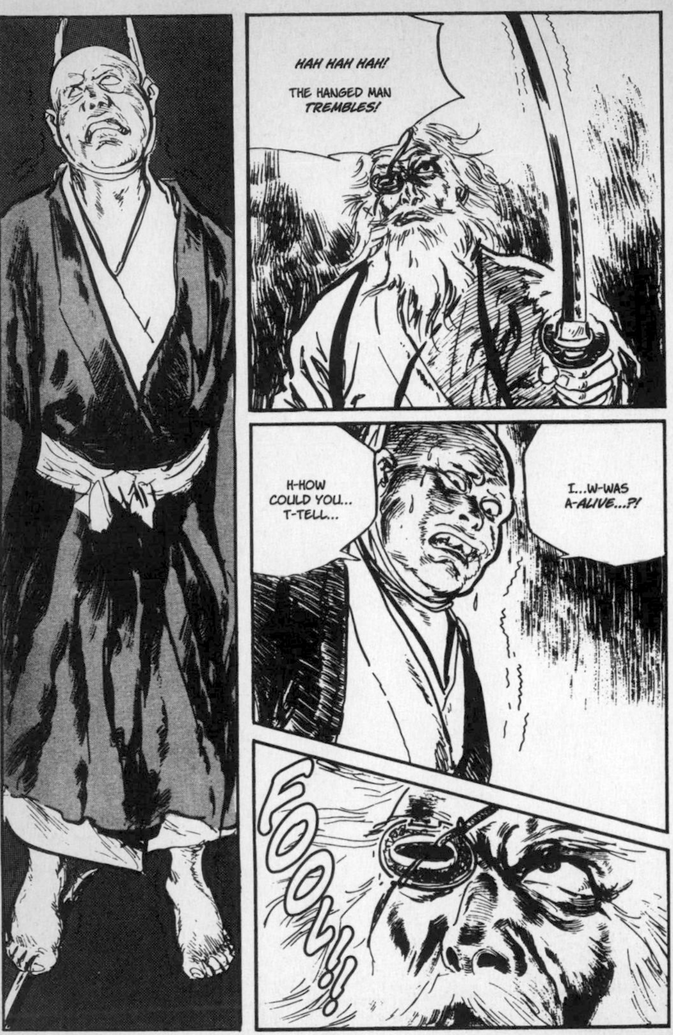
HAH HAH HAH!
THE HANGED MAN TREMBLES!
H-HOW COULD YOU... T-TELL...
I...W-WAS A-ALIVE...?!
FOOM!!

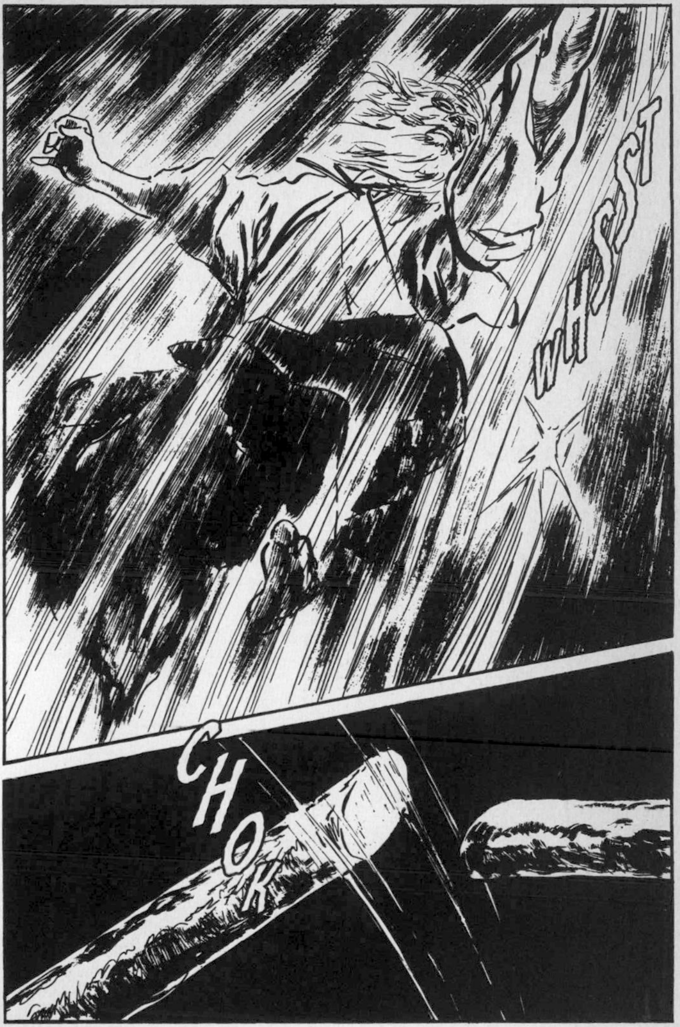
WHSSST
CHOK

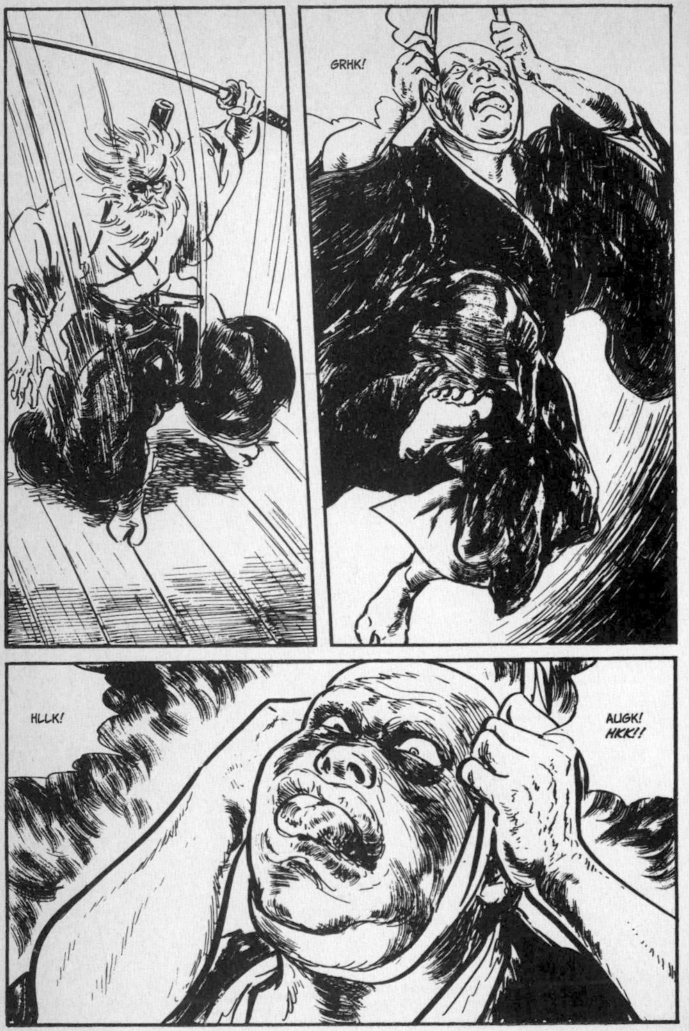
GRHK!
AUGK! HKK!!
HLLK!

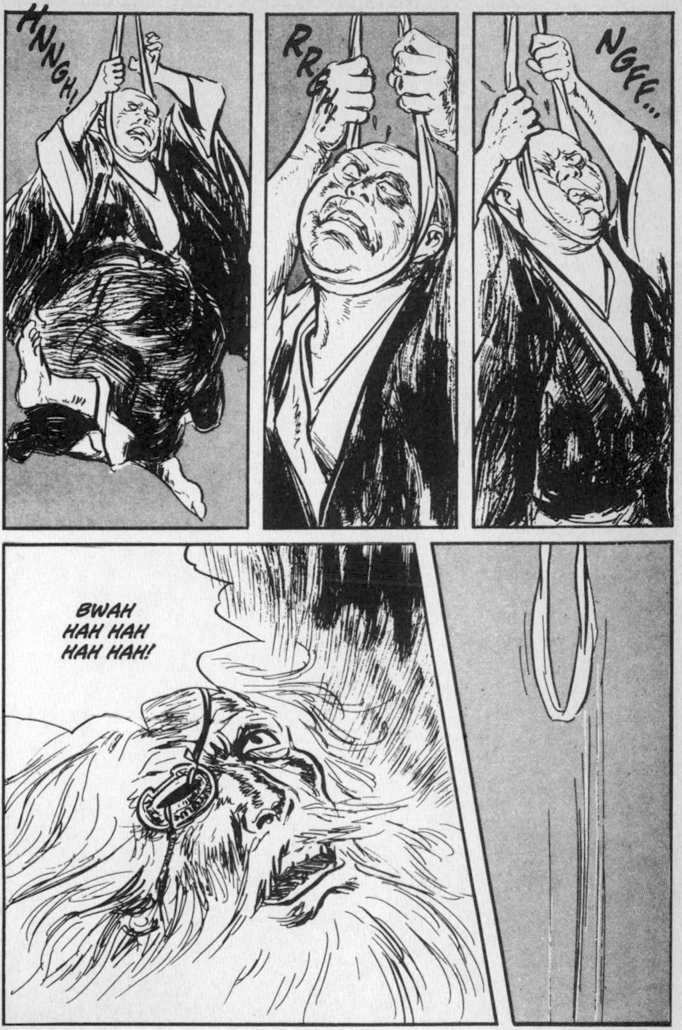
HNNGH!
RRGH!
NGFFF...
BWAH HAH HAH HAH HAH!

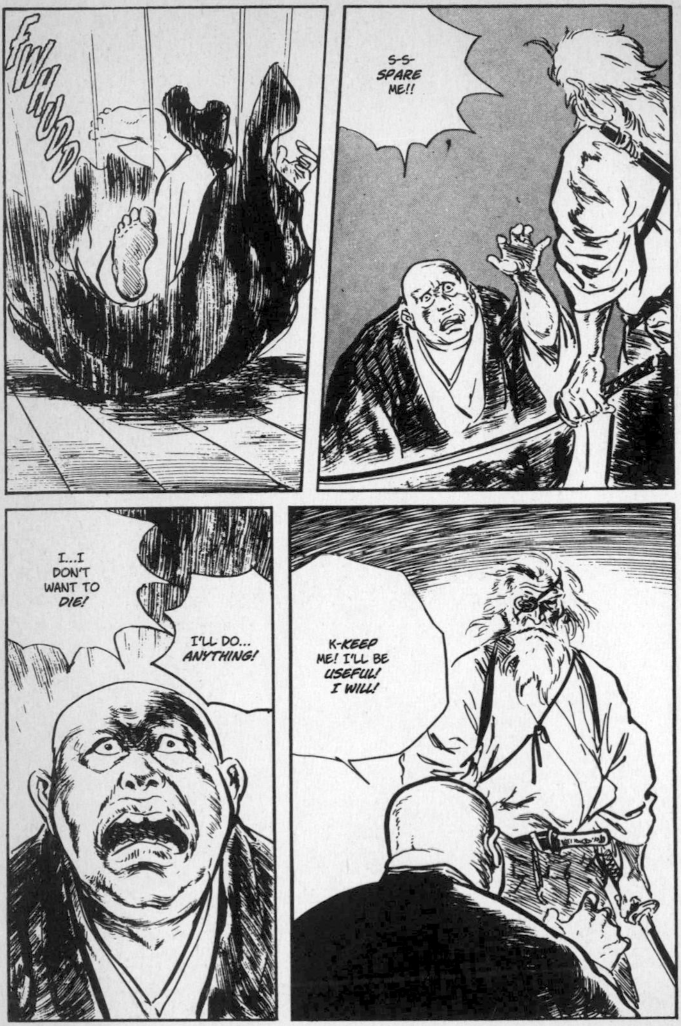
S-S-SPARE ME!!
FWHOOO
K-KEEP ME! I'LL BE USEFUL! I WILL!
I...I DON'T WANT TO DIE!
I'LL DO... ANYTHING!

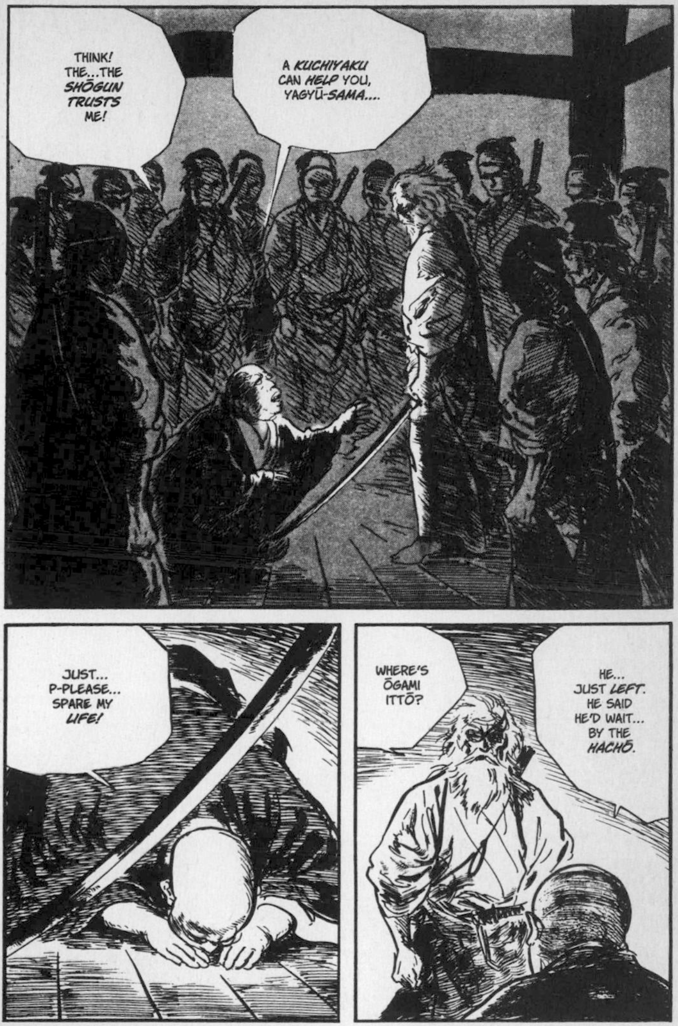
A *KUCHIYAKU* CAN *HELP* YOU, YAGYŪ-*SAMA*....
THINK! THE...THE *SHŌGUN* *TRUSTS* ME!
WHERE'S ŌGAMI ITTŌ?
HE... JUST *LEFT*. HE SAID HE'D WAIT... BY THE *HACHŌ*.
JUST... P-PLEASE... SPARE MY *LIFE!*

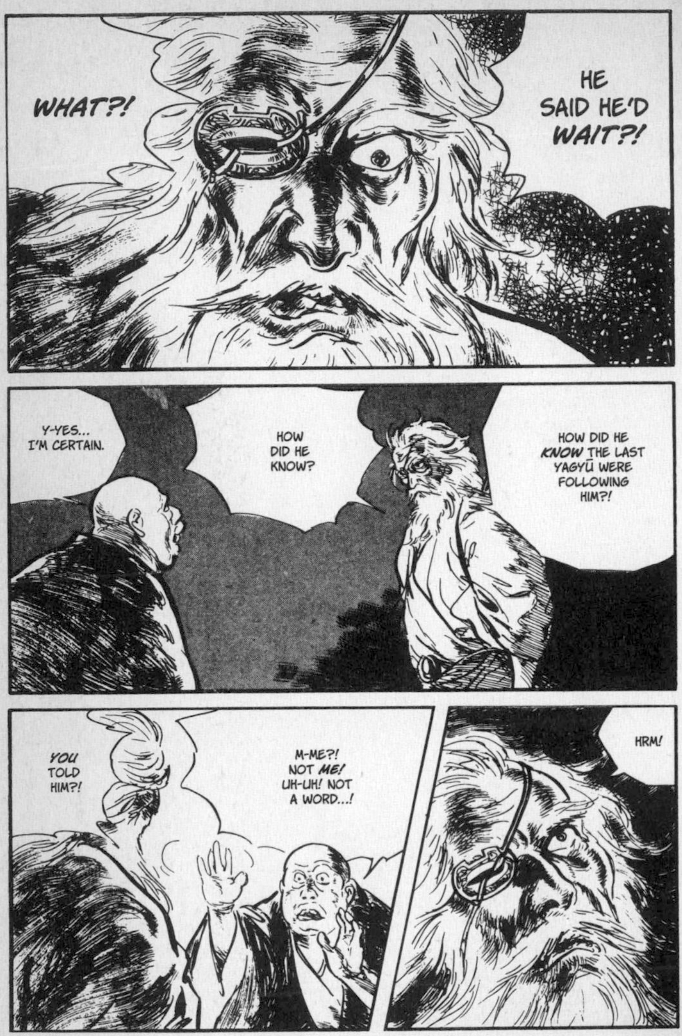
HE SAID HE'D *WAIT?!*
WHAT?!
HOW DID HE *KNOW* THE LAST YAGYŪ WERE FOLLOWING HIM?!
HOW DID HE KNOW?
Y-YES... I'M CERTAIN.
HRM!
M-ME?! NOT *ME!* UH-UH! NOT A WORD...!
YOU TOLD HIM?!

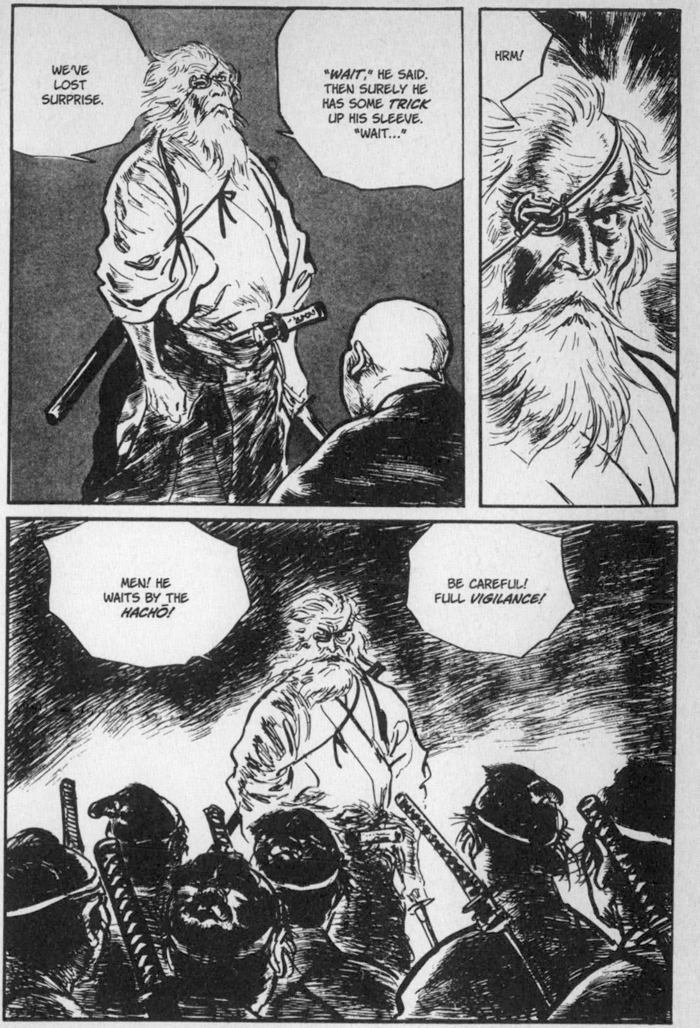
WE'VE LOST SURPRISE.
"WAIT," HE SAID. THEN SURELY HE HAS SOME TRICK UP HIS SLEEVE. "WAIT..."
HRM!
MEN! HE WAITS BY THE HACHŌ!
BE CAREFUL! FULL VIGILANCE!

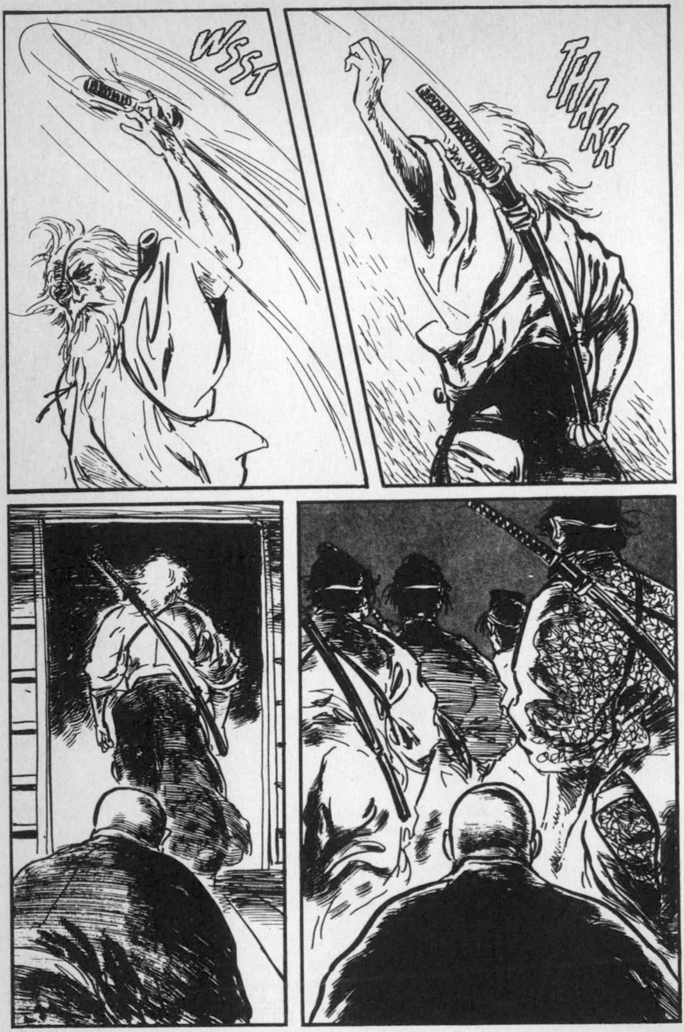
THAKK
WSST

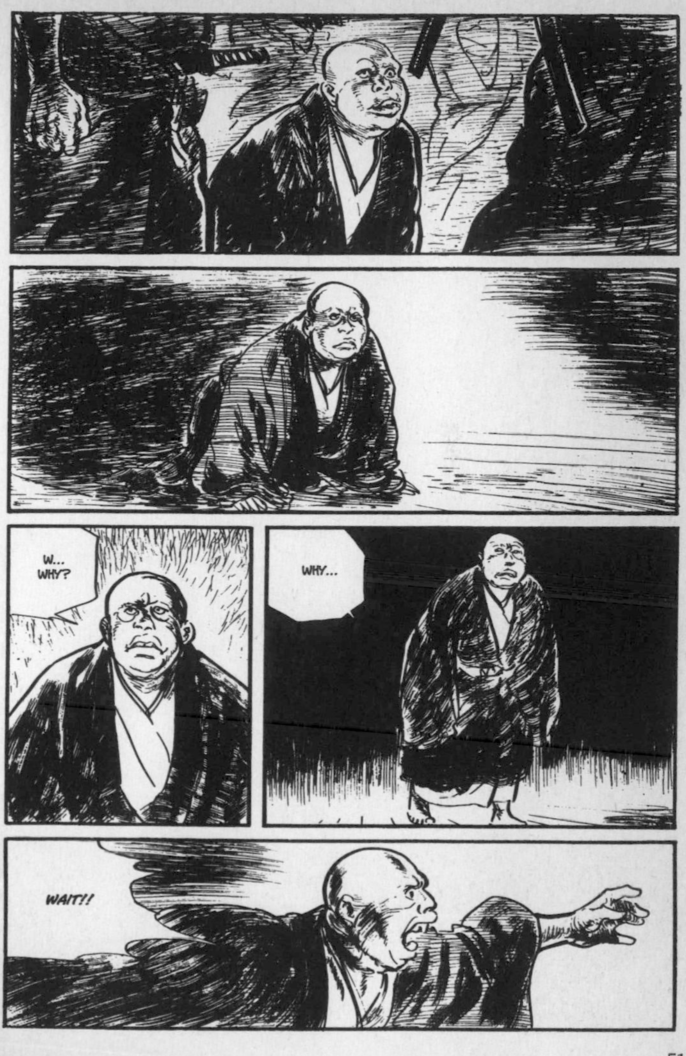
WHY...
W... WHY?
WAIT!!

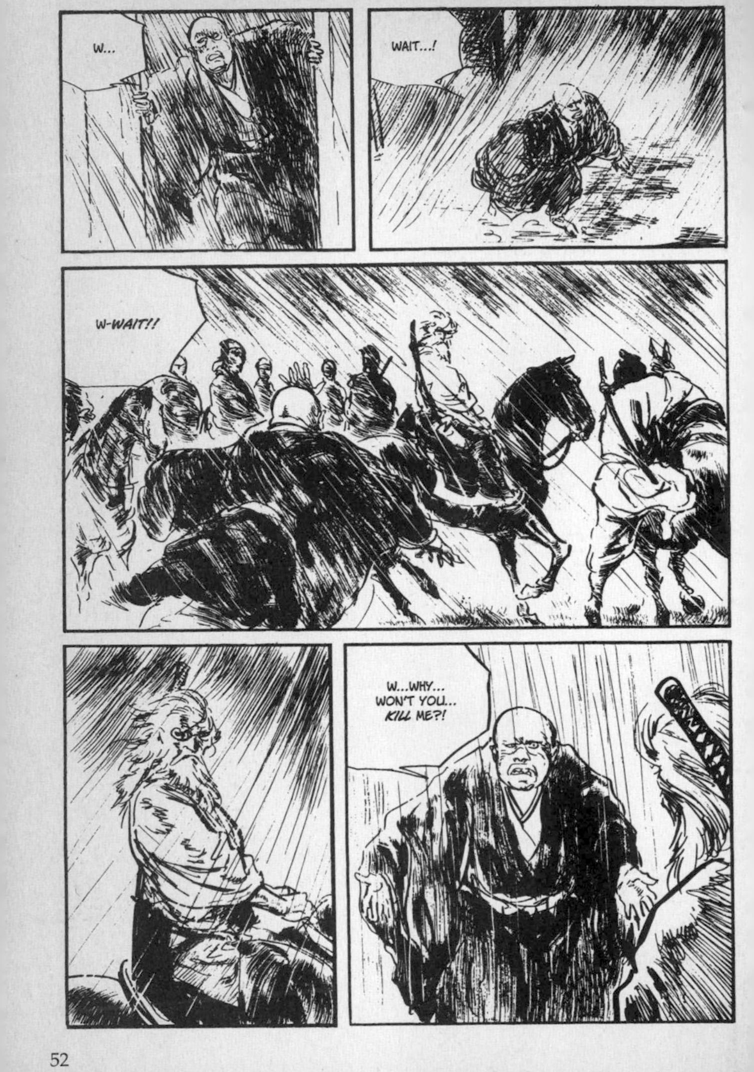
W...
WAIT...!
W-WAIT!!
W...WHY... WON'T YOU... KILL ME?!

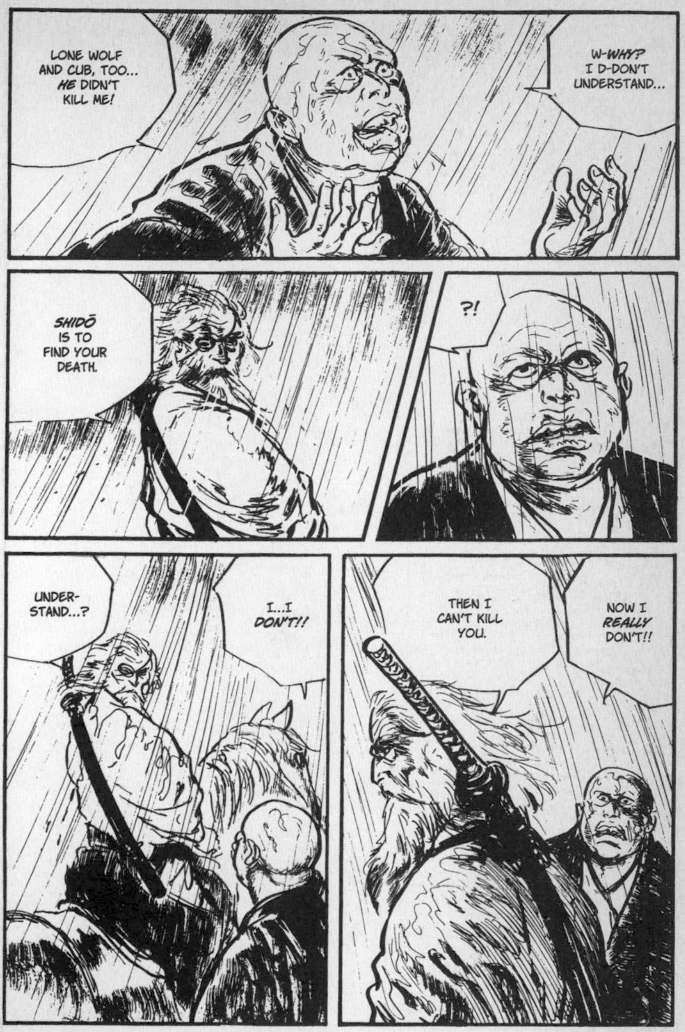

LONE WOLF AND CUB, TOO... *HE* DIDN'T KILL ME!
W-*WHY?* I D-DON'T UNDERSTAND...
SHIDŌ IS TO FIND YOUR DEATH.
?!
UNDER-STAND...?
I...I *DON'T!!*
THEN I CAN'T KILL YOU.
NOW I *REALLY* DON'T!!

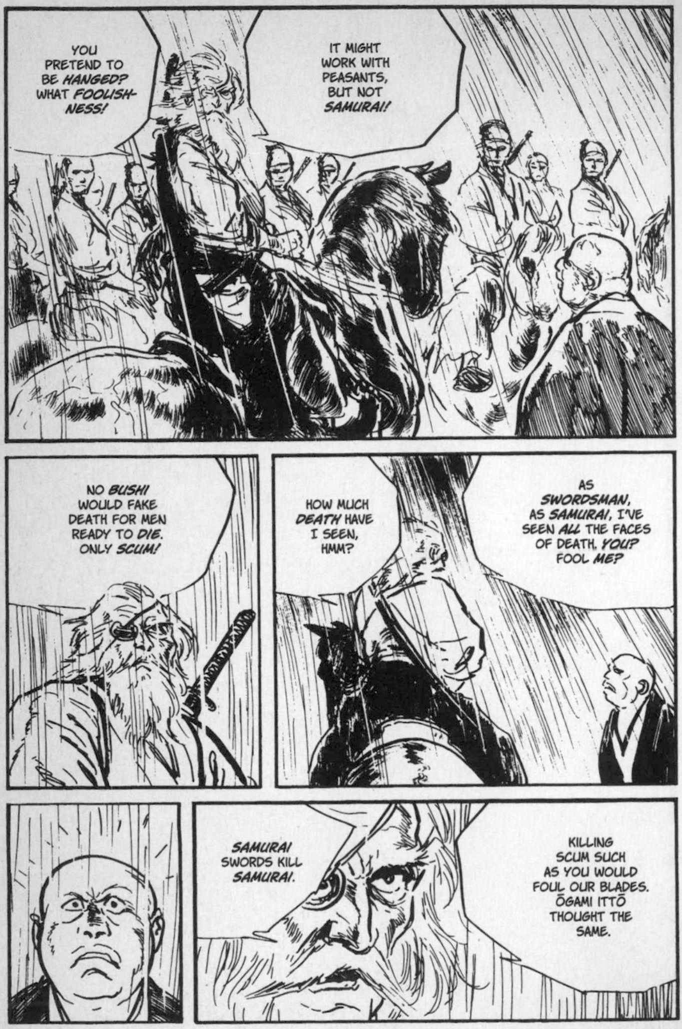
YOU PRETEND TO BE HANGED? WHAT FOOLISHNESS!
IT MIGHT WORK WITH PEASANTS, BUT NOT SAMURAI!
NO BUSHI WOULD FAKE DEATH FOR MEN READY TO DIE. ONLY SCUM!
HOW MUCH DEATH HAVE I SEEN, HMM?
AS SWORDSMAN, AS SAMURAI, I'VE SEEN ALL THE FACES OF DEATH. YOU? FOOL ME?
SAMURAI SWORDS KILL SAMURAI.
KILLING SCUM SUCH AS YOU WOULD FOUL OUR BLADES. ŌGAMI ITTŌ THOUGHT THE SAME.

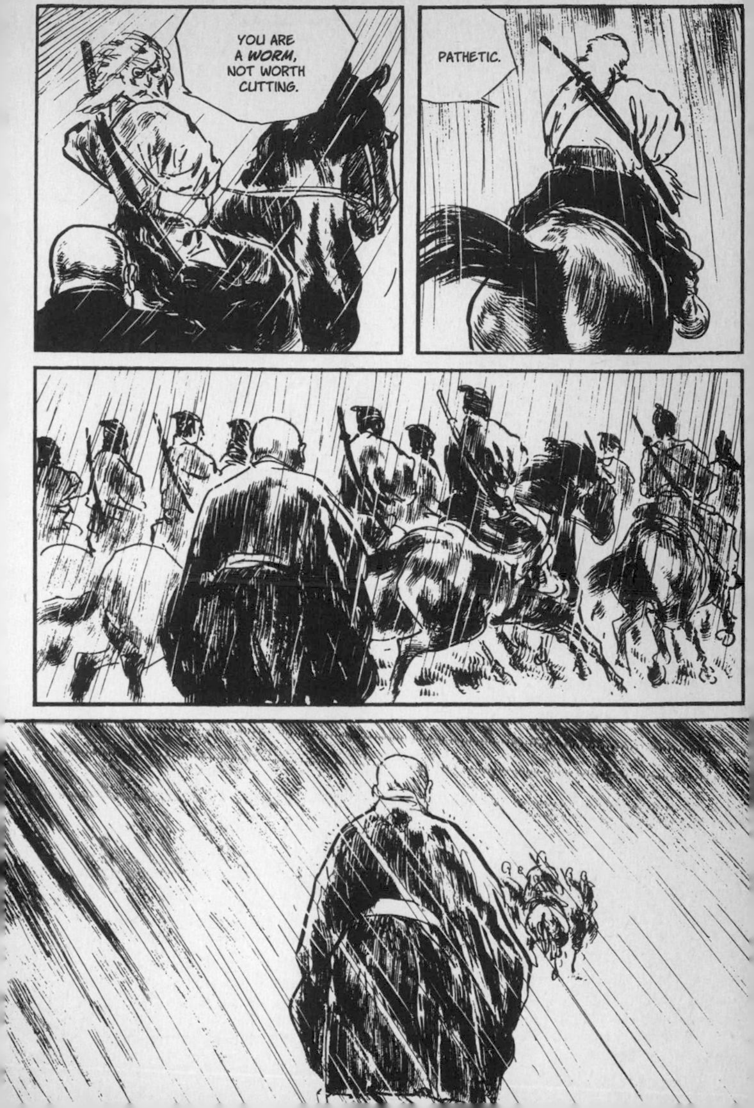
YOU ARE A *WORM*, NOT WORTH CUTTING.
PATHETIC.

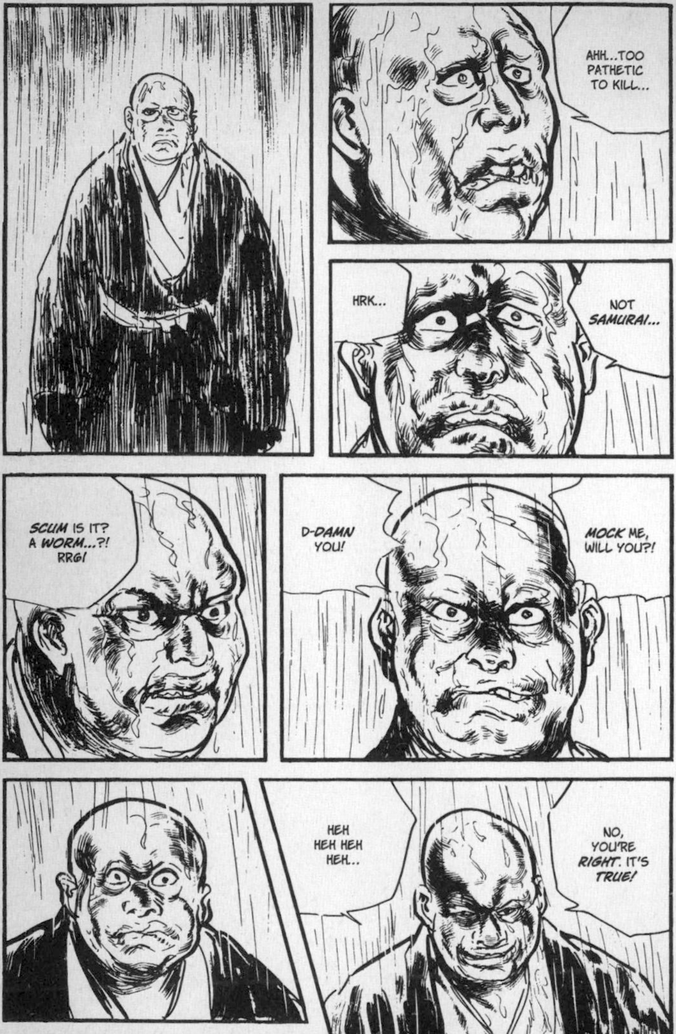
AHH...TOO PATHETIC TO KILL...
HRK...
NOT SAMURAI...
SCUM IS IT? A WORM...?! RRG!
D-DAMN YOU!
MOCK ME, WILL YOU?!
HEH HEH HEH HEH...
NO, YOU'RE RIGHT. IT'S TRUE!

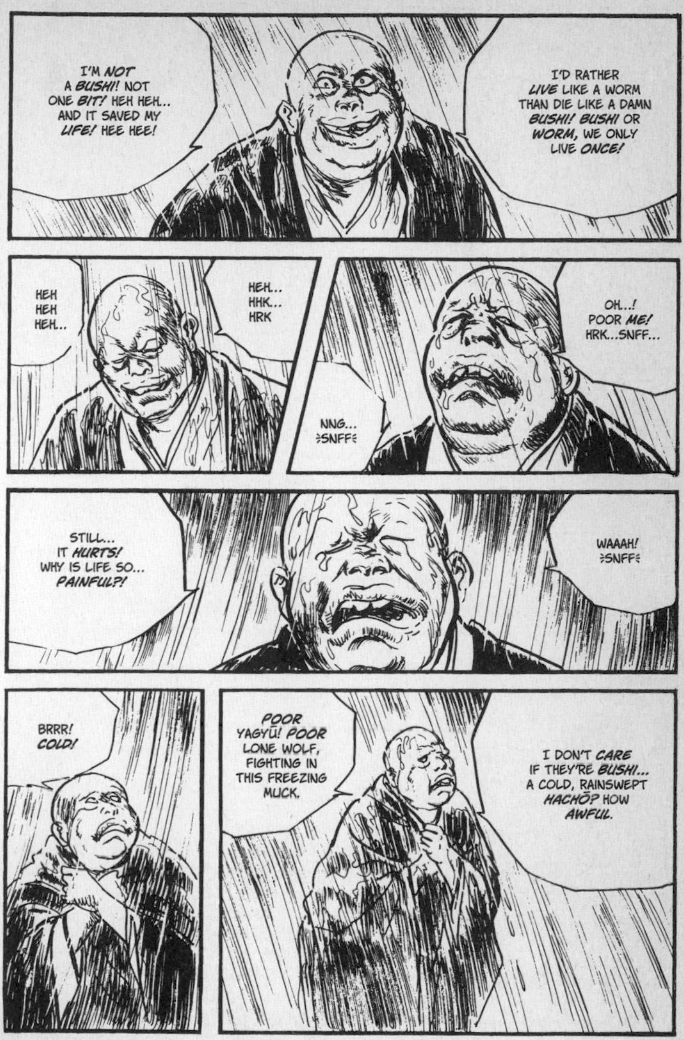
I'M NOT A BUSHI! NOT ONE BIT! HEH HEH... AND IT SAVED MY LIFE! HEE HEE!
I'D RATHER LIVE LIKE A WORM THAN DIE LIKE A DAMN BUSHI! BUSHI OR WORM, WE ONLY LIVE ONCE!
HEH HEH HEH...
HEH... HHK... HRK
OH...! POOR ME! HRK...SNFF...
NNG... SNFF
STILL... IT HURTS! WHY IS LIFE SO... PAINFUL?!
WAAAH! SNFF
BRRR! COLD!
POOR YAGYŪ! POOR LONE WOLF, FIGHTING IN THIS FREEZING MUCK.
I DON'T CARE IF THEY'RE BUSHI... A COLD, RAINSWEPT HACHŌ? HOW AWFUL.

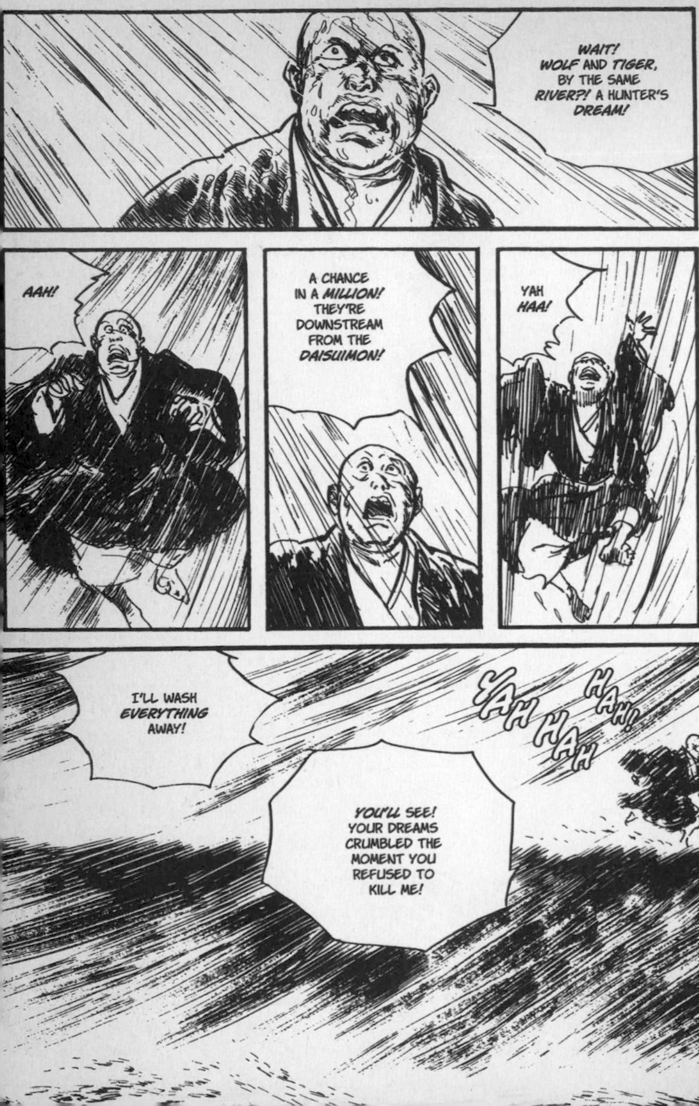
WAIT! WOLF AND TIGER, BY THE SAME RIVER?! A HUNTER'S DREAM!
AAH!
A CHANCE IN A MILLION! THEY'RE DOWNSTREAM FROM THE DAISUIMON!
YAH HAA!
I'LL WASH EVERYTHING AWAY!
YAH HAH HAH!
YOU'LL SEE! YOUR DREAMS CRUMBLED THE MOMENT YOU REFUSED TO KILL ME!

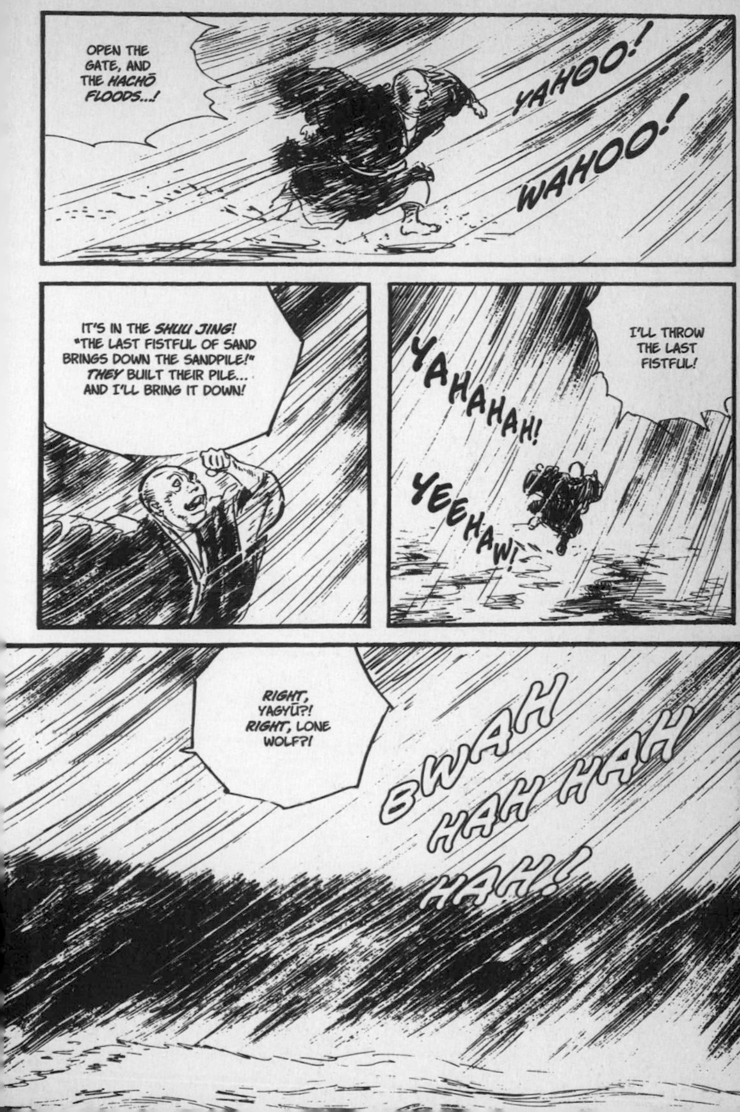
YAHOO!
WAHOO!
OPEN THE GATE, AND THE HACHŌ FLOODS...!
I'LL THROW THE LAST FISTFUL!
YAHAHAH!
YEEHAW!
IT'S IN THE SHUU JING! "THE LAST FISTFUL OF SAND BRINGS DOWN THE SANDPILE!" THEY BUILT THEIR PILE... AND I'LL BRING IT DOWN!
RIGHT, YAGYŪ?! RIGHT, LONE WOLF?!
BWAH HAH HAH HAH!

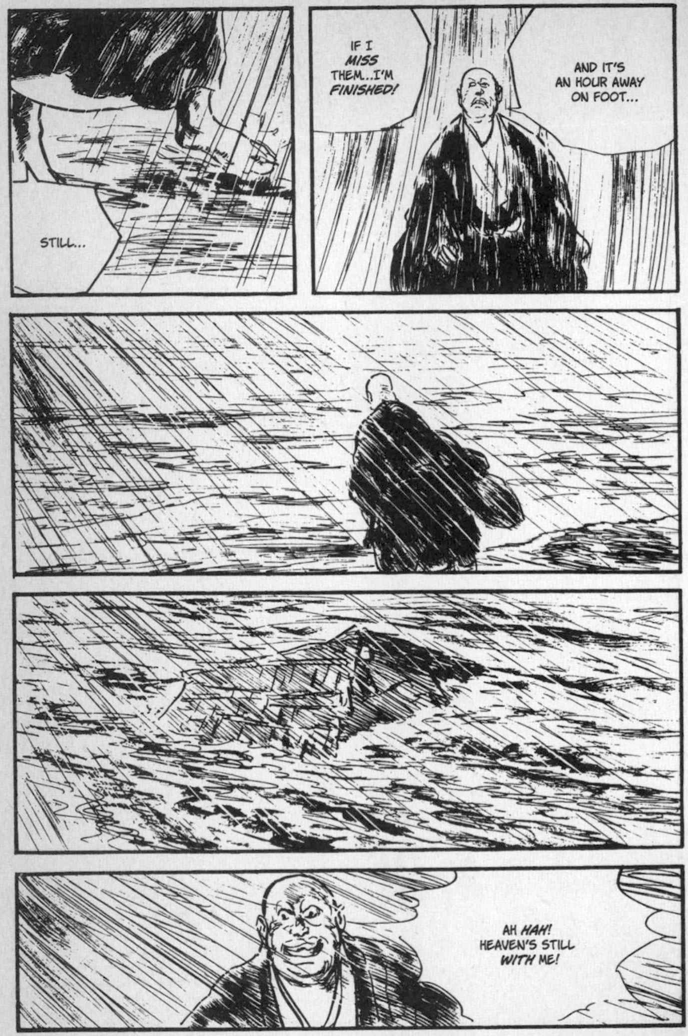
AND IT'S AN HOUR AWAY ON FOOT...
IF I *MISS* THEM...I'M *FINISHED!*
STILL...
AH *HAH!* HEAVEN'S STILL *WITH* ME!

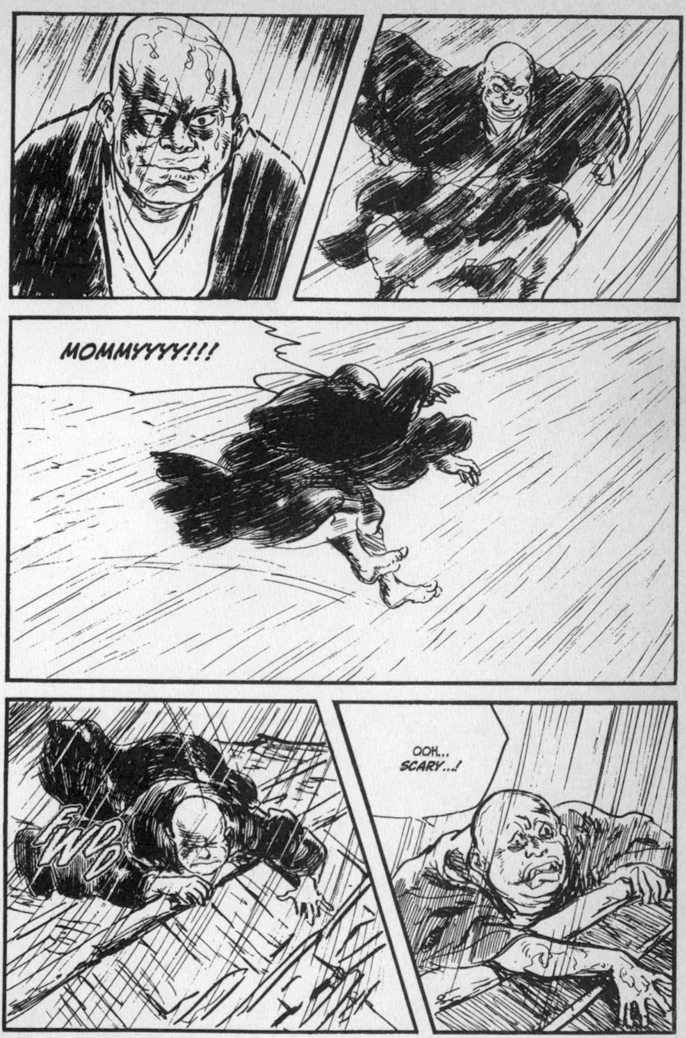
MOMMYYYY!!!
OOH... SCARY...!
FWS

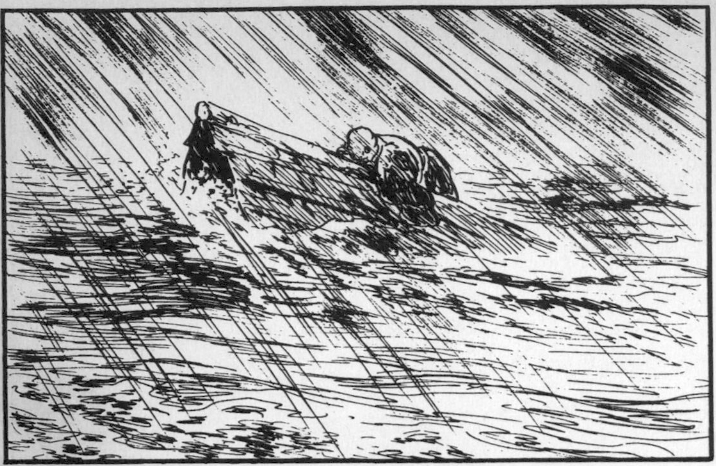
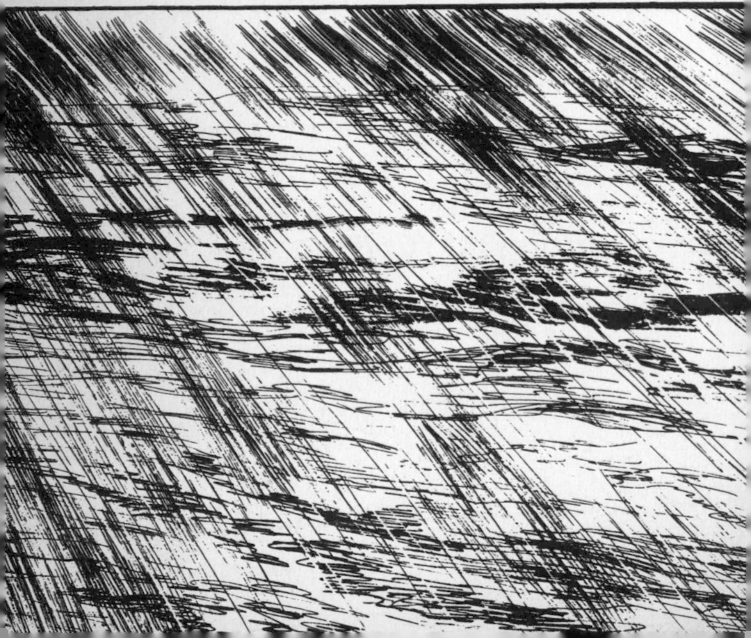

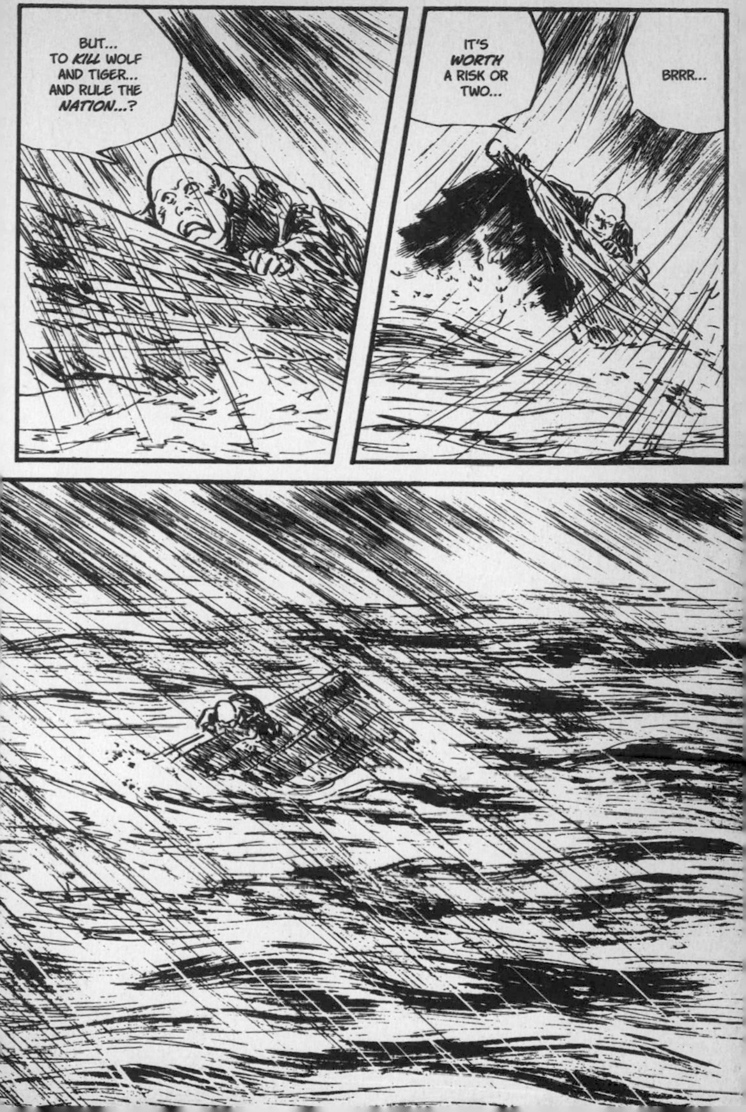
BUT... TO KILL WOLF AND TIGER... AND RULE THE NATION...?
IT'S WORTH A RISK OR TWO...
BRRR...

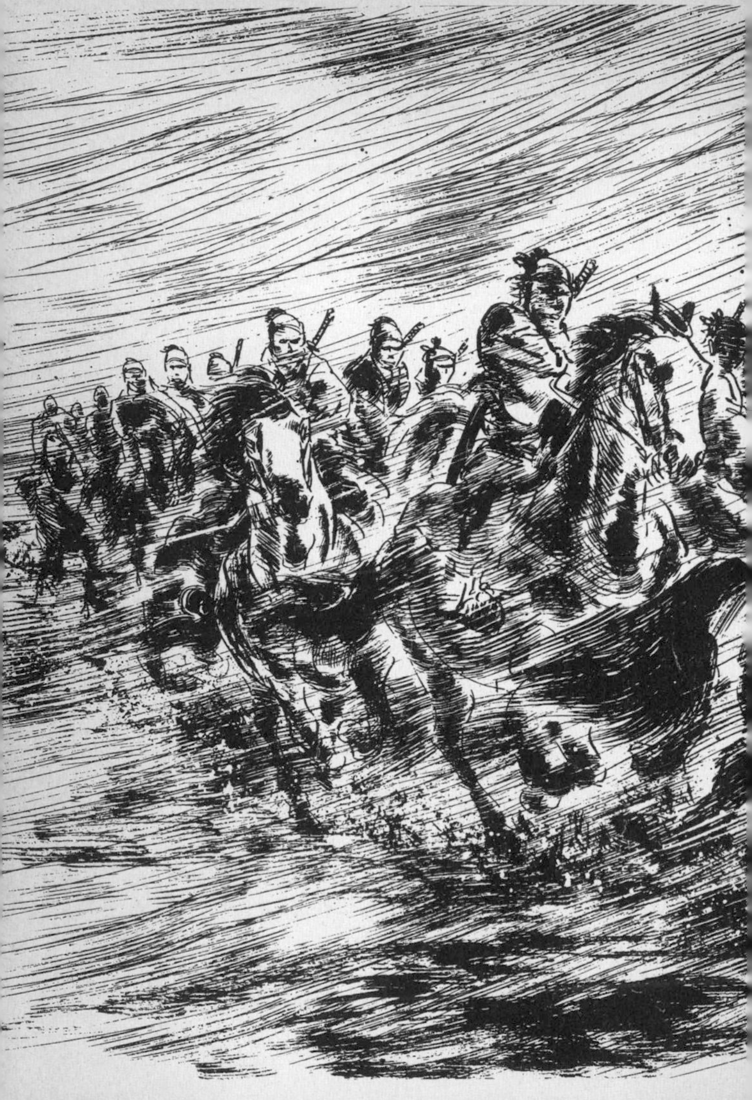

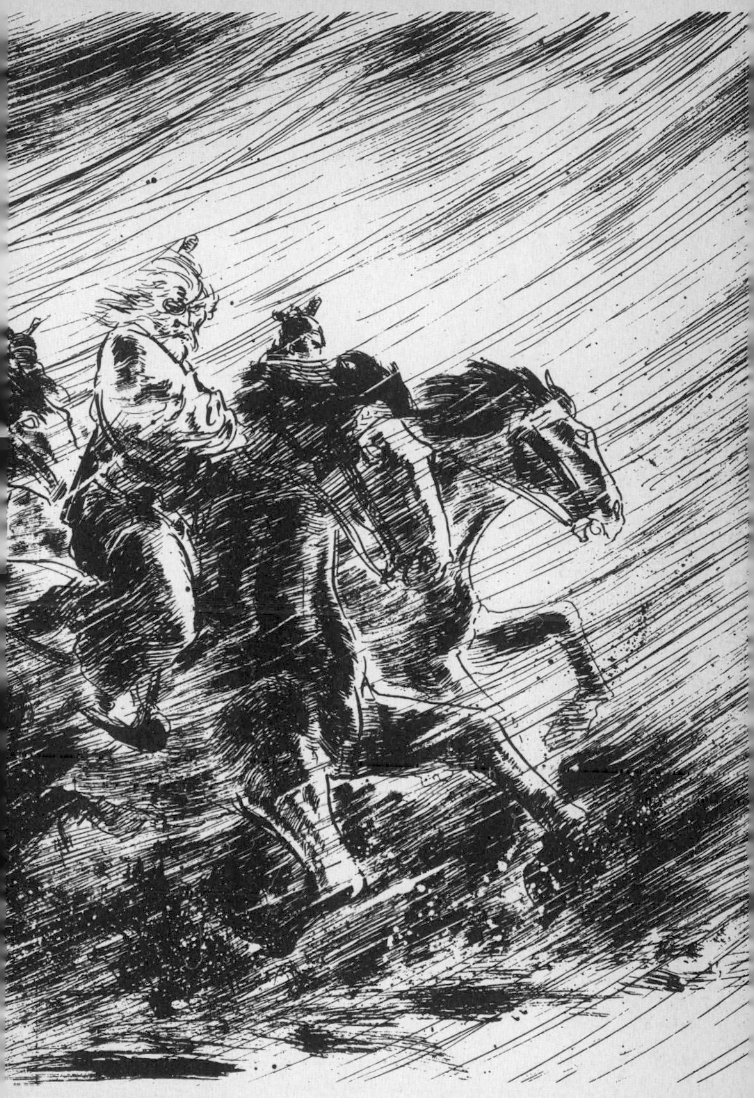

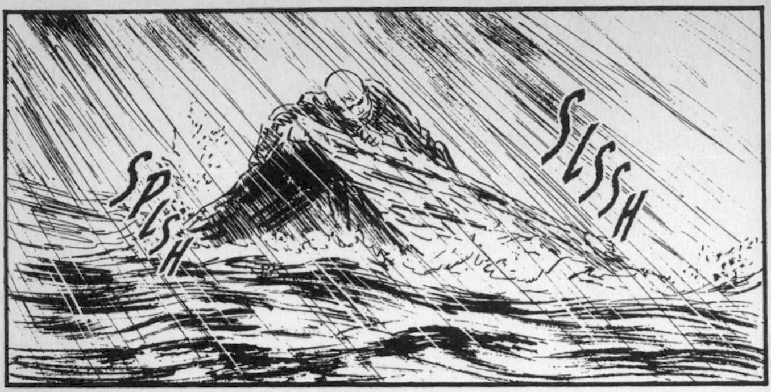
SISSH
SPLSH
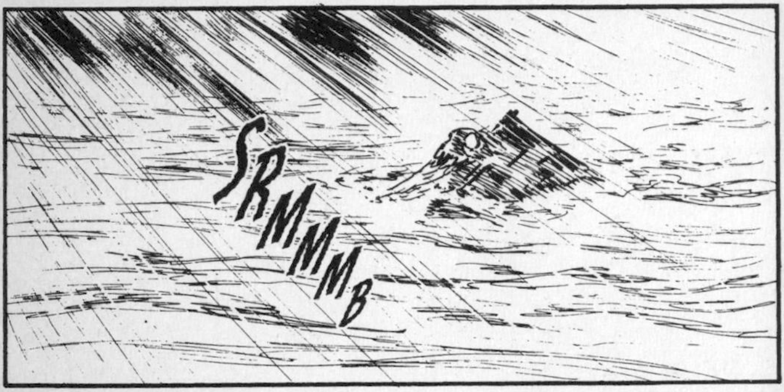
SRMMMB
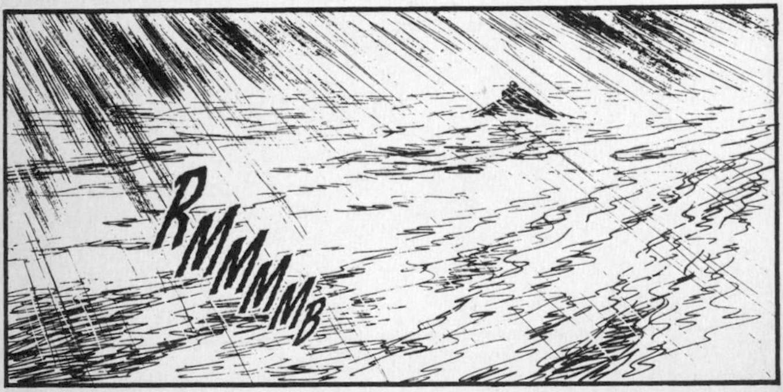
RMMMMB

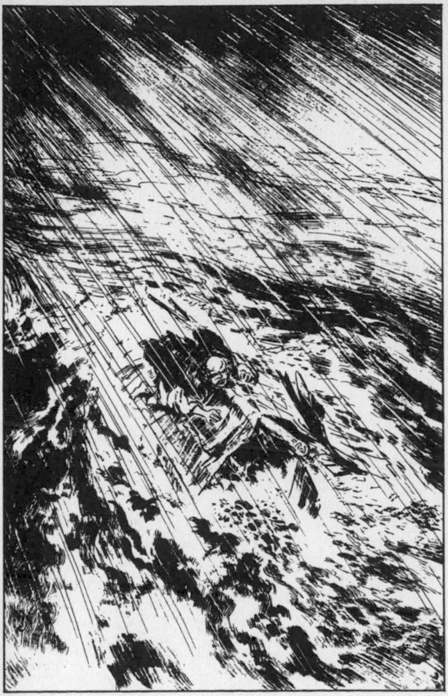

the hundred
and ninth

Tōtekizai

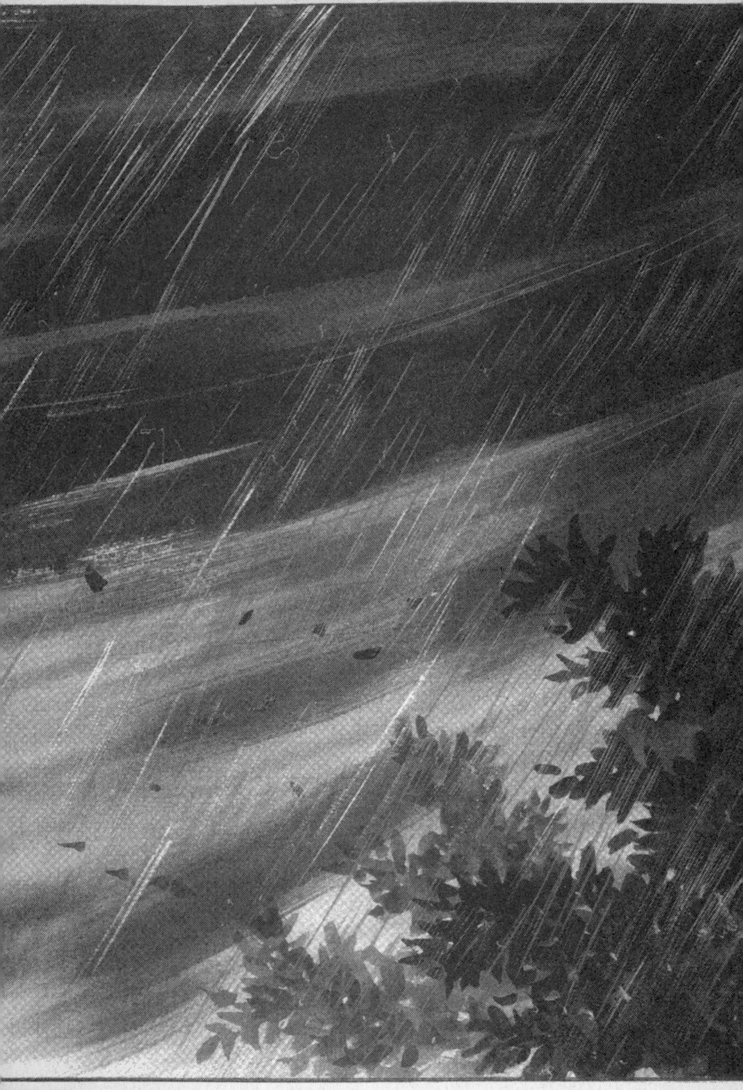

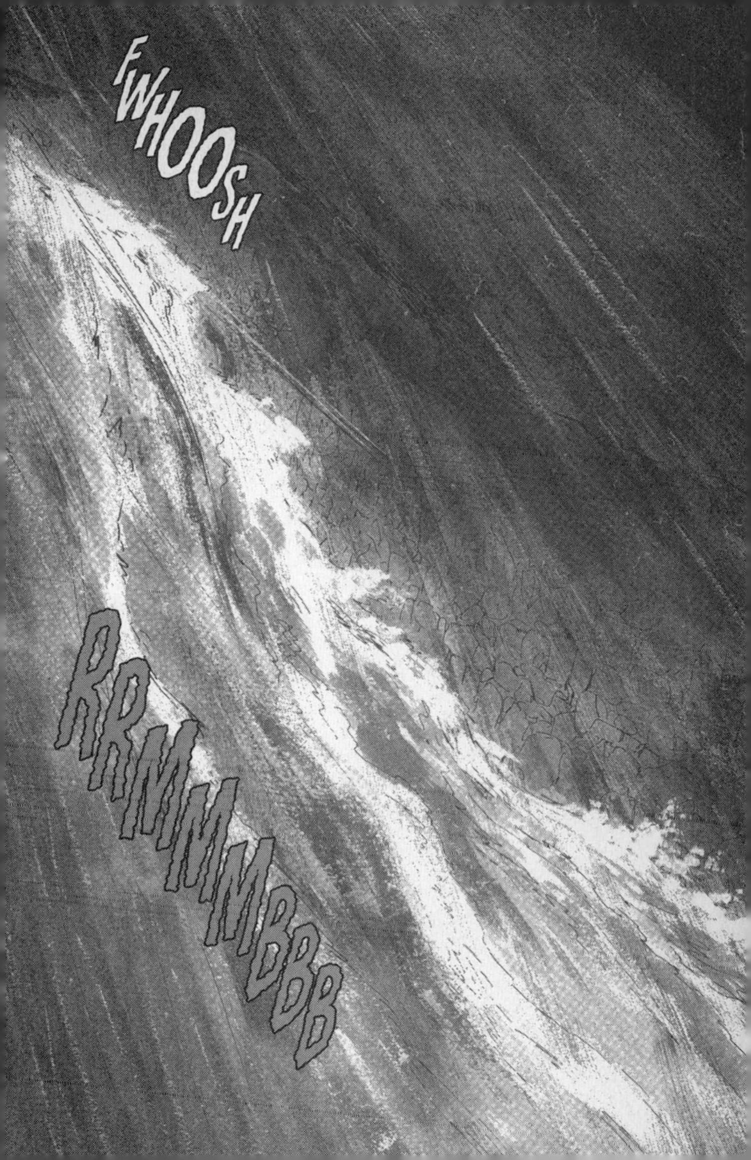
FWHOOSH
RRMMMBBB

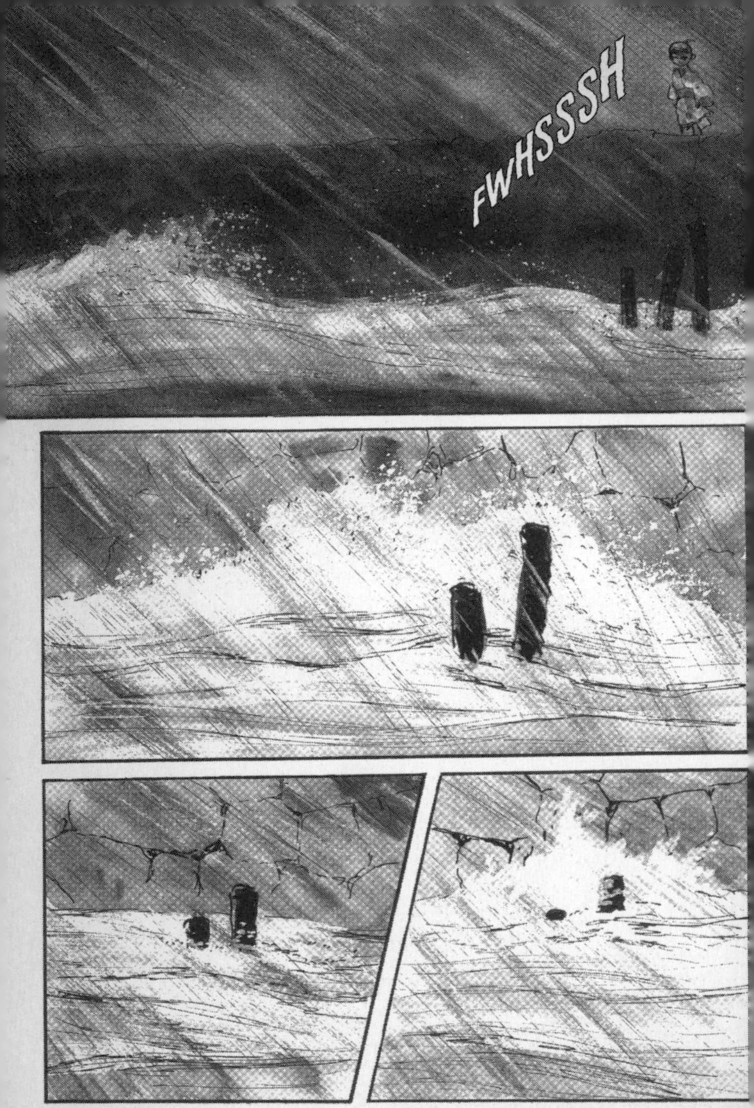
FWHSSSH

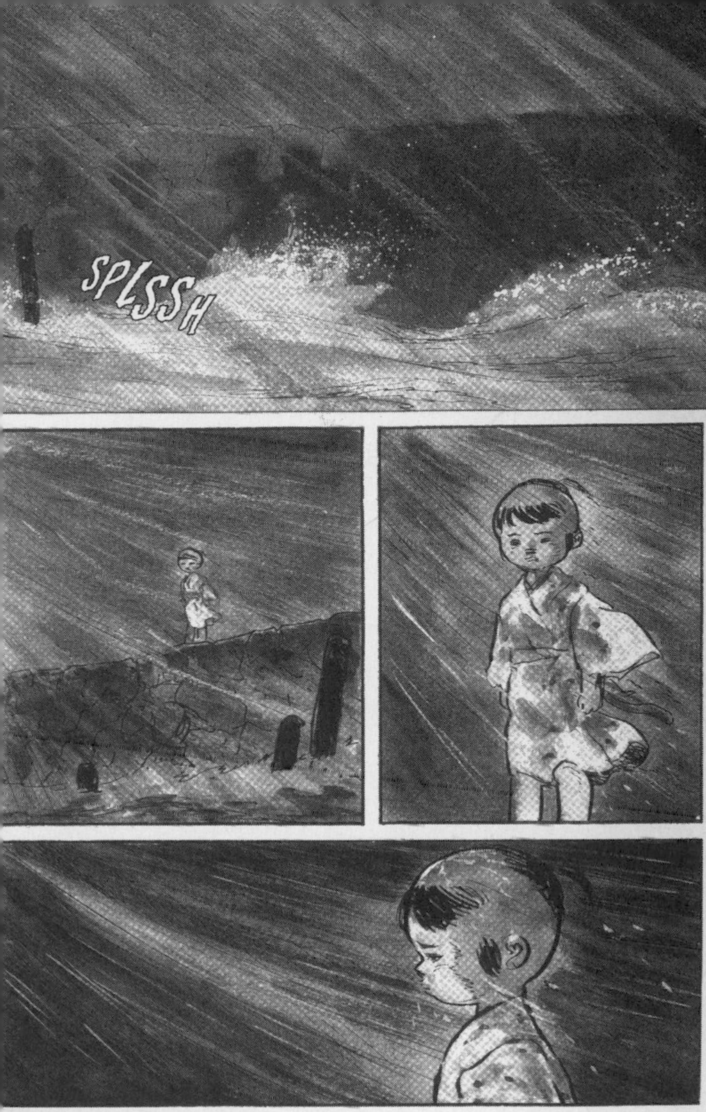
SPLSSH

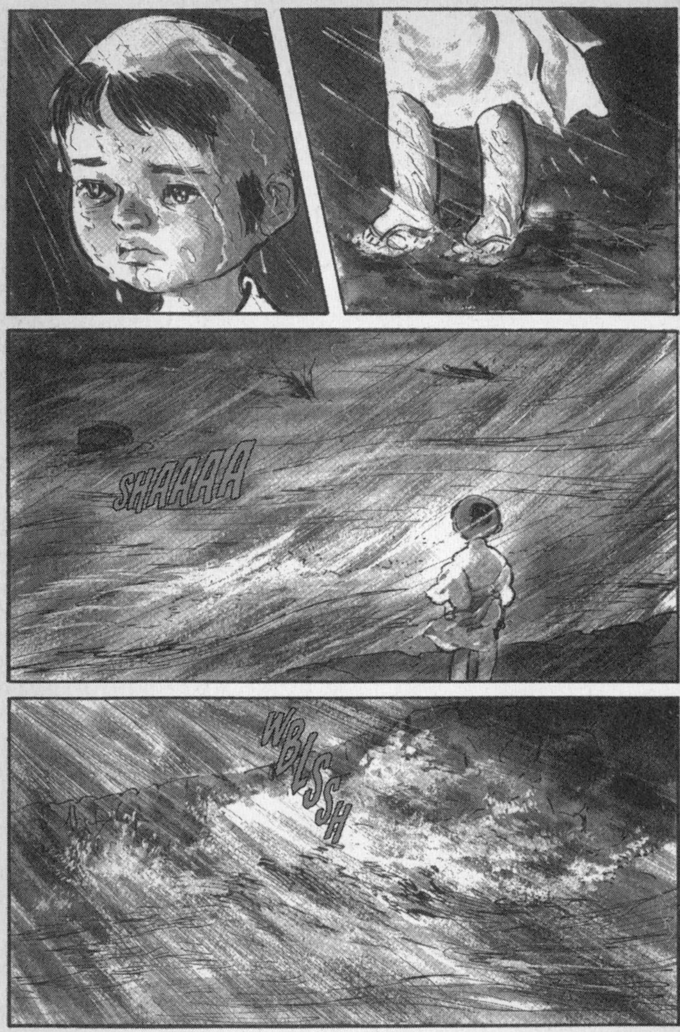
SHAAAA
WBLSSH

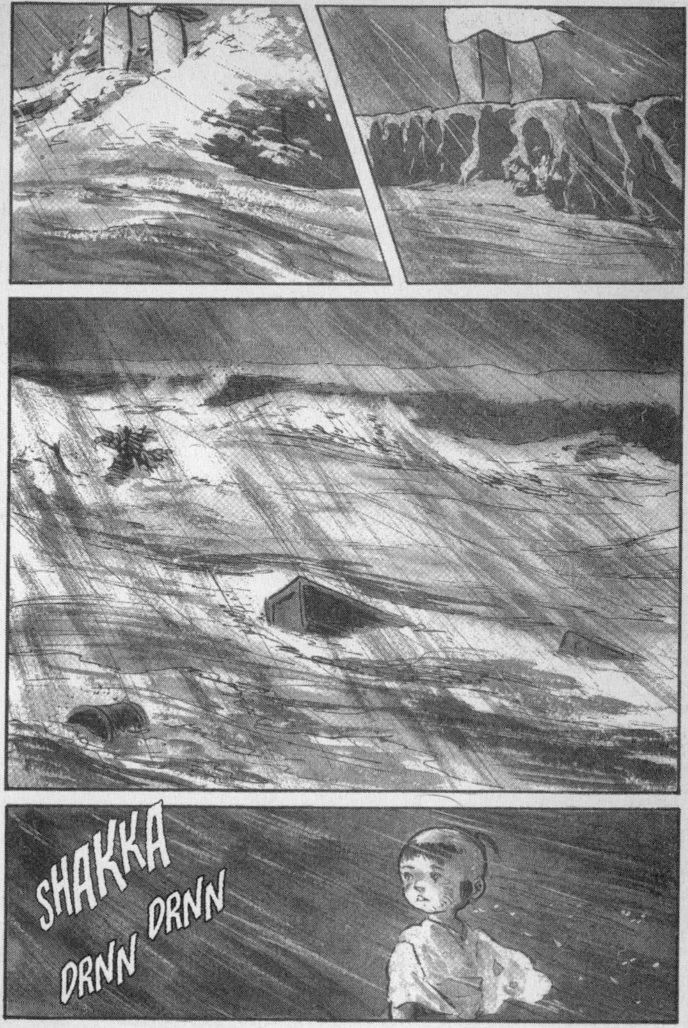
SHAKKA
DRNN DRNN

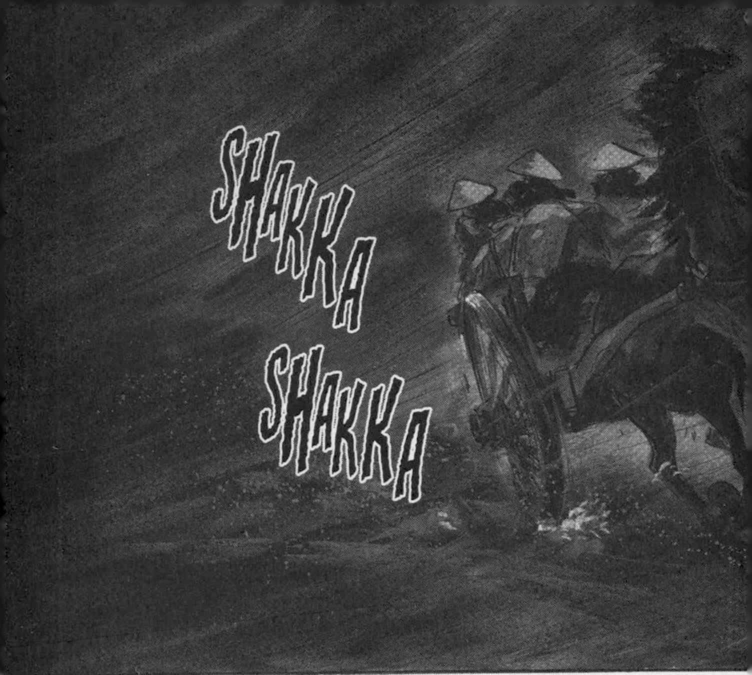
SHAKKA
SHAKKA

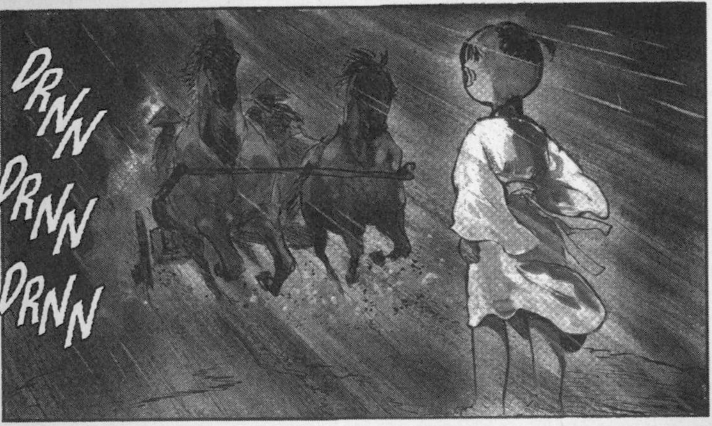
DRNN
DRNN
DRNN

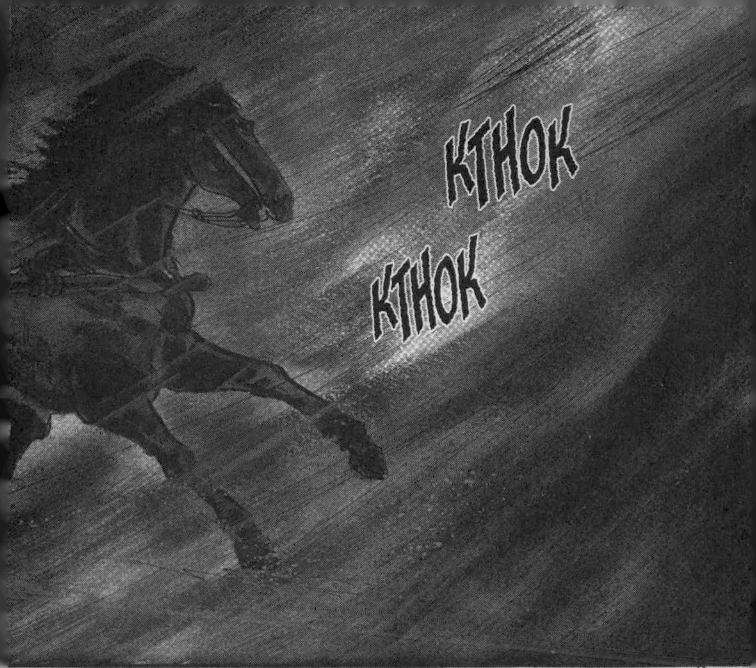
KTHOK
KTHOK

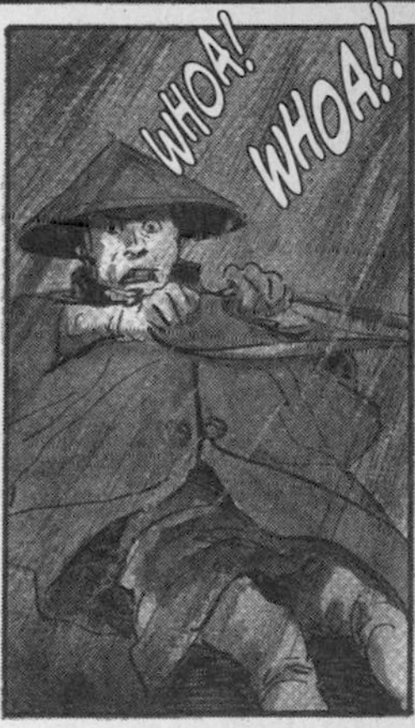
WHOA!
WHOA!!

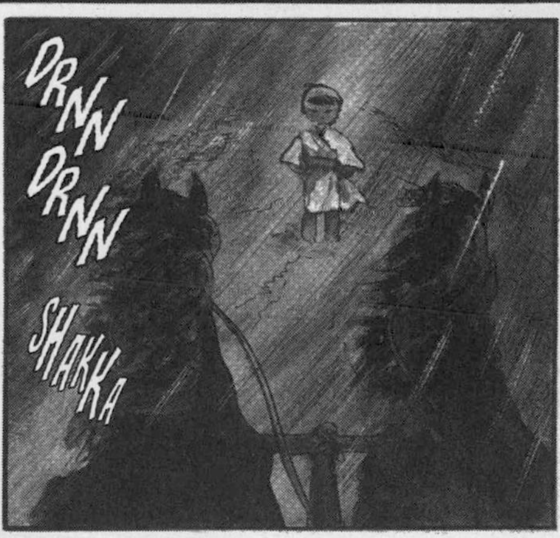
DRNN DRNN
SHAKKA

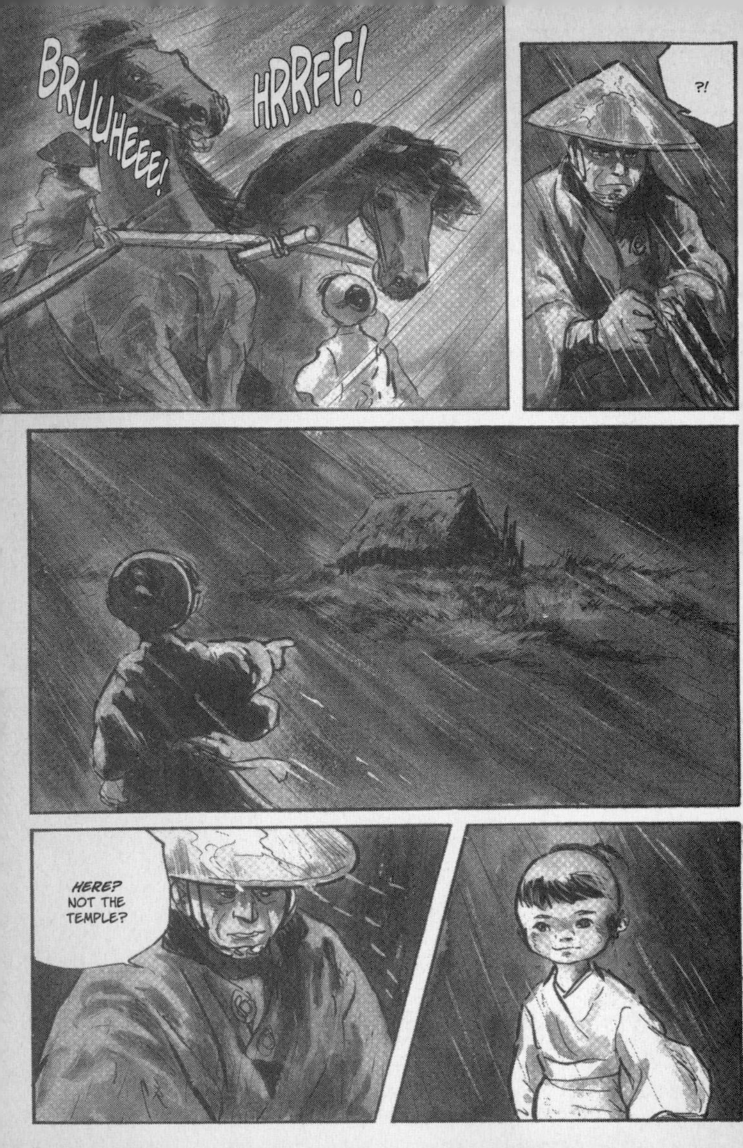
BRUUHEEEE!
HRRFF!
?!
HERE? NOT THE TEMPLE?

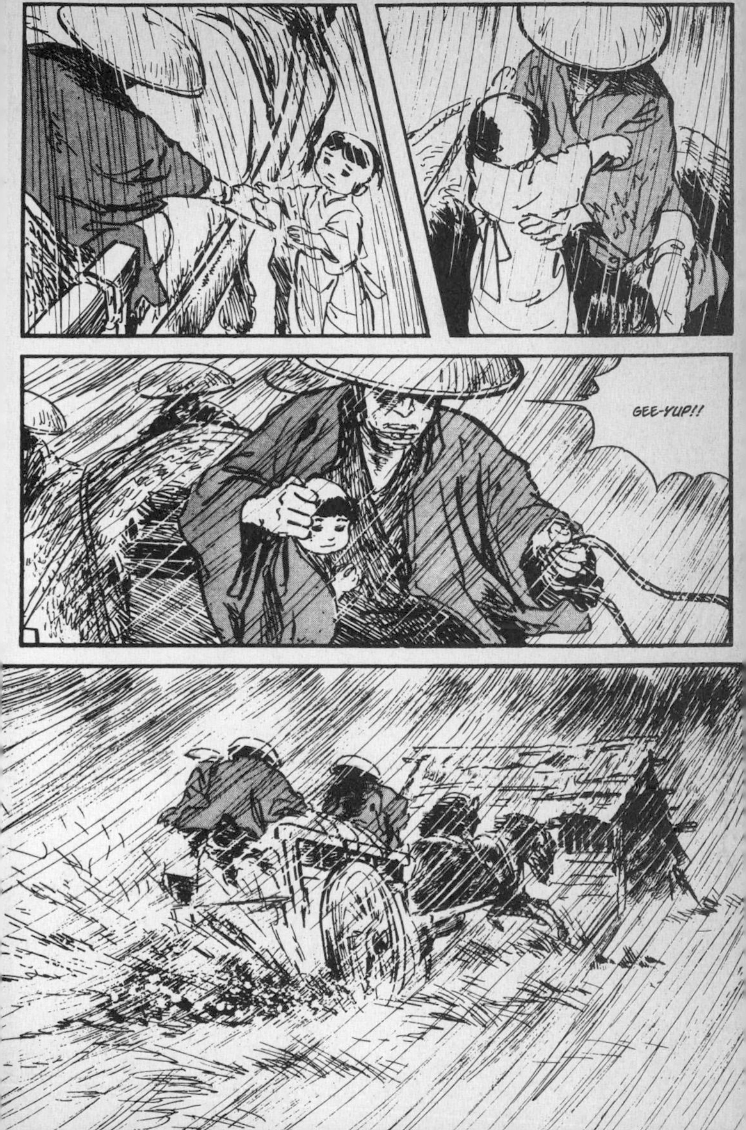
GEE-YUP!!

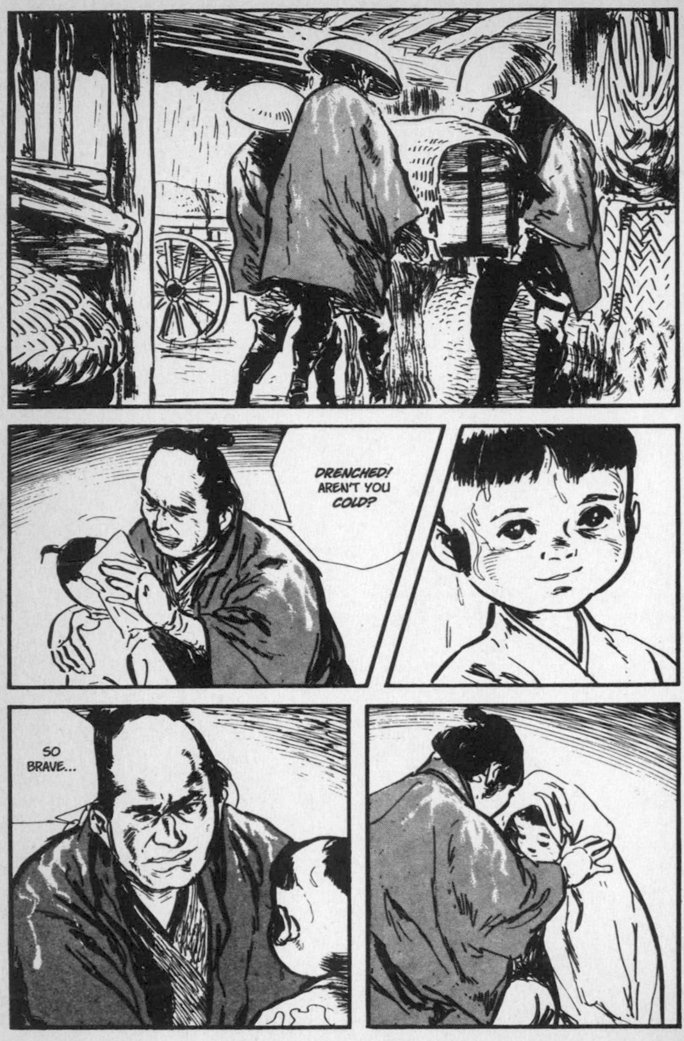
DRENCHED! AREN'T YOU COLD?
SO BRAVE...

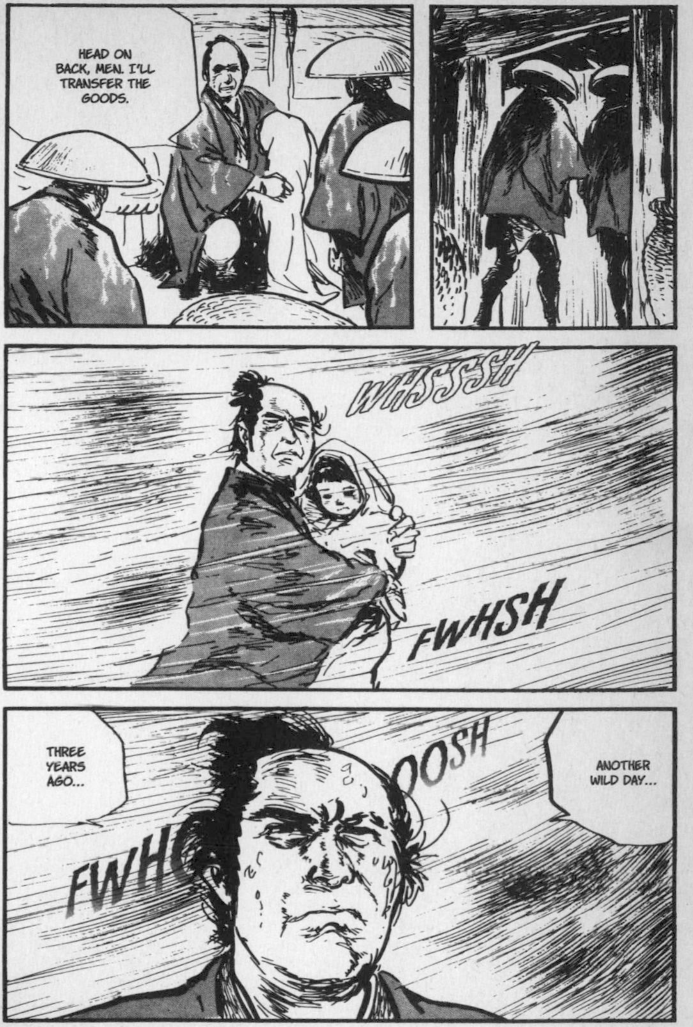
HEAD ON BACK, MEN. I'LL TRANSFER THE GOODS.
WHSSSH
FWHSH
ANOTHER WILD DAY...
OOSH
THREE YEARS AGO...
FWH

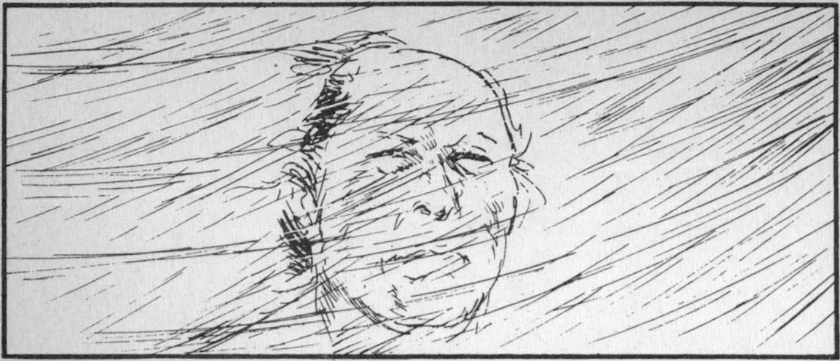
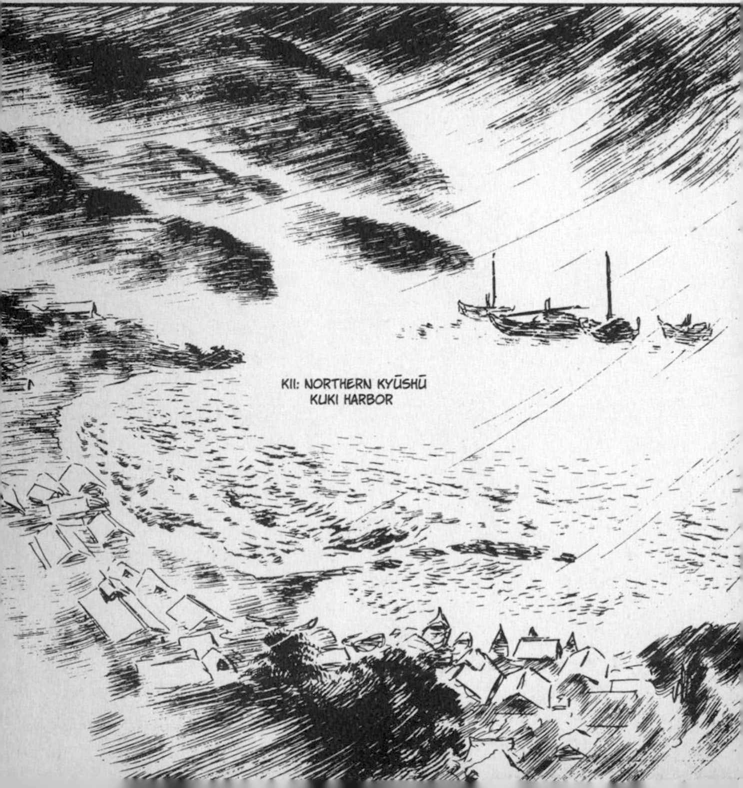
KII: NORTHERN KYŪSHŪ
KUKI HARBOR

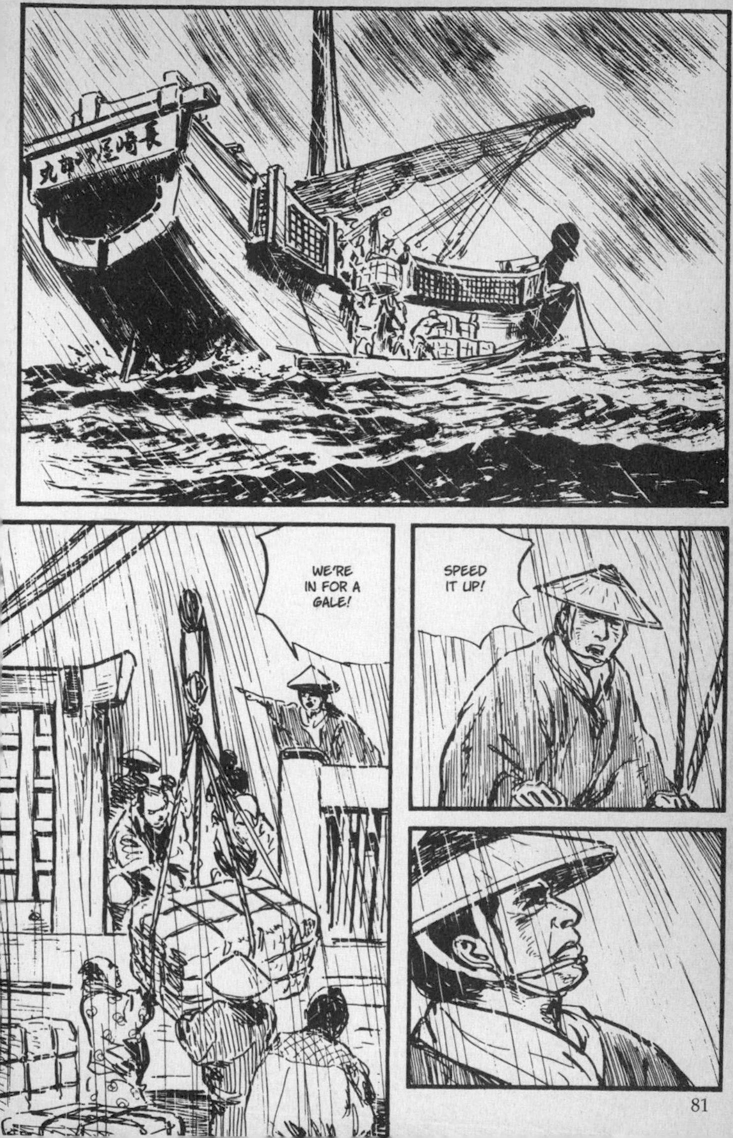
WE'RE IN FOR A GALE!
SPEED IT UP!

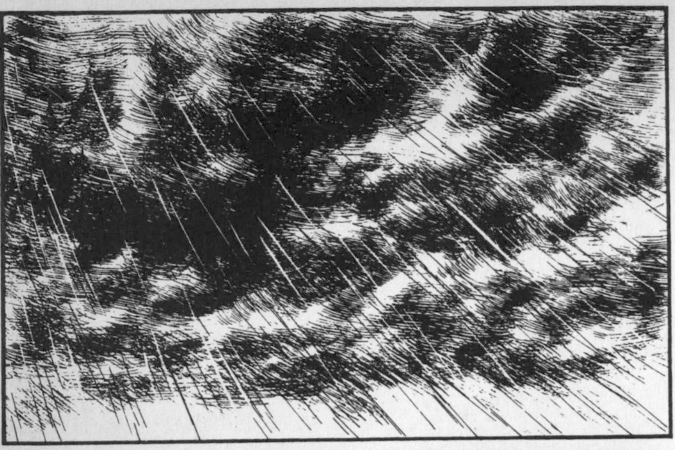
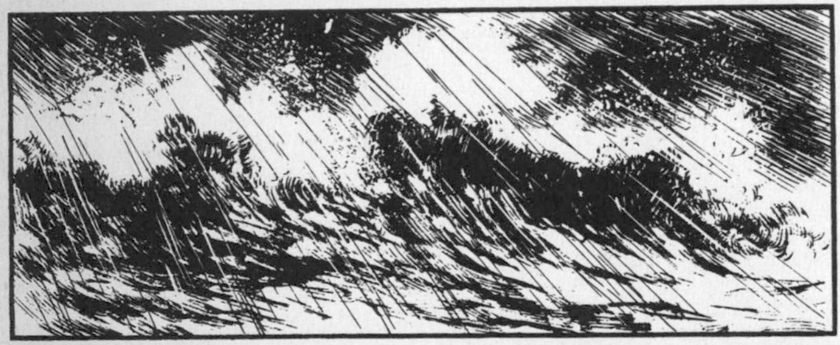
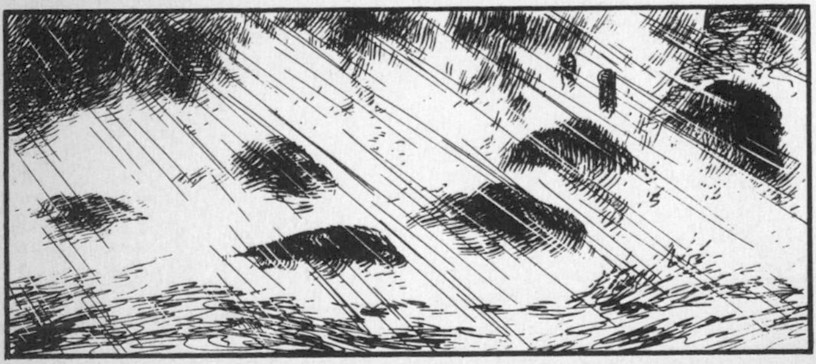

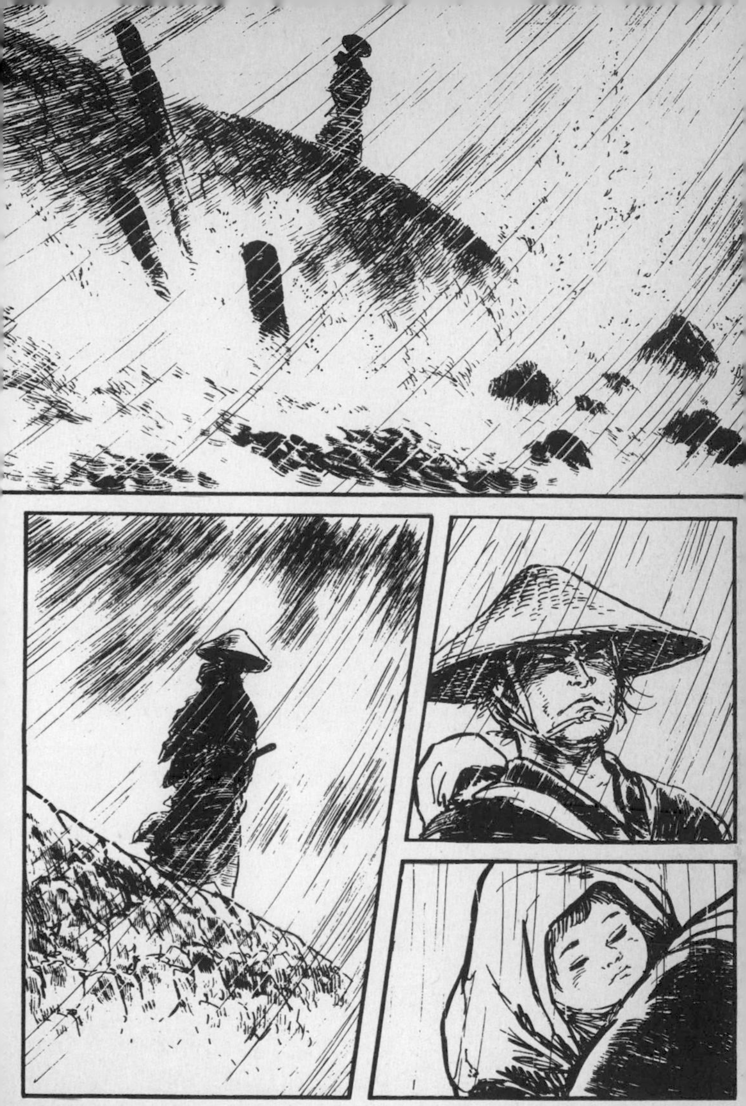

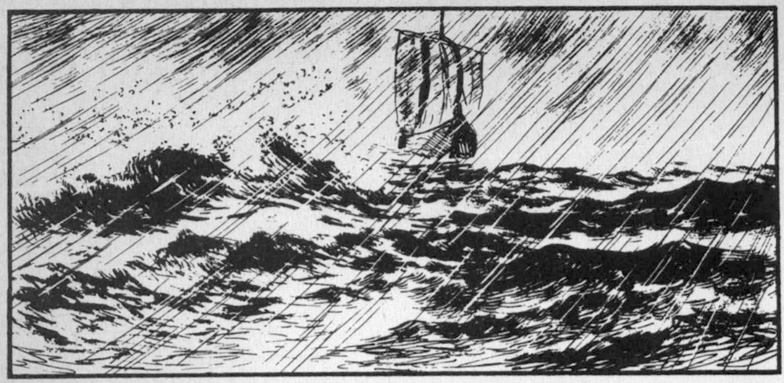

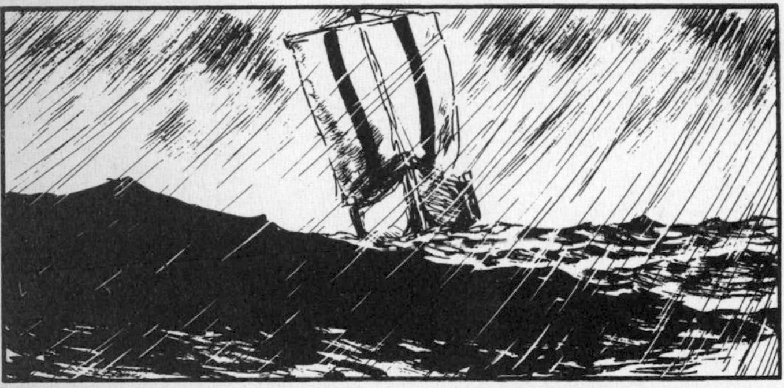

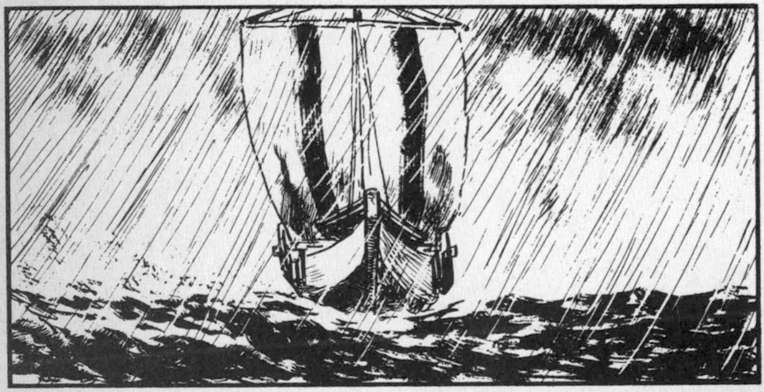

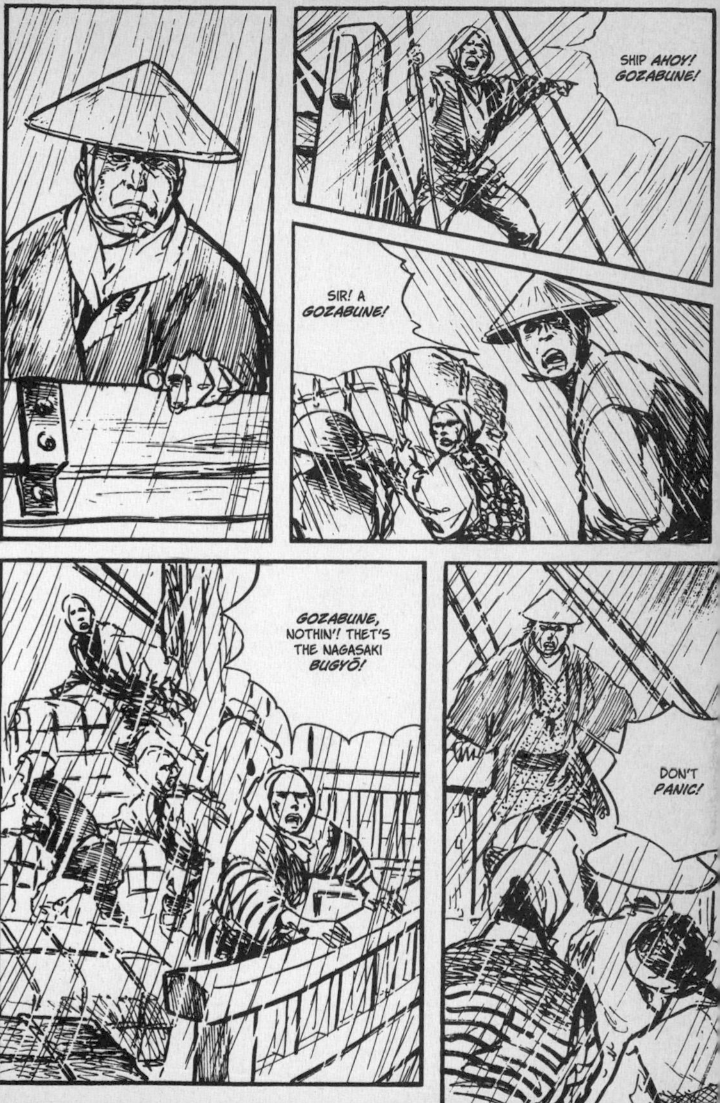
SHIP AHOY! GOZABUNE!
SIR! A GOZABUNE!
GOZABUNE, NOTHIN'! THET'S THE NAGASAKI BUGYŌ!
DON'T PANIC!

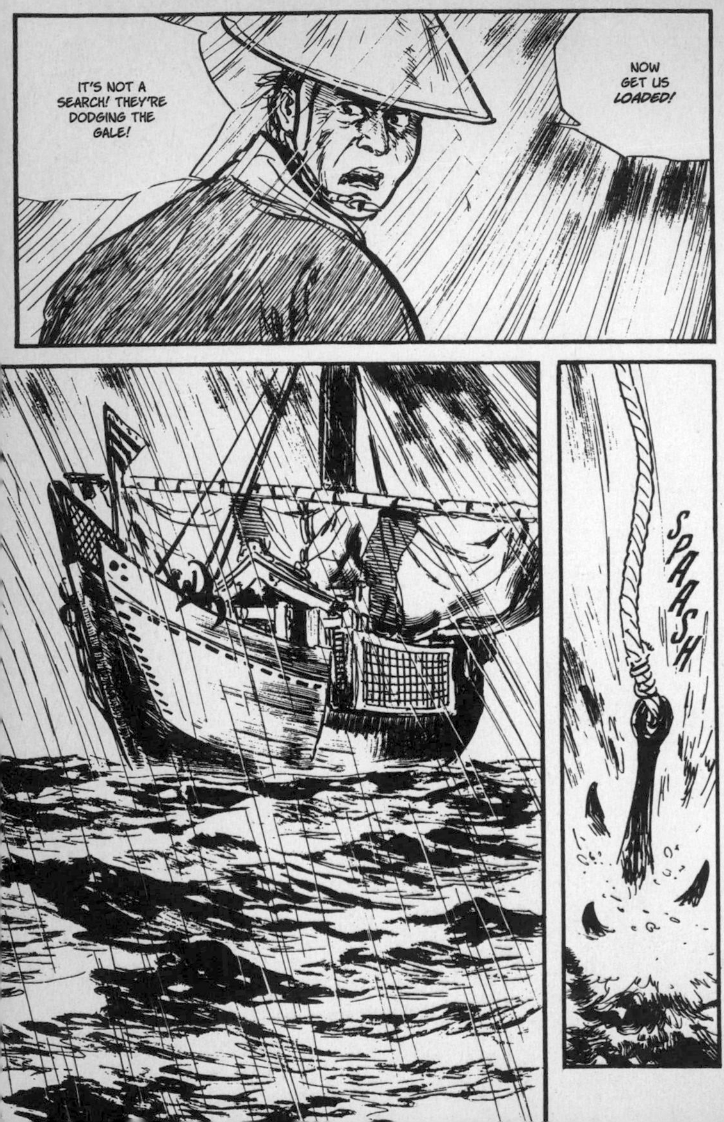
IT'S NOT A SEARCH! THEY'RE DODGING THE GALE!
NOW GET US *LOADED!*
SPAASH

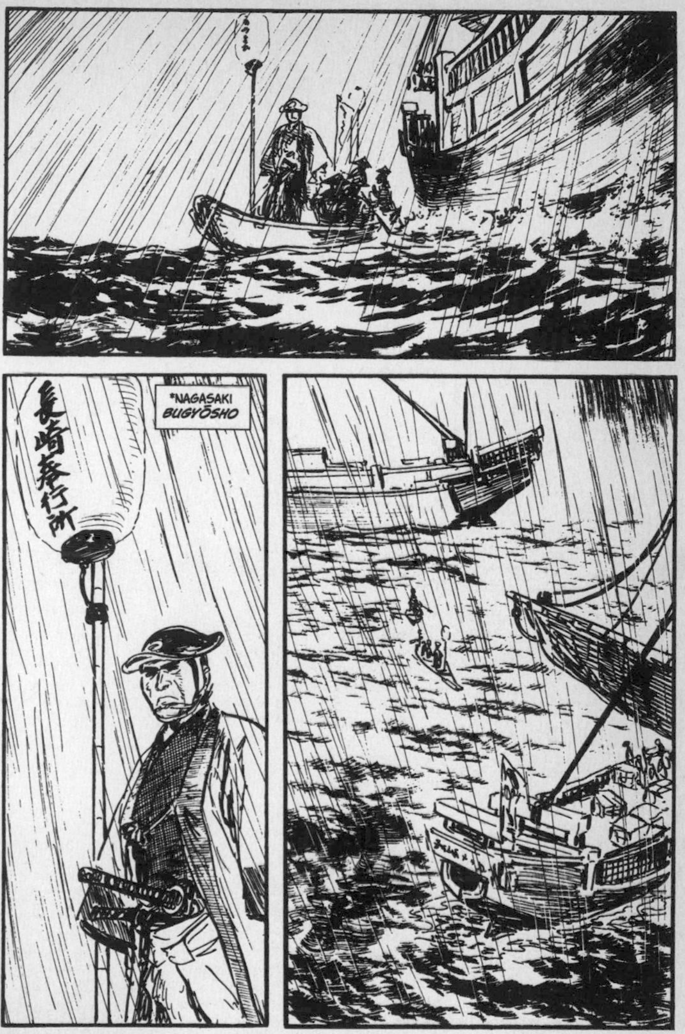
*NAGASAKI BUGYŌSHO
長崎奉行所

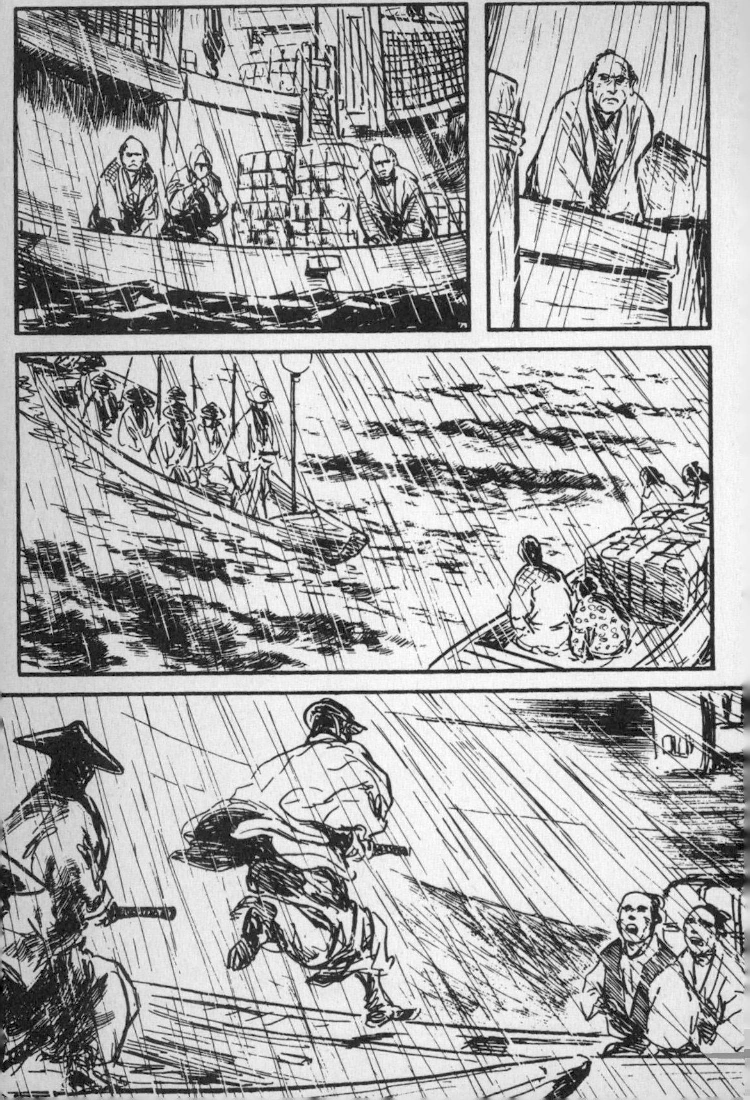

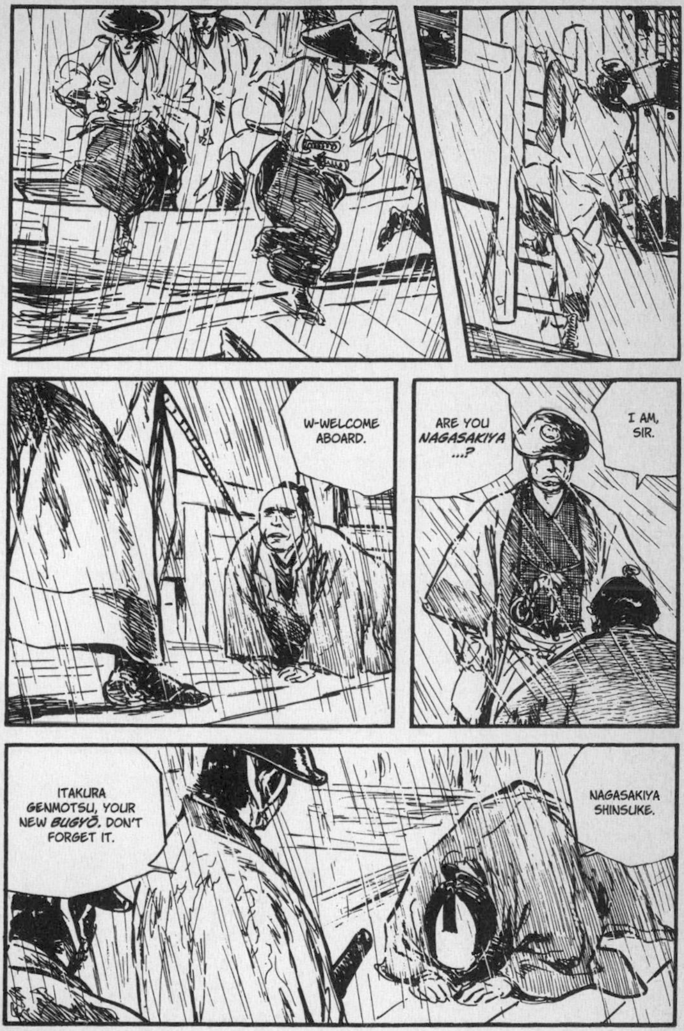
W-WELCOME ABOARD.
ARE YOU *NAGASAKIYA* ...?
I AM, SIR.
ITAKURA GENMOTSU, YOUR NEW *BUGYŌ*. DON'T FORGET IT.
NAGASAKIYA SHINSUKE.

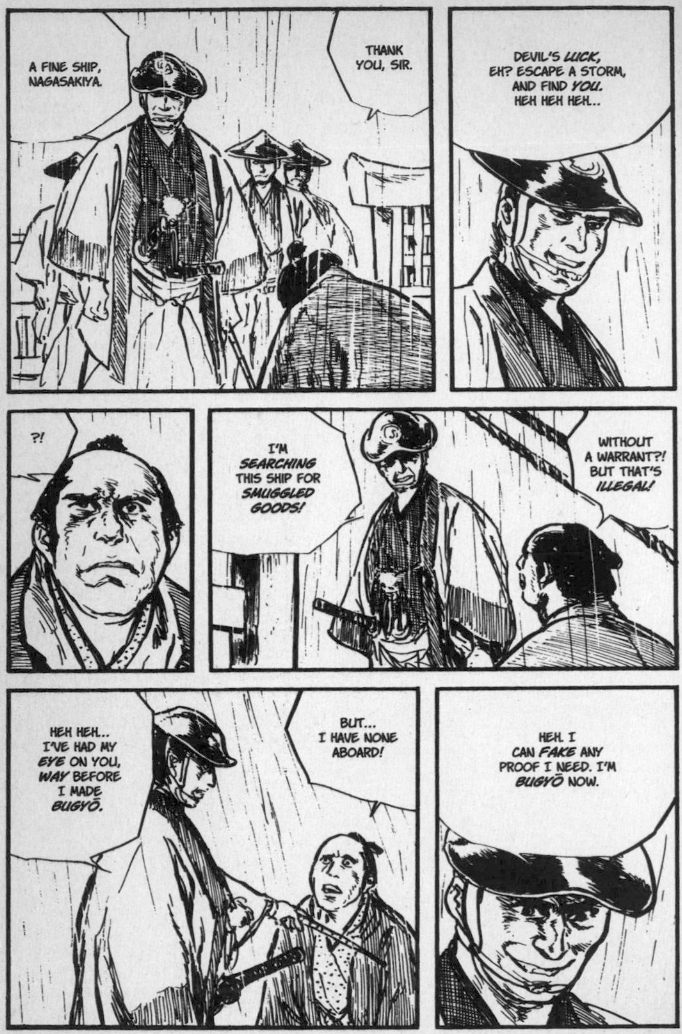
A FINE SHIP, NAGASAKIYA.
THANK YOU, SIR.
DEVIL'S *LUCK*, EH? ESCAPE A STORM, AND FIND *YOU*. HEH HEH HEH...
?!
I'M *SEARCHING* THIS SHIP FOR *SMUGGLED GOODS!*
WITHOUT A WARRANT?! BUT THAT'S *ILLEGAL!*
HEH HEH... I'VE HAD MY *EYE* ON YOU, *WAY* BEFORE I MADE *BUGYŌ*.
BUT... I HAVE NONE ABOARD!
HEH. I CAN *FAKE* ANY PROOF I NEED. I'M *BUGYŌ* NOW.

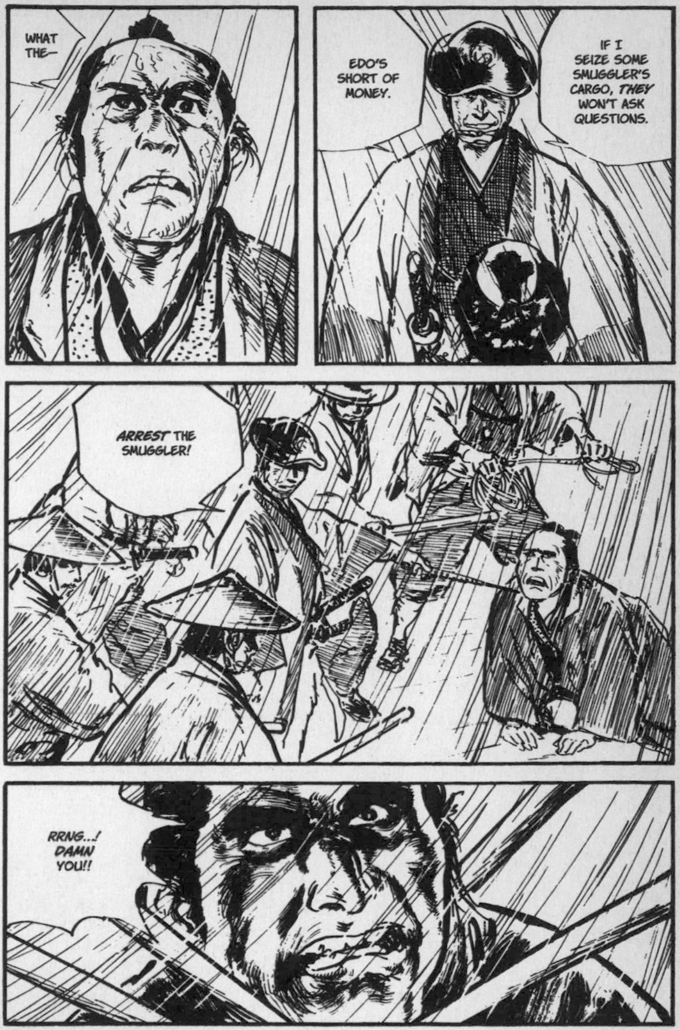
WHAT THE—
EDO'S SHORT OF MONEY.
IF I SEIZE SOME SMUGGLER'S CARGO, *THEY* WON'T ASK QUESTIONS.
ARREST THE SMUGGLER!
RRNG...! DAMN YOU!!

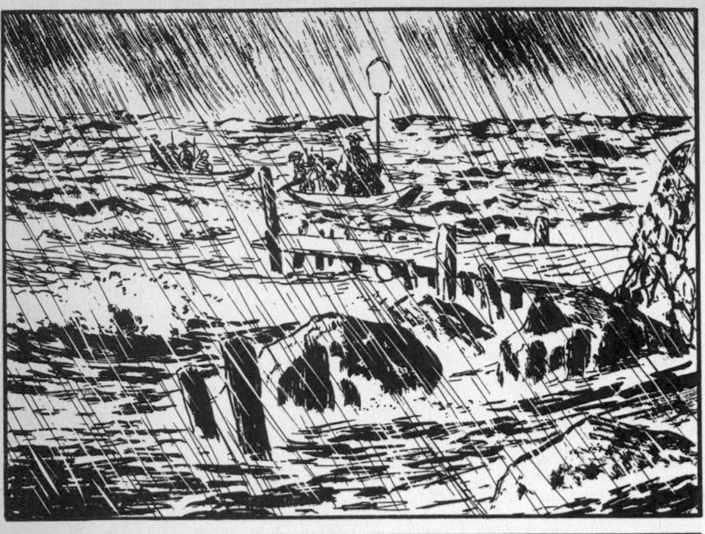
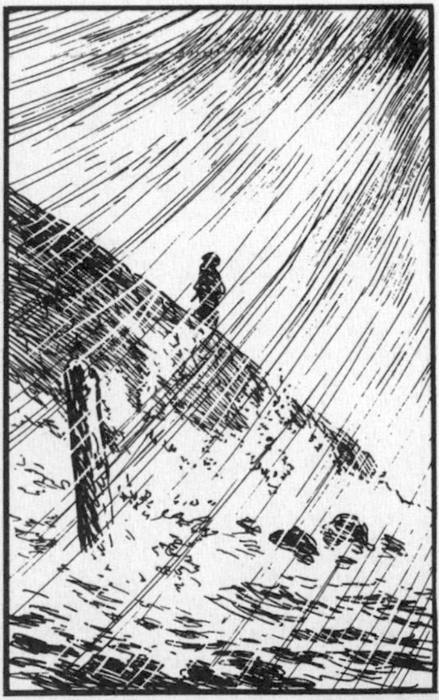
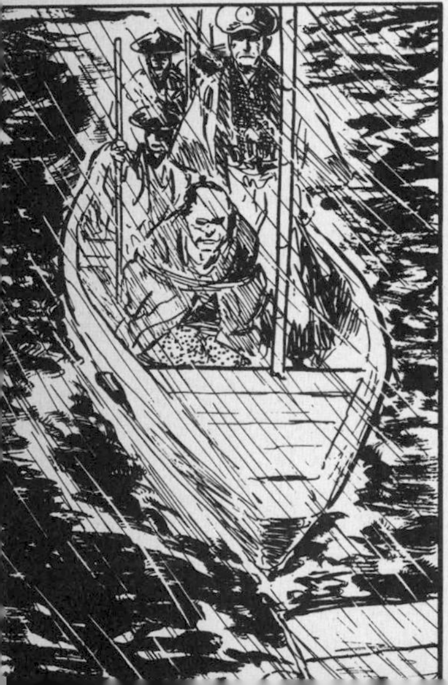

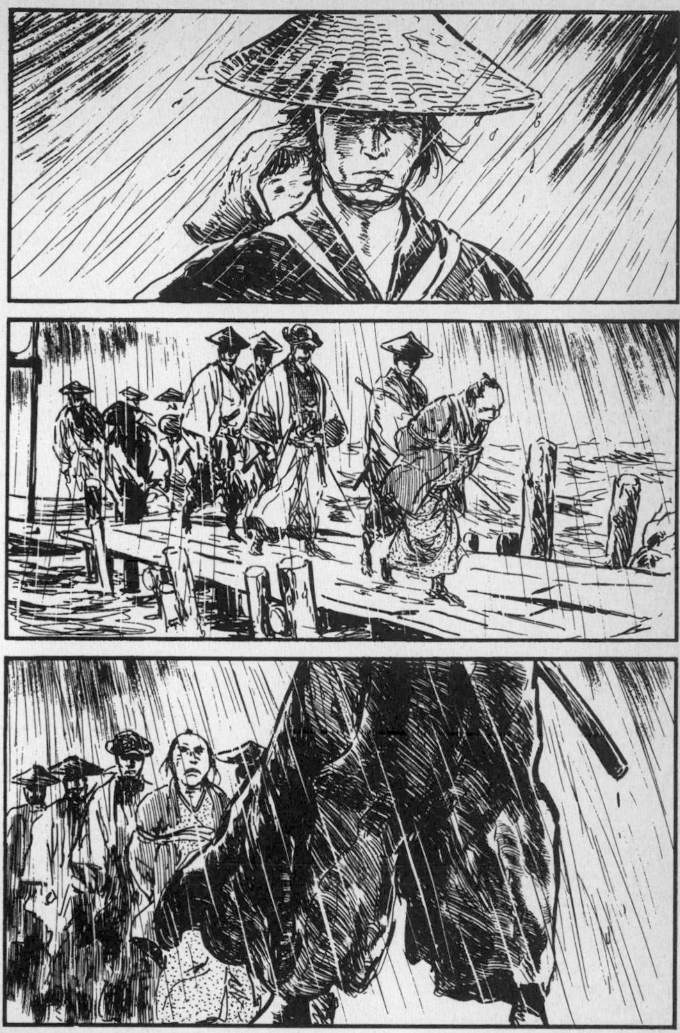

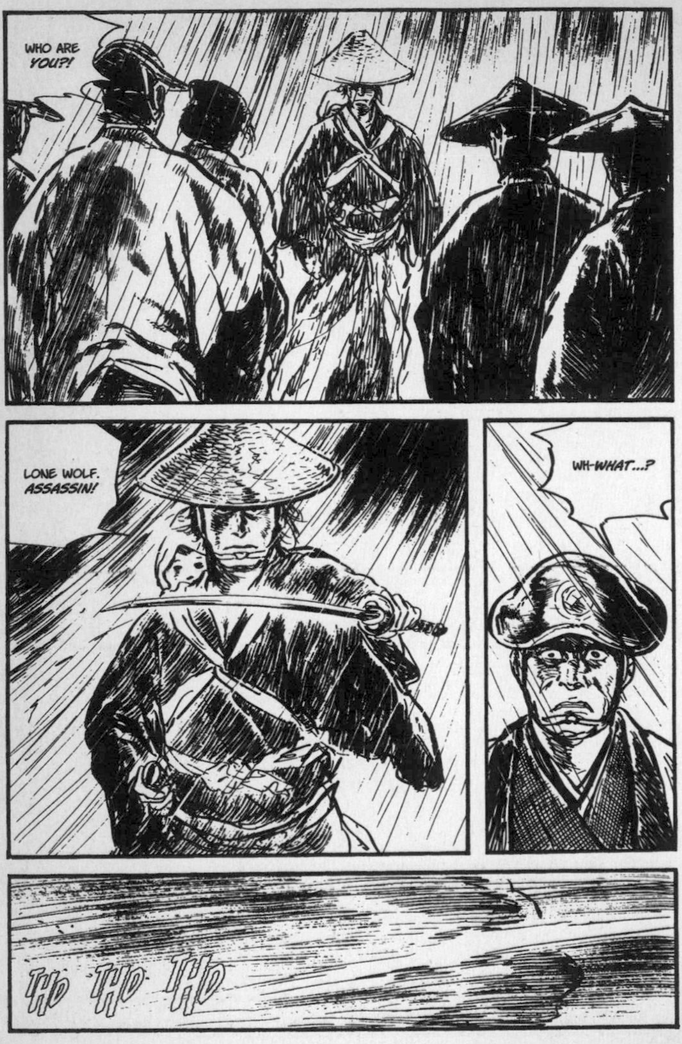
WHO ARE YOU?!
LONE WOLF. ASSASSIN!
WH-WHAT...?
THD THD THD

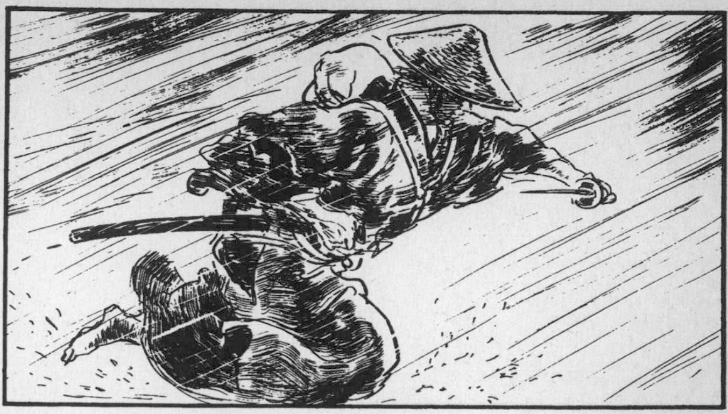
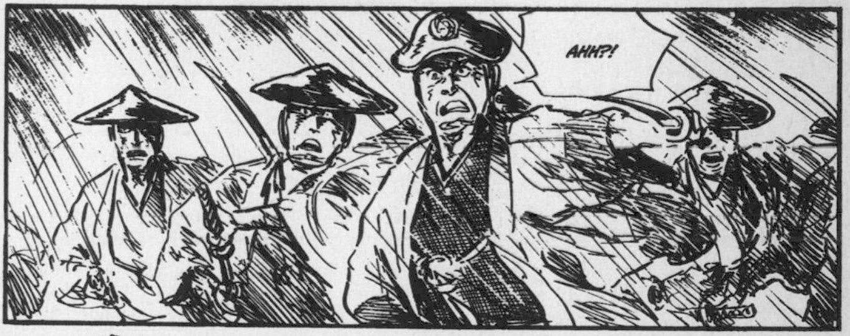
AHH?!
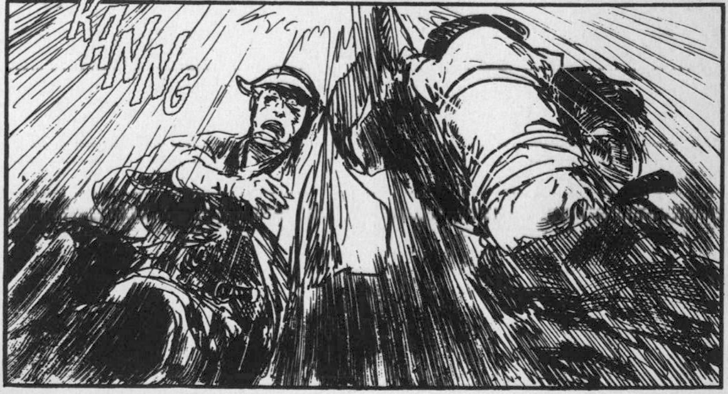
KANNG

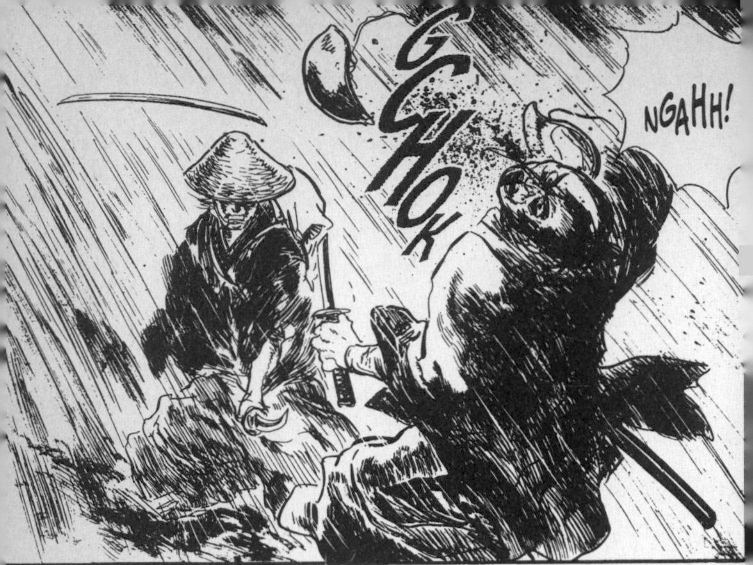
NGAHH!
GSHOK

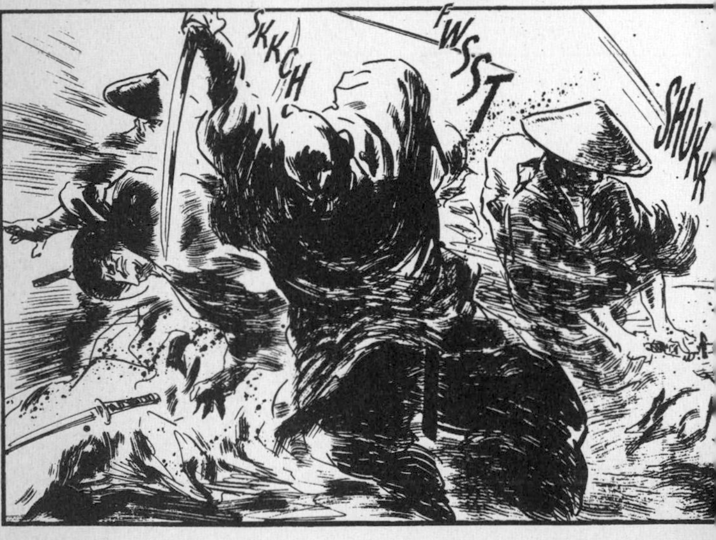
SHUKK
FWSST
SKKCH

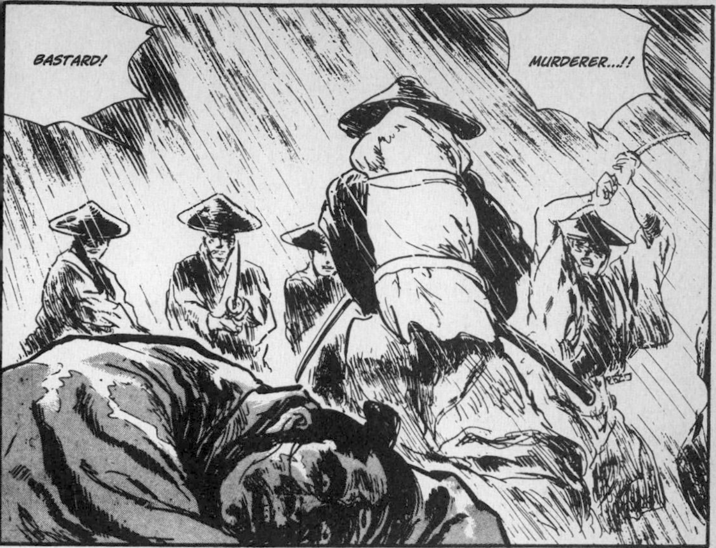
MURDERER...!!
BASTARD!
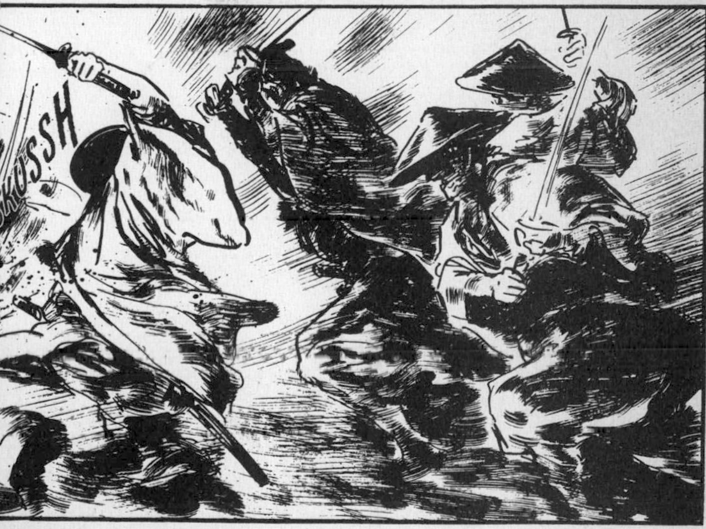
KUSSH

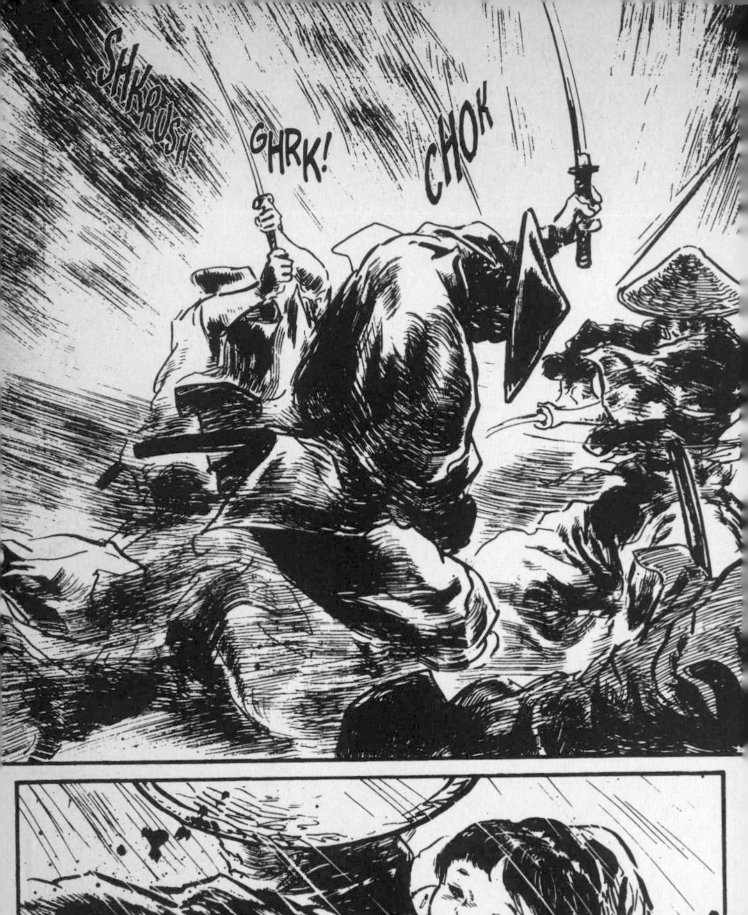
SHKRUSH
GHRK!
CHOK
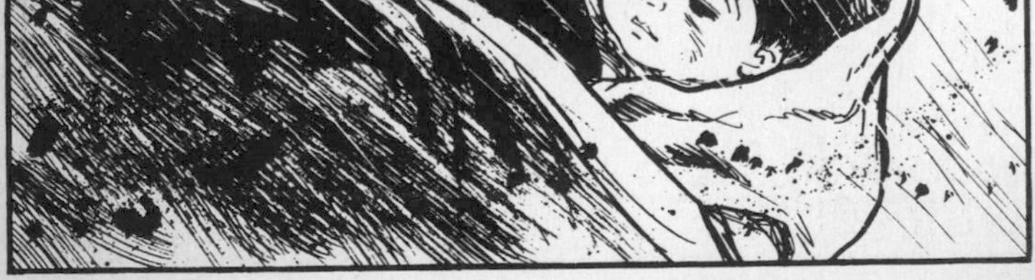

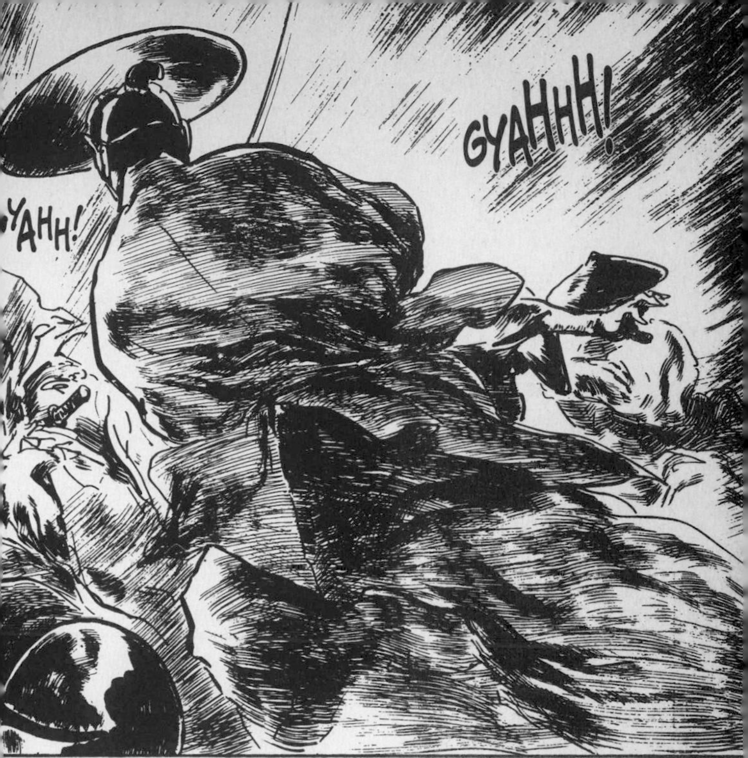
GYAHHH!
YAHH!

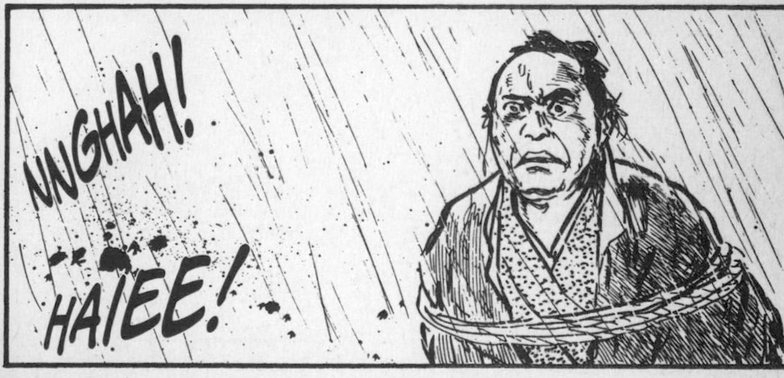
NNGHAH!
HAIEE!

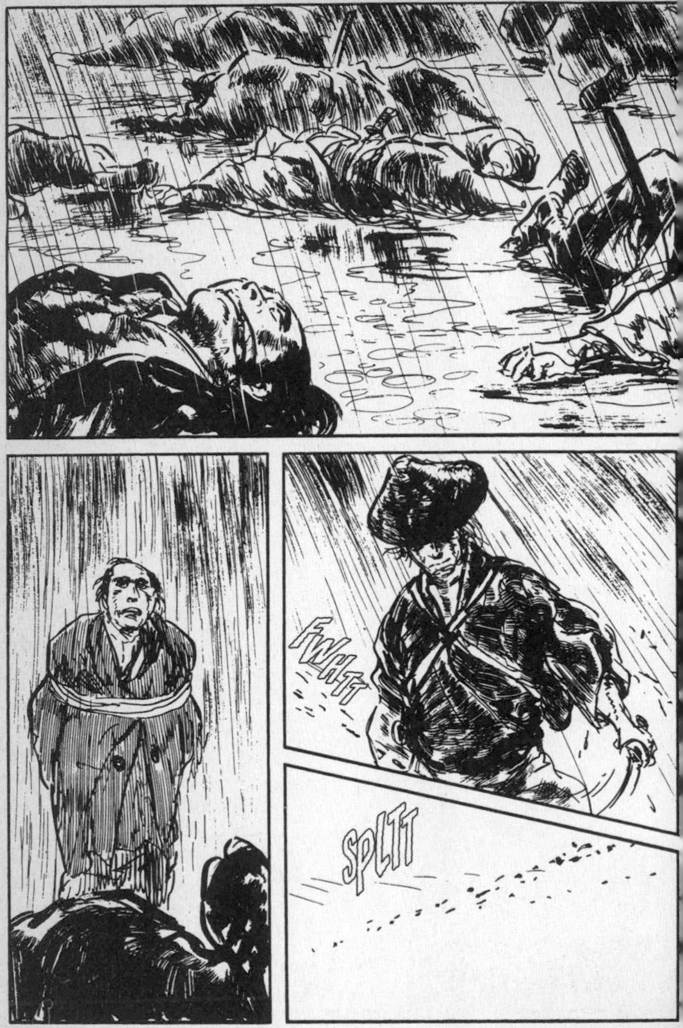
FWHTT
SPLTT

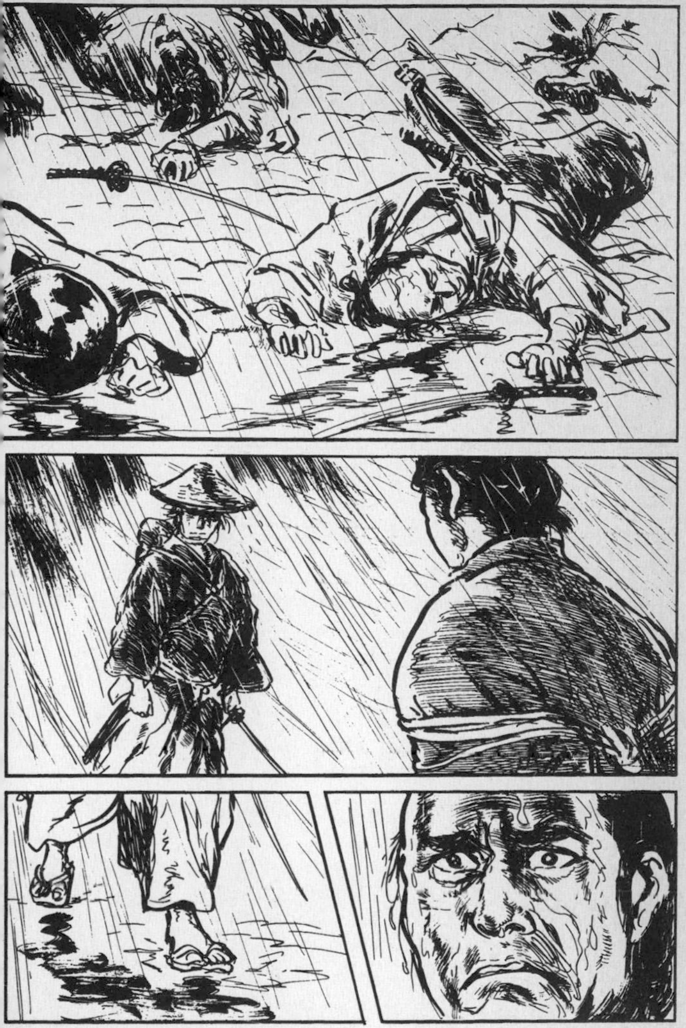

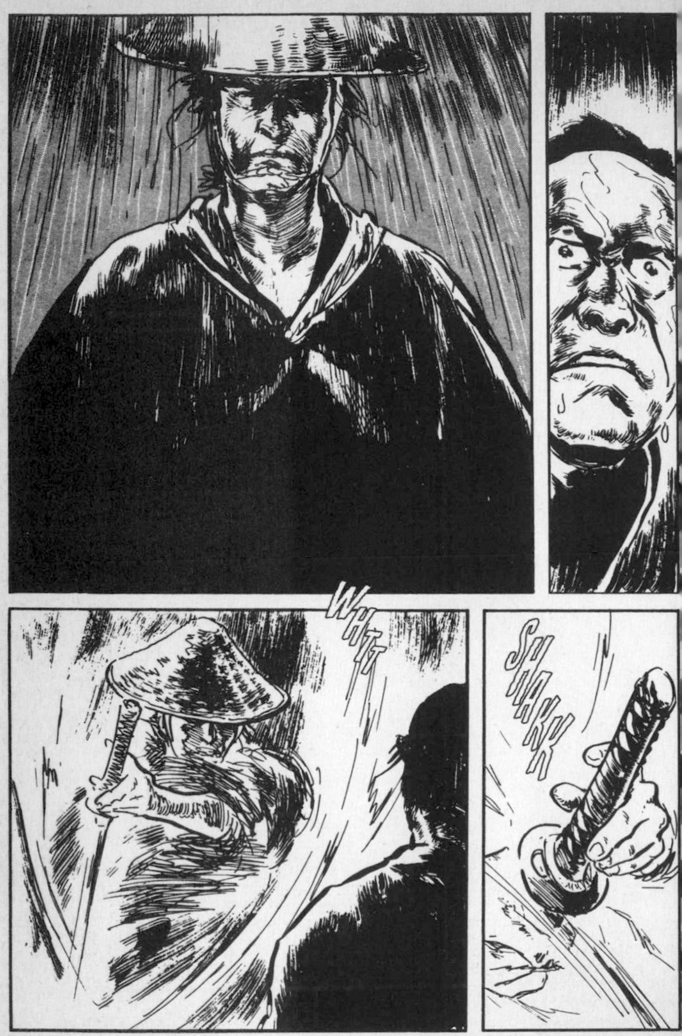
SHAKK
WHTT

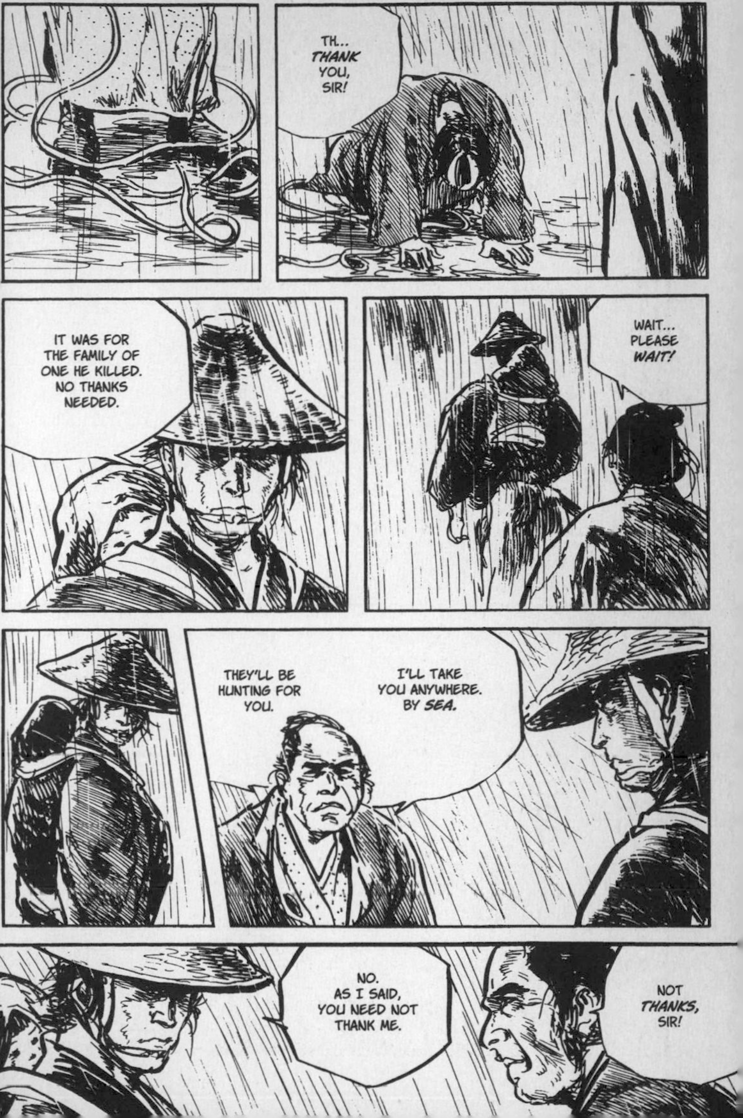
TH... *THANK* YOU, SIR!
IT WAS FOR THE FAMILY OF ONE HE KILLED. NO THANKS NEEDED.
WAIT... PLEASE *WAIT!*
THEY'LL BE HUNTING FOR YOU.
I'LL TAKE YOU ANYWHERE. BY *SEA.*
NO. AS I SAID, YOU NEED NOT THANK ME.
NOT *THANKS,* SIR!

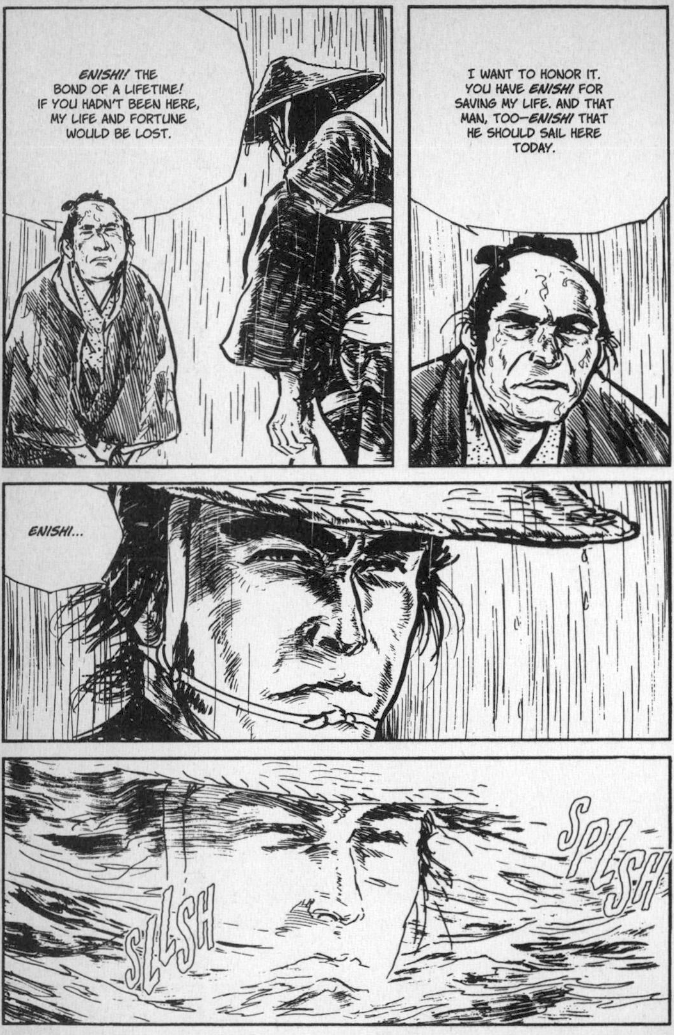
ENISHI! THE BOND OF A LIFETIME! IF YOU HADN'T BEEN HERE, MY LIFE AND FORTUNE WOULD BE LOST.
I WANT TO HONOR IT. YOU HAVE ENISHI FOR SAVING MY LIFE. AND THAT MAN, TOO—ENISHI THAT HE SHOULD SAIL HERE TODAY.
ENISHI...
SPLSH
SLLSH

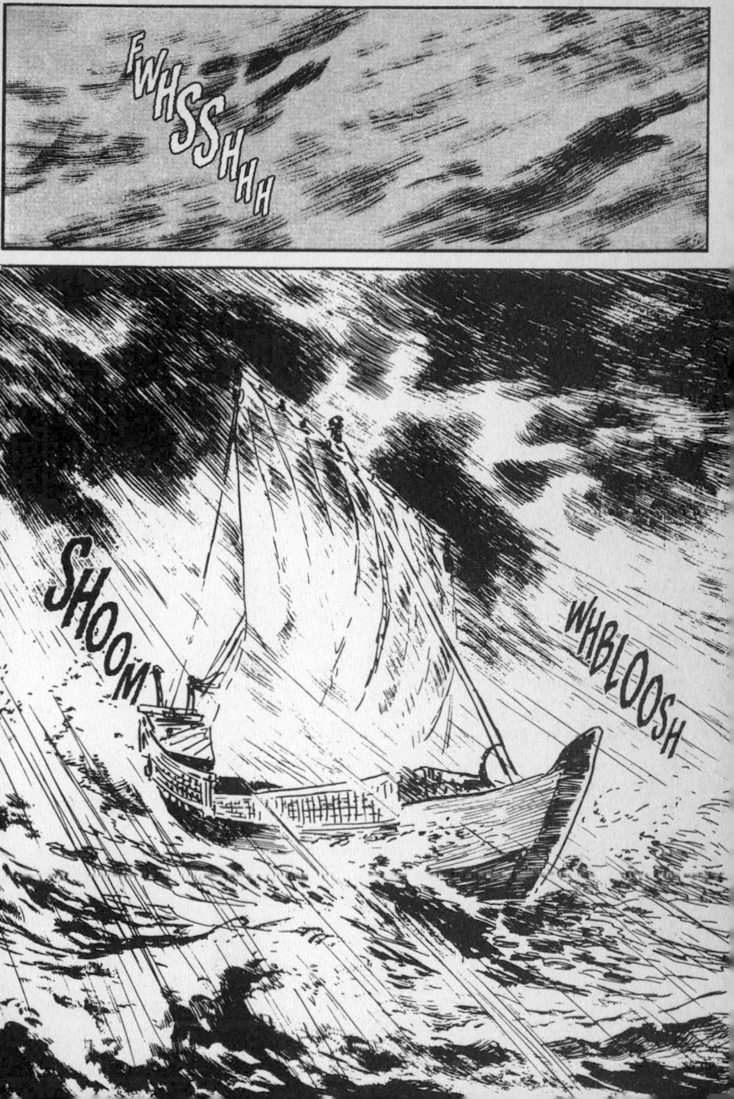
FWHSSHHH
WHBLOOSH
SHOOM

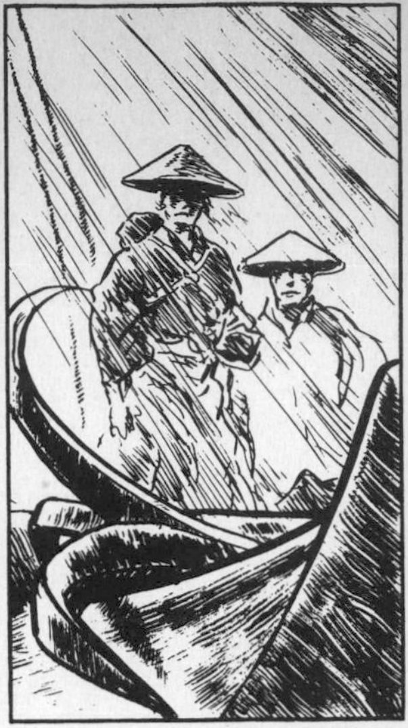
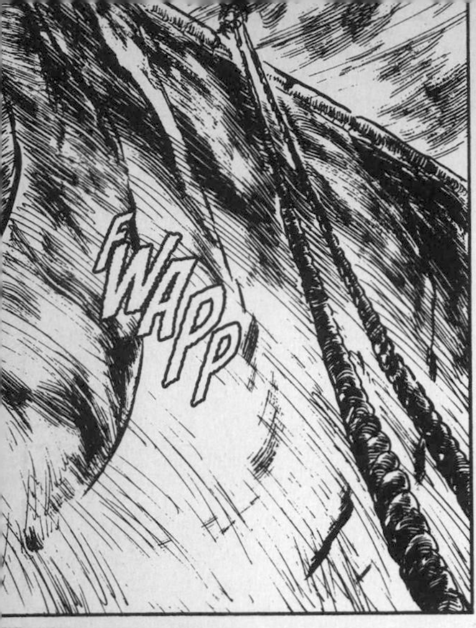
FWAPP
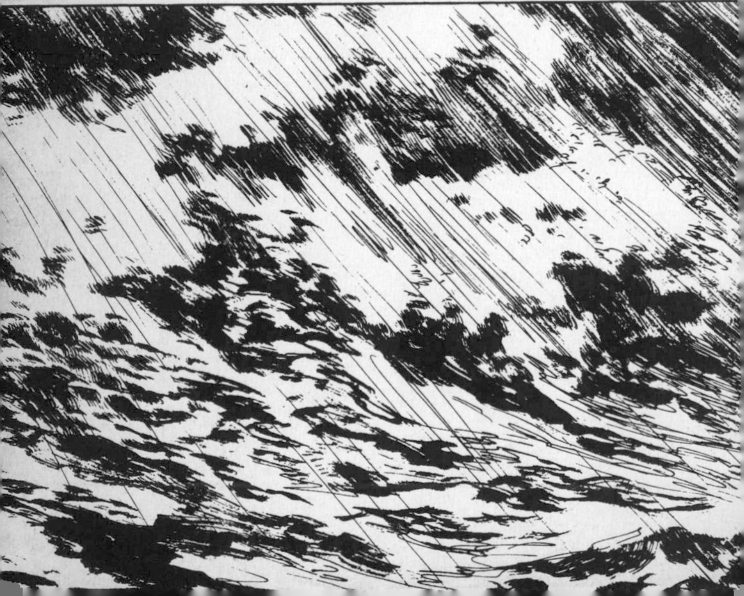

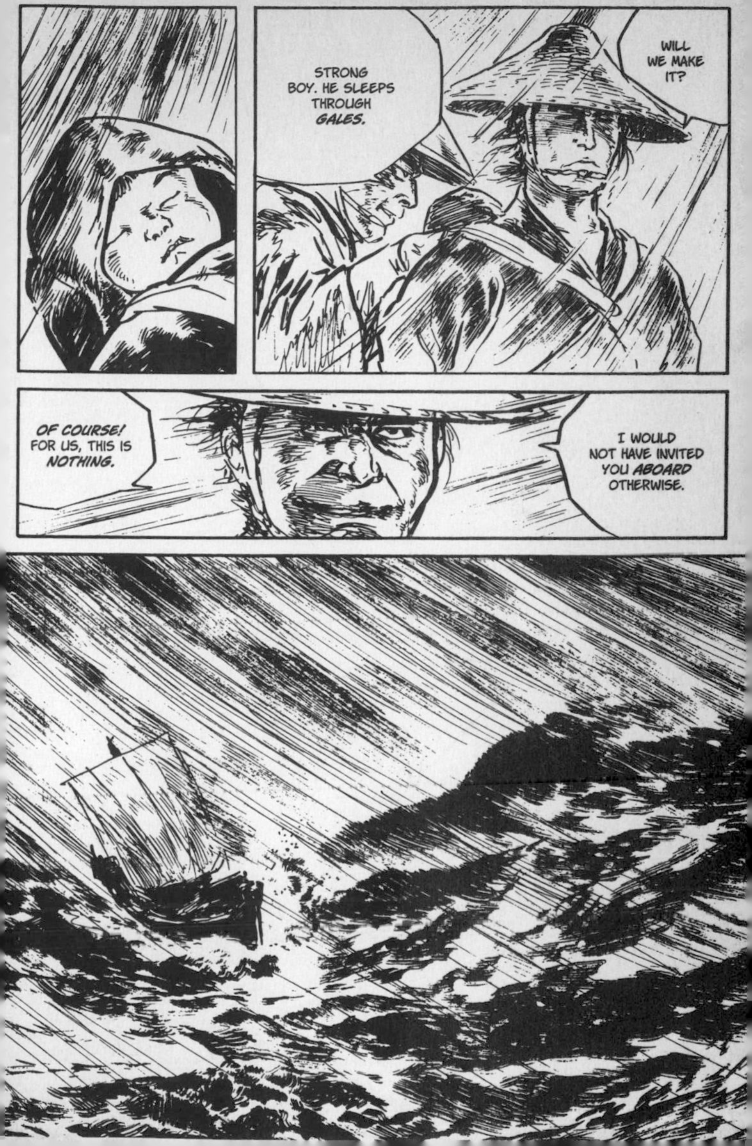
STRONG BOY. HE SLEEPS THROUGH *GALES.*
WILL WE MAKE IT?
OF COURSE! FOR US, THIS IS *NOTHING.*
I WOULD NOT HAVE INVITED YOU *ABOARD* OTHERWISE.

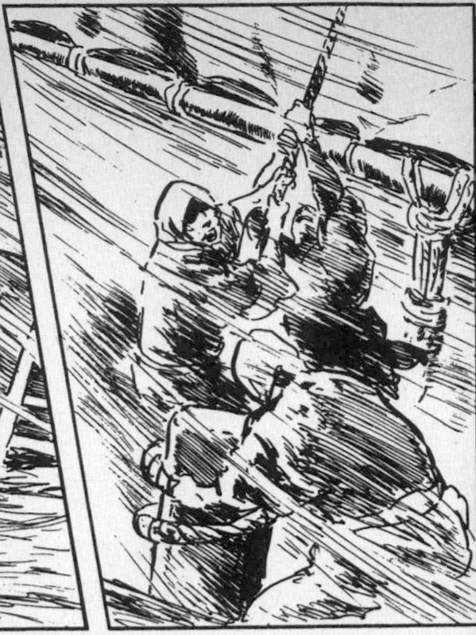
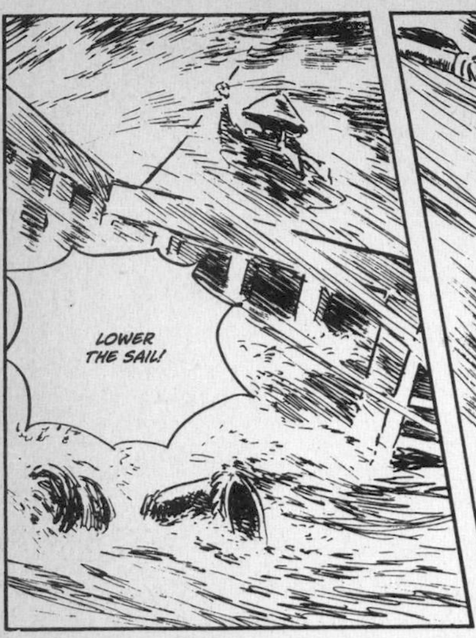
LOWER THE SAIL!
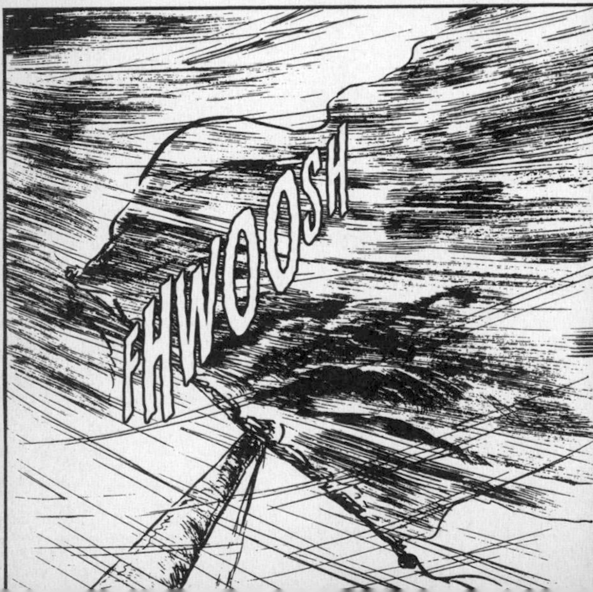
FHWOOSH
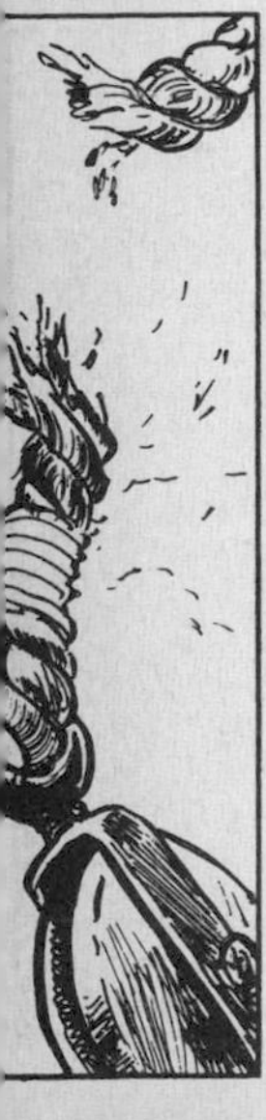

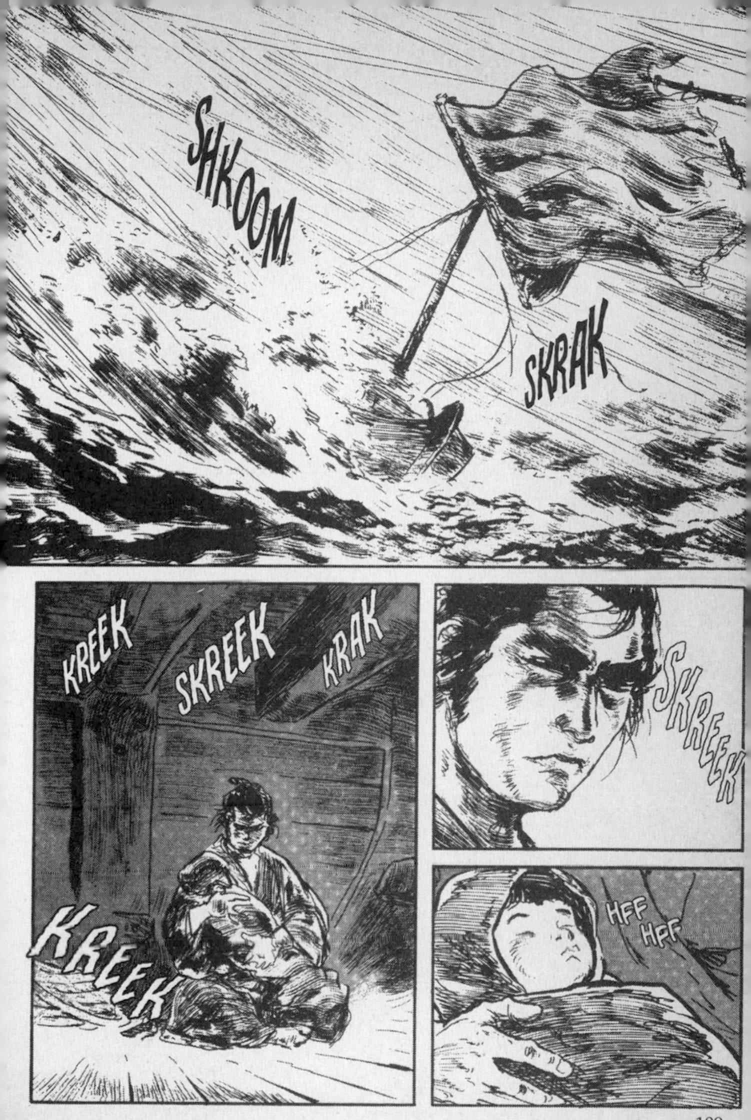
SHKOOM
SKRAK
SKREEK
HFF HPF
KRAK
SKREEK
KREEK
KREEK

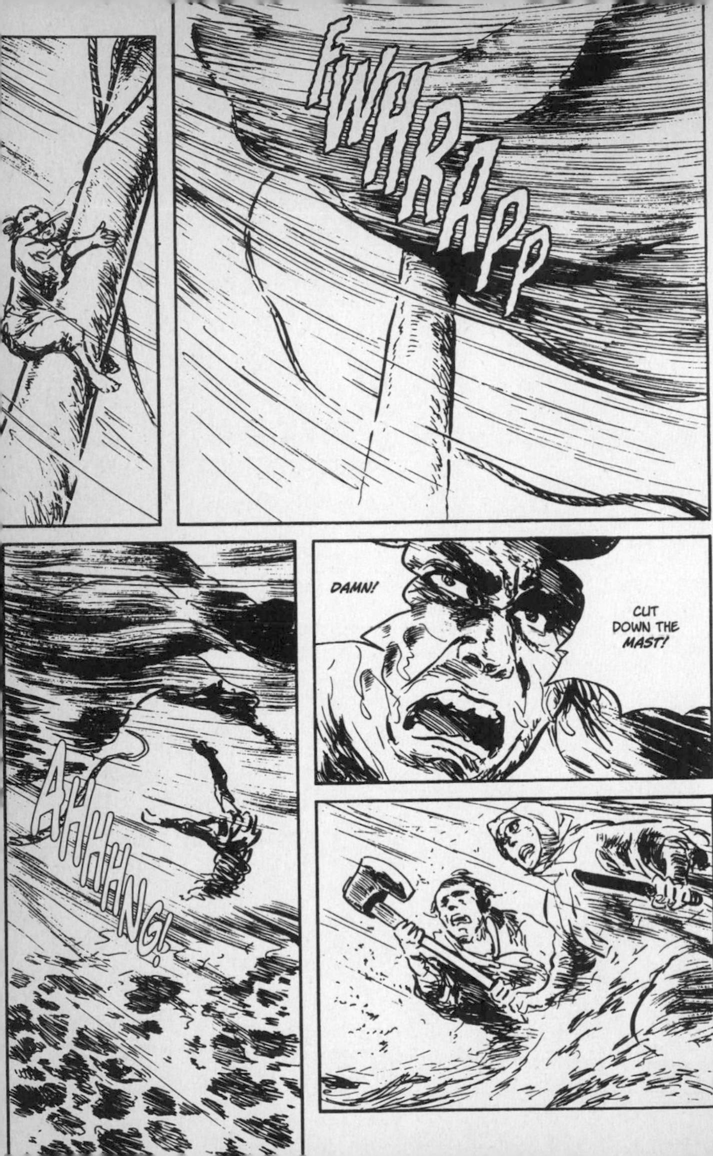
FWHRAPP
DAMN!
CUT DOWN THE MAST!
AHHHHNG!

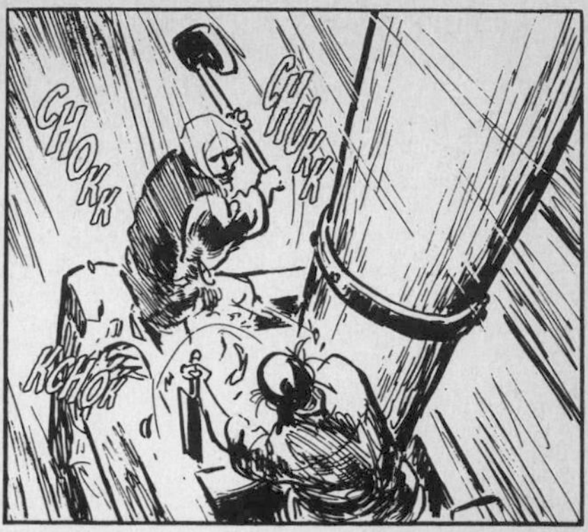
CHUKK
CHOKK
KCHOK
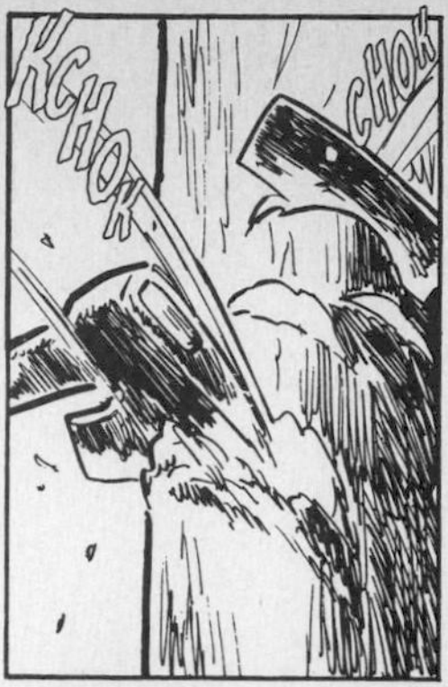
CHOK
KCHOK
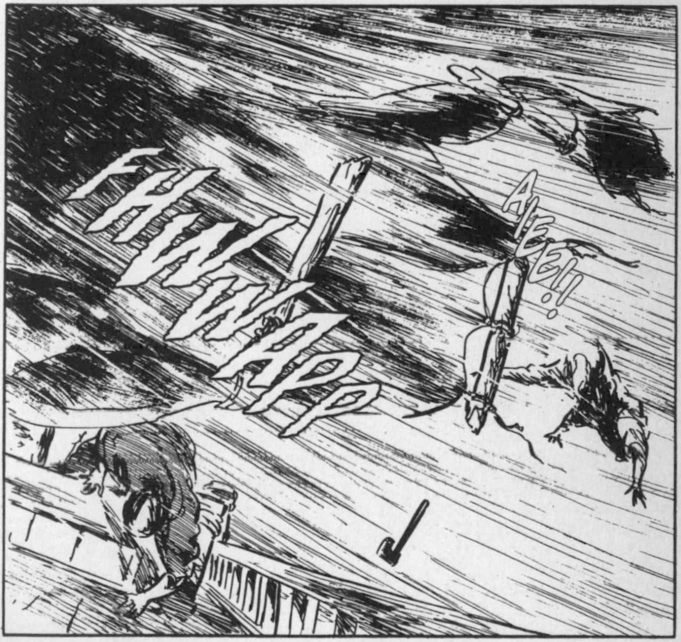
AIEE!!
THWAPP

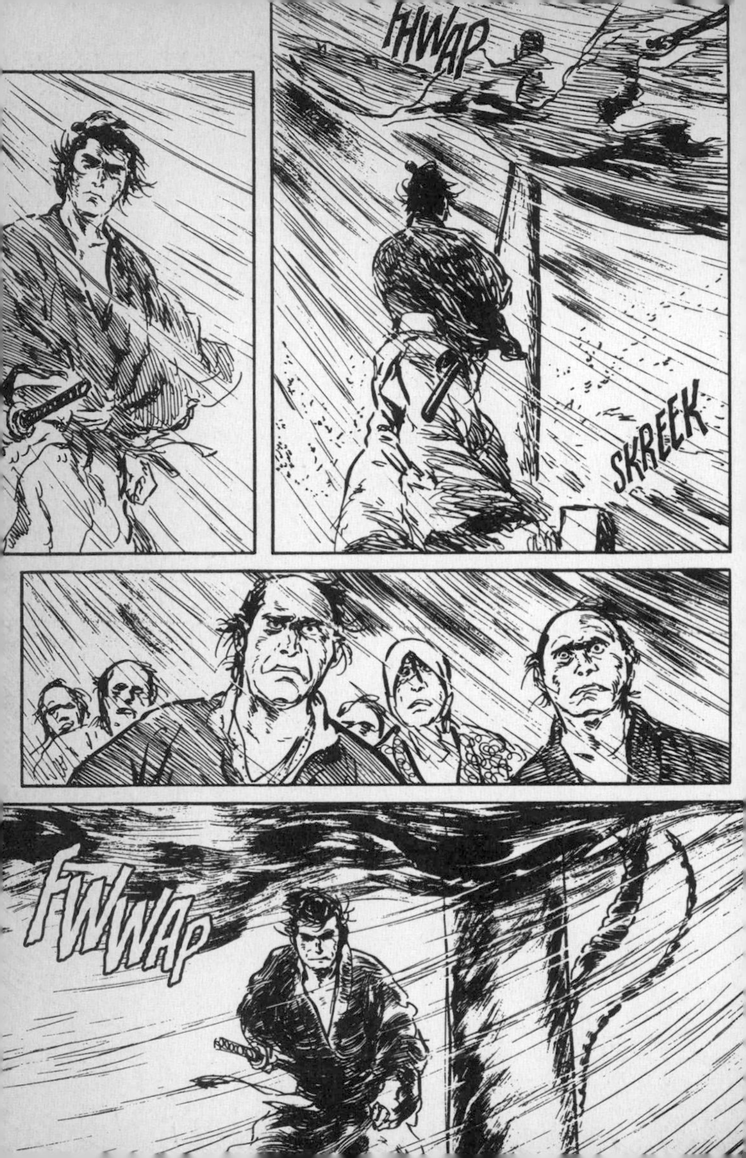
FHWAP
SKREEK
FWWAP

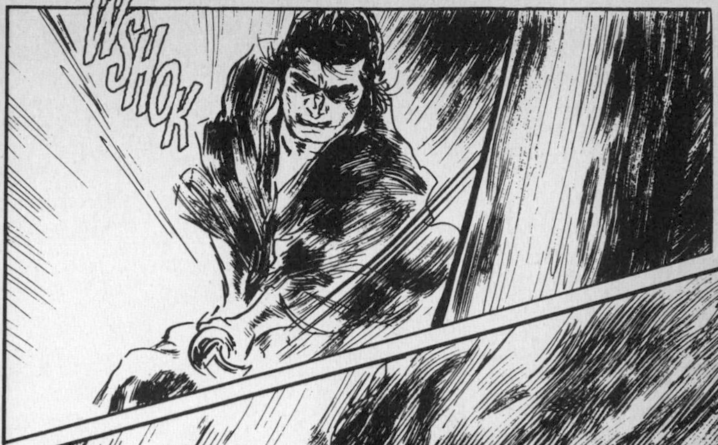
WSHOK
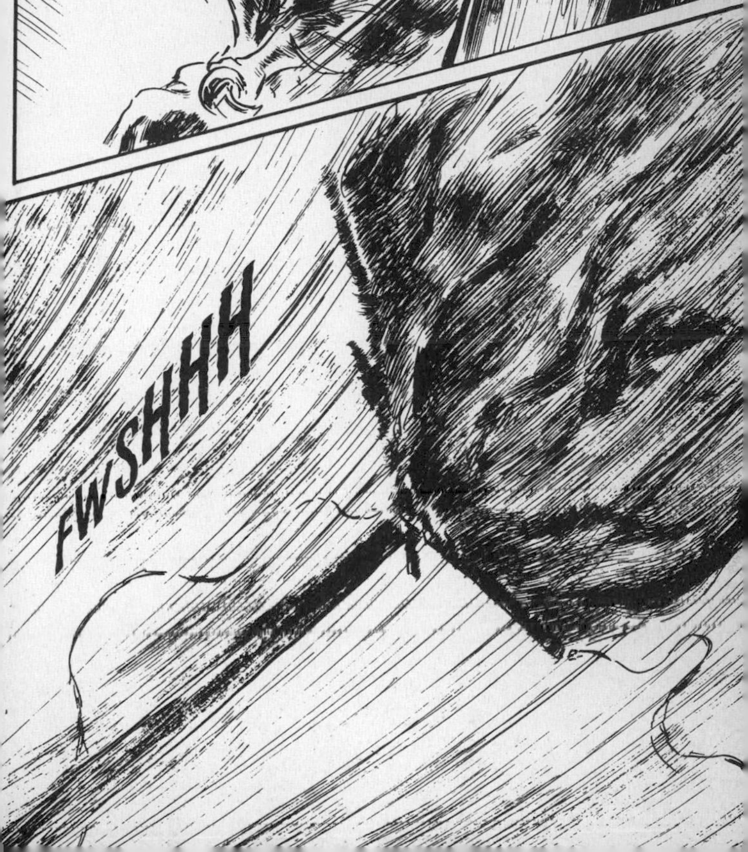
FWSHHH

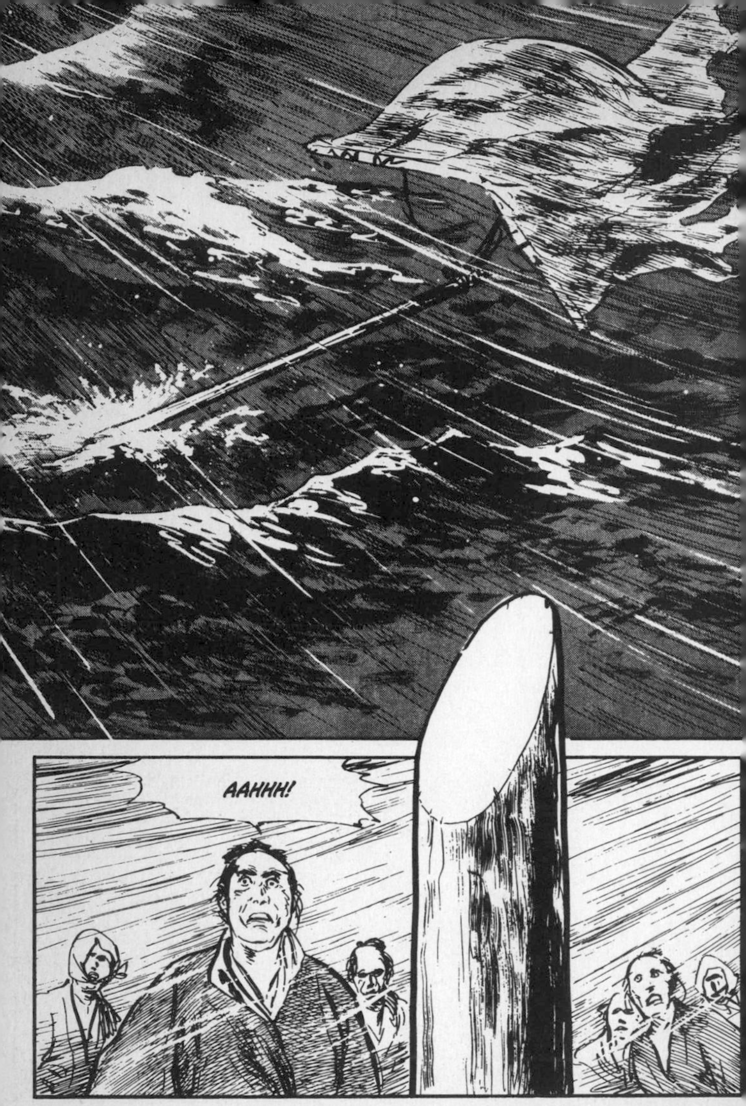
AAHHH!

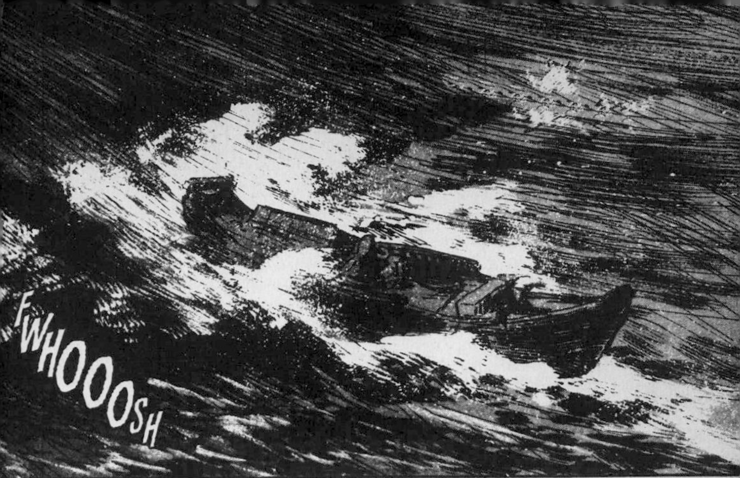
FWHOOOSH

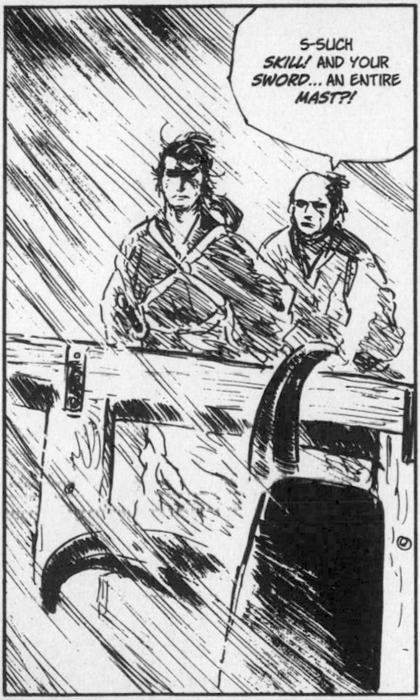
S-SUCH SKILL! AND YOUR SWORD... AN ENTIRE MAST?!

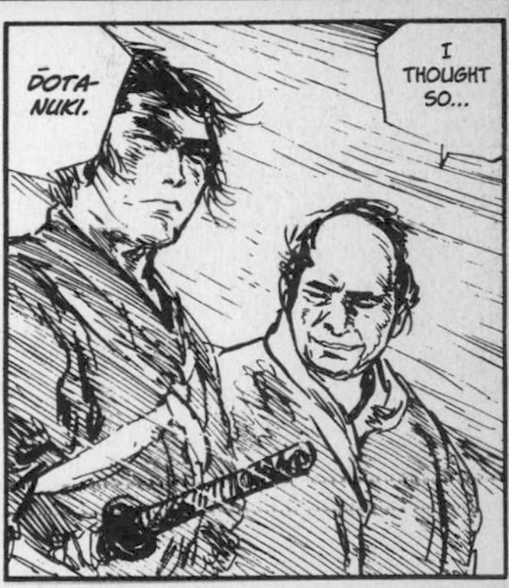
DŌTANUKI.
I THOUGHT SO...

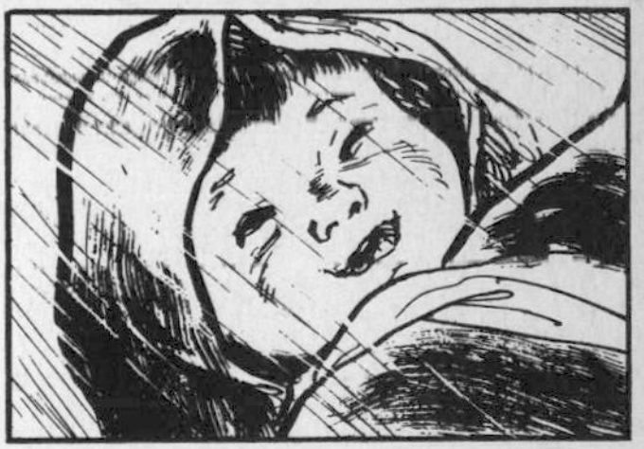

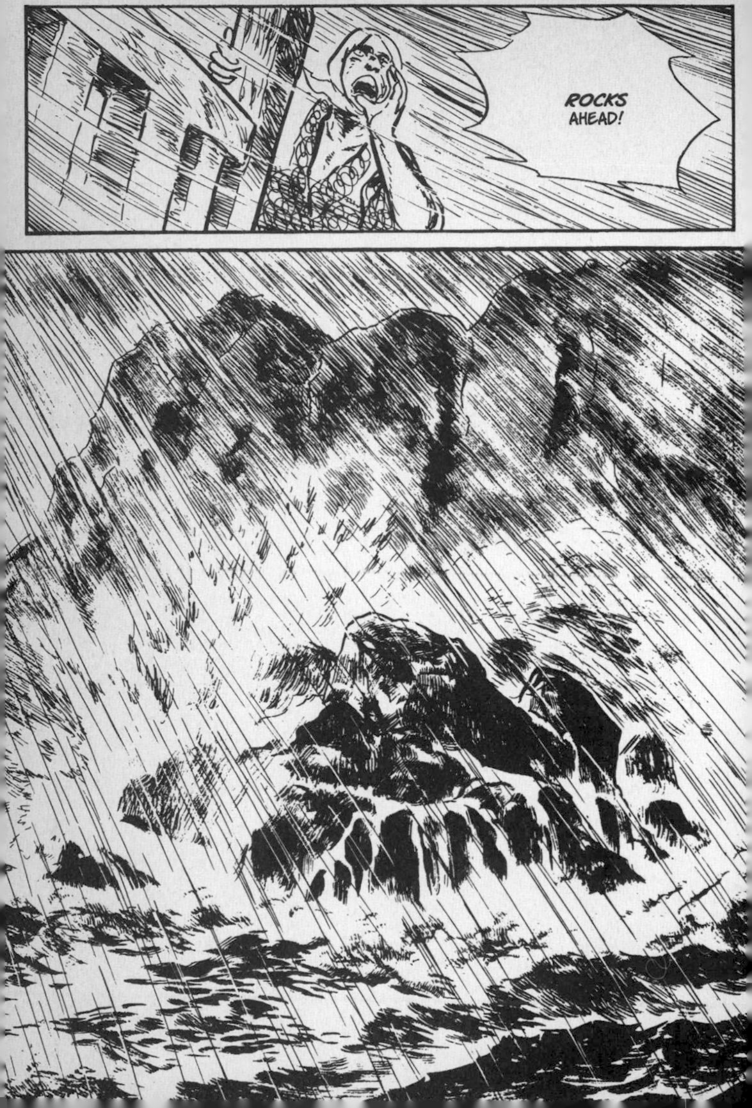
ROCKS AHEAD!

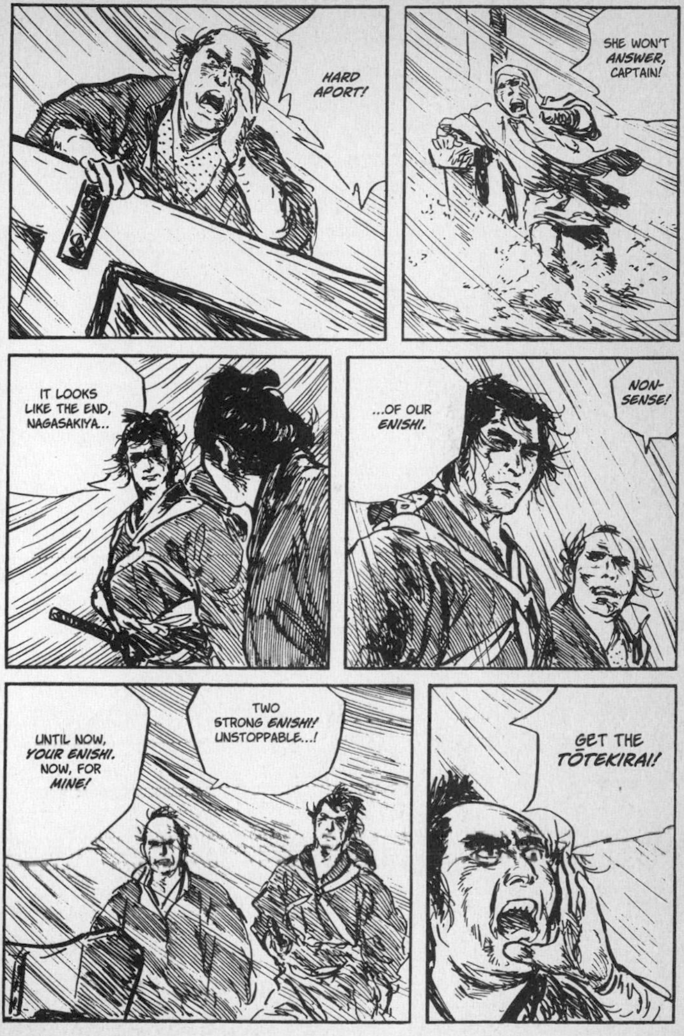
HARD APORT!
SHE WON'T ANSWER, CAPTAIN!
IT LOOKS LIKE THE END, NAGASAKIYA...
...OF OUR ENISHI.
NON-SENSE!
UNTIL NOW, YOUR ENISHI. NOW, FOR MINE!
TWO STRONG ENISHI! UNSTOPPABLE...!
GET THE TŌTEKIRAI!

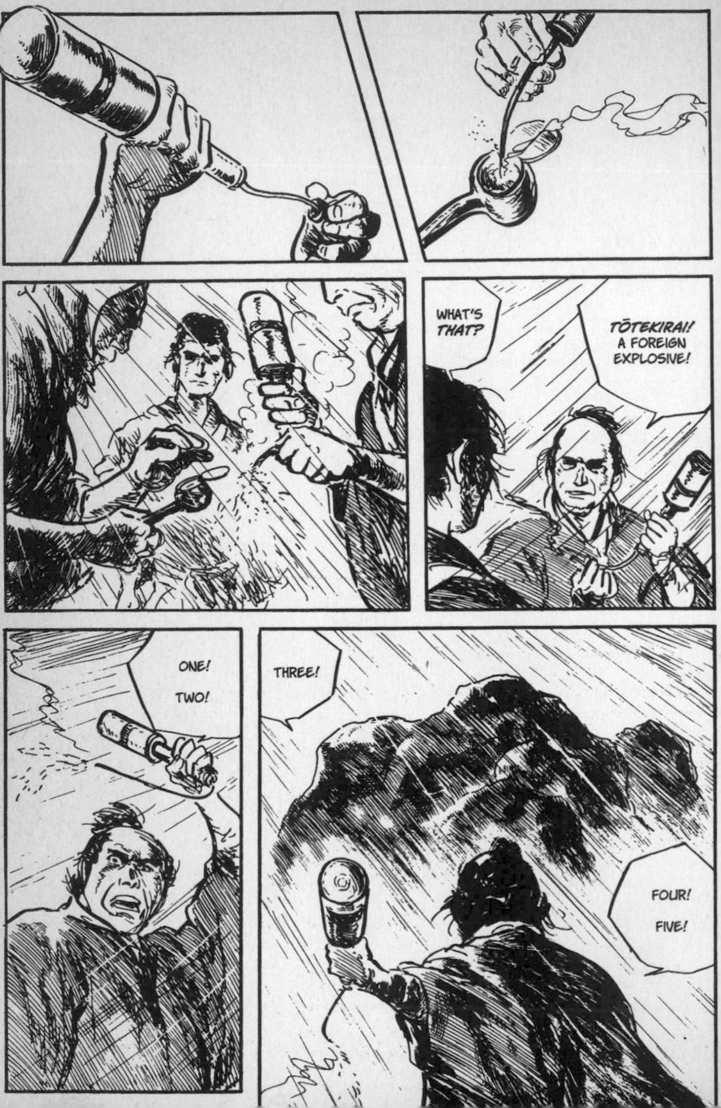
WHAT'S *THAT?*
TŌTEKIRAI! A FOREIGN EXPLOSIVE!
ONE!
TWO!
THREE!
FOUR!
FIVE!

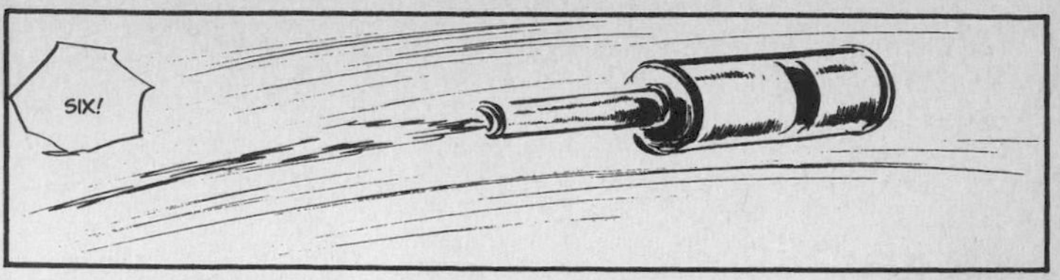
SIX!
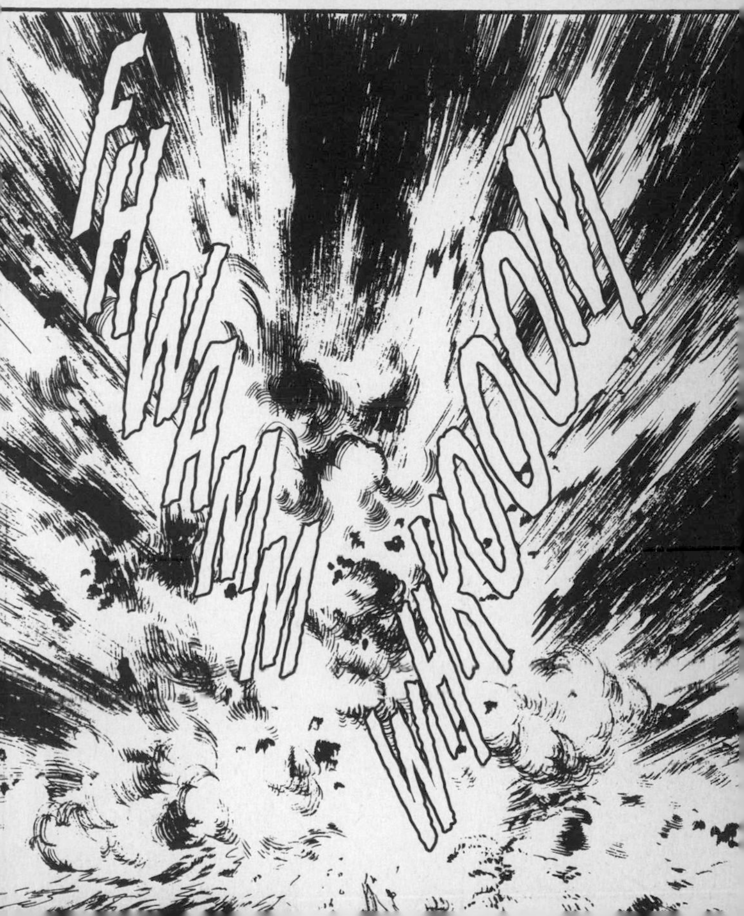
FWAAM
WHOOOM

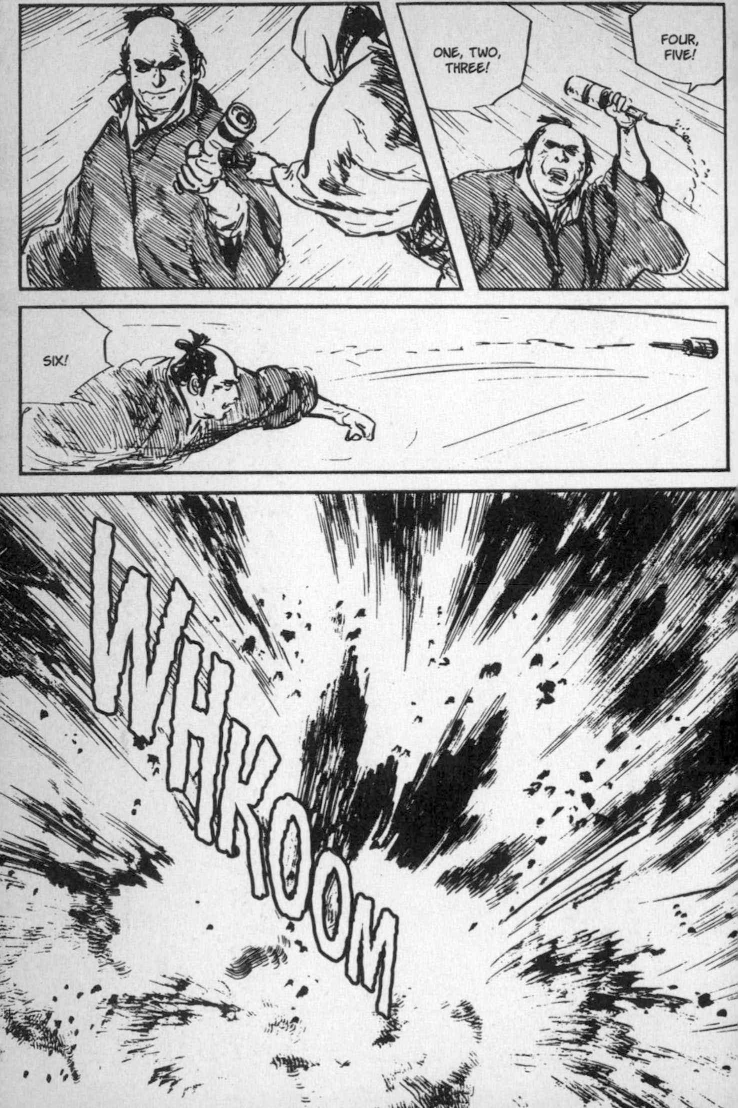
ONE, TWO, THREE!
FOUR, FIVE!
SIX!
WHKOOM

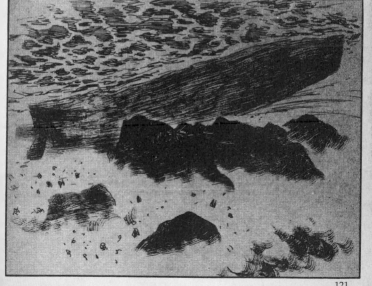

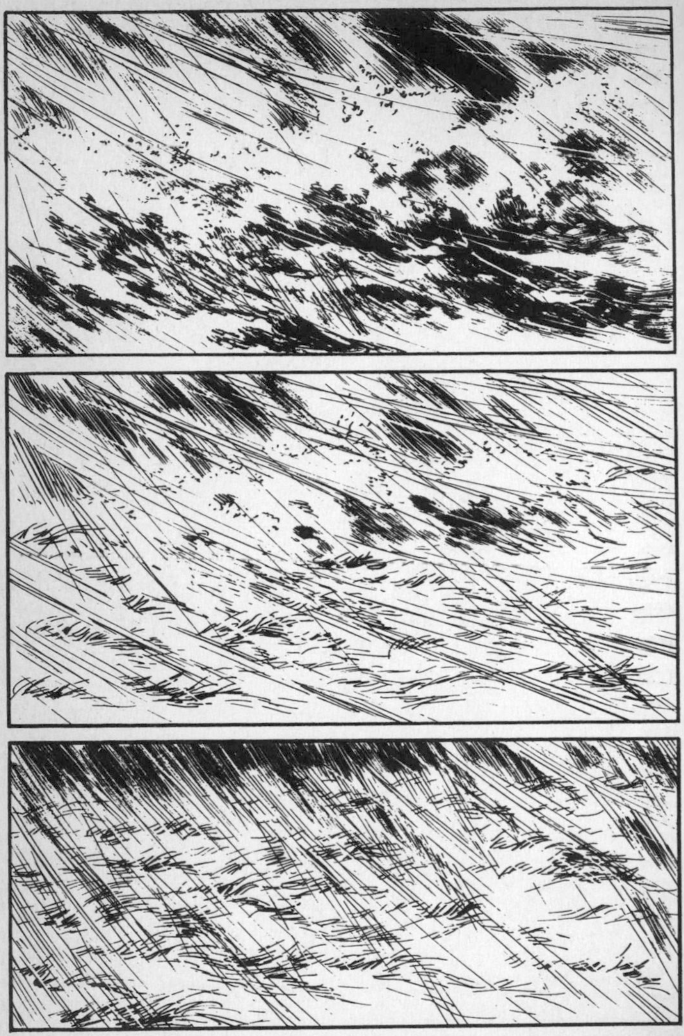

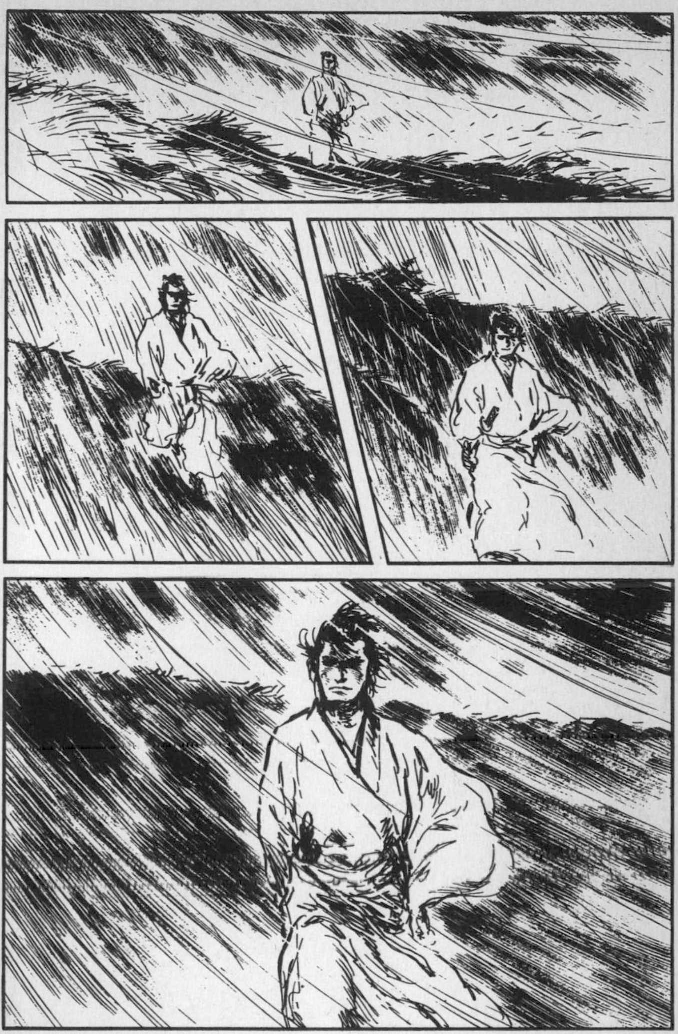

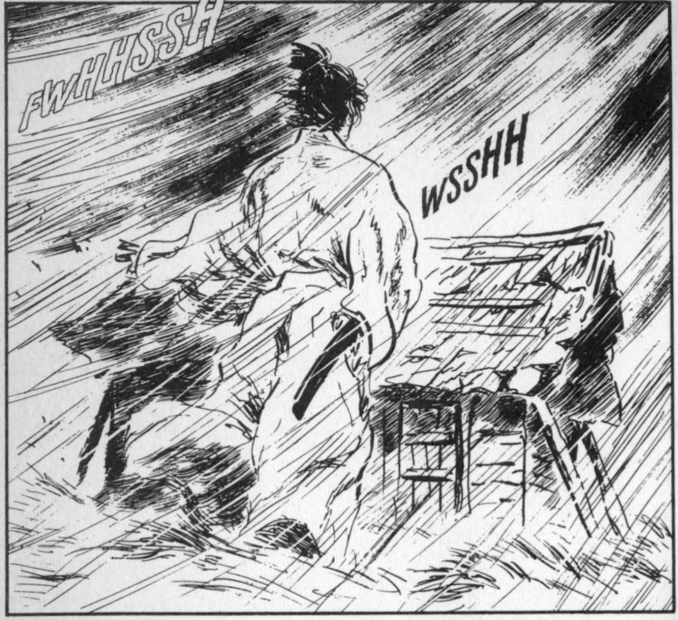
FWHHSSH
WSSHH
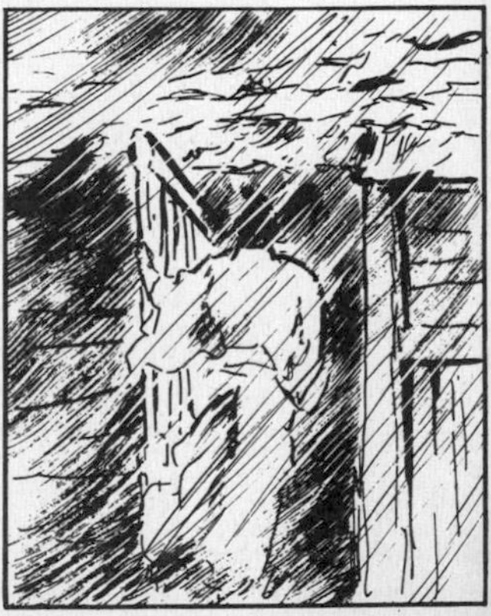
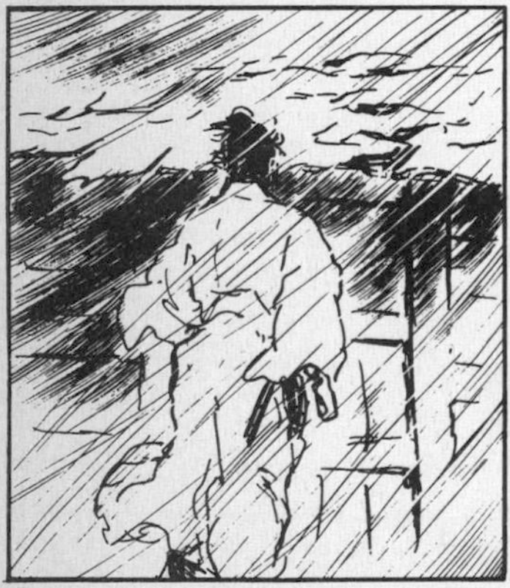

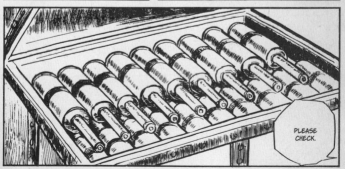

PLEASE
CHECK.

125

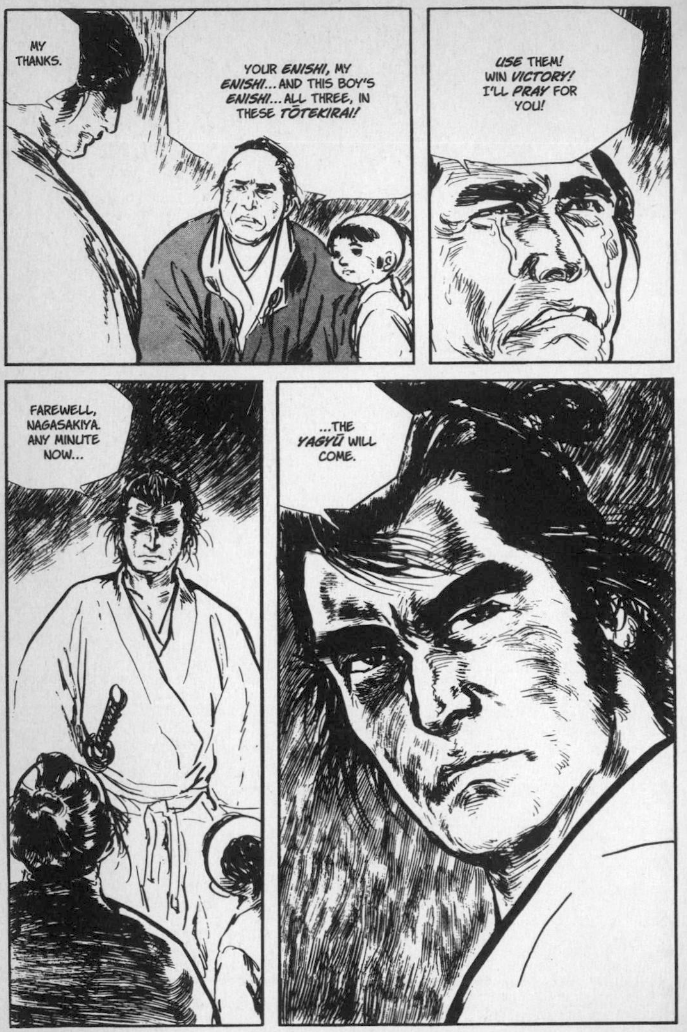
MY THANKS.
YOUR *ENISHI*, MY *ENISHI*... AND THIS BOY'S *ENISHI*... ALL THREE, IN THESE *TŌTEKIRAI!*
USE THEM! WIN *VICTORY!* I'LL *PRAY* FOR YOU!
FAREWELL, NAGASAKIYA. ANY MINUTE NOW...
...THE *YAGYŪ* WILL COME.

the hundred
and tenth

Heaven
and
Earth

128

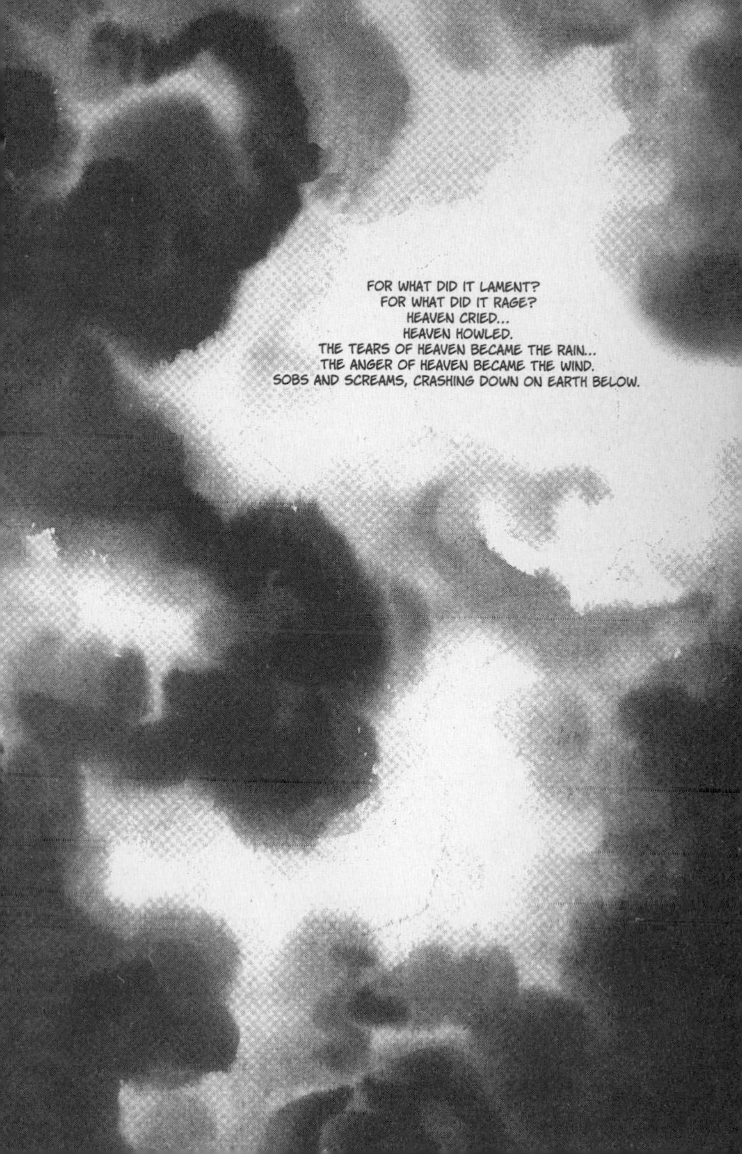
FOR WHAT DID IT LAMENT?
FOR WHAT DID IT RAGE?
HEAVEN CRIED...
HEAVEN HOWLED.
THE TEARS OF HEAVEN BECAME THE RAIN...
THE ANGER OF HEAVEN BECAME THE WIND.
SOBS AND SCREAMS, CRASHING DOWN ON EARTH BELOW.

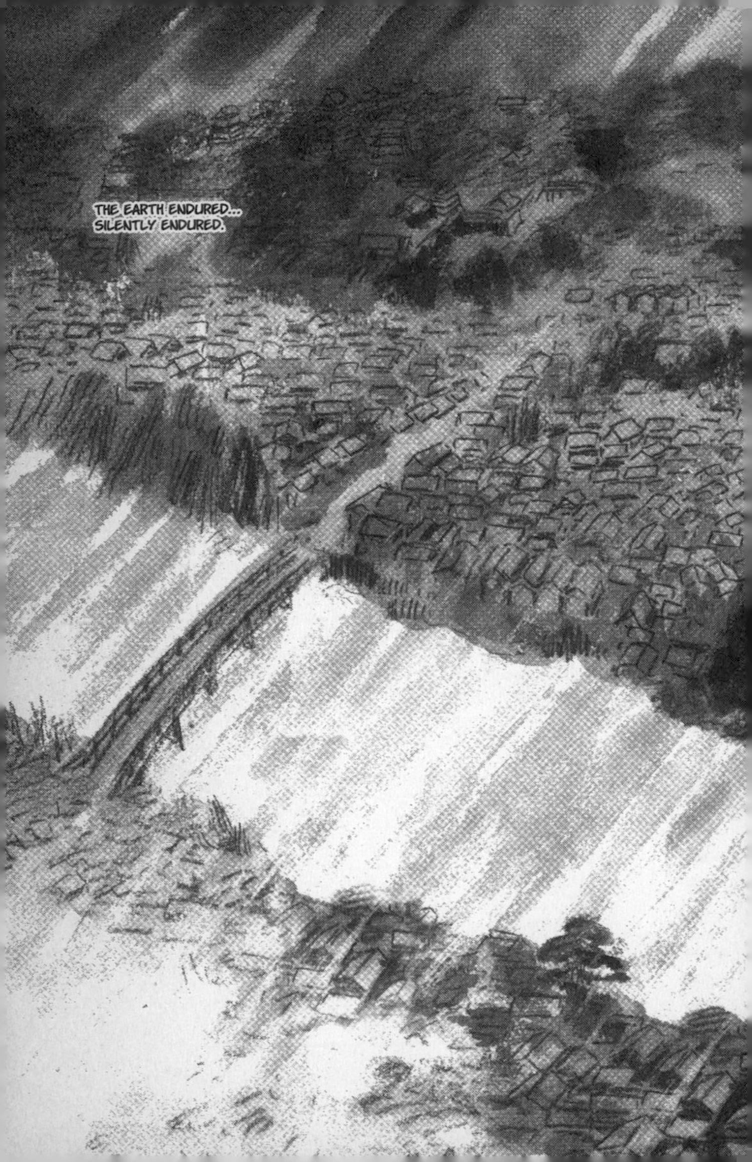
THE EARTH ENDURED...
SILENTLY ENDURED.

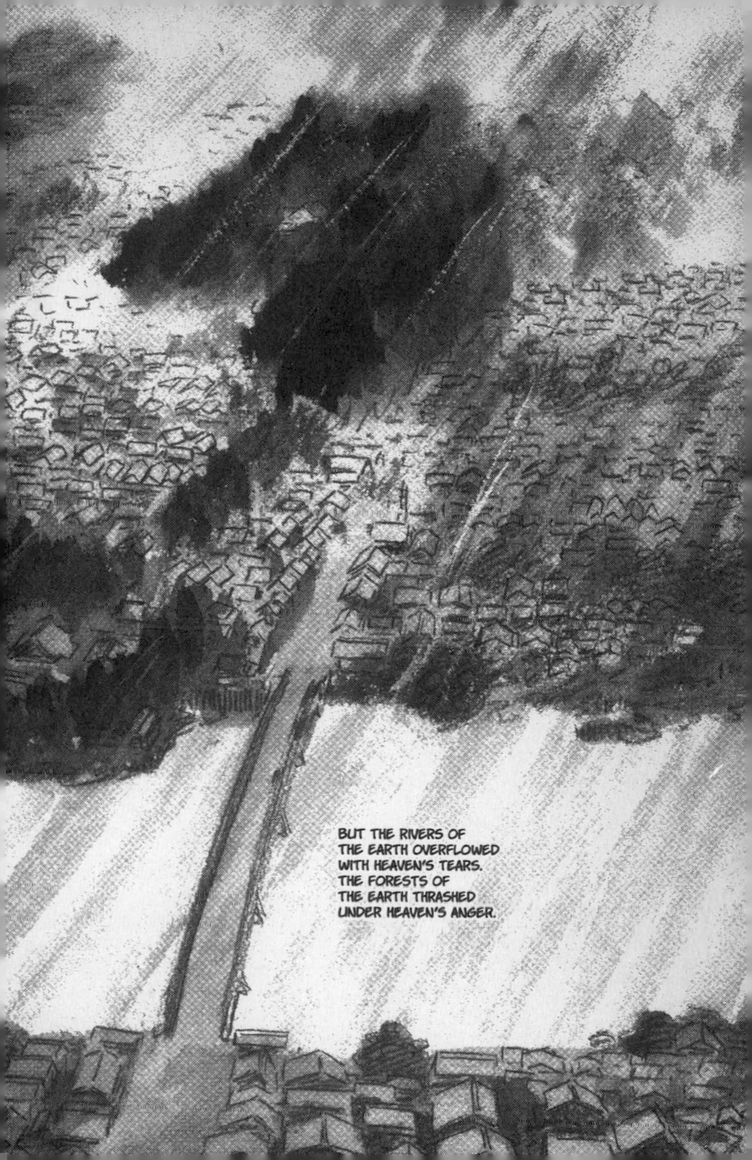
BUT THE RIVERS OF THE EARTH OVERFLOWED WITH HEAVEN'S TEARS. THE FORESTS OF THE EARTH THRASHED UNDER HEAVEN'S ANGER.

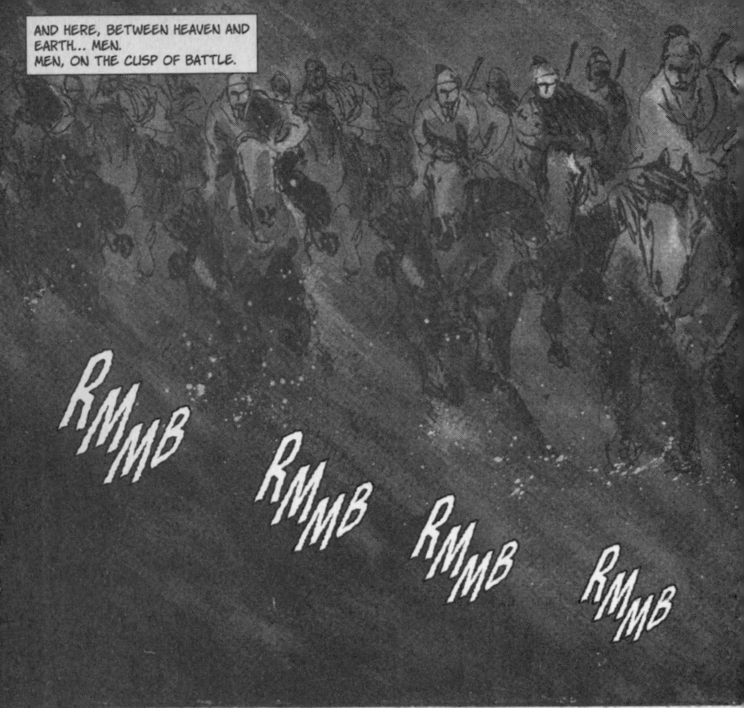
AND HERE, BETWEEN HEAVEN AND EARTH... MEN.
MEN, ON THE CUSP OF BATTLE.
RMMB
RMMB
RMMB
RMMB

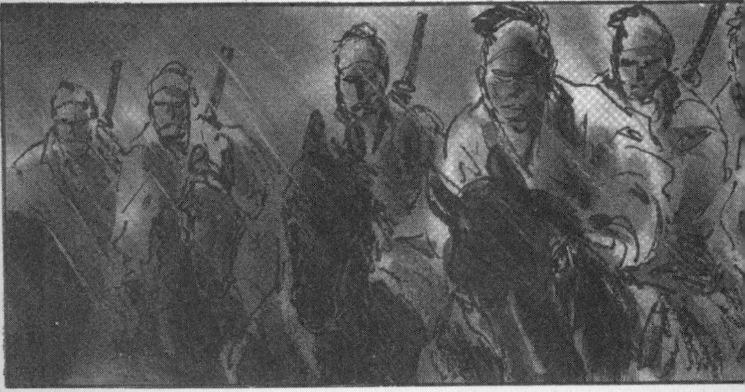

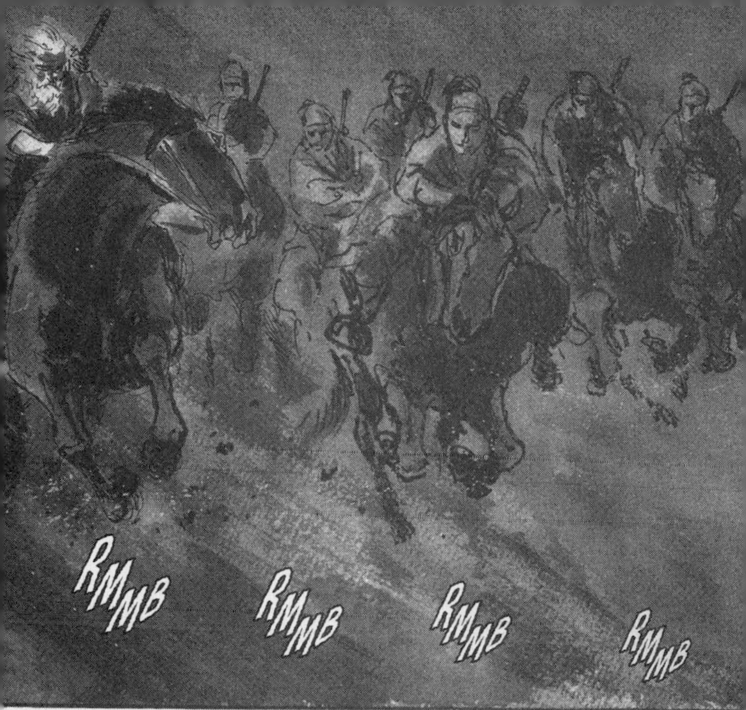
RMMB
RMMB
RMMB
RMMB

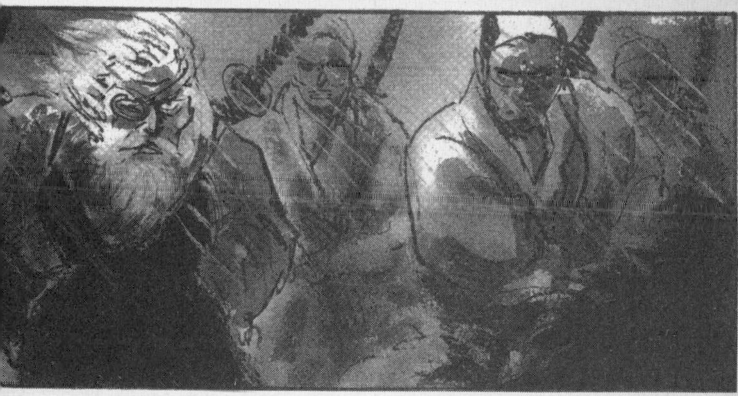

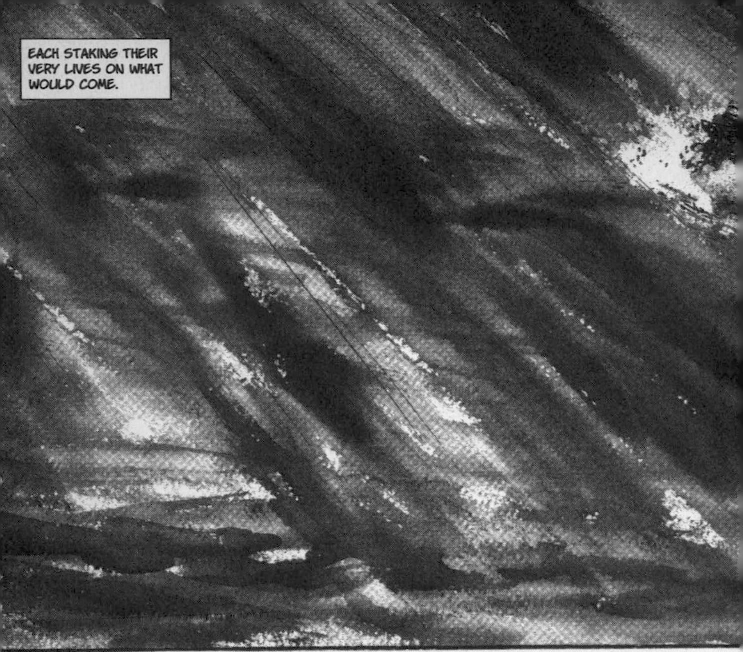
EACH STAKING THEIR VERY LIVES ON WHAT WOULD COME.

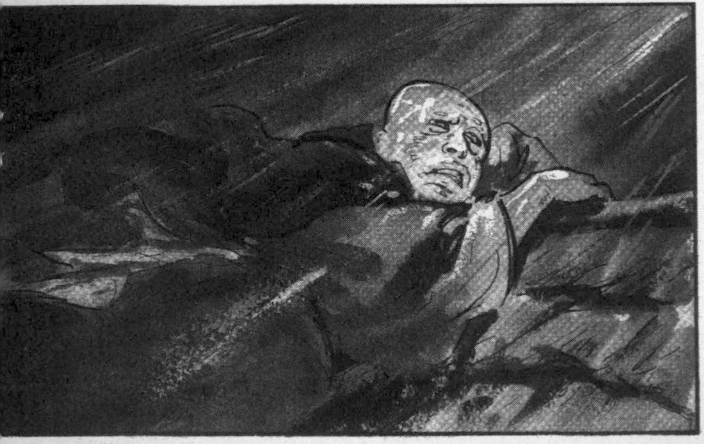

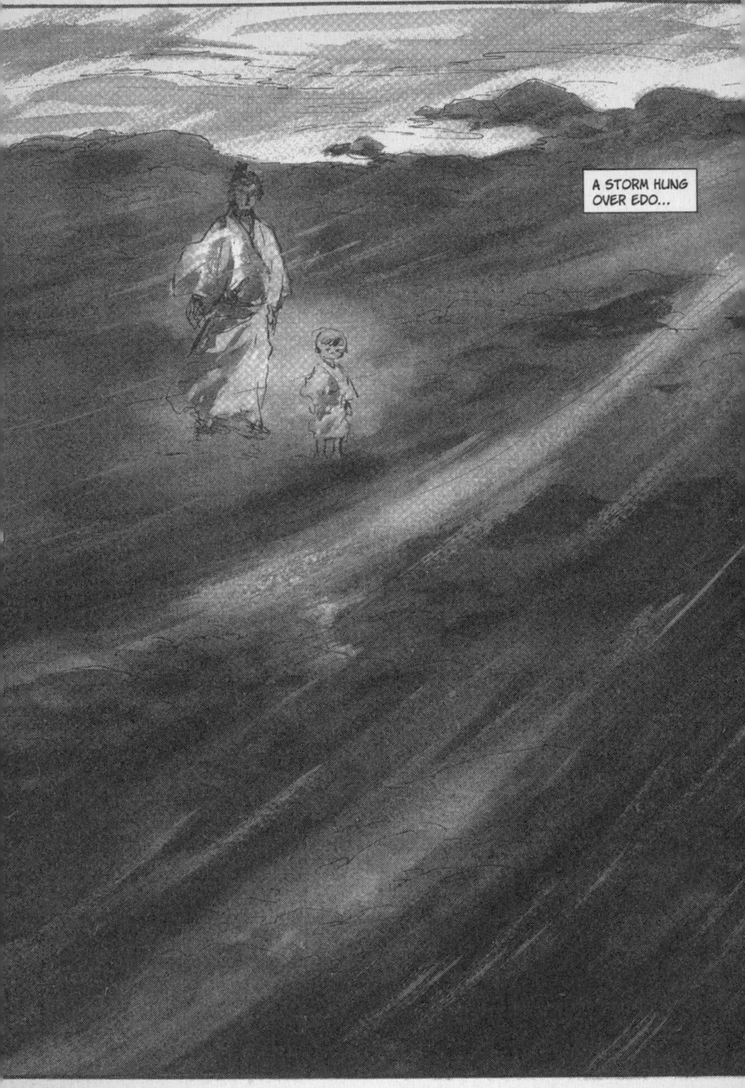
A STORM HUNG
OVER EDO...

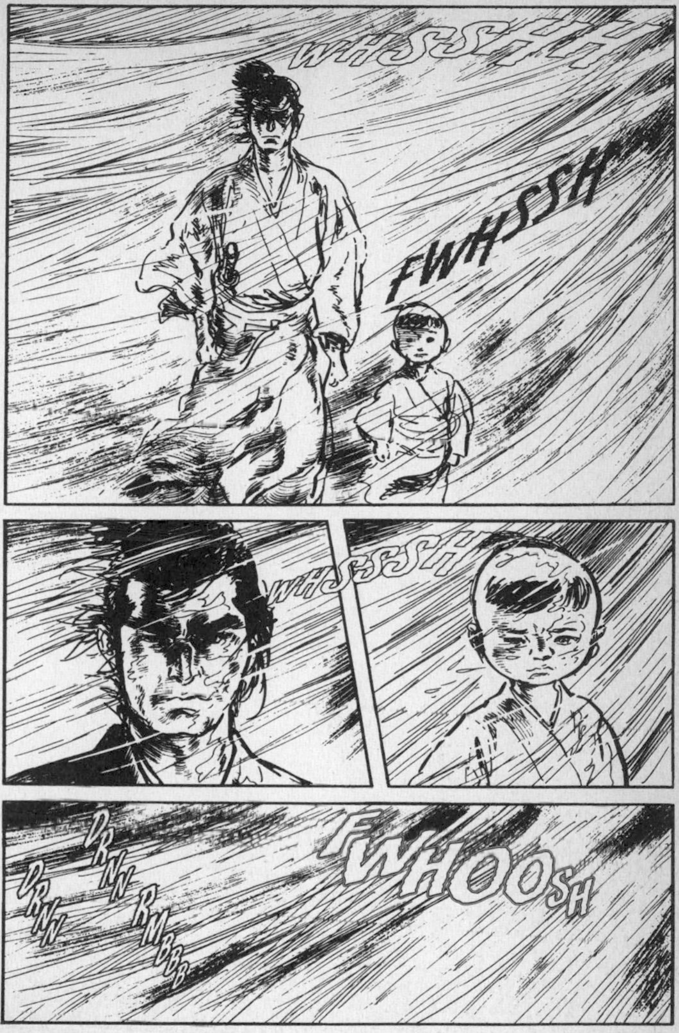
WHSSHH
FWHSSH
WHSSSH
FWHOOSH
DRNN
DRNN
RMBBB

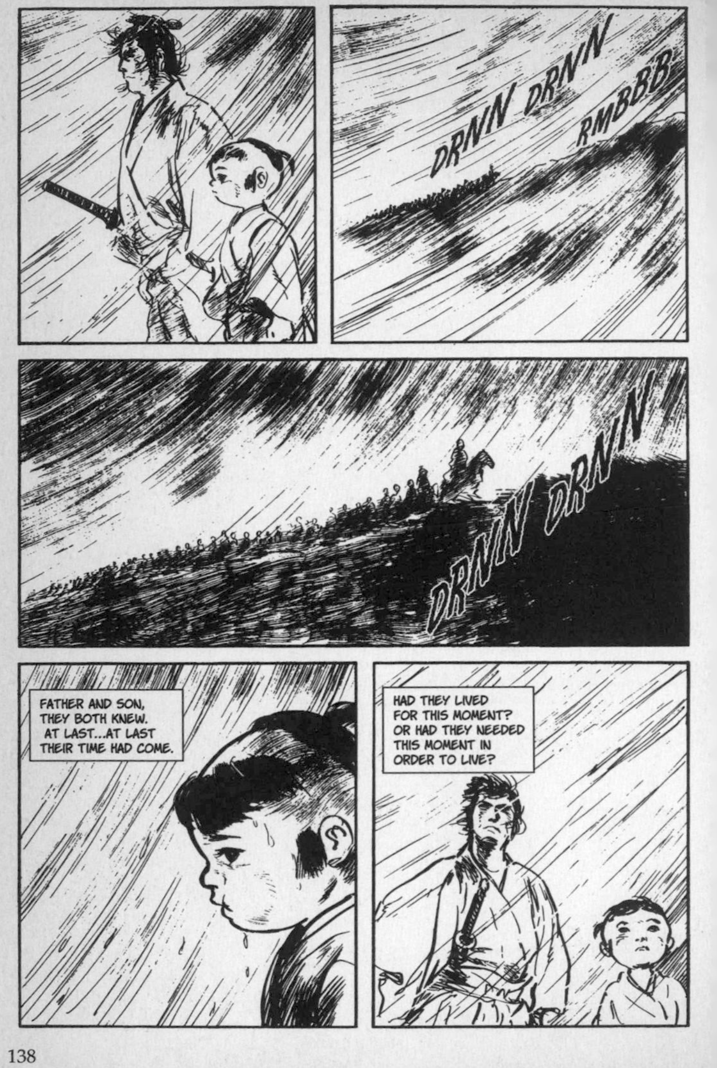
DRNN DRNN
RMBBB
DRNN DRNN
FATHER AND SON, THEY BOTH KNEW. AT LAST...AT LAST THEIR TIME HAD COME.
HAD THEY LIVED FOR THIS MOMENT? OR HAD THEY NEEDED THIS MOMENT IN ORDER TO LIVE?

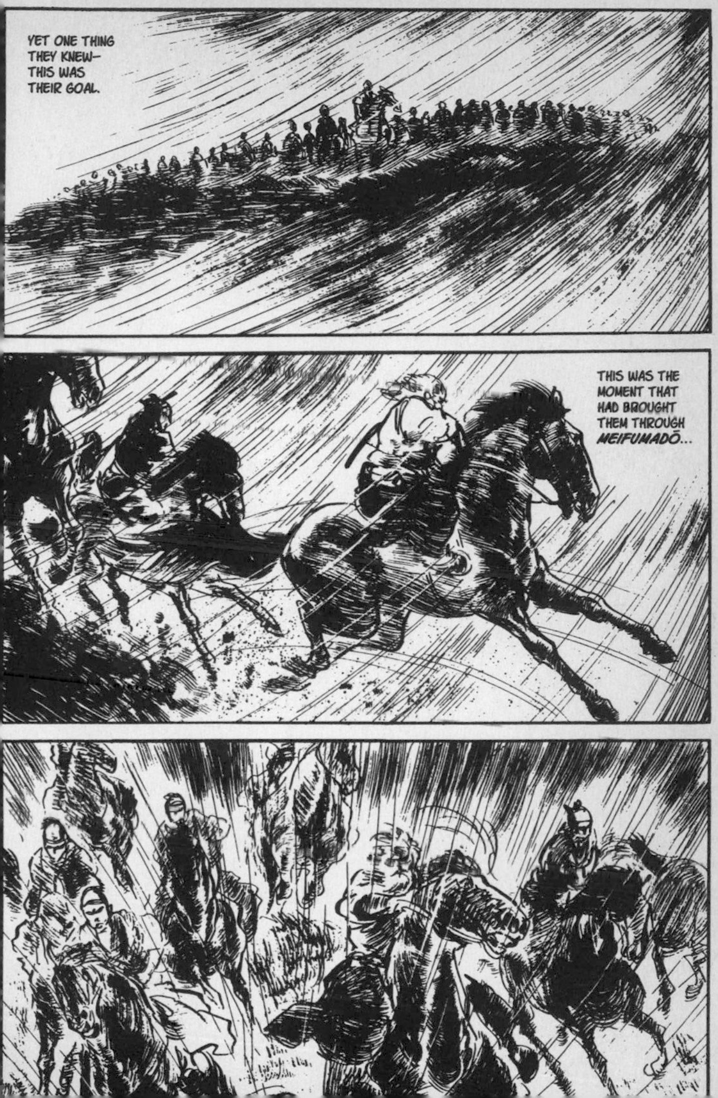
YET ONE THING THEY KNEW— THIS WAS THEIR GOAL.
THIS WAS THE MOMENT THAT HAD BROUGHT THEM THROUGH *MEIFUMADŌ*...

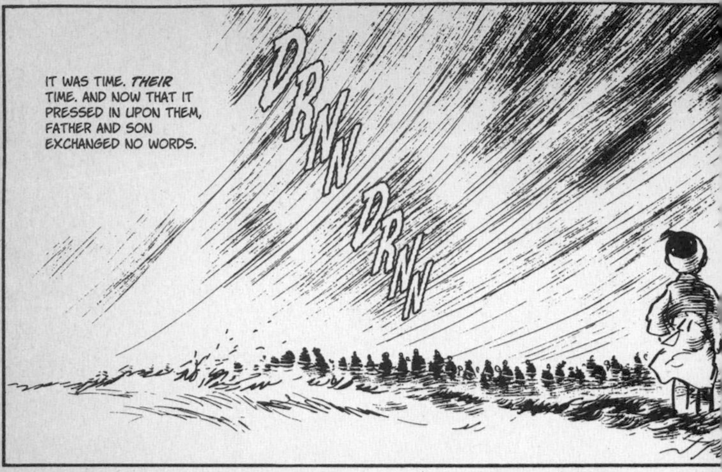
IT WAS TIME. *THEIR* TIME. AND NOW THAT IT PRESSED IN UPON THEM, FATHER AND SON EXCHANGED NO WORDS.
DRNN DRNN

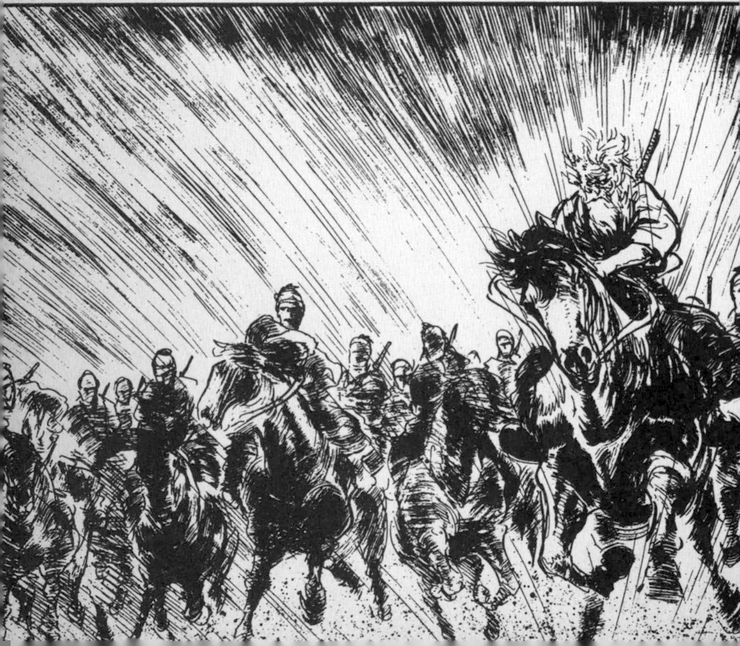

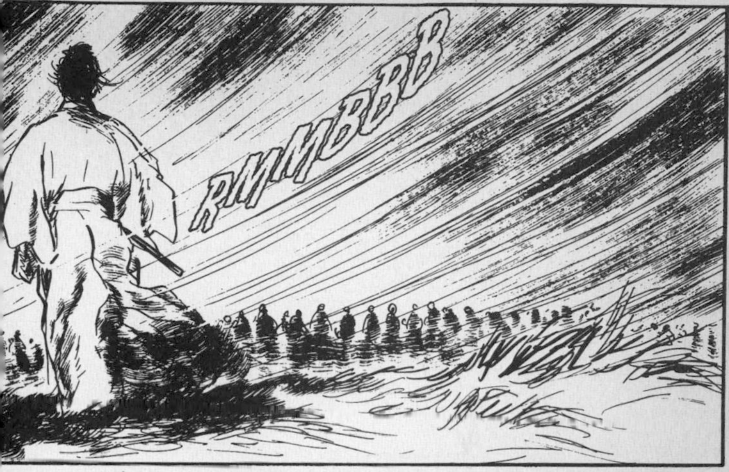
RMMBBB

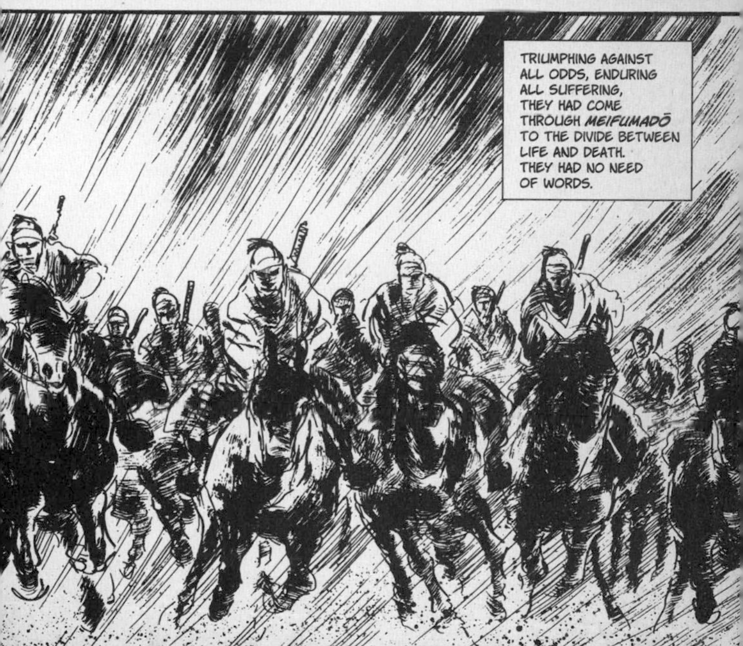
TRIUMPHING AGAINST ALL ODDS, ENDURING ALL SUFFERING, THEY HAD COME THROUGH *MEIFUMADŌ* TO THE DIVIDE BETWEEN LIFE AND DEATH. THEY HAD NO NEED OF WORDS.

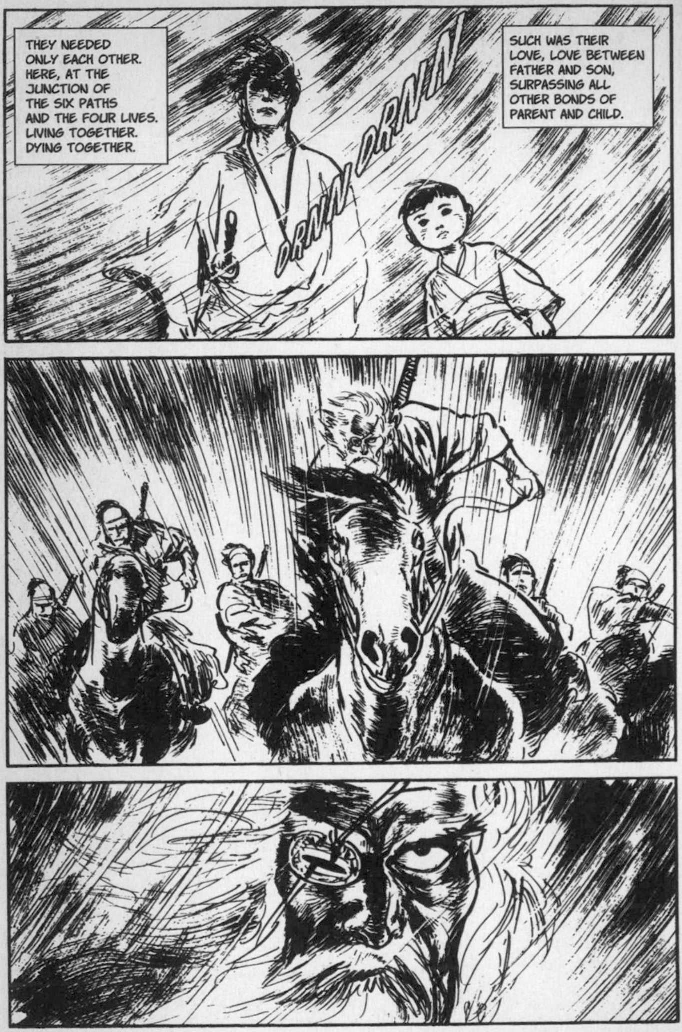
THEY NEEDED ONLY EACH OTHER. HERE, AT THE JUNCTION OF THE SIX PATHS AND THE FOUR LIVES. LIVING TOGETHER. DYING TOGETHER.
SUCH WAS THEIR LOVE, LOVE BETWEEN FATHER AND SON, SURPASSING ALL OTHER BONDS OF PARENT AND CHILD.

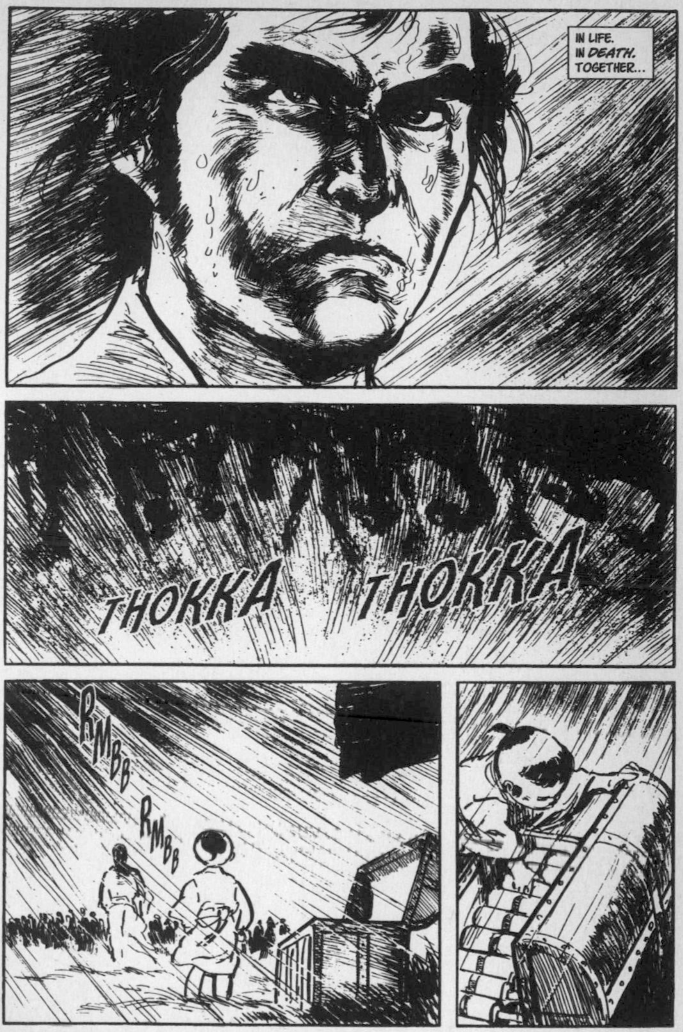
IN LIFE.
IN *DEATH.*
TOGETHER...
THOKKA THOKKA
RMBB
RMBB

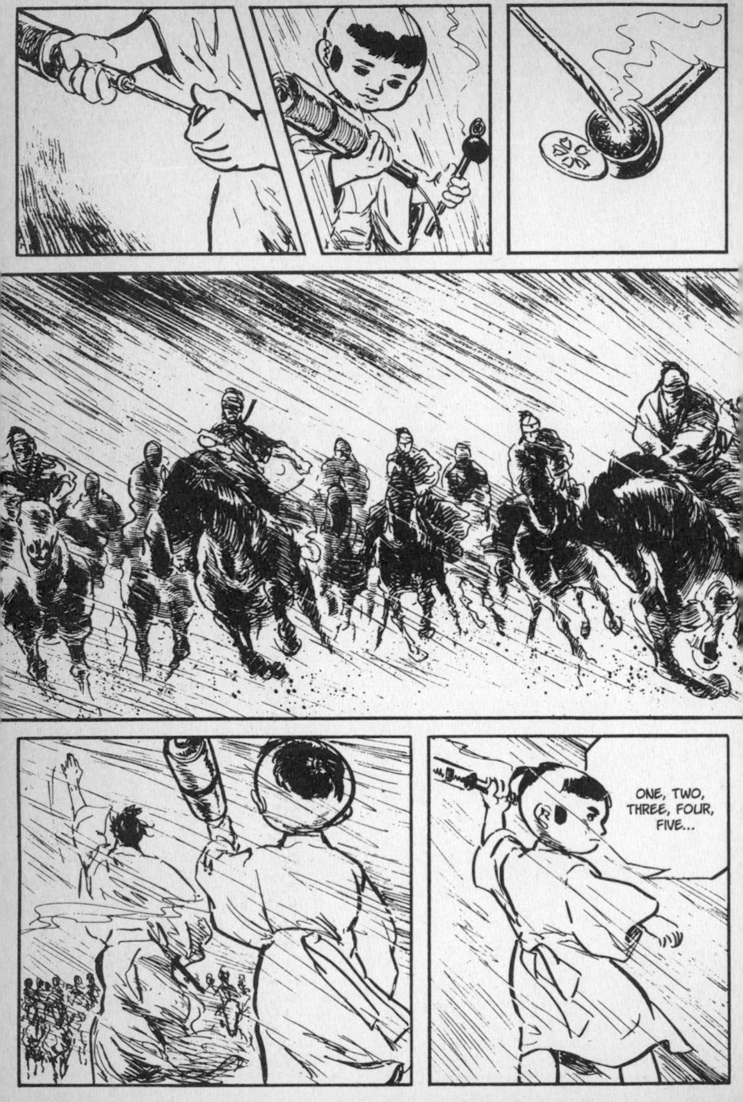
ONE, TWO, THREE, FOUR, FIVE...

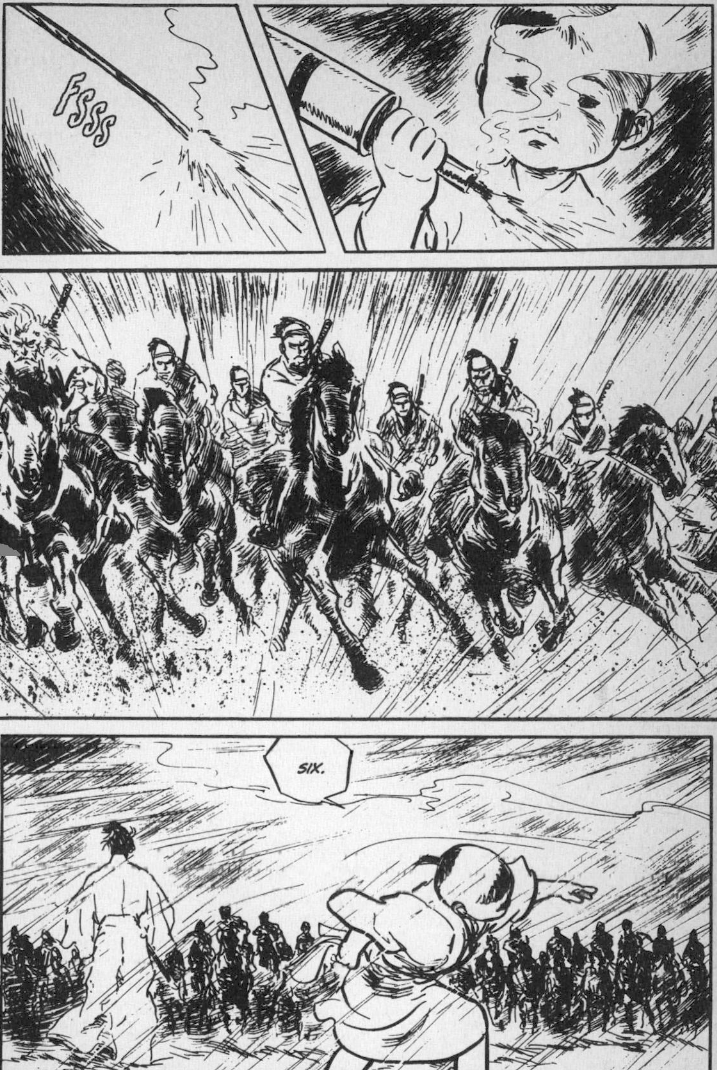
FSSS
SIX.

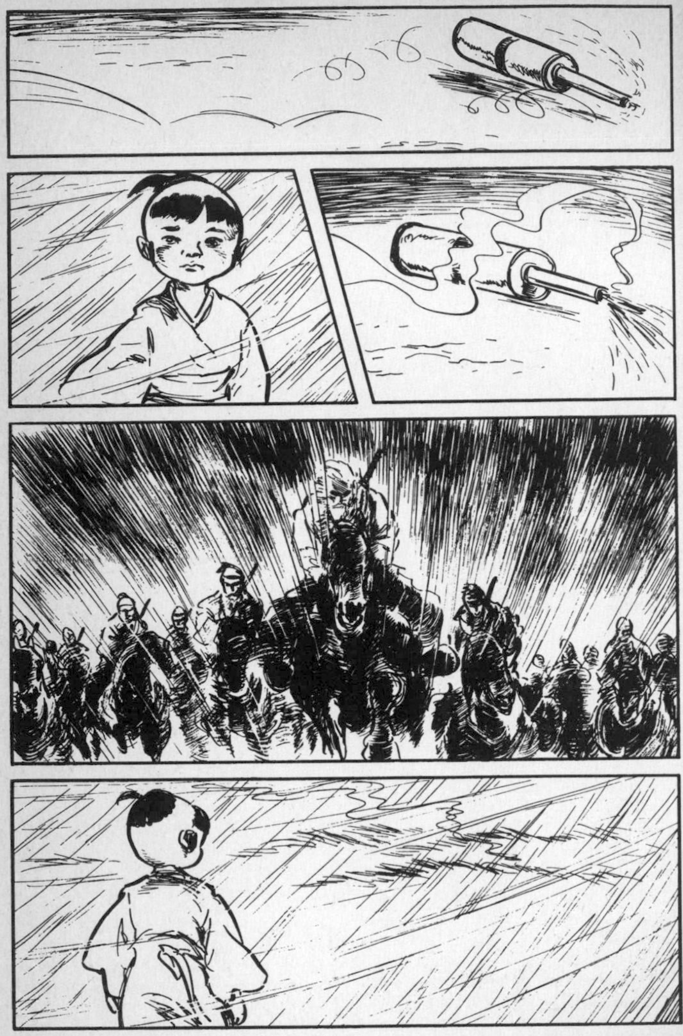

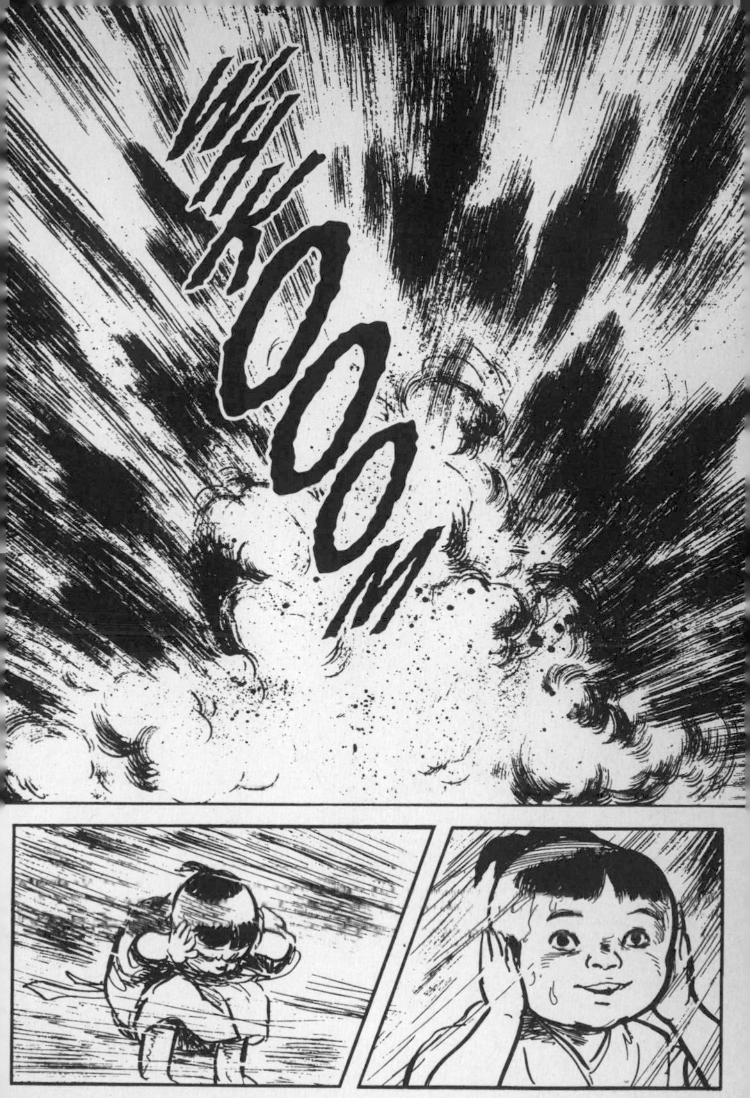
WHOOOM

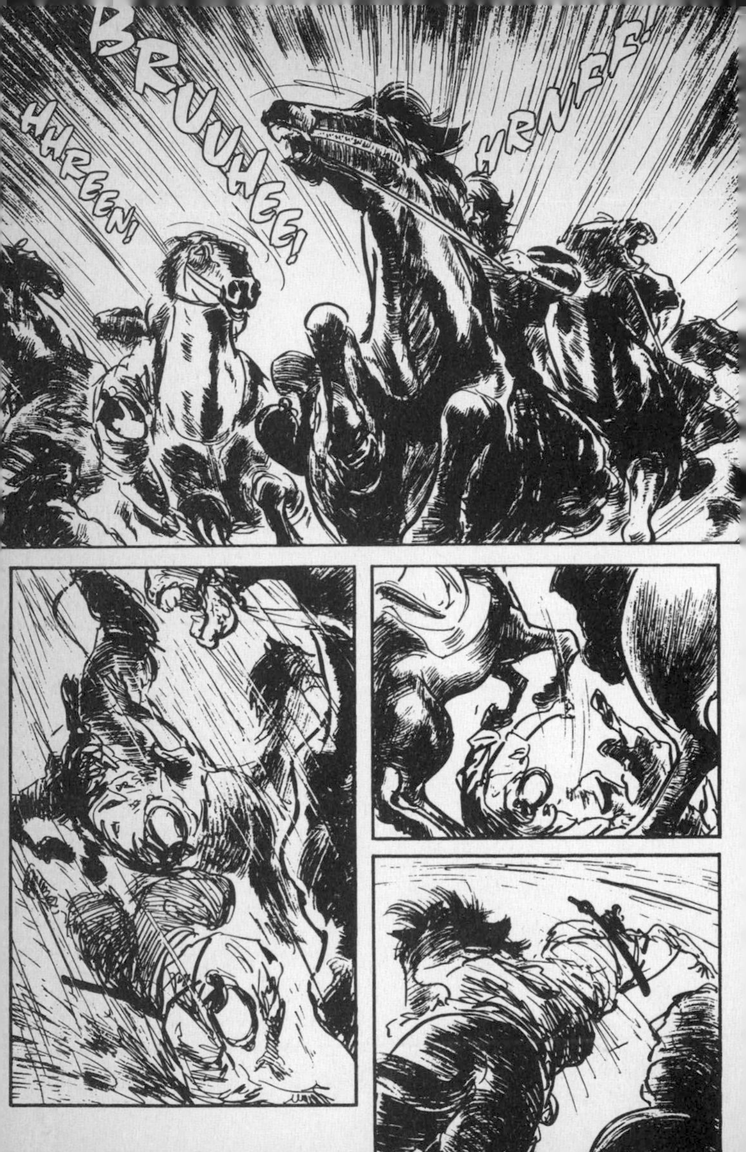
HRNFF!
BRUUHEEE!
HHREEN!

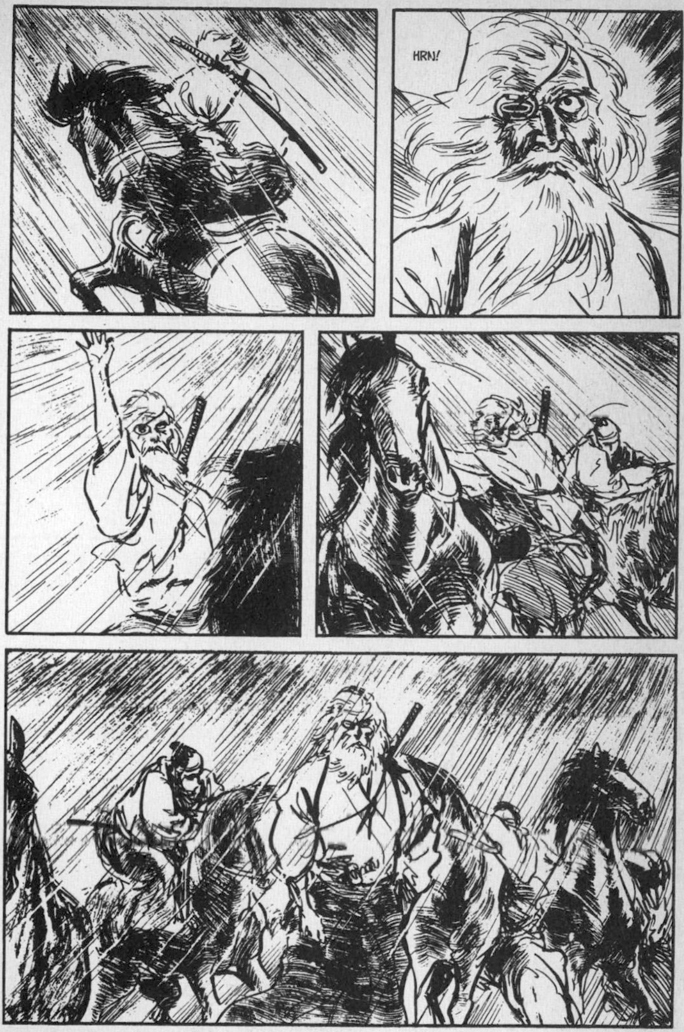
HRN!

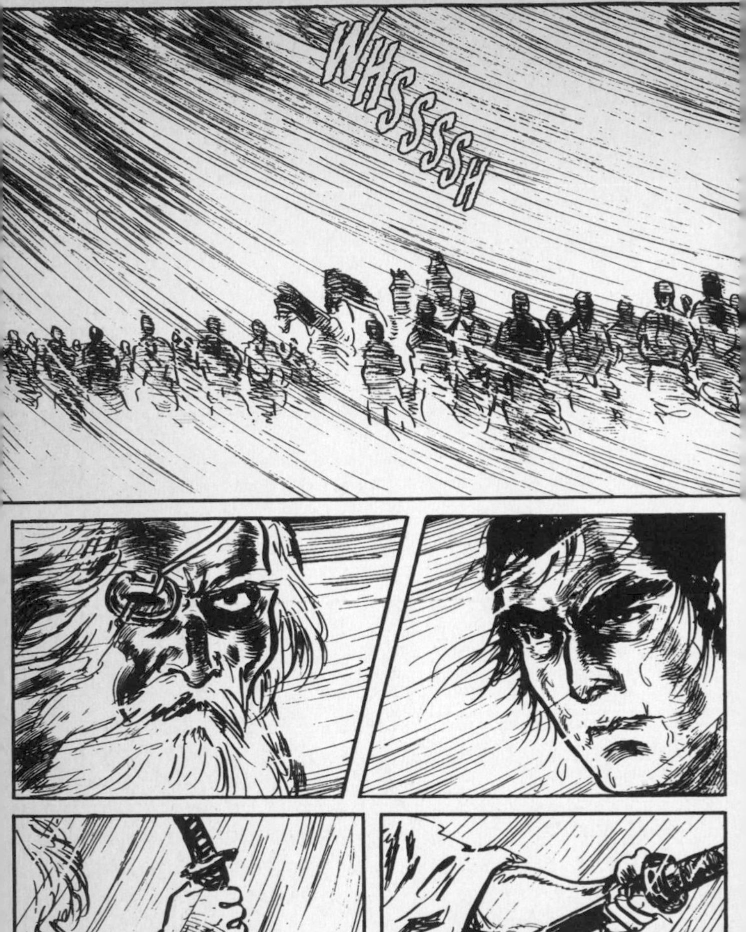
WHSSSSH

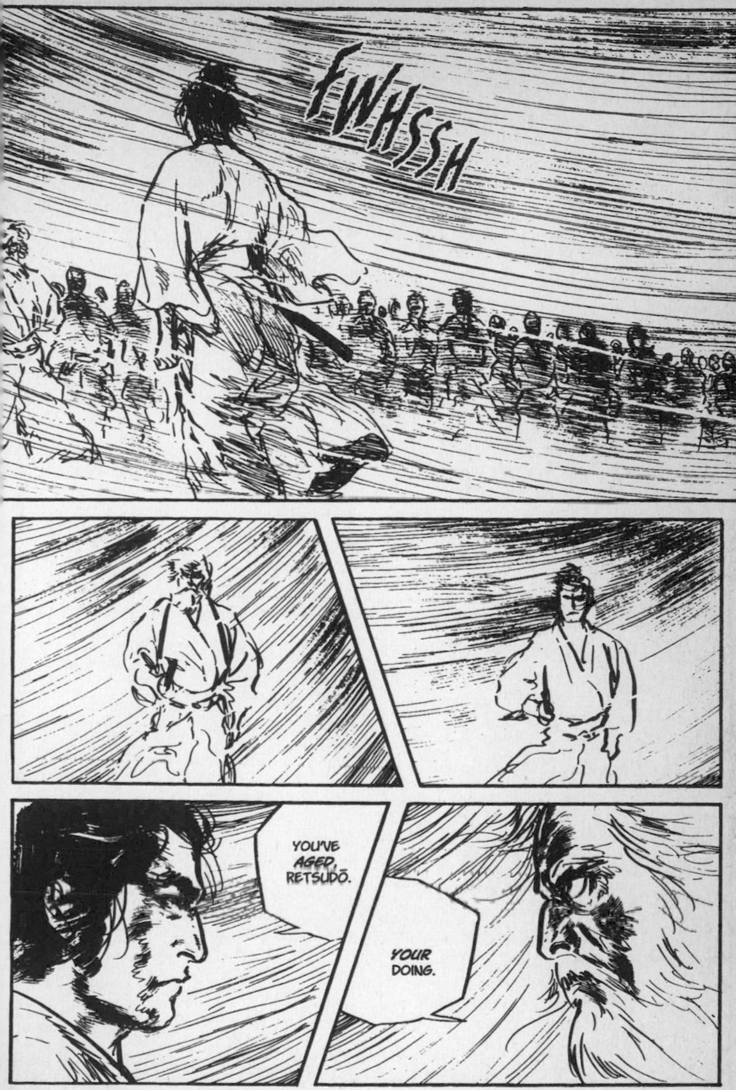
FWHSSH
YOUR DOING.
YOU'VE AGED, RETSUDŌ.

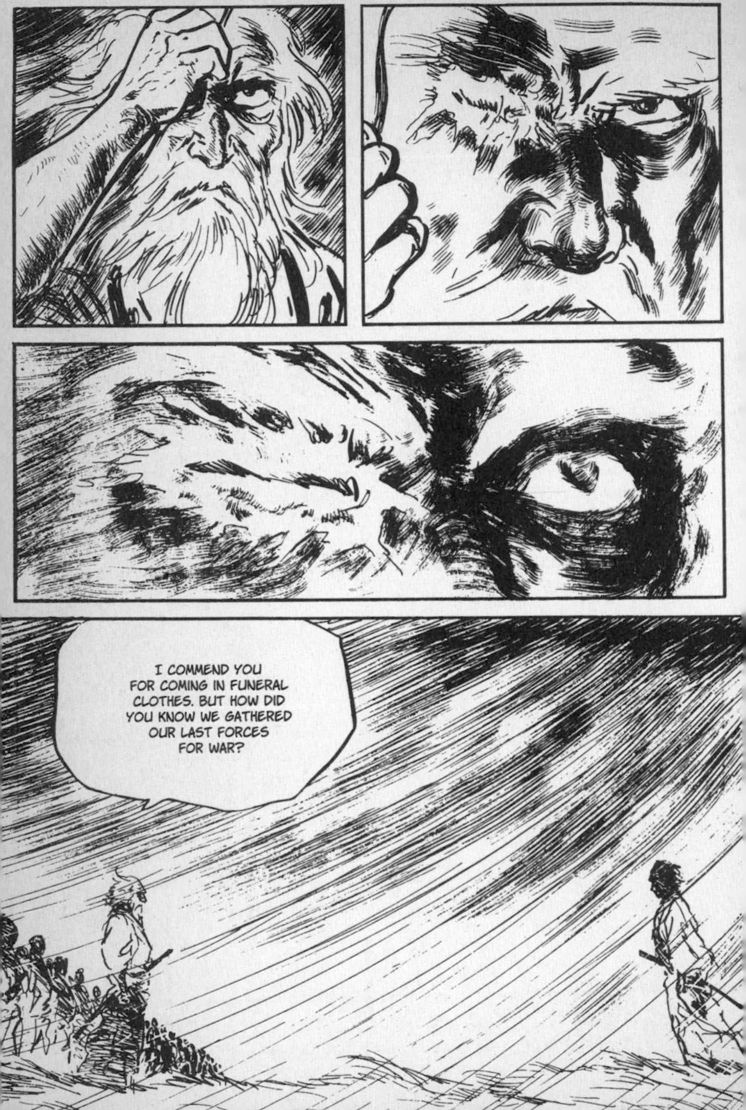
I COMMEND YOU FOR COMING IN FUNERAL CLOTHES. BUT HOW DID YOU KNOW WE GATHERED OUR LAST FORCES FOR WAR?

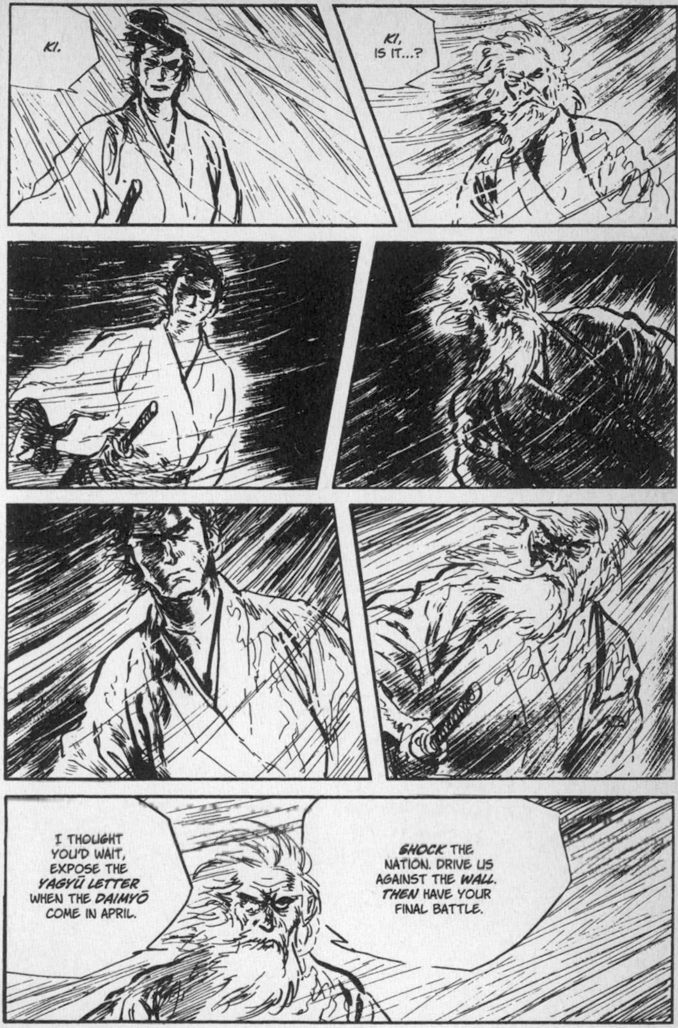
KI.
KI, IS IT...?
I THOUGHT YOU'D WAIT, EXPOSE THE *YAGYŪ LETTER* WHEN THE *DAIMYŌ* COME IN APRIL.
SHOCK THE NATION. DRIVE US AGAINST THE *WALL*. *THEN* HAVE YOUR FINAL BATTLE.

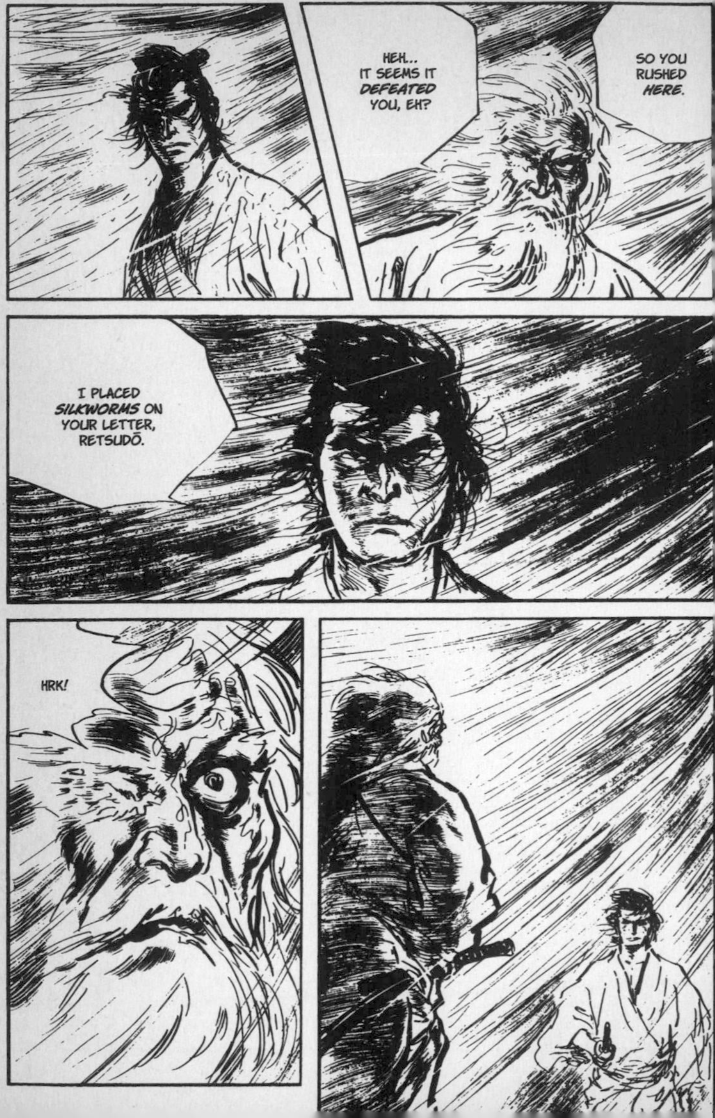
HEH.. IT SEEMS IT DEFEATED YOU, EH?
SO YOU RUSHED HERE.
I PLACED SILKWORMS ON YOUR LETTER, RETSUDŌ.
HRK!

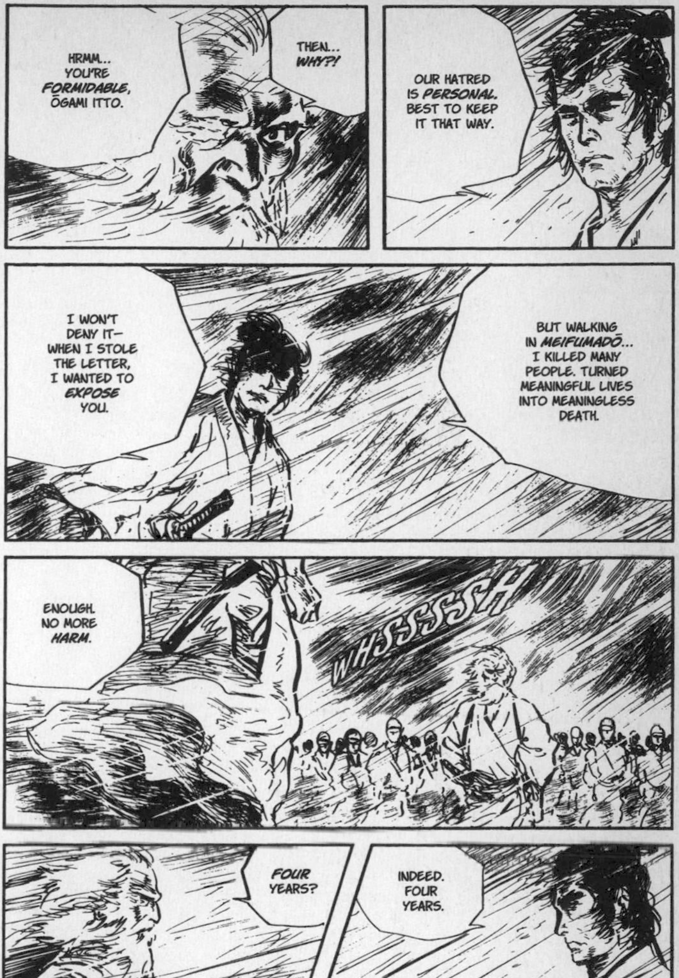
HRMM... YOU'RE FORMIDABLE, ŌGAMI ITTO.
THEN... WHY?!
OUR HATRED IS PERSONAL. BEST TO KEEP IT THAT WAY.
I WON'T DENY IT— WHEN I STOLE THE LETTER, I WANTED TO EXPOSE YOU.
BUT WALKING IN MEIFUMADŌ... I KILLED MANY PEOPLE. TURNED MEANINGFUL LIVES INTO MEANINGLESS DEATH.
ENOUGH. NO MORE HARM.
WHSSSSSH
FOUR YEARS?
INDEED. FOUR YEARS.

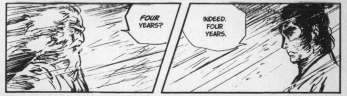

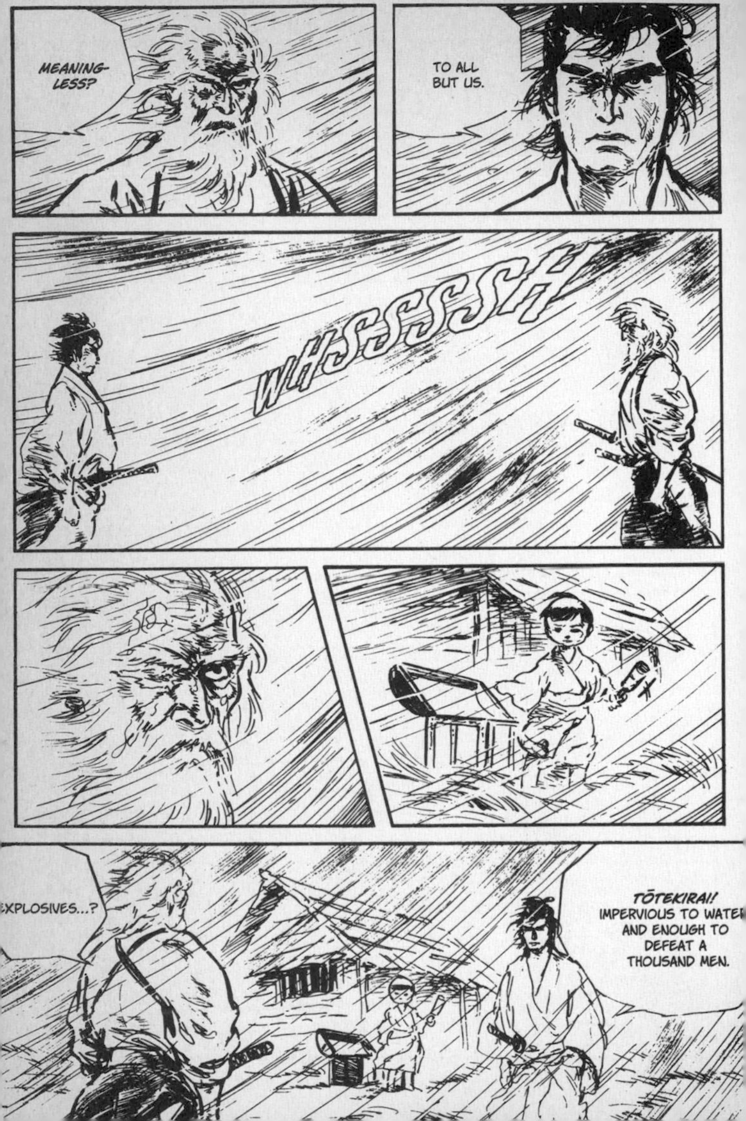
MEANING-LESS?
TO ALL BUT US.
WHSSSSSH
XPLOSIVES...?
TŌTEKIRAI! IMPERVIOUS TO WATE AND ENOUGH TO DEFEAT A THOUSAND MEN.

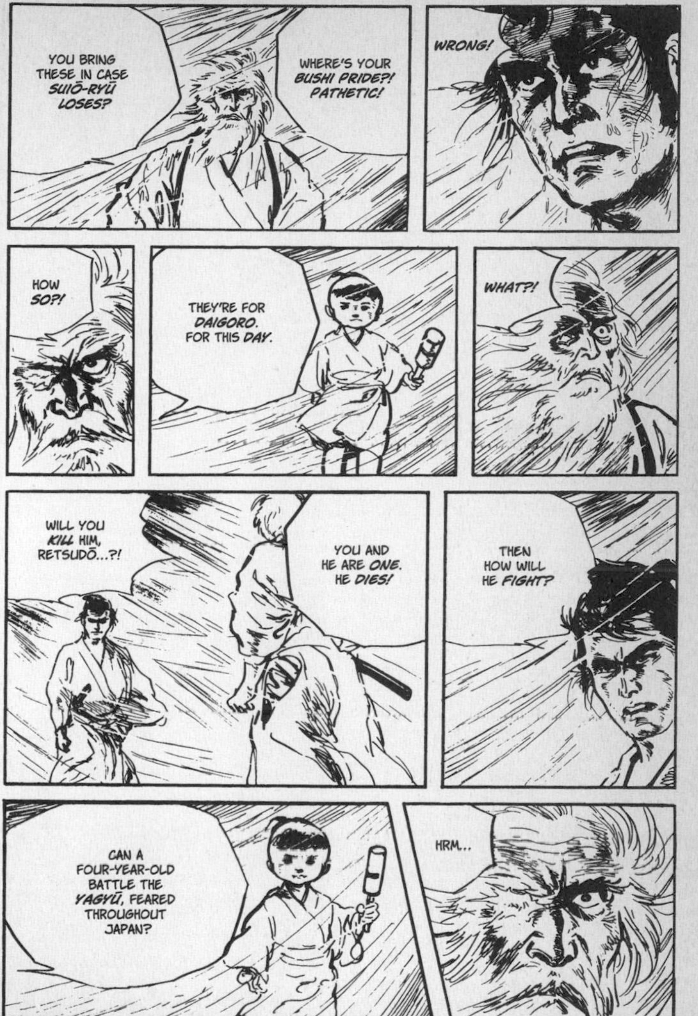

YOU BRING THESE IN CASE SUIŌ-RYŪ LOSES?
WHERE'S YOUR BUSHI PRIDE?! PATHETIC!
WRONG!
HOW SO?!
THEY'RE FOR DAIGORO. FOR THIS DAY.
WHAT?!
WILL YOU KILL HIM, RETSUDŌ...?!
YOU AND HE ARE ONE. HE DIES!
THEN HOW WILL HE FIGHT?
CAN A FOUR-YEAR-OLD BATTLE THE YAGYŪ, FEARED THROUGHOUT JAPAN?
HRM...

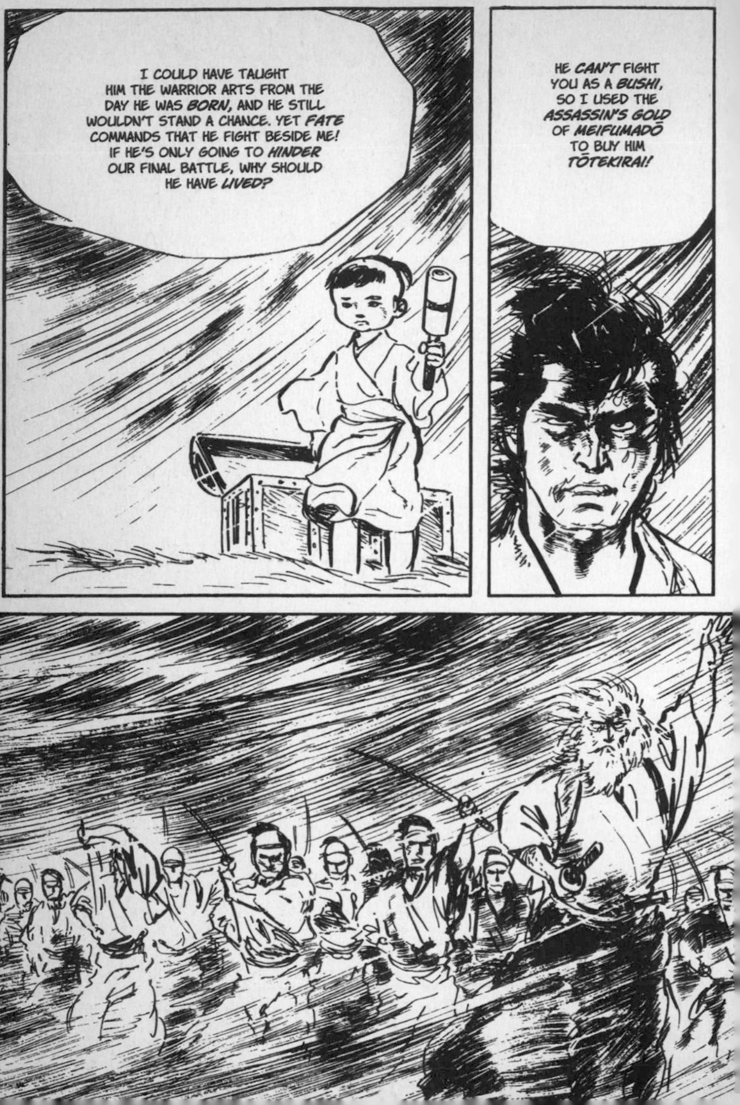
HE CAN'T FIGHT YOU AS A BUSHI, SO I USED THE ASSASSIN'S GOLD OF MEIFUMADŌ TO BUY HIM TŌTEKIRAI!
I COULD HAVE TAUGHT HIM THE WARRIOR ARTS FROM THE DAY HE WAS BORN, AND HE STILL WOULDN'T STAND A CHANCE. YET FATE COMMANDS THAT HE FIGHT BESIDE ME! IF HE'S ONLY GOING TO HINDER OUR FINAL BATTLE, WHY SHOULD HE HAVE LIVED?

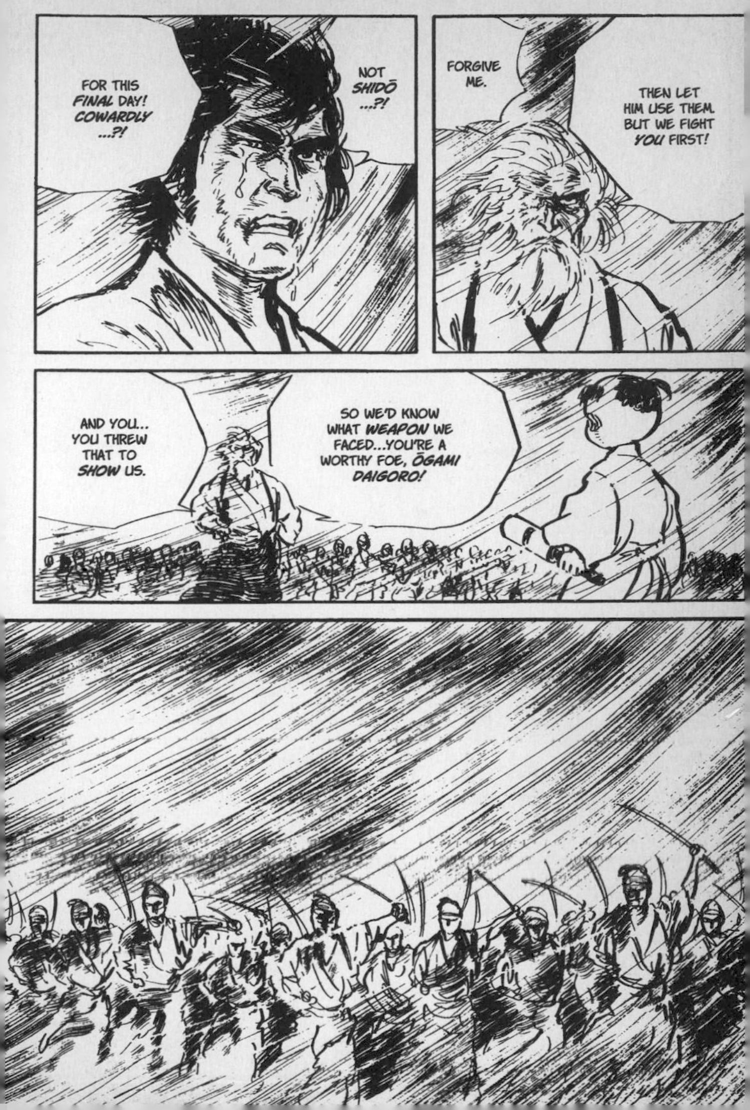
FOR THIS *FINAL* DAY! *COWARDLY* ...?!
NOT *SHIDŌ* ...?!
FORGIVE ME.
THEN LET HIM USE THEM BUT WE FIGHT *YOU* FIRST!
AND YOU... YOU THREW THAT TO *SHOW* US.
SO WE'D KNOW WHAT *WEAPON* WE FACED...YOU'RE A WORTHY FOE, *ŌGAMI DAIGORO!*

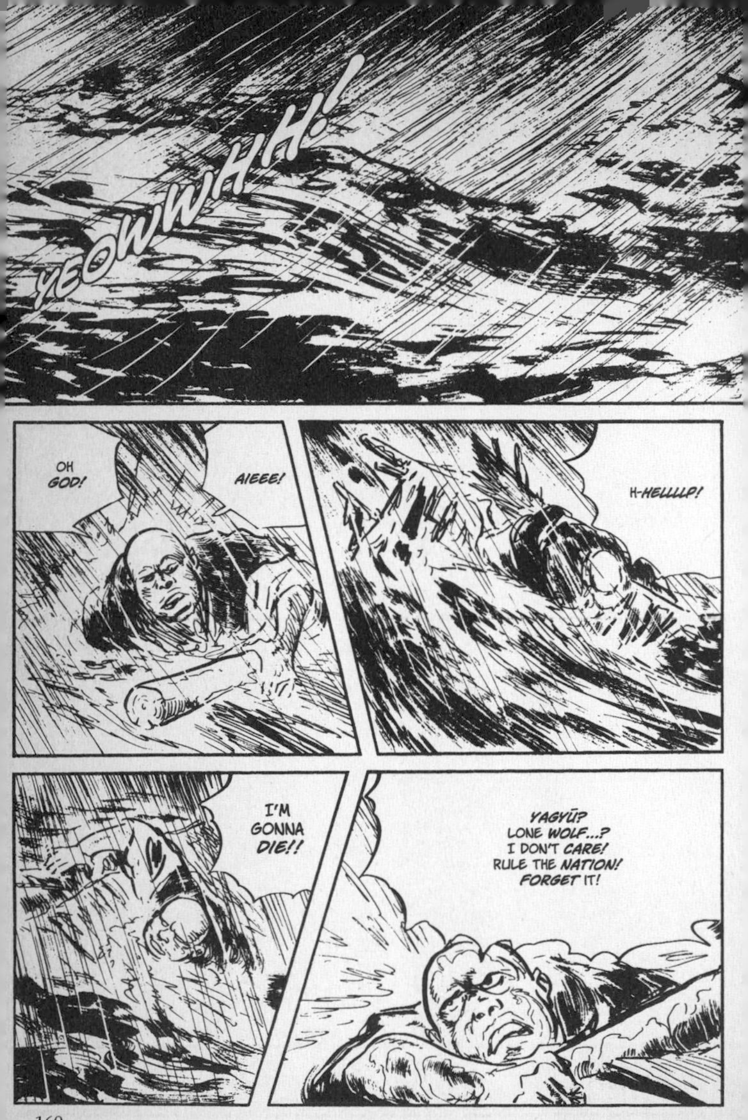
YEOWWHH!!
H-HELLLLP!
AIEEE!
OH GOD!
YAGYŪ? LONE WOLF...? I DON'T CARE! RULE THE NATION! FORGET IT!
I'M GONNA DIE!!

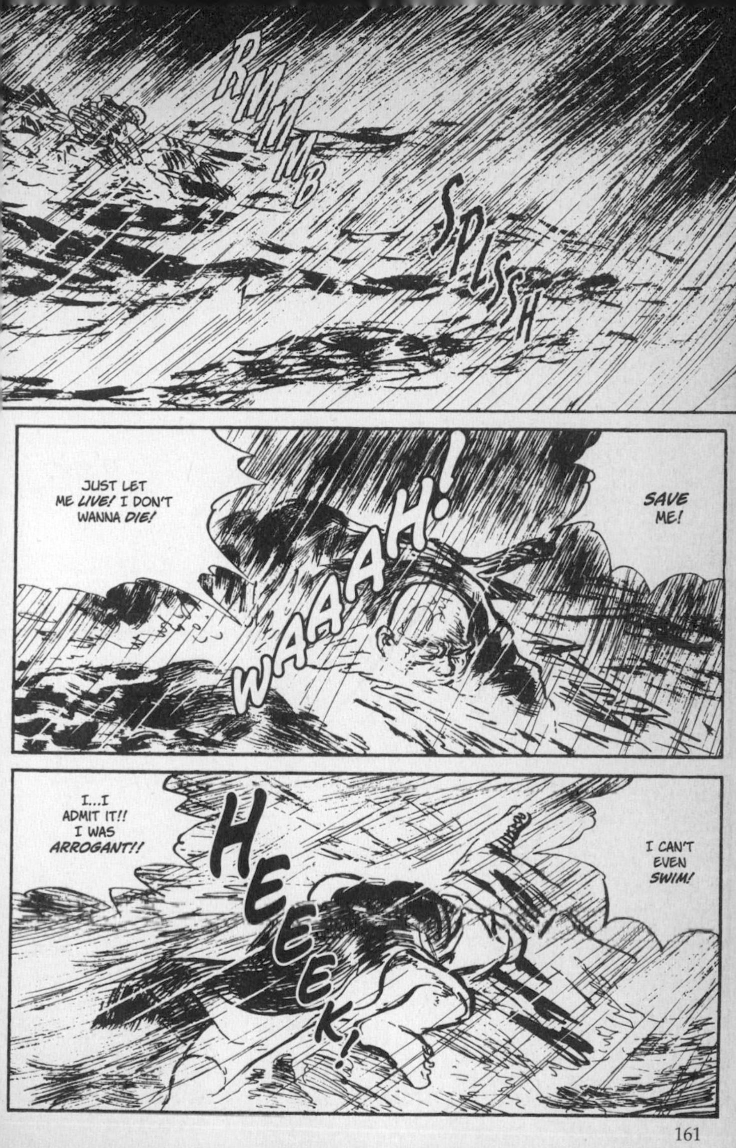
RMMMB
SPLSSH
SAVE ME!
WAAAAH!
JUST LET ME LIVE! I DON'T WANNA DIE!
I CAN'T EVEN SWIM!
HEEEEK!
I...I ADMIT IT!! I WAS ARROGANT!!

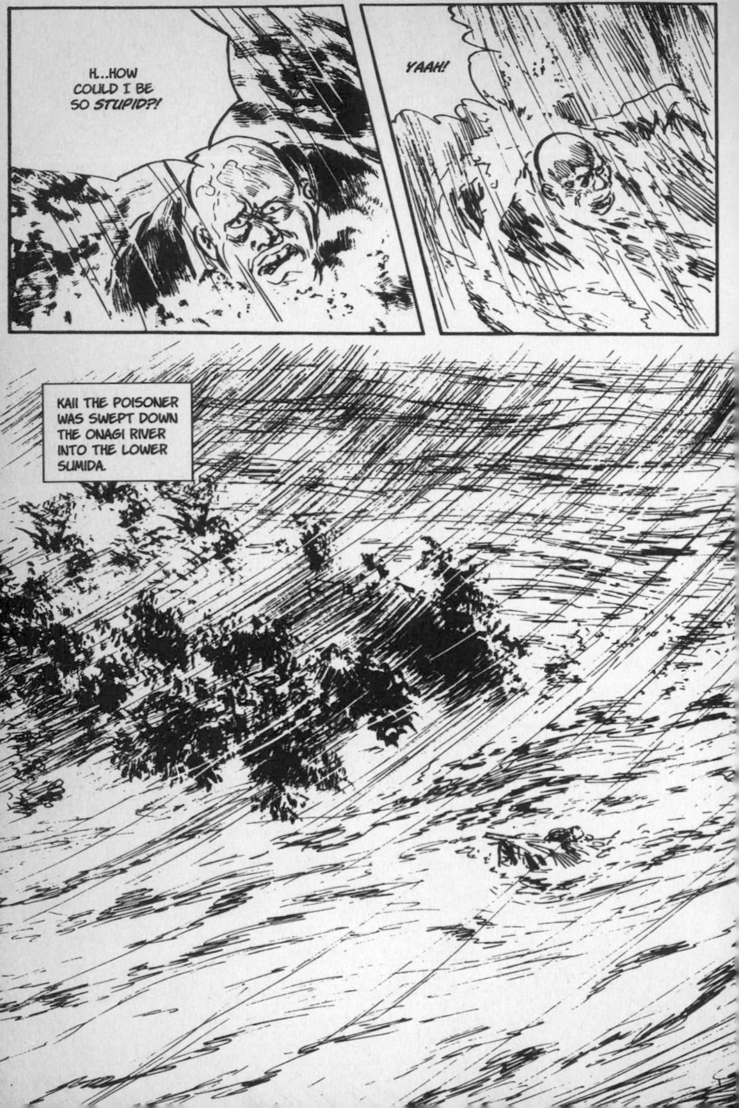
H..HOW COULD I BE SO STUPID?!
YAAH!
KAII THE POISONER WAS SWEPT DOWN THE ONAGI RIVER INTO THE LOWER SUMIDA.

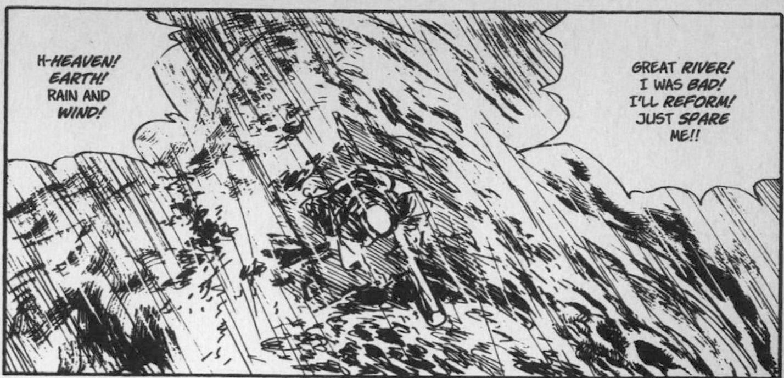
GREAT RIVER! I WAS BAD! I'LL REFORM! JUST SPARE ME!!
H-HEAVEN! EARTH! RAIN AND WIND!

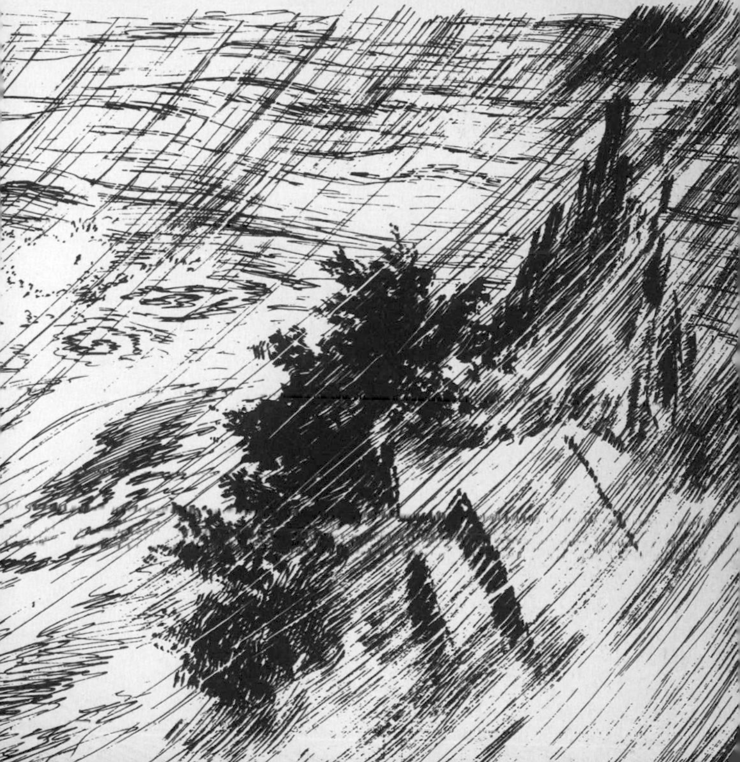

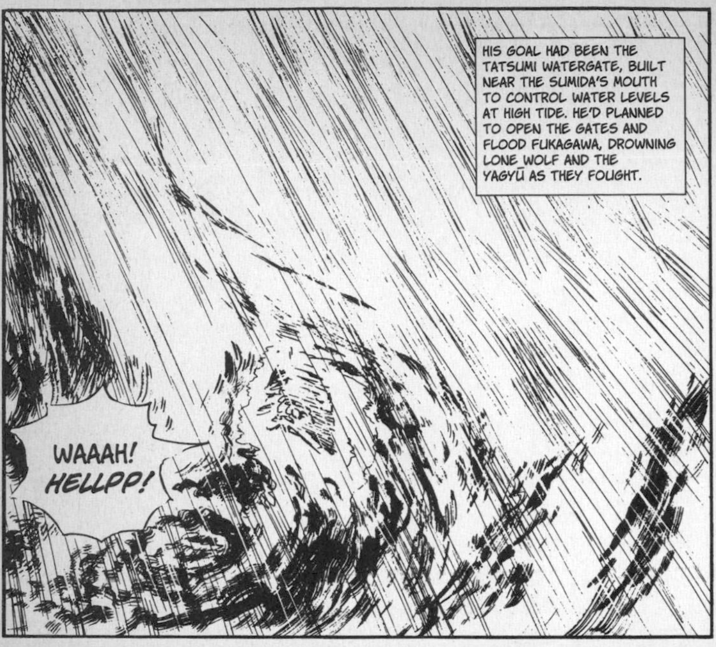
HIS GOAL HAD BEEN THE TATSUMI WATERGATE, BUILT NEAR THE SUMIDA'S MOUTH TO CONTROL WATER LEVELS AT HIGH TIDE. HE'D PLANNED TO OPEN THE GATES AND FLOOD FUKAGAWA, DROWNING LONE WOLF AND THE YAGYŪ AS THEY FOUGHT.
WAAAH! *HELLPP!*
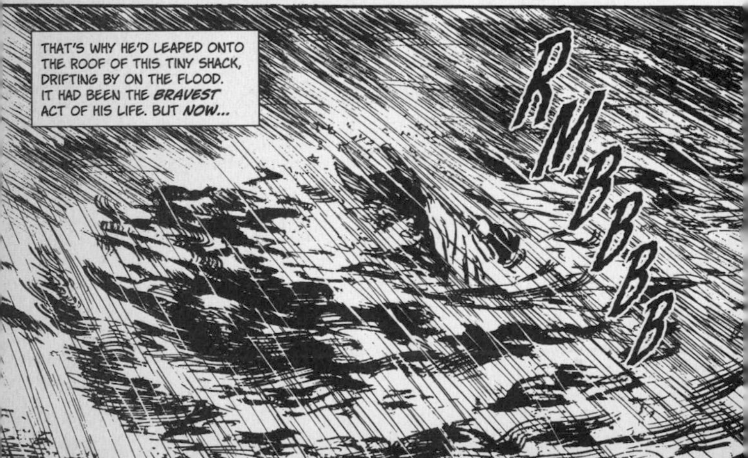
THAT'S WHY HE'D LEAPED ONTO THE ROOF OF THIS TINY SHACK, DRIFTING BY ON THE FLOOD. IT HAD BEEN THE *BRAVEST* ACT OF HIS LIFE. BUT *NOW...*
RMBBBB

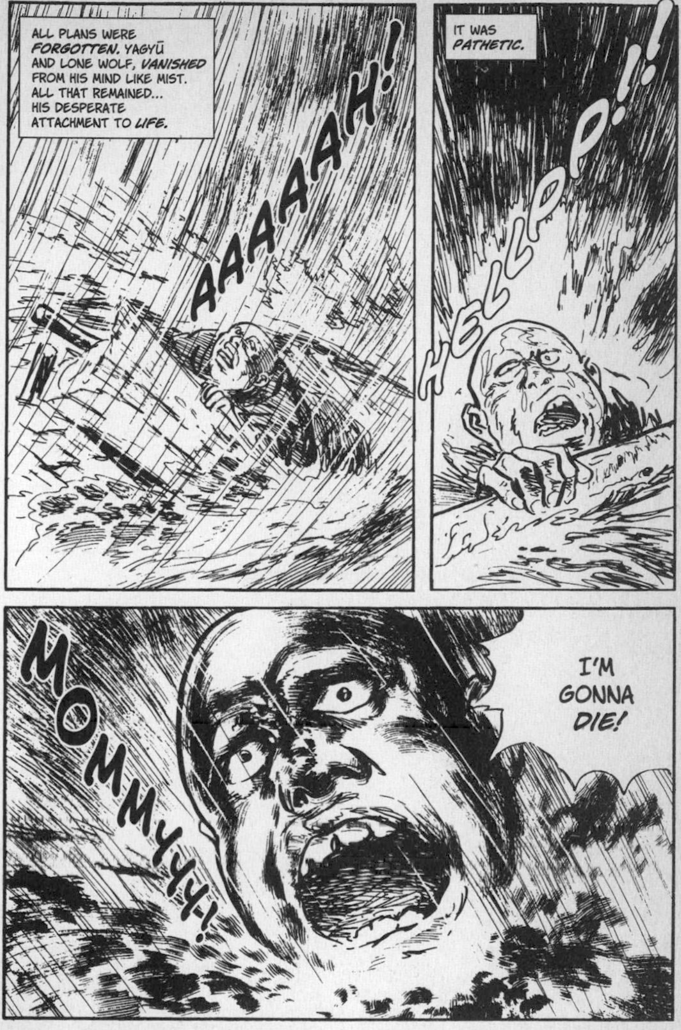
ALL PLANS WERE FORGOTTEN. YAGYŪ AND LONE WOLF, VANISHED FROM HIS MIND LIKE MIST. ALL THAT REMAINED... HIS DESPERATE ATTACHMENT TO LIFE.
AAAAAH!
IT WAS PATHETIC.
HELLLPP!!!
MOMMYYY-!
I'M GONNA DIE!

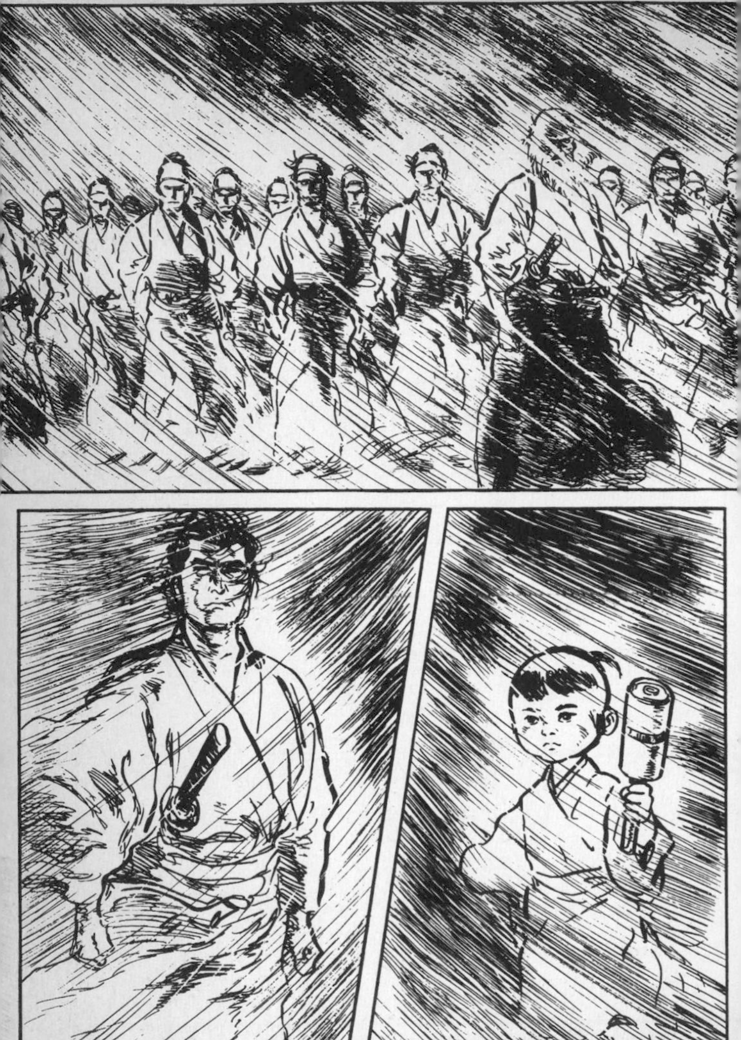

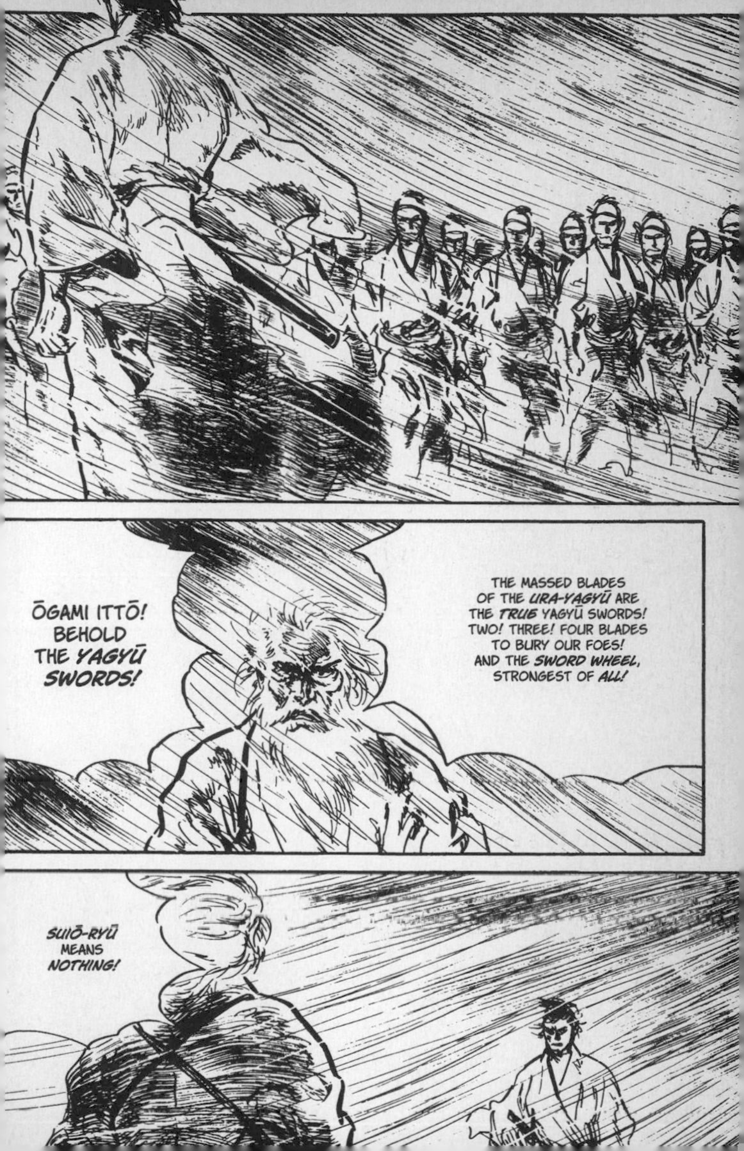
THE MASSED BLADES OF THE URA-YAGYŪ ARE THE TRUE YAGYŪ SWORDS! TWO! THREE! FOUR BLADES TO BURY OUR FOES! AND THE SWORD WHEEL, STRONGEST OF ALL!
ŌGAMI ITTŌ! BEHOLD THE YAGYŪ SWORDS!
SUIŌ-RYŪ MEANS NOTHING!

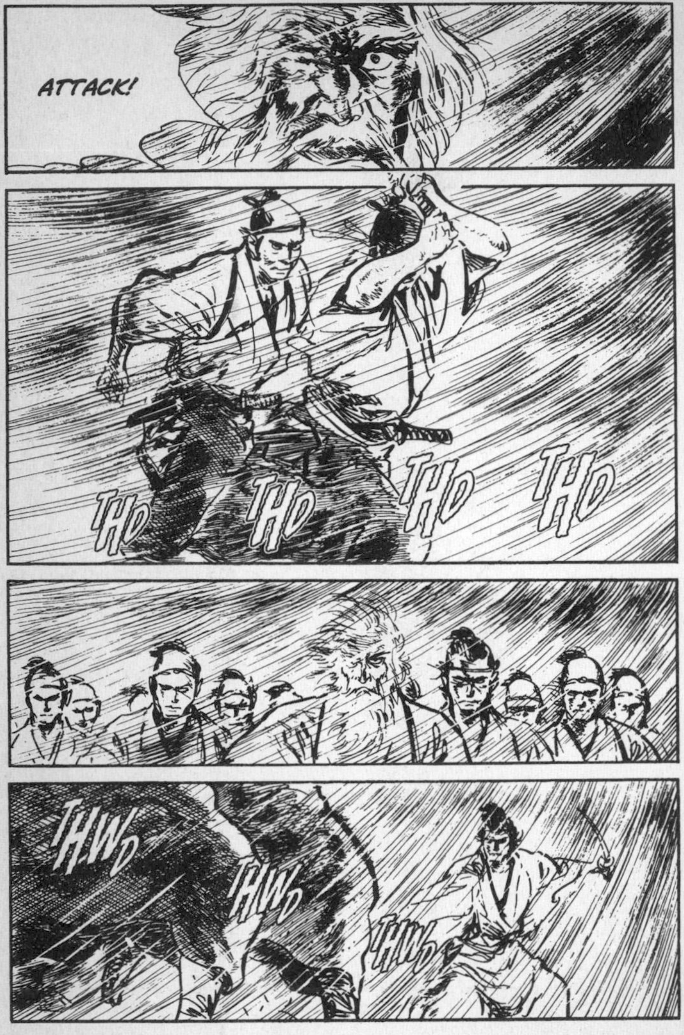
ATTACK!
THD
THD
THD
THD
THWD
THWD
THWD

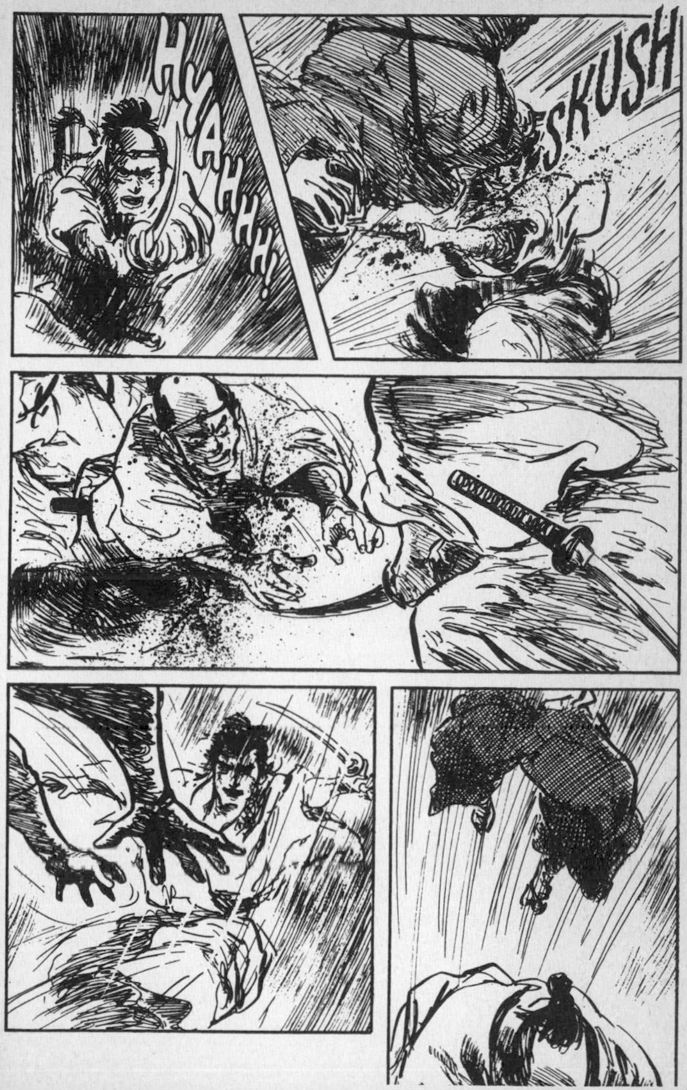
SKUSH
HYAHHH!

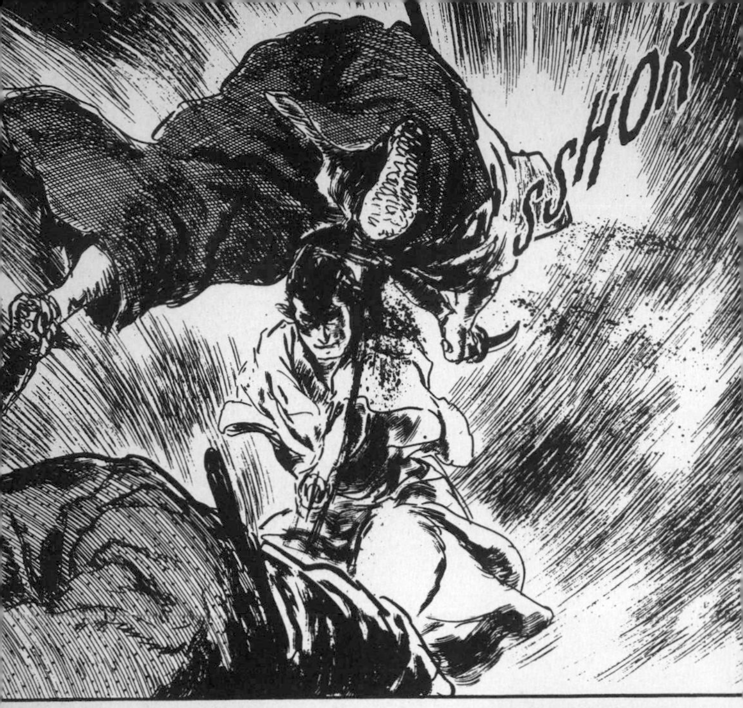
SSHOK

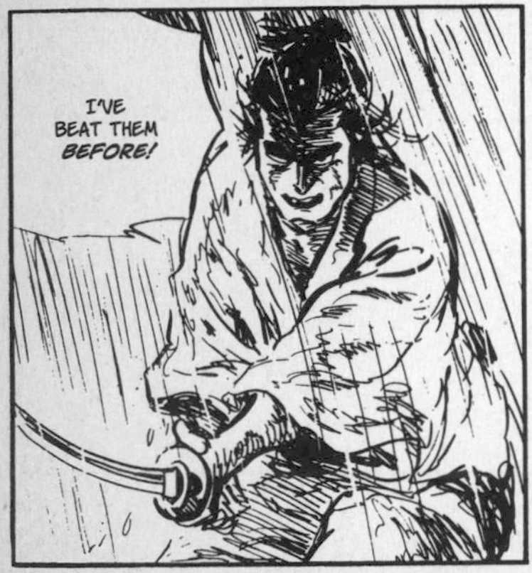
I'VE BEAT THEM BEFORE!

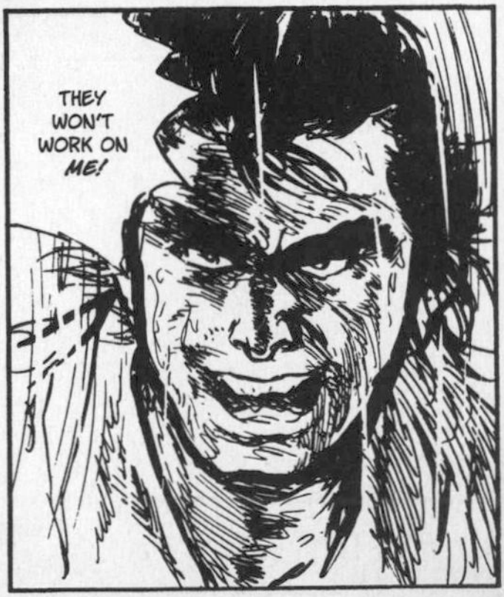
THEY WON'T WORK ON ME!

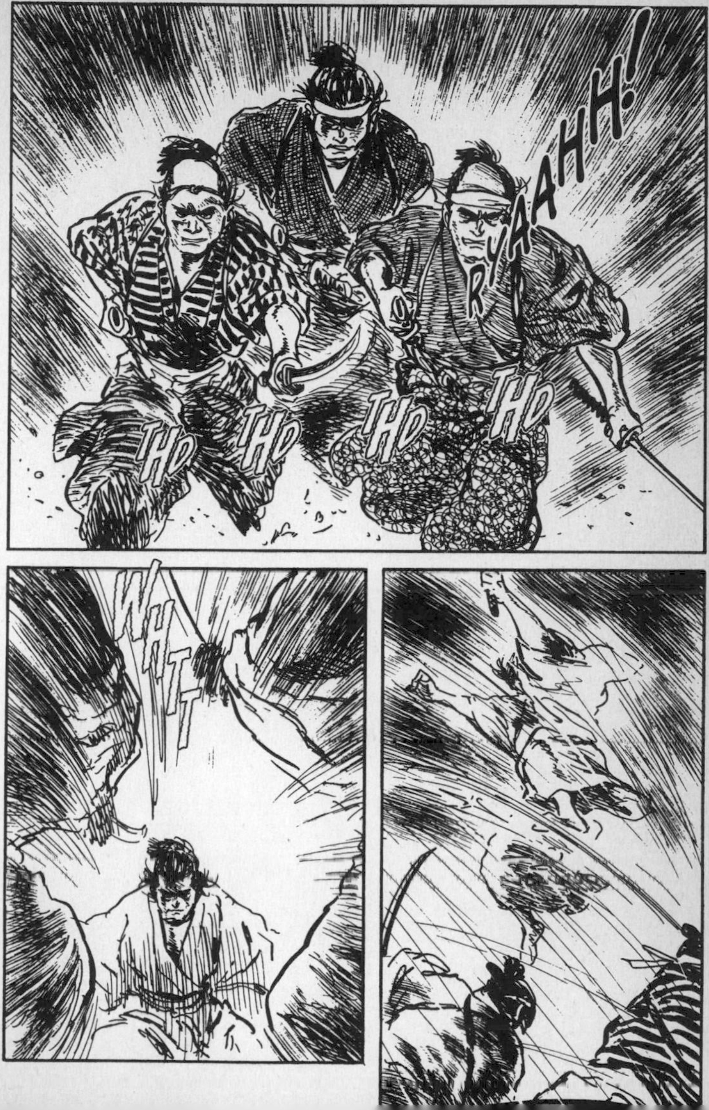
RYAAHH!
THD
THD
THD
THD
WHTT

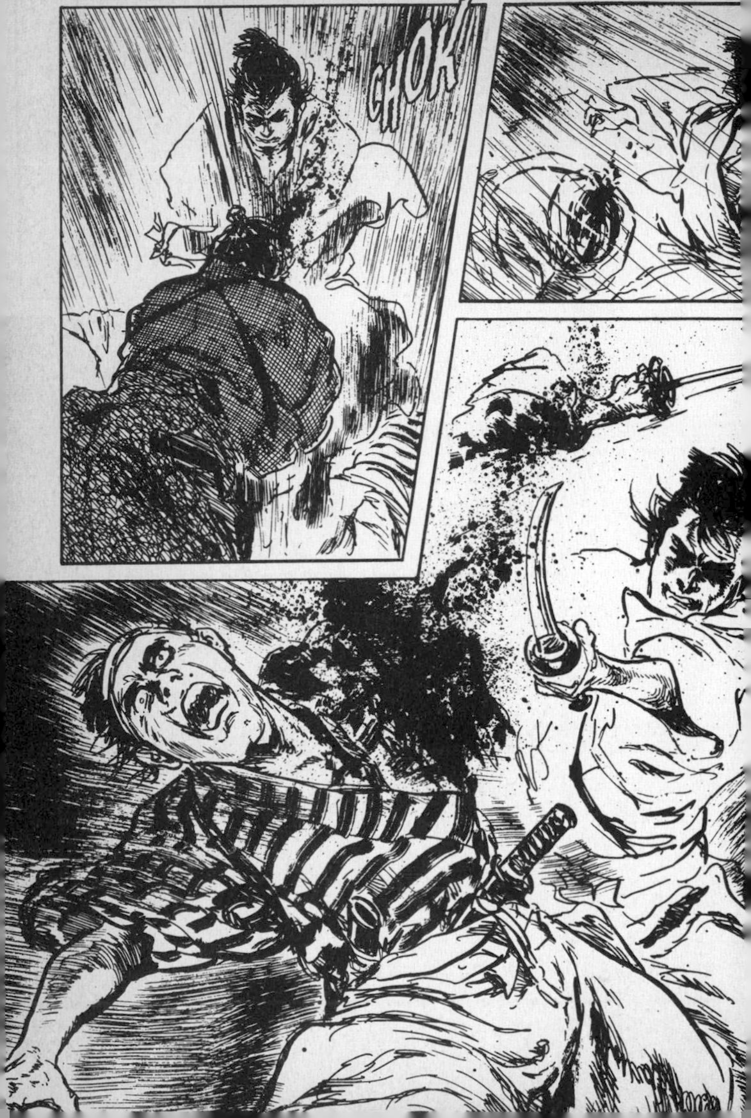
CHOK!

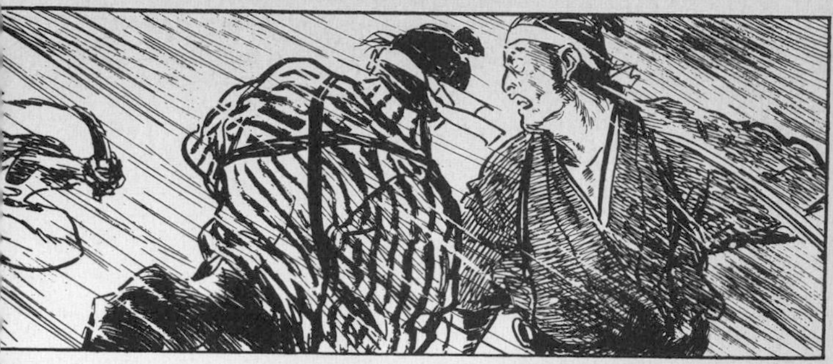
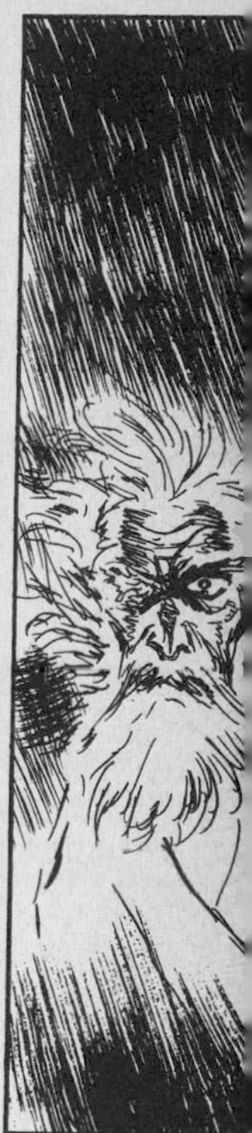
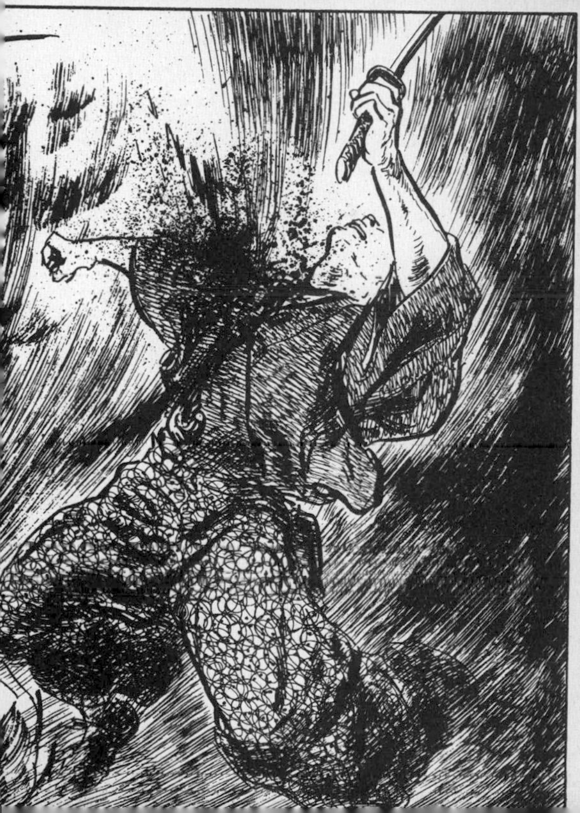

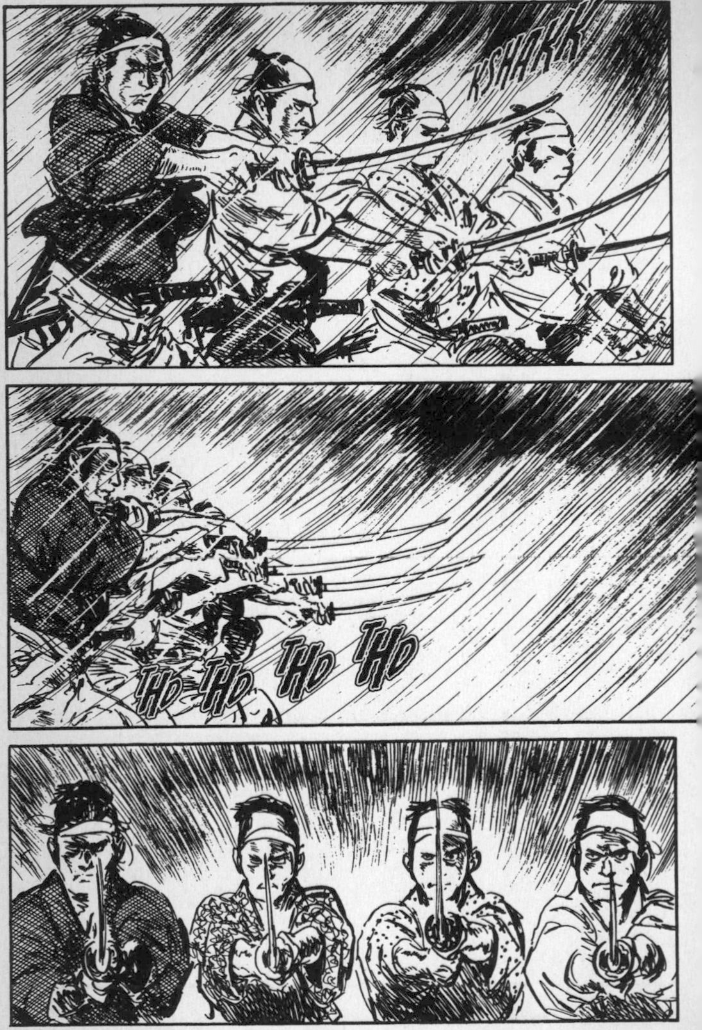
KSHAKK!
THD
THD
THD
THD

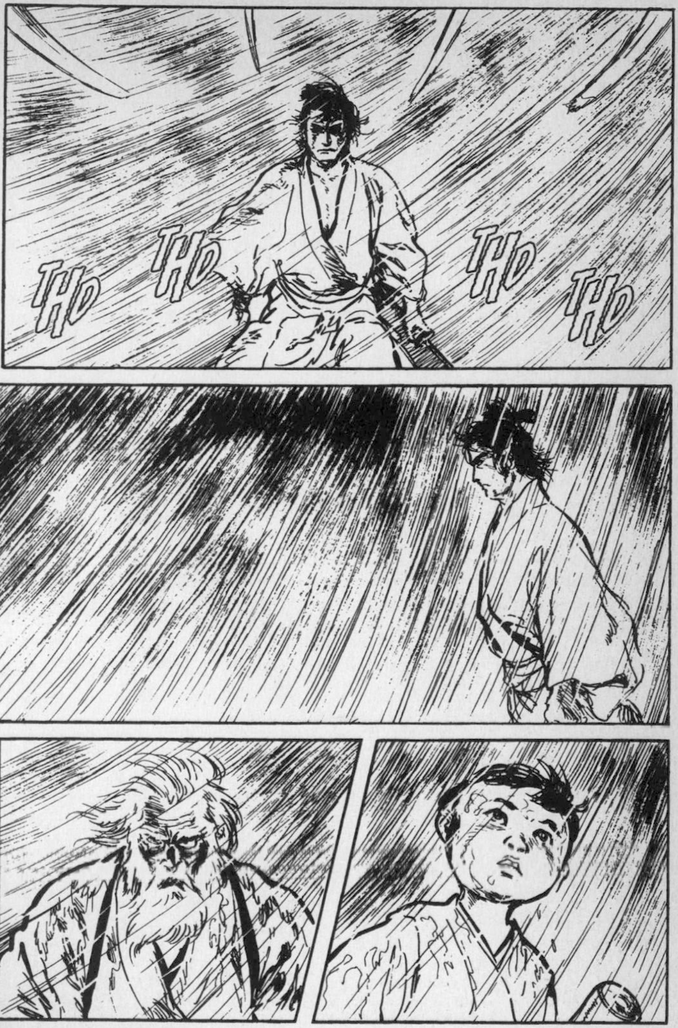
THD
THD
THD
THD

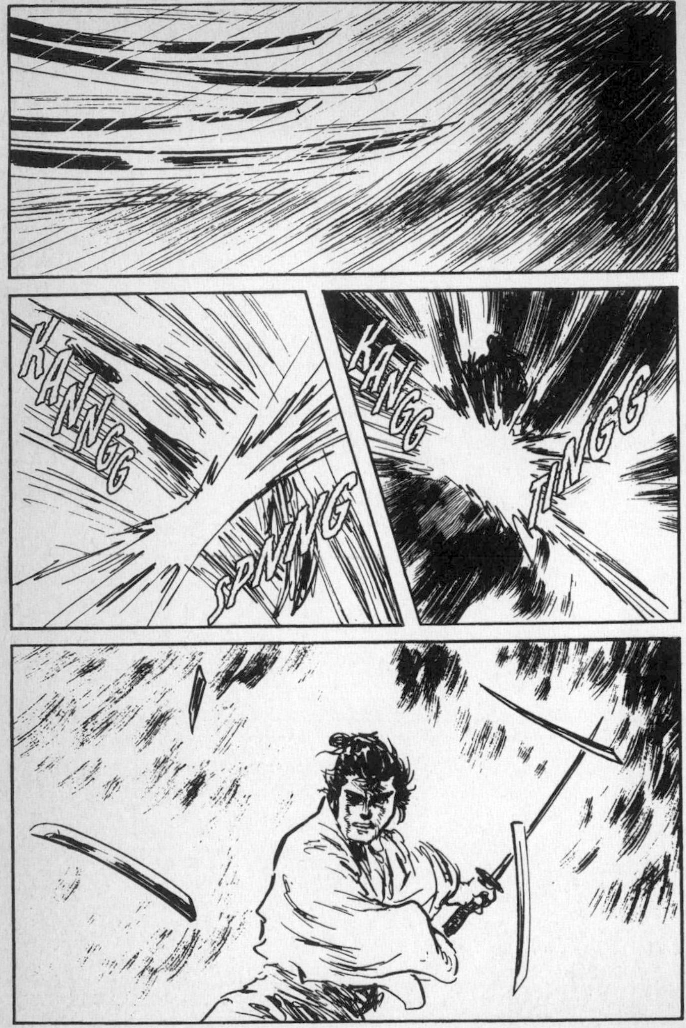
KANGG
TINGG
KANNGG
SPNNG

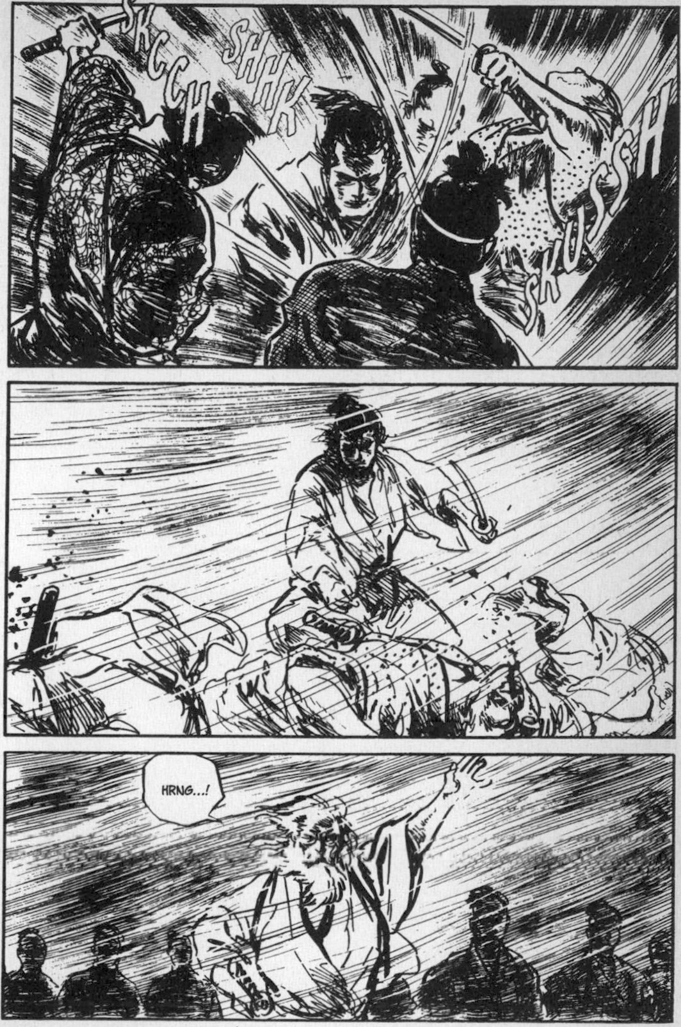
SKUSSH
SHHK
SKCCH
HRNG...!

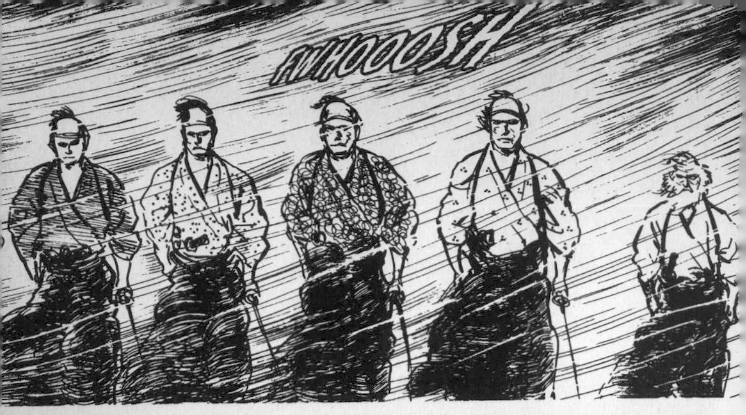
FWHOOOSH
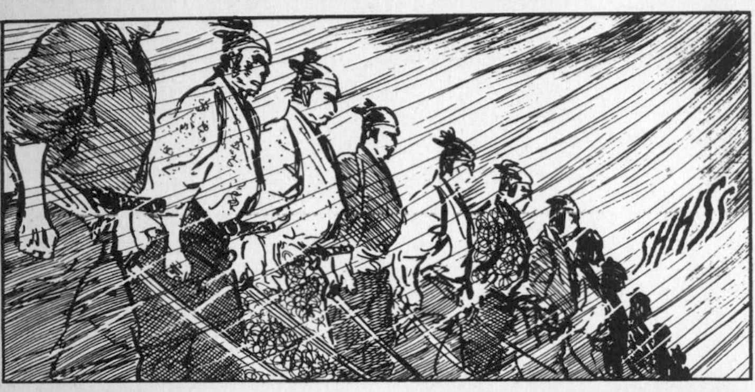
SHHSS
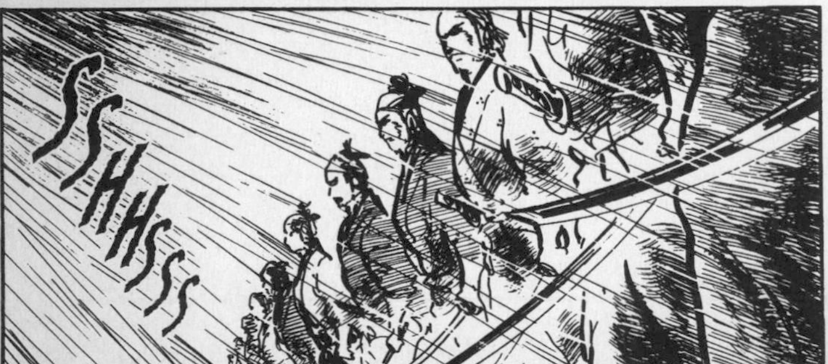
SSHHSSSS

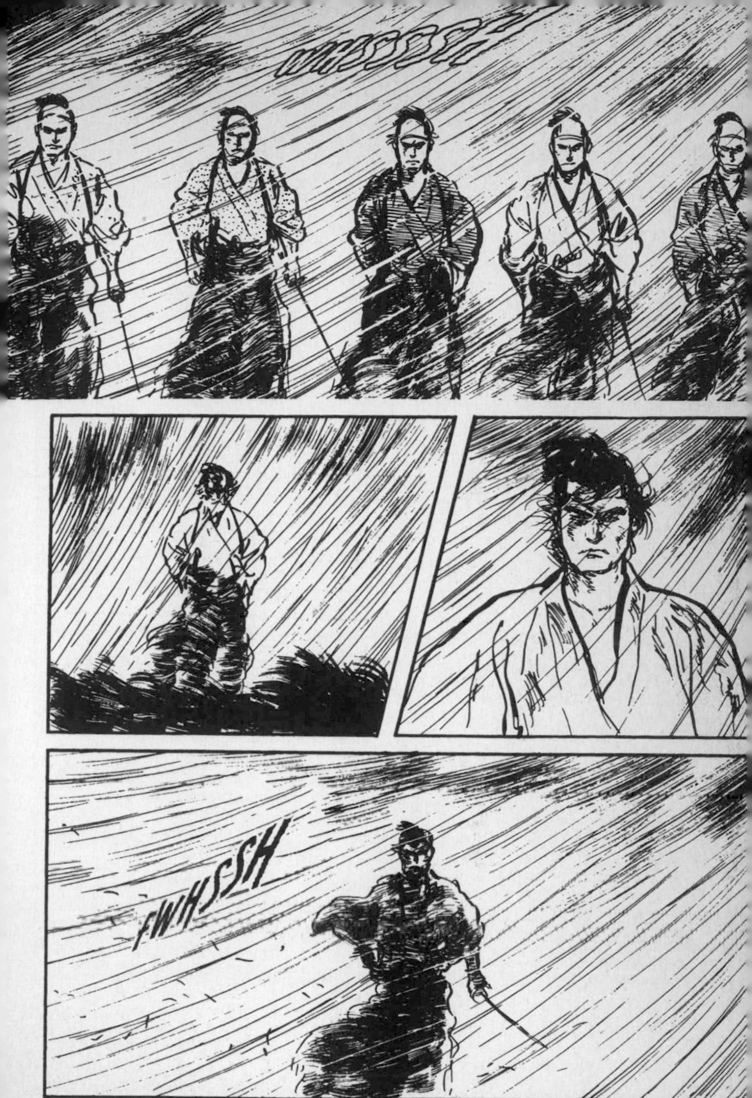
FWHSSH

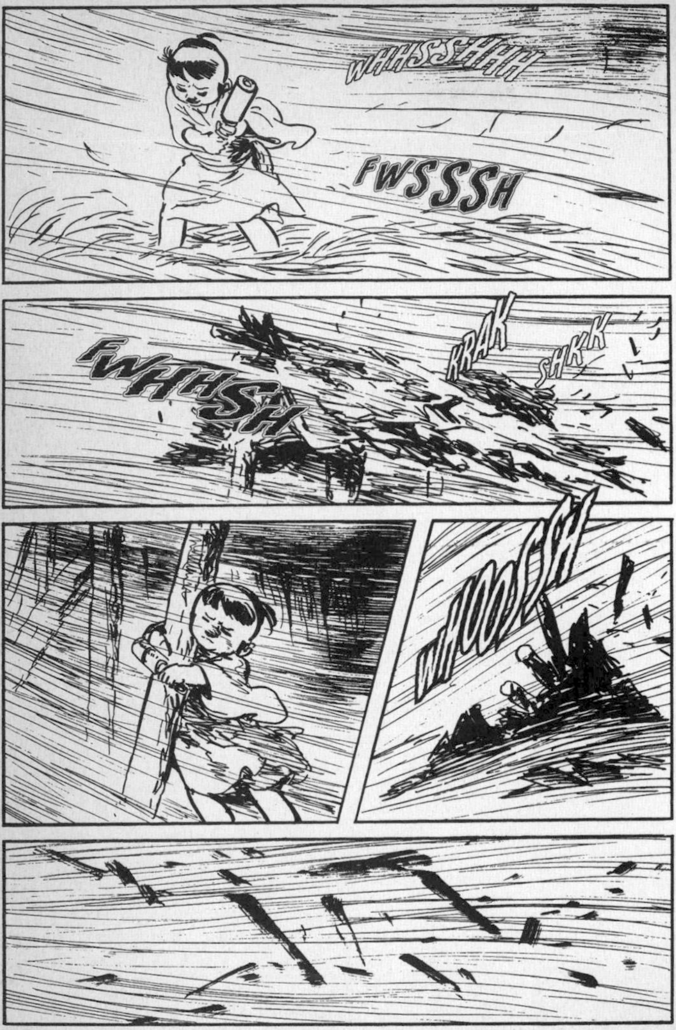
WHHSSHHH
FWSSSH
KRAK
SHKK
FWHHSH
WHOOSH

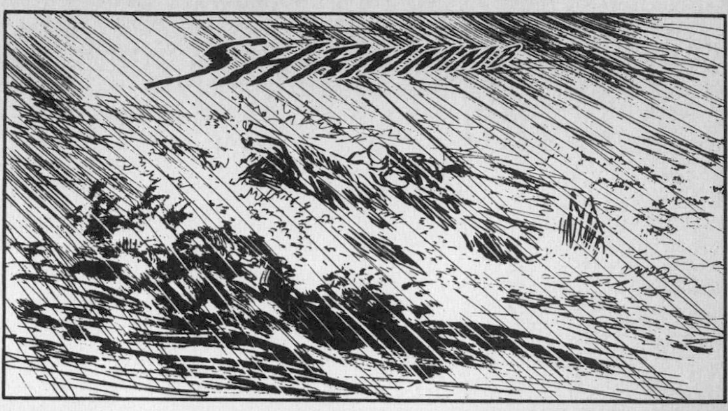
SHRMMMB
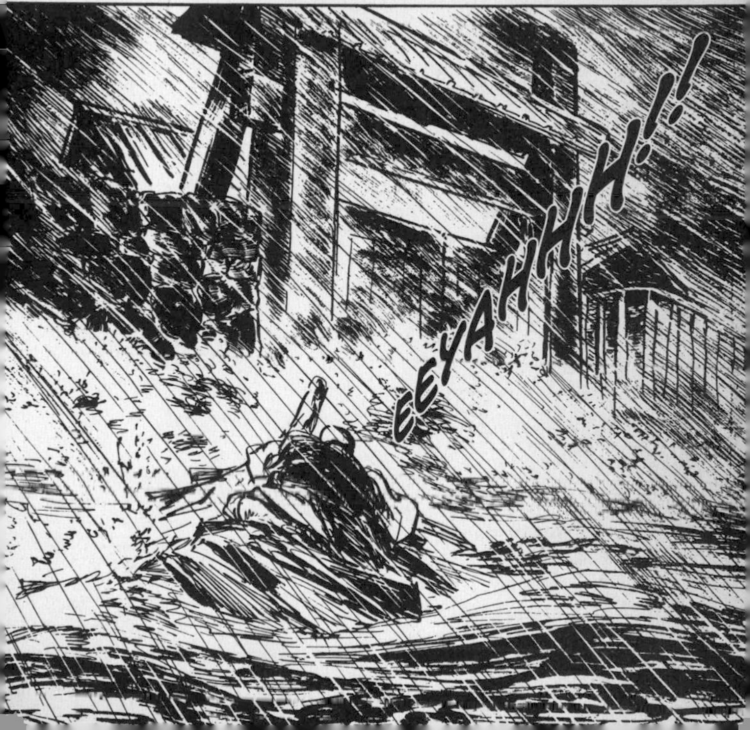
EEYAHHHH!!!

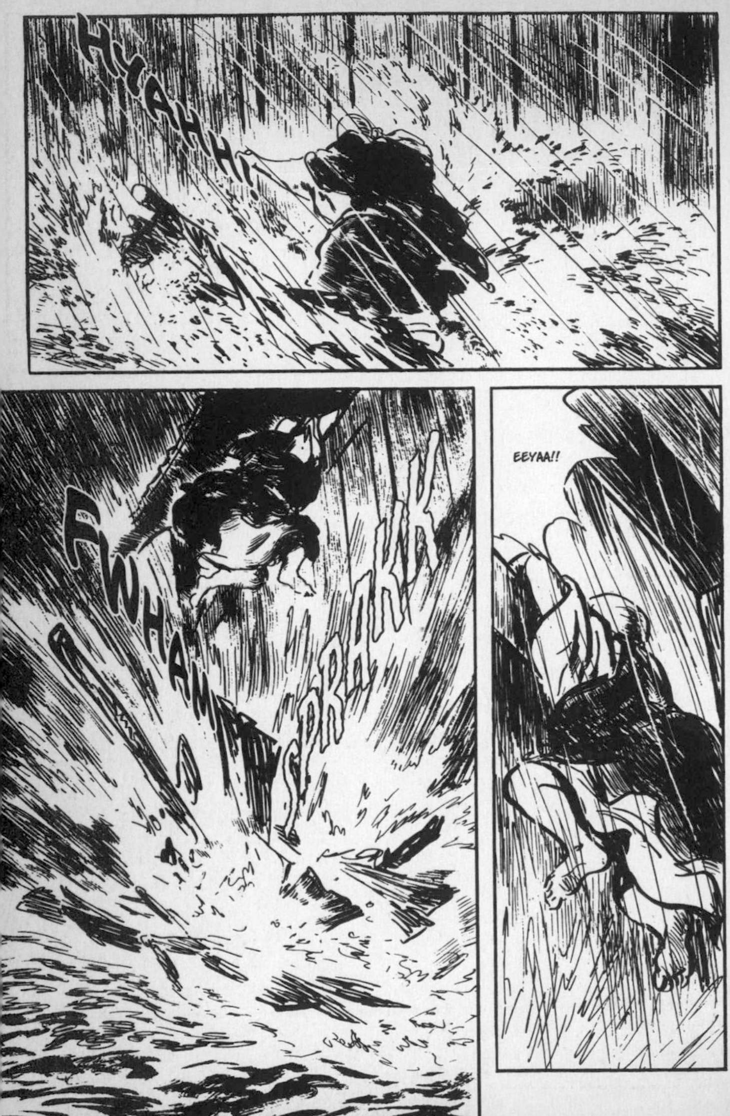
HIYAAHH!
EEYAA!!
FWHAMM
SPRAKK

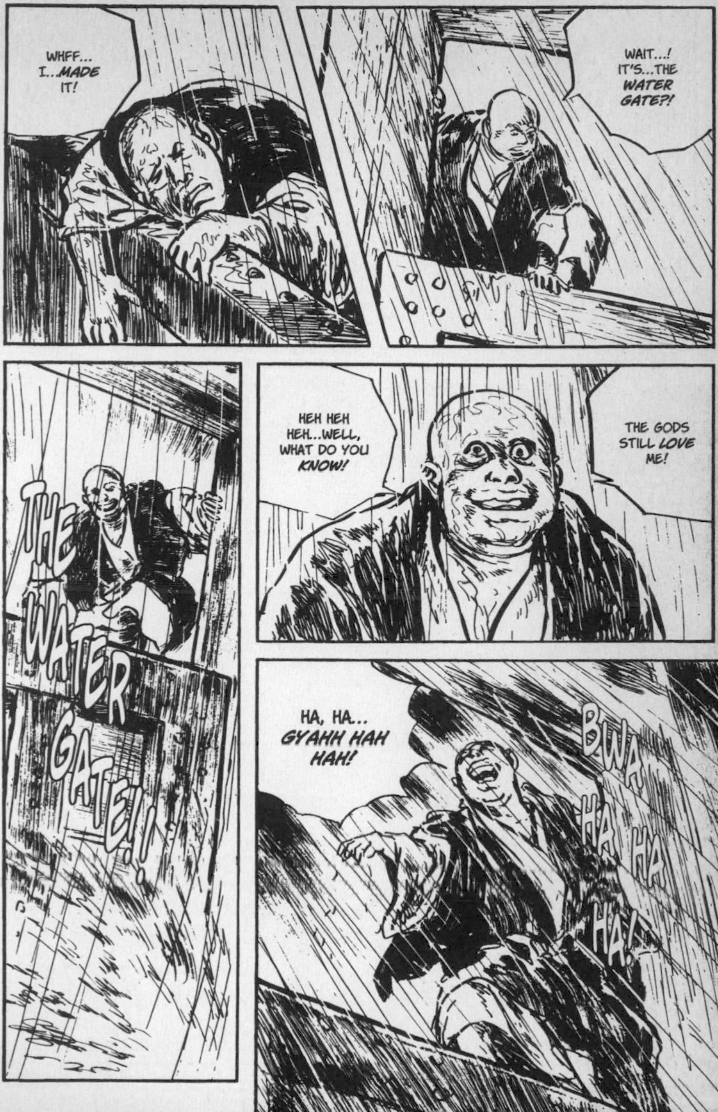
WHFF... I...MADE IT!
WAIT...! IT'S...THE WATER GATE?!
THE WATER GATE!!
HEH HEH HEH...WELL, WHAT DO YOU KNOW!
THE GODS STILL LOVE ME!
HA, HA... GYAHH HAH HAH!
BWA HA HA HA!

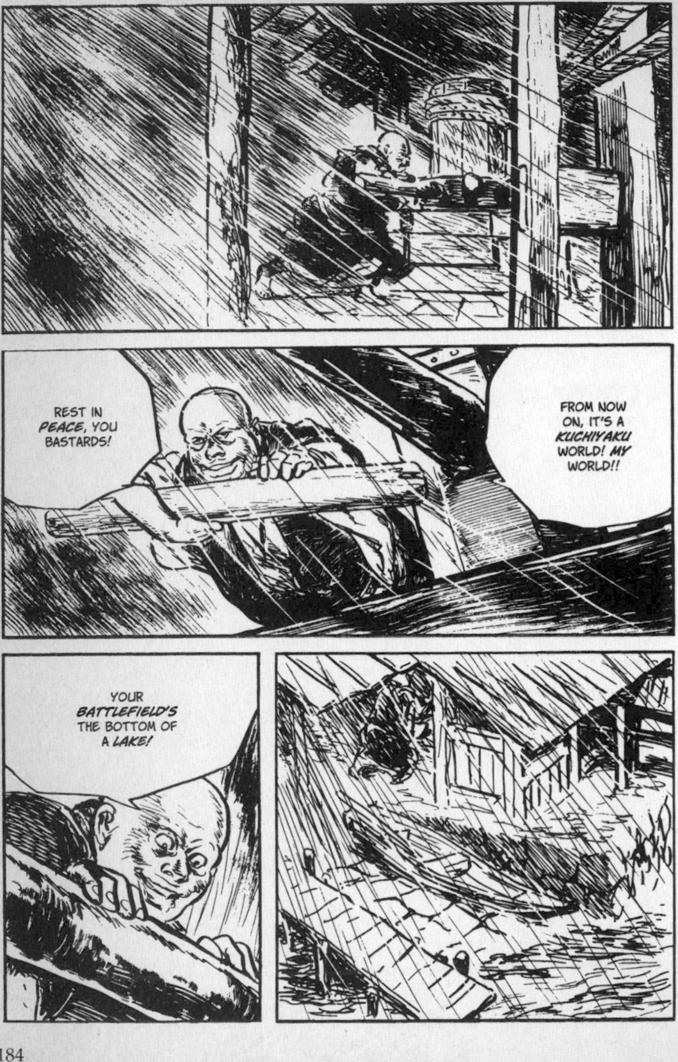
REST IN PEACE, YOU BASTARDS!
FROM NOW ON, IT'S A KUCHIYAKU WORLD! MY WORLD!!
YOUR BATTLEFIELD'S THE BOTTOM OF A LAKE!

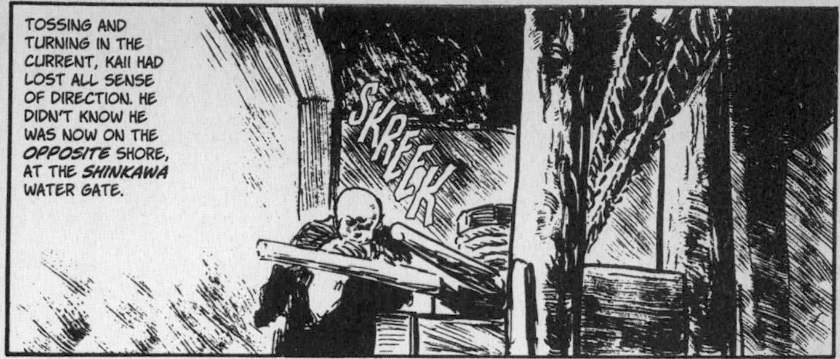
TOSSING AND TURNING IN THE CURRENT, KAII HAD LOST ALL SENSE OF DIRECTION. HE DIDN'T KNOW HE WAS NOW ON THE *OPPOSITE* SHORE, AT THE *SHINKAWA* WATER GATE.
SKREEK

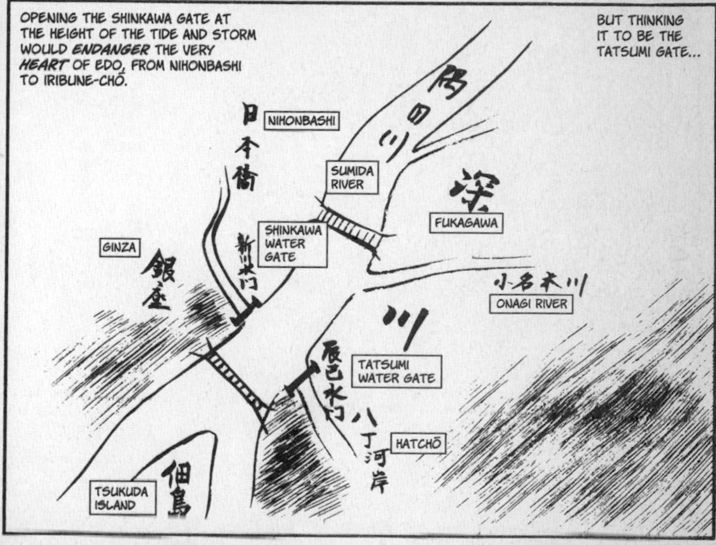
OPENING THE SHINKAWA GATE AT THE HEIGHT OF THE TIDE AND STORM WOULD *ENDANGER* THE VERY *HEART* OF EDO, FROM NIHONBASHI TO IRIBUNE-CHŌ.
BUT THINKING IT TO BE THE TATSUMI GATE...
日本橋
NIHONBASHI
SUMIDA RIVER
FUKAGAWA
SHINKAWA WATER GATE
GINZA
銀座
小名木川
ONAGI RIVER
TATSUMI WATER GATE
HATCHŌ
八丁河岸
佃島
TSUKUDA ISLAND

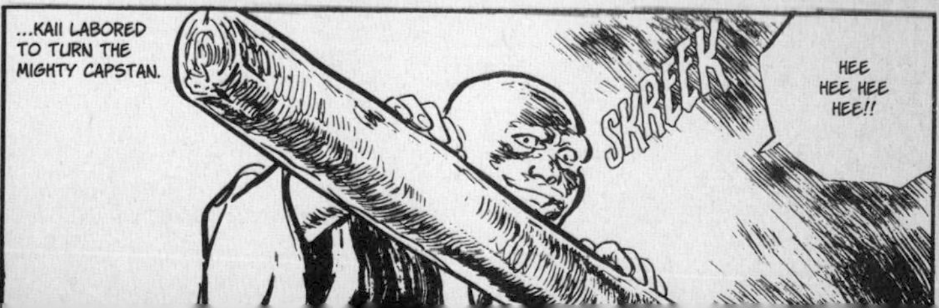
...KAII LABORED TO TURN THE MIGHTY CAPSTAN.
SKREEK
HEE HEE HEE HEE!!

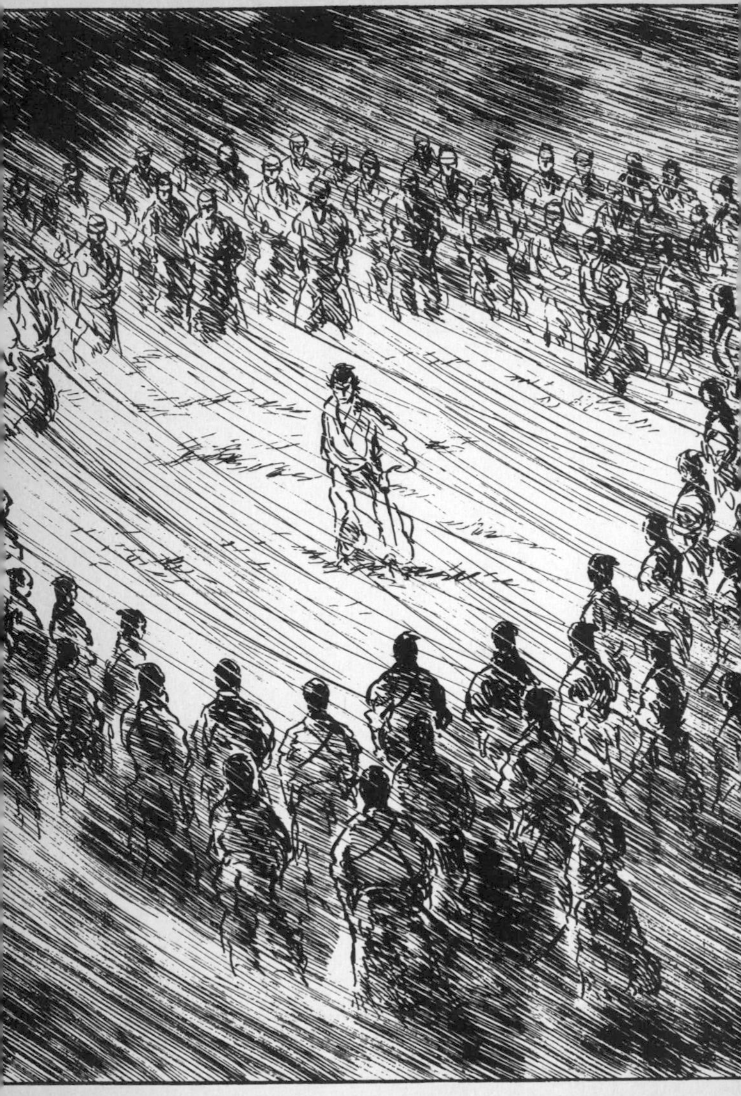

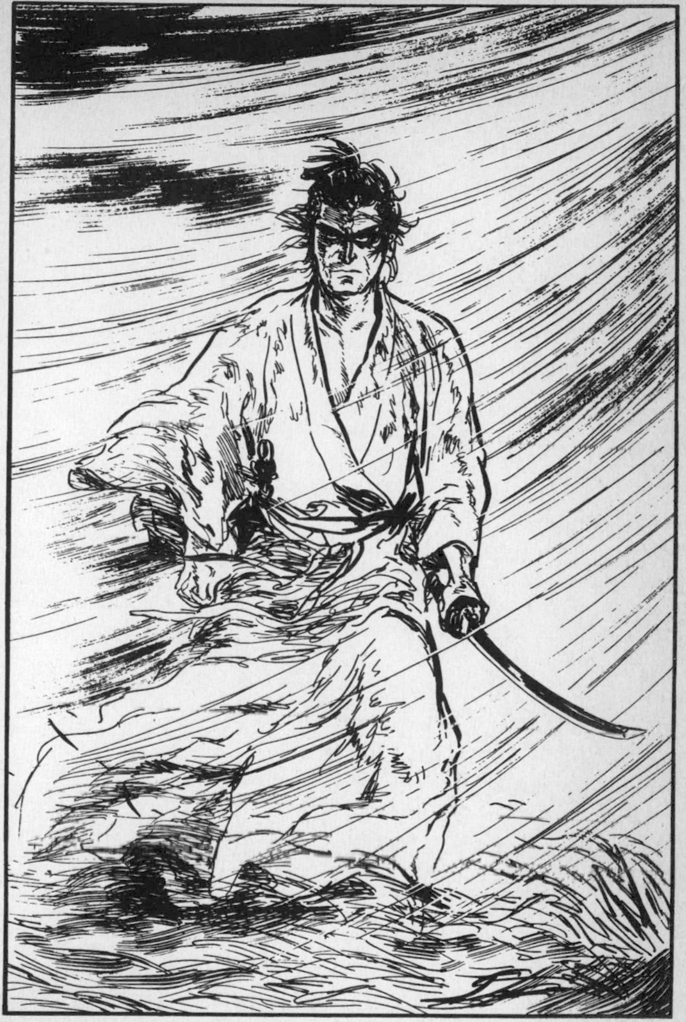

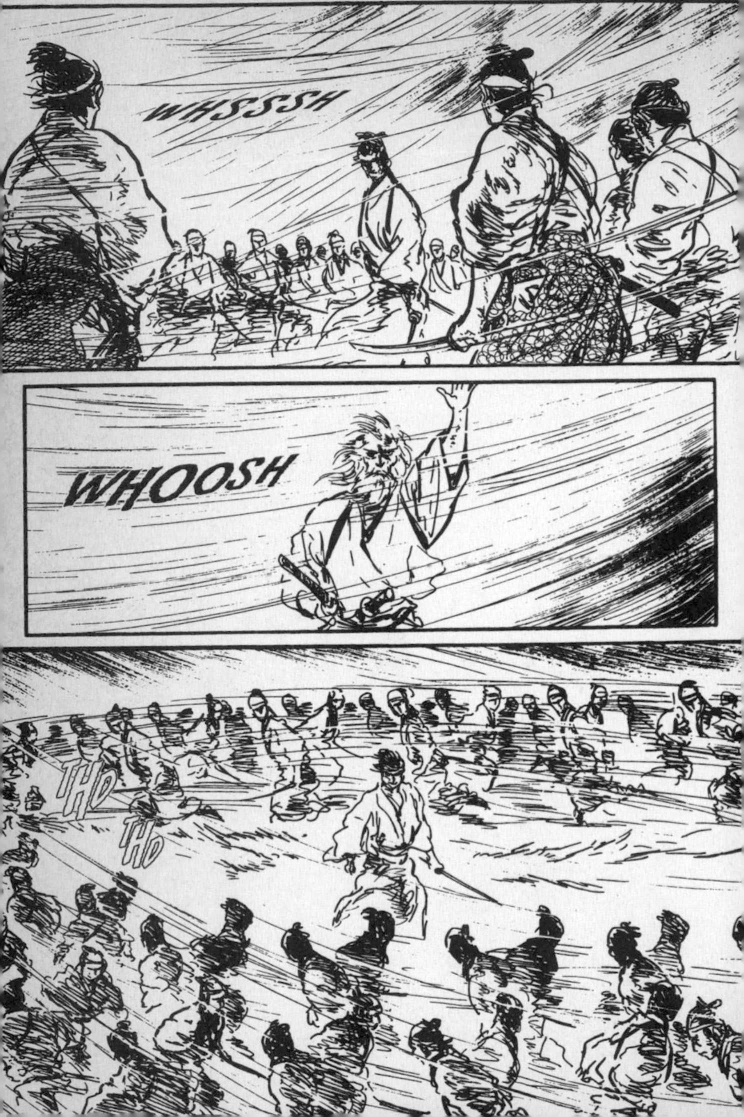
WHSSSH
WHOOSH
THD
THD

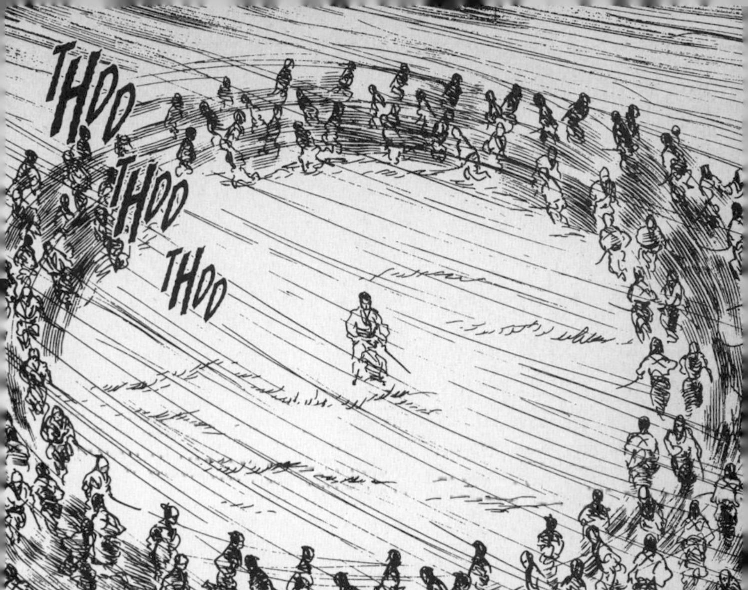
THOO
THOO
THOO
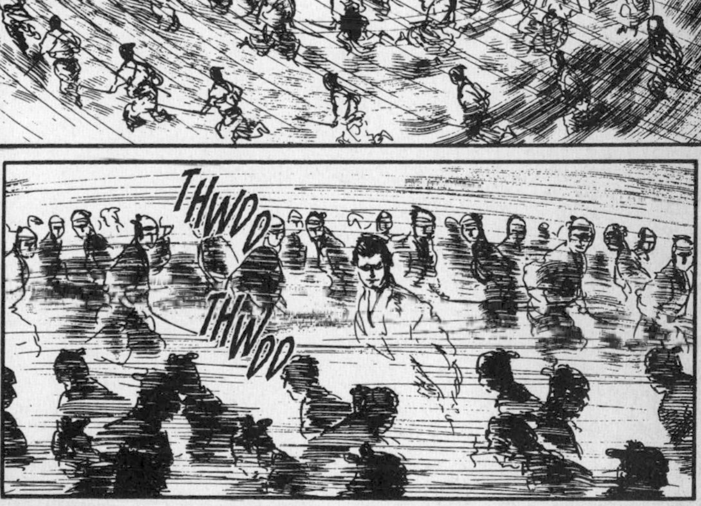
THWOO
THWOO

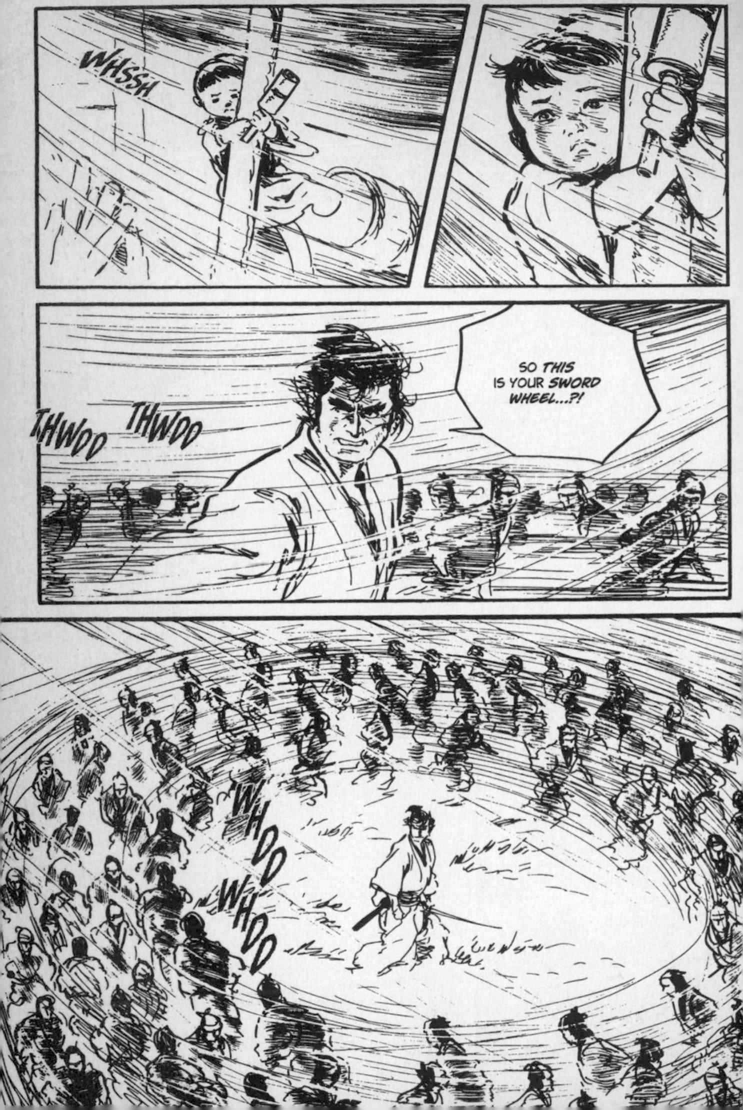
WHSSH
SO THIS IS YOUR SWORD WHEEL...?!
THWOO
THWOO
WHOO
WHOO

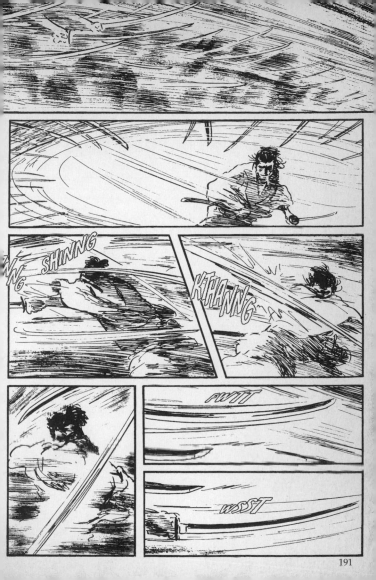

SHINNG

NG

KTHANNG

FWTT

WSST

191

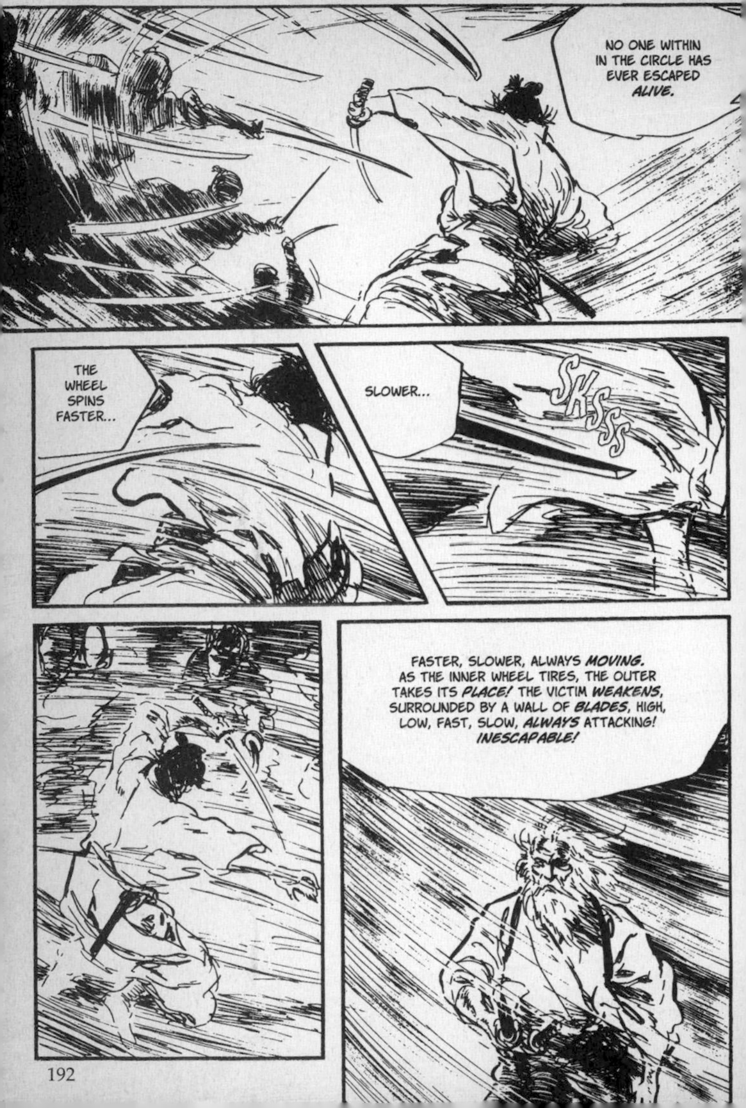
NO ONE WITHIN IN THE CIRCLE HAS EVER ESCAPED *ALIVE.*
THE WHEEL SPINS FASTER...
SLOWER...
SKSSS
FASTER, SLOWER, ALWAYS *MOVING.* AS THE INNER WHEEL TIRES, THE OUTER TAKES ITS *PLACE!* THE VICTIM *WEAKENS,* SURROUNDED BY A WALL OF *BLADES,* HIGH, LOW, FAST, SLOW, *ALWAYS* ATTACKING! *INESCAPABLE!*

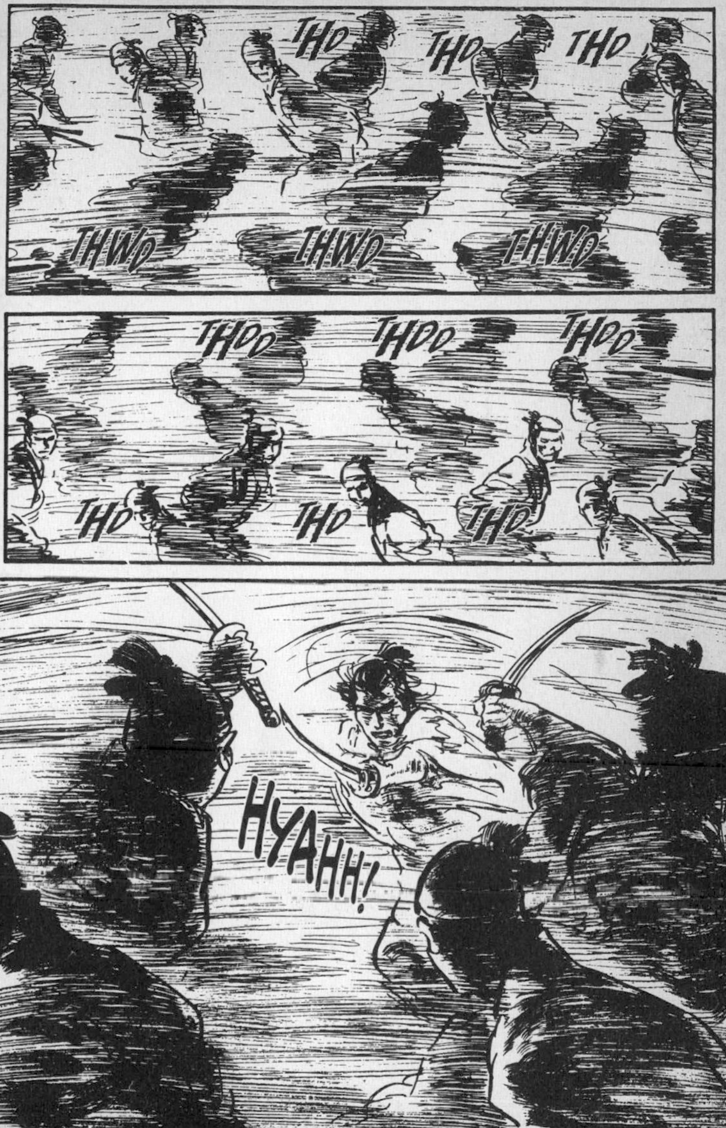
THO
THO
THO
THWD
THWD
THWD
THOO
THOO
THOO
THO
THO
THO
HYAHH!

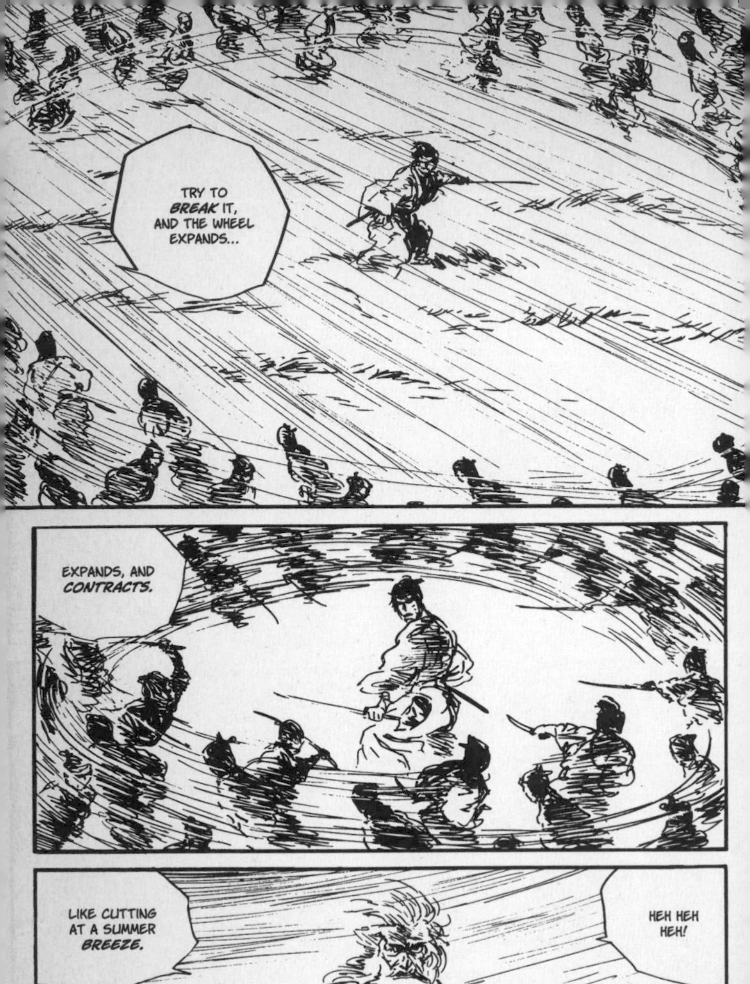
TRY TO *BREAK* IT, AND THE WHEEL EXPANDS...
EXPANDS, AND *CONTRACTS.*
LIKE CUTTING AT A SUMMER *BREEZE.*
HEH HEH HEH!

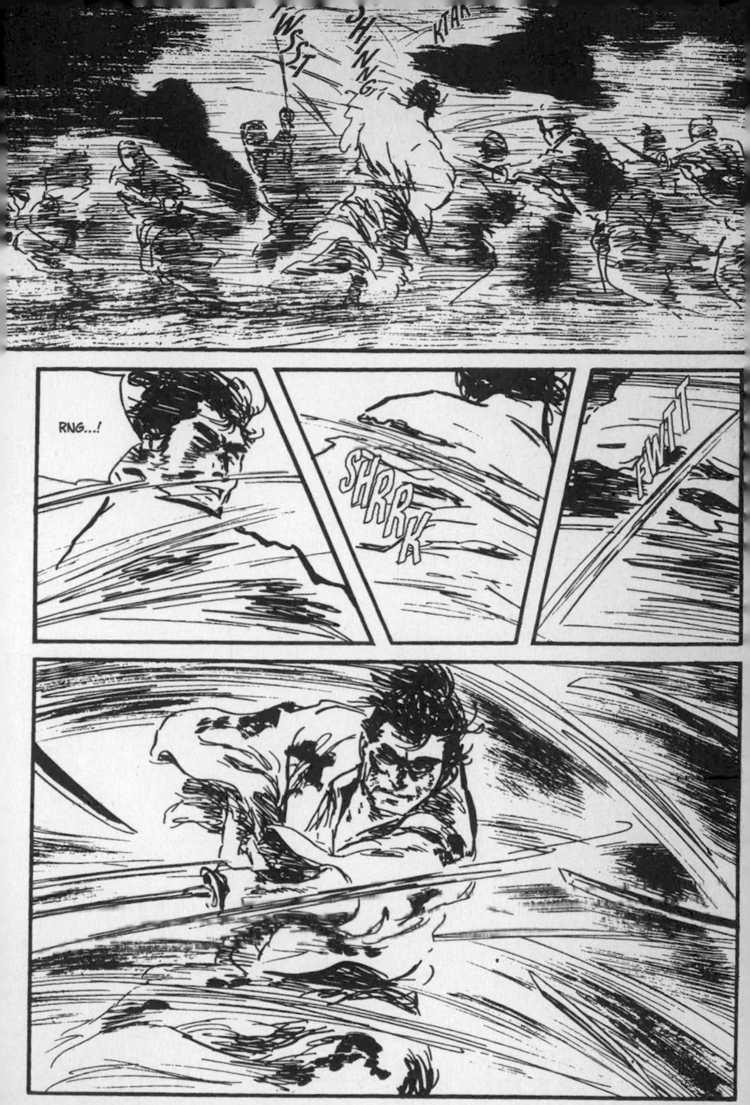
SHINNG
TWSST
FWTT
SHRRK
RNG...!

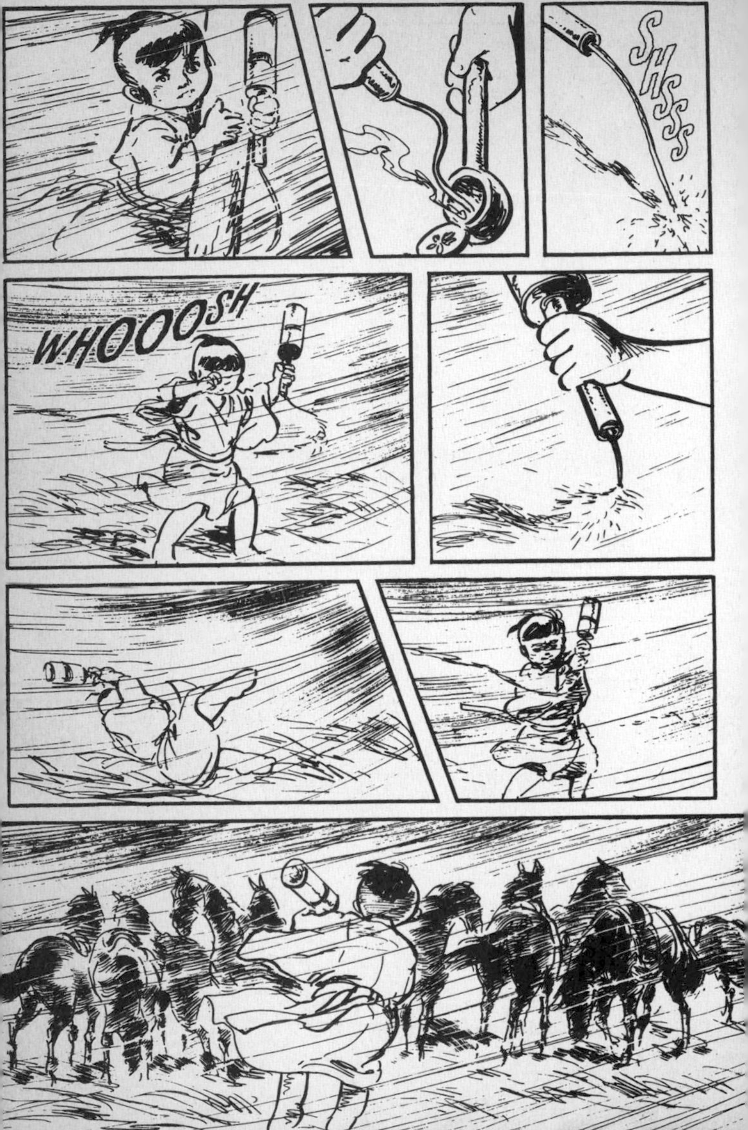
SHSSS
WHOOOSH

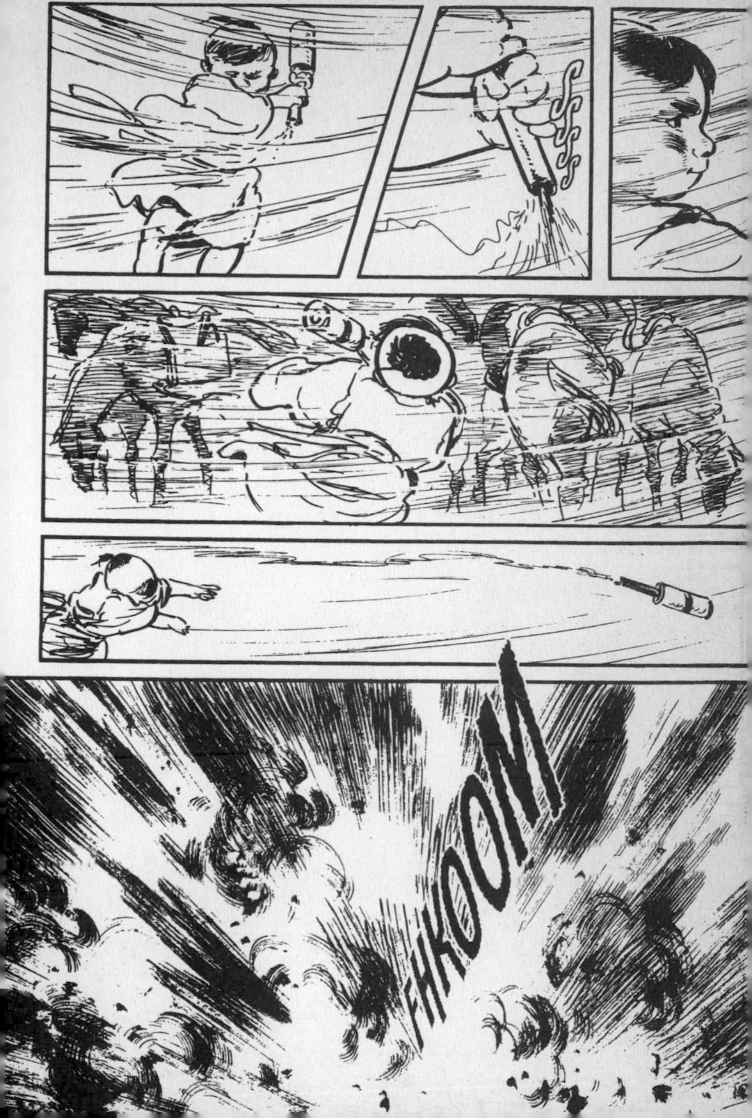
FHKOOM

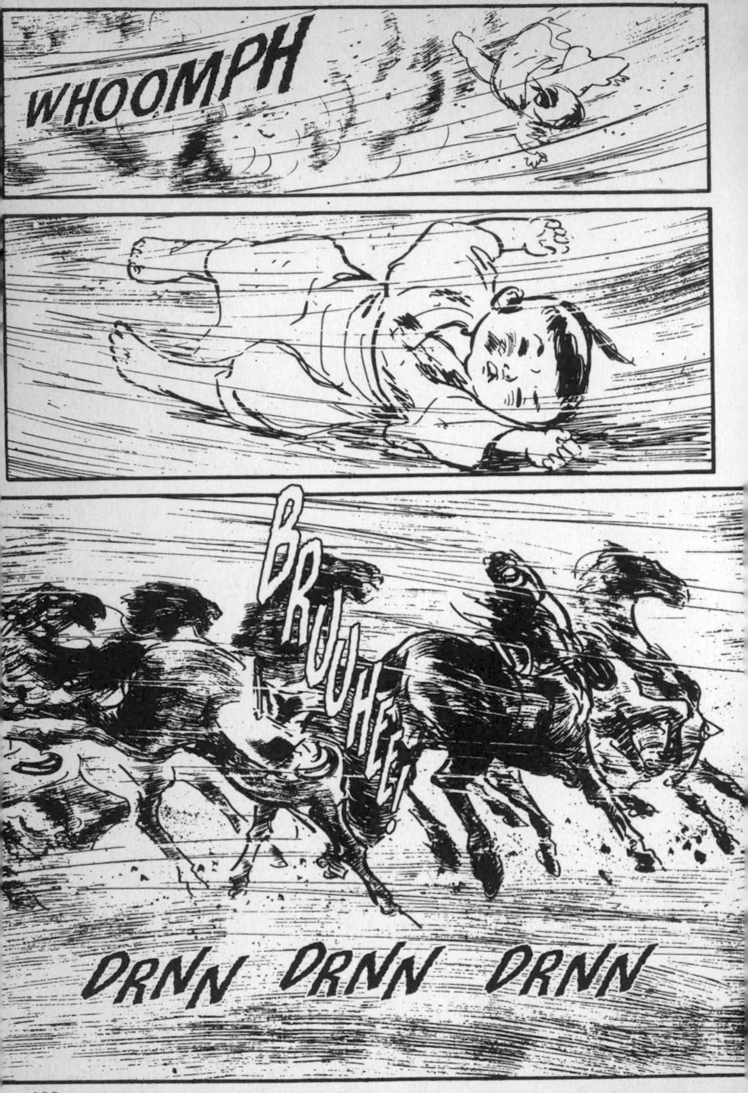
WHOOMPH
BRUHEE!
DRNN DRNN DRNN

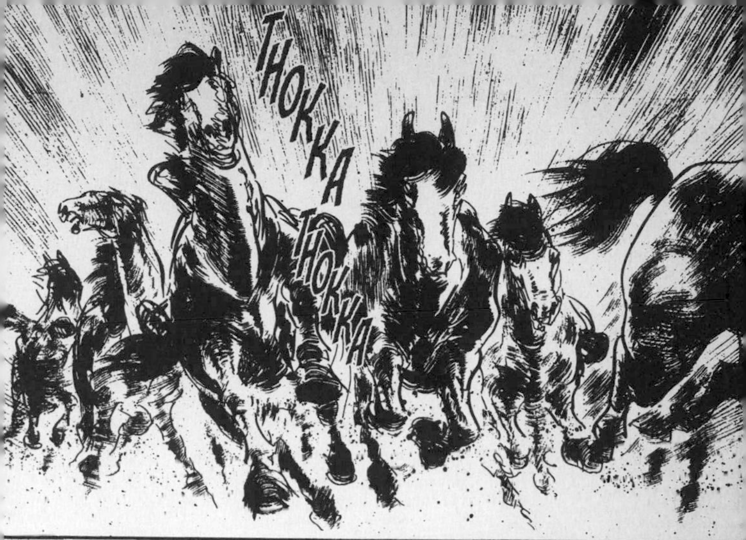
THOKKA
THOKKA
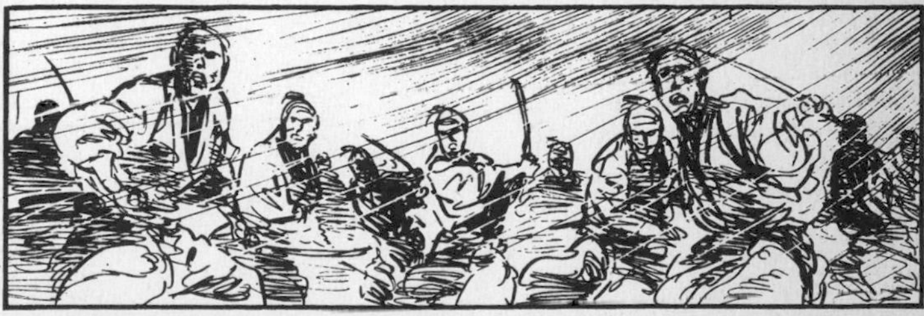
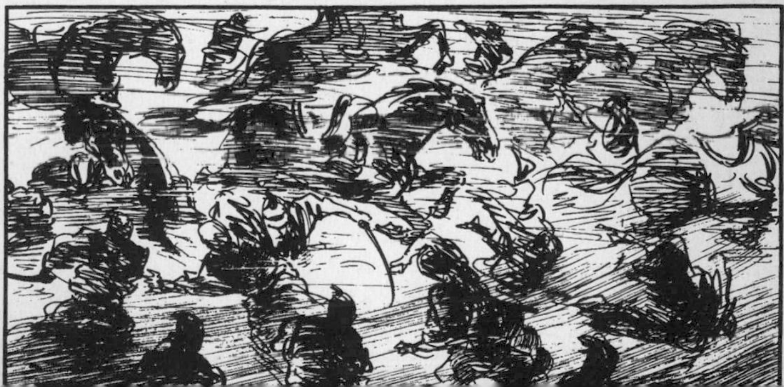

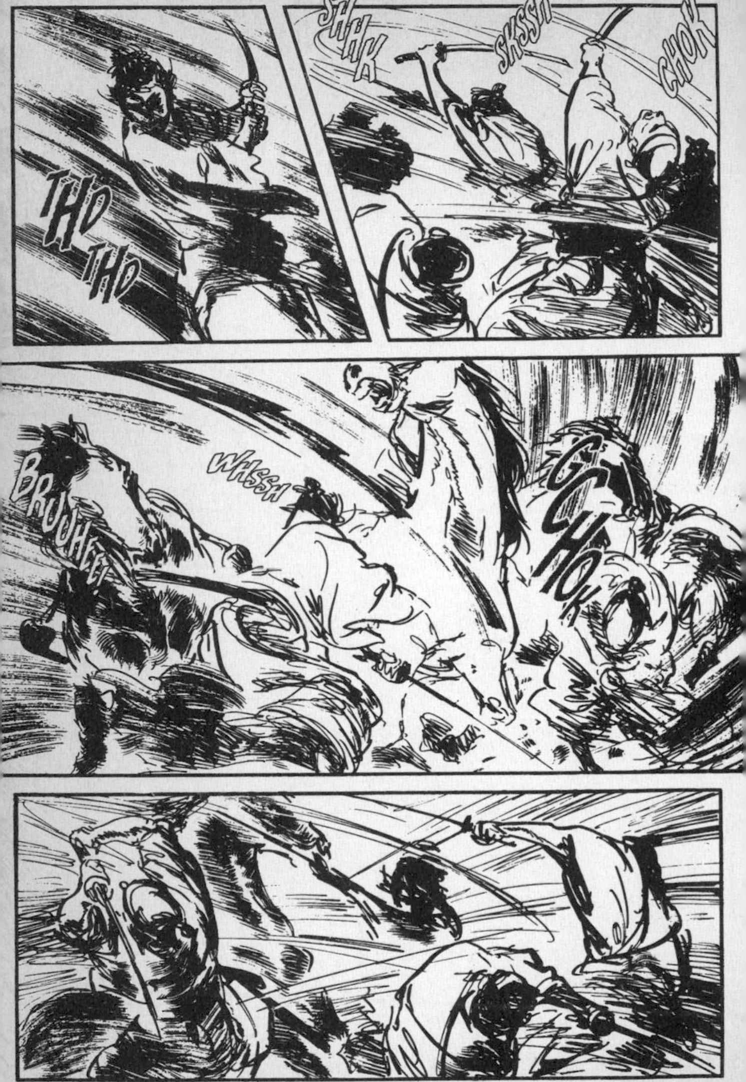
CHOK
SKSSH
SHHK
THO
THO
GCHOK
WHSSH
BRUUHEEI

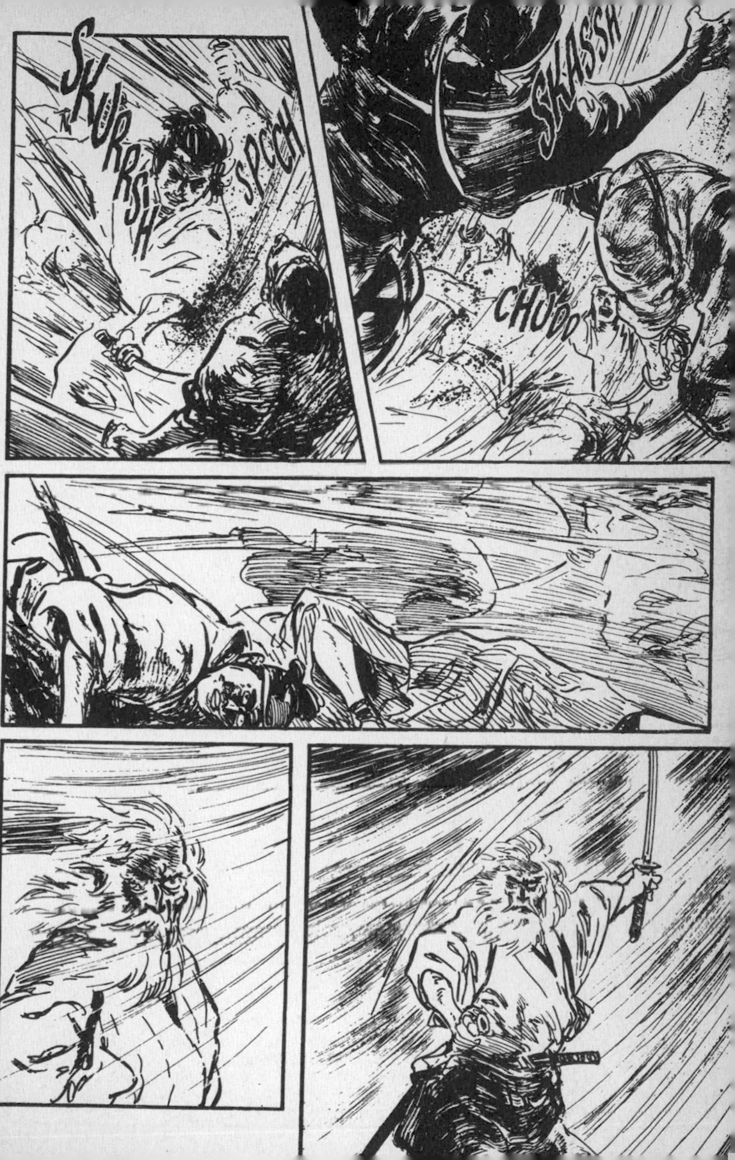
SKASSH
CHUDD
SKURRSH
SPCCH

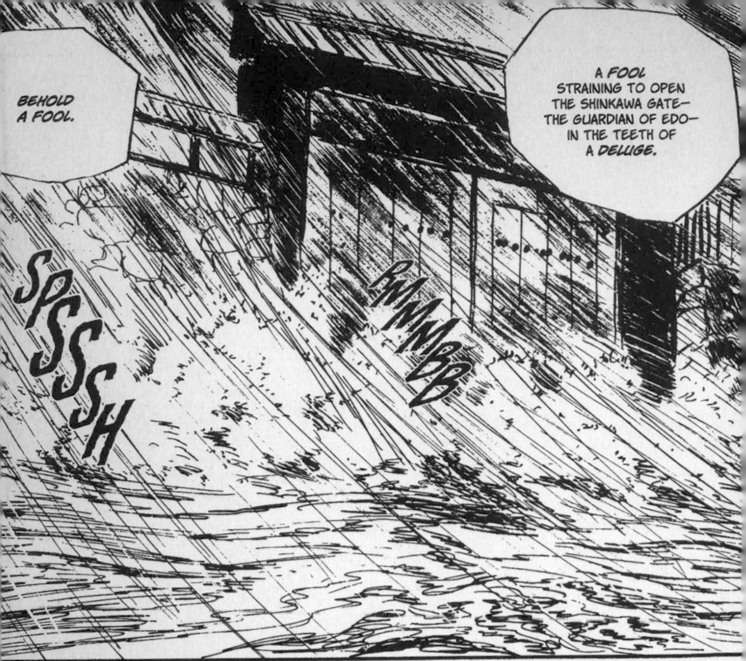
BEHOLD A FOOL.
A FOOL STRAINING TO OPEN THE SHINKAWA GATE—THE GUARDIAN OF EDO—IN THE TEETH OF A DELUGE.
SPSSSH
RMMMBB

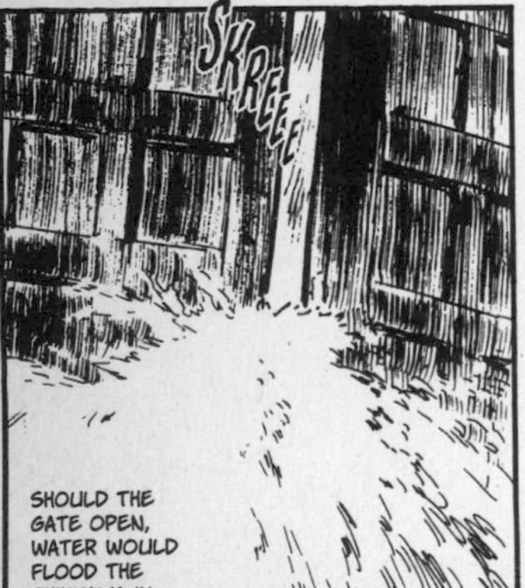
SKREEE
SHOULD THE GATE OPEN, WATER WOULD FLOOD THE SHINKAWA IN THE HEART OF EDO.

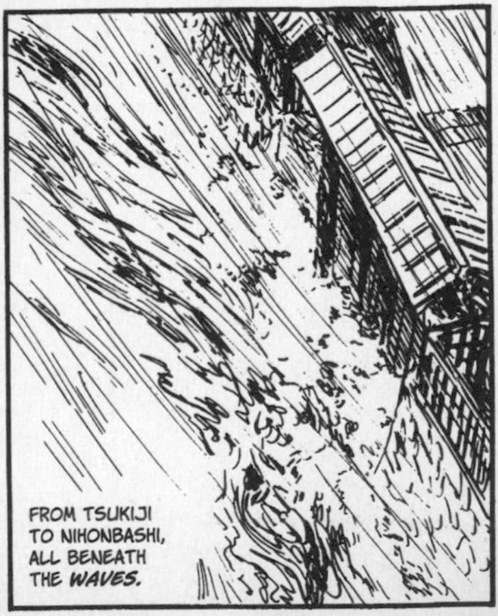
FROM TSUKIJI TO NIHONBASHI, ALL BENEATH THE WAVES.

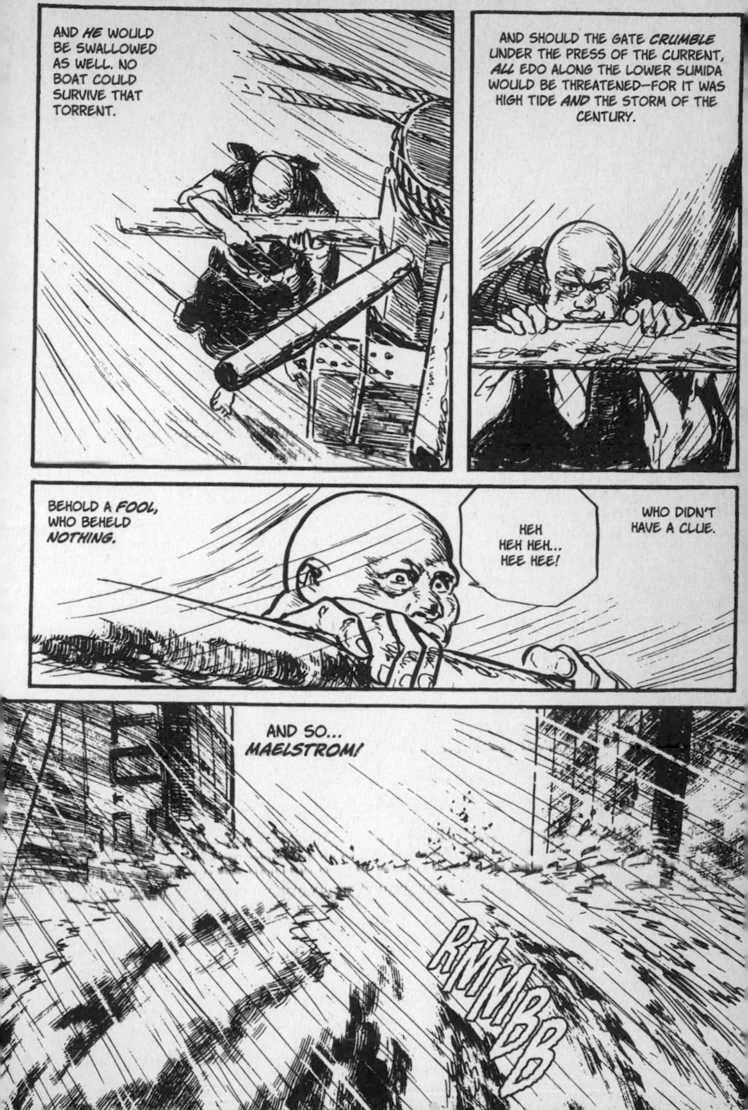
AND *HE* WOULD BE SWALLOWED AS WELL. NO BOAT COULD SURVIVE THAT TORRENT.
AND SHOULD THE GATE *CRUMBLE* UNDER THE PRESS OF THE CURRENT, *ALL* EDO ALONG THE LOWER SUMIDA WOULD BE THREATENED—FOR IT WAS HIGH TIDE *AND* THE STORM OF THE CENTURY.
BEHOLD A *FOOL,* WHO BEHELD *NOTHING.*
HEH HEH HEH.. HEE HEE!
WHO DIDN'T HAVE A CLUE.
AND SO... *MAELSTROM!*
RMMBB

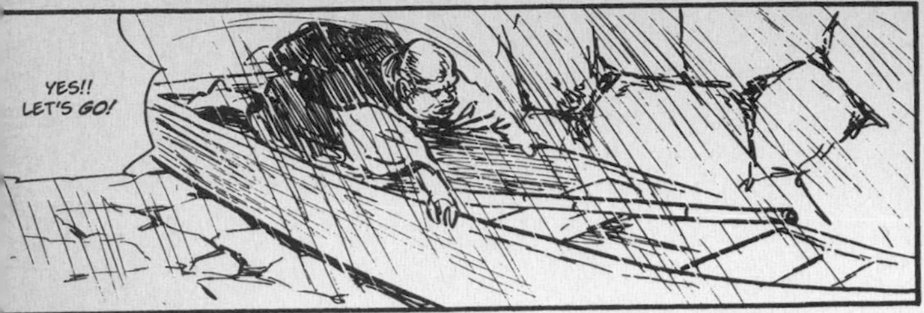
YES!!
LET'S GO!

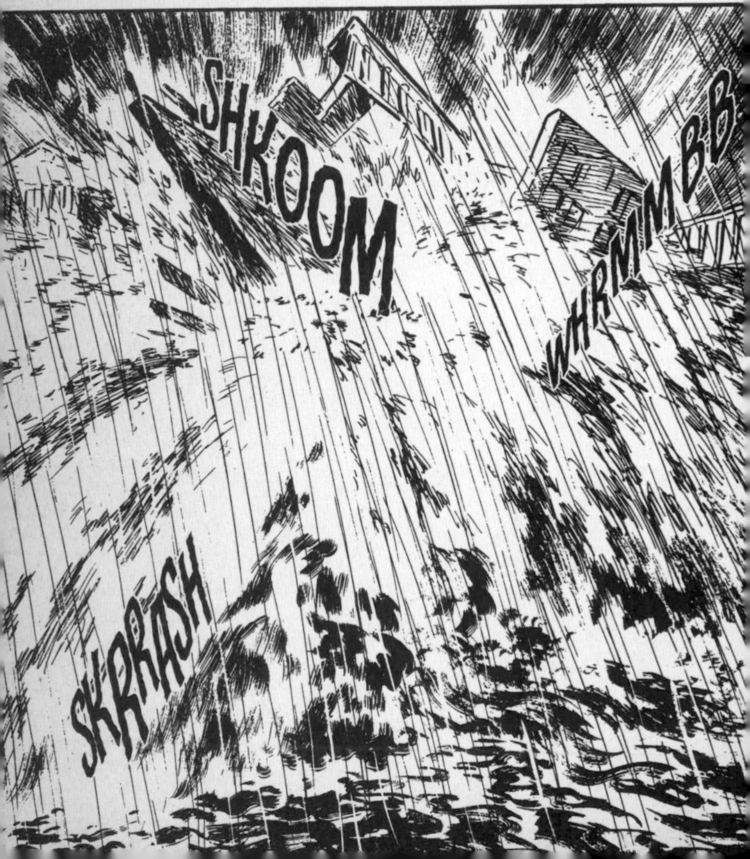
WHRMMBB
SHKOOM
SKRASH

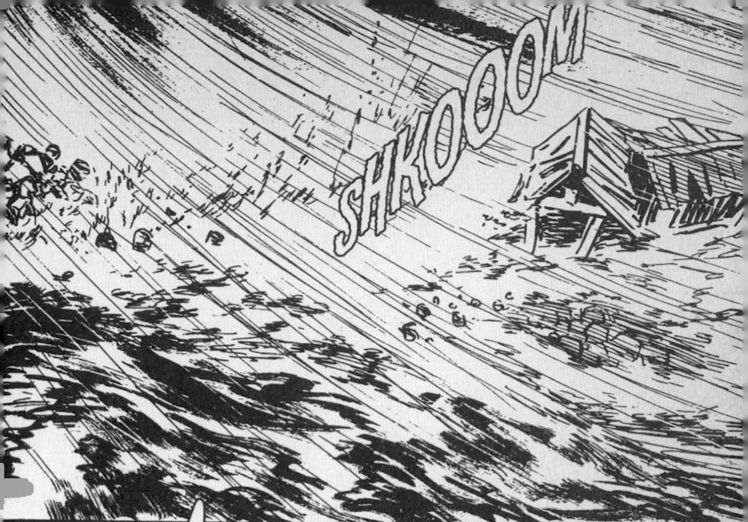
SHKOOOM
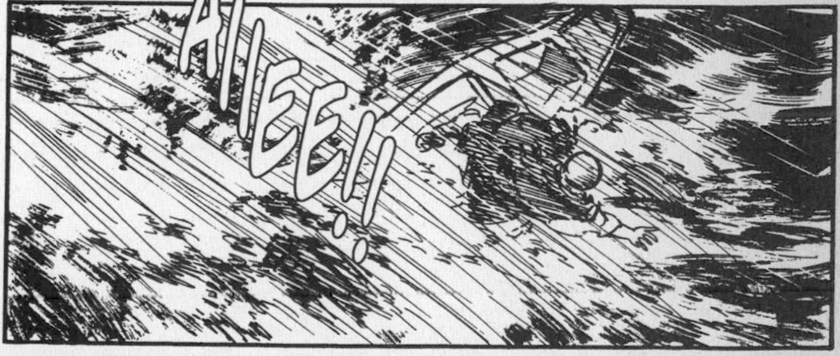
AIIEE!!
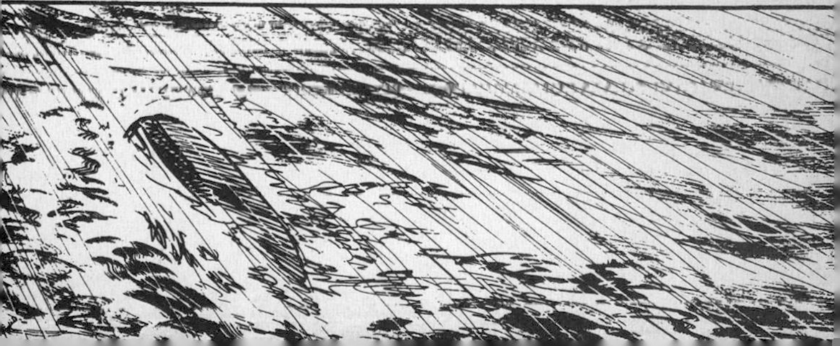

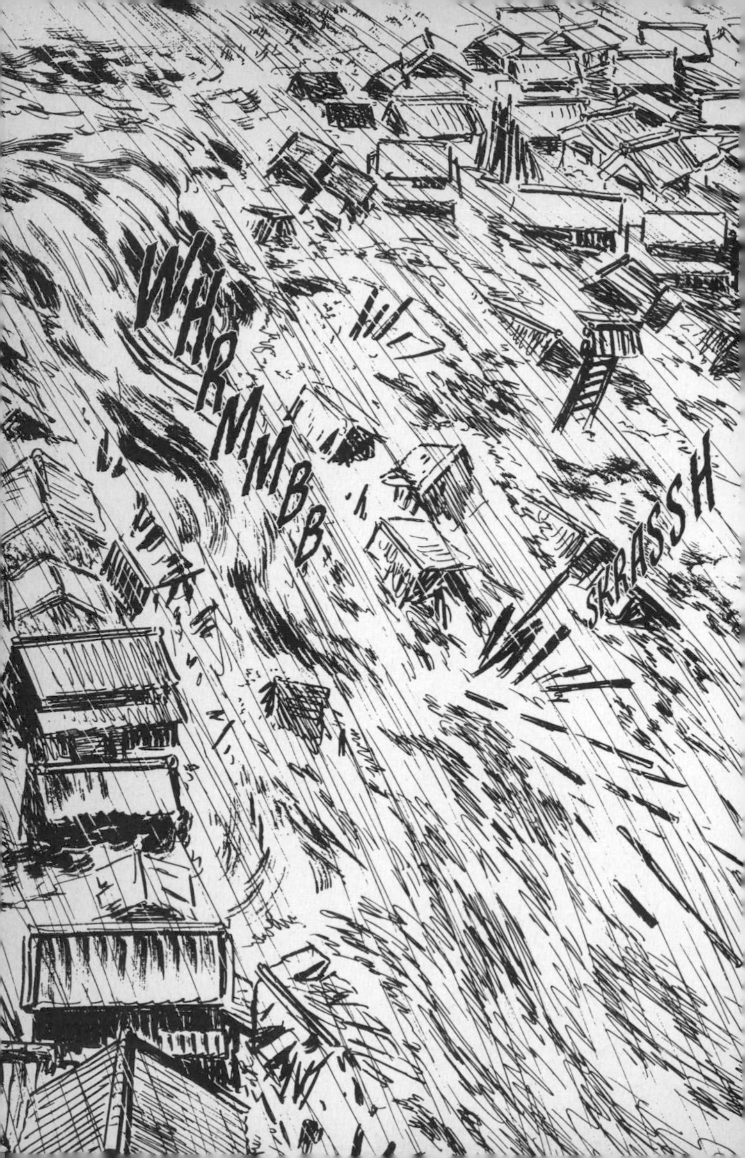
WHRMMBB
SKRASSH

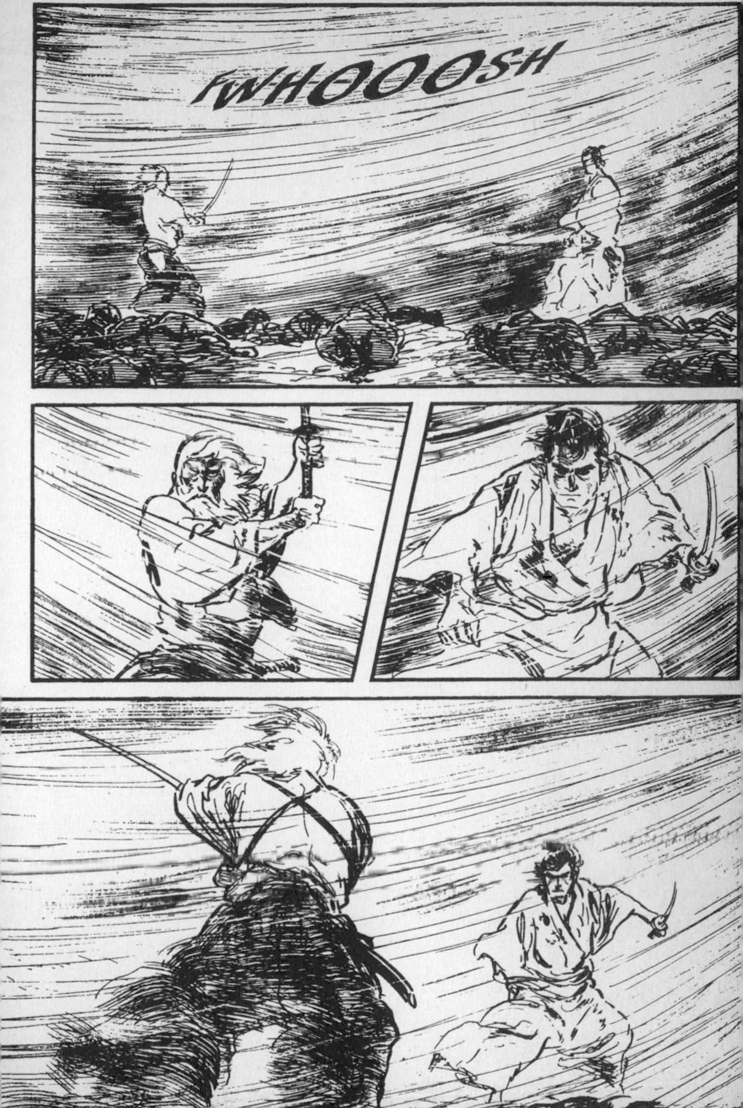
FWHOOOOSH

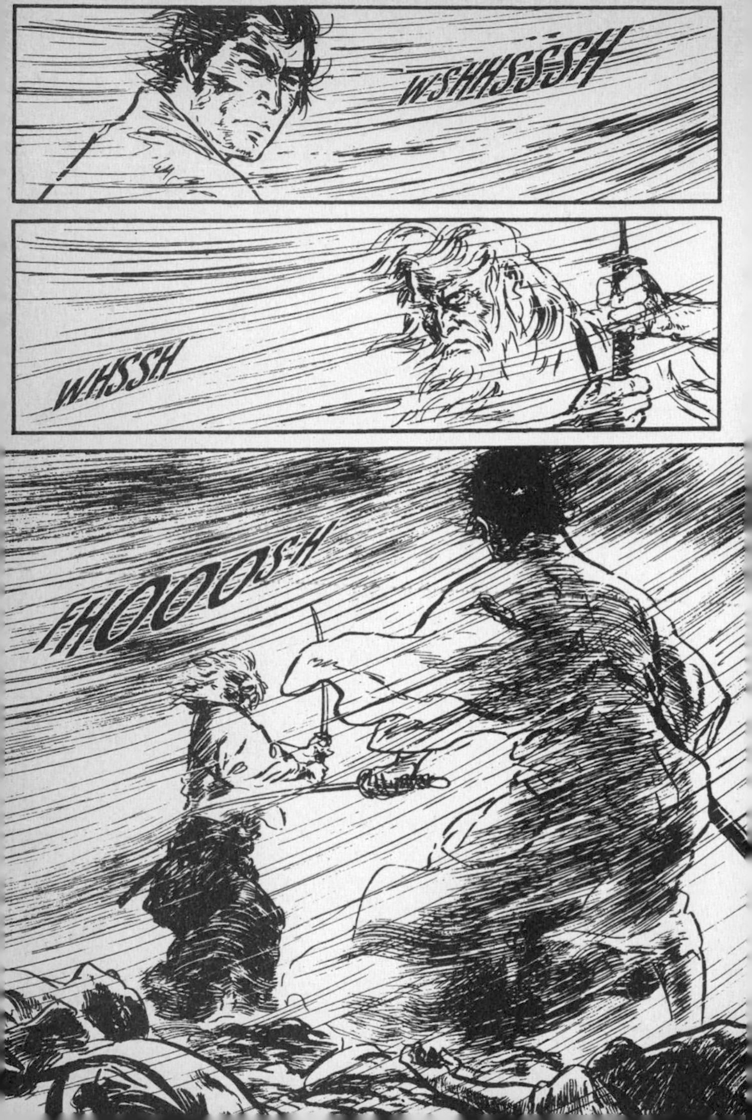
WSHHSSSH
WHSSH
FHOOOSH

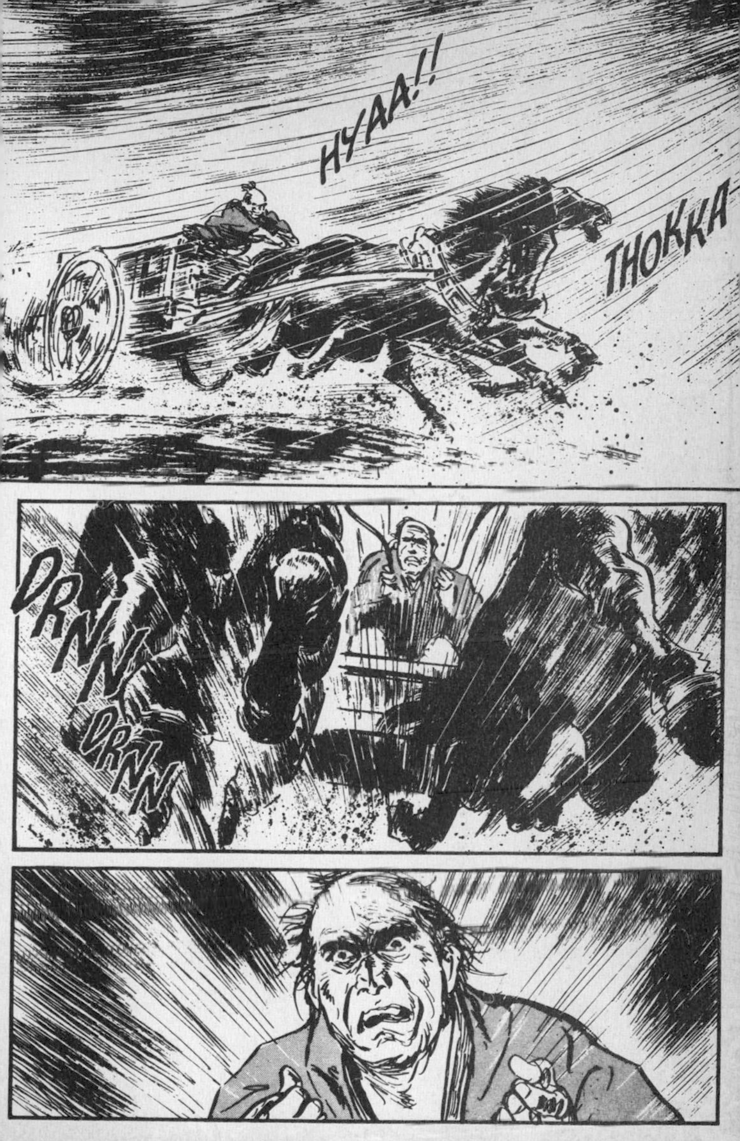
HYAA!!
THOKKA
DRNN
DRNN

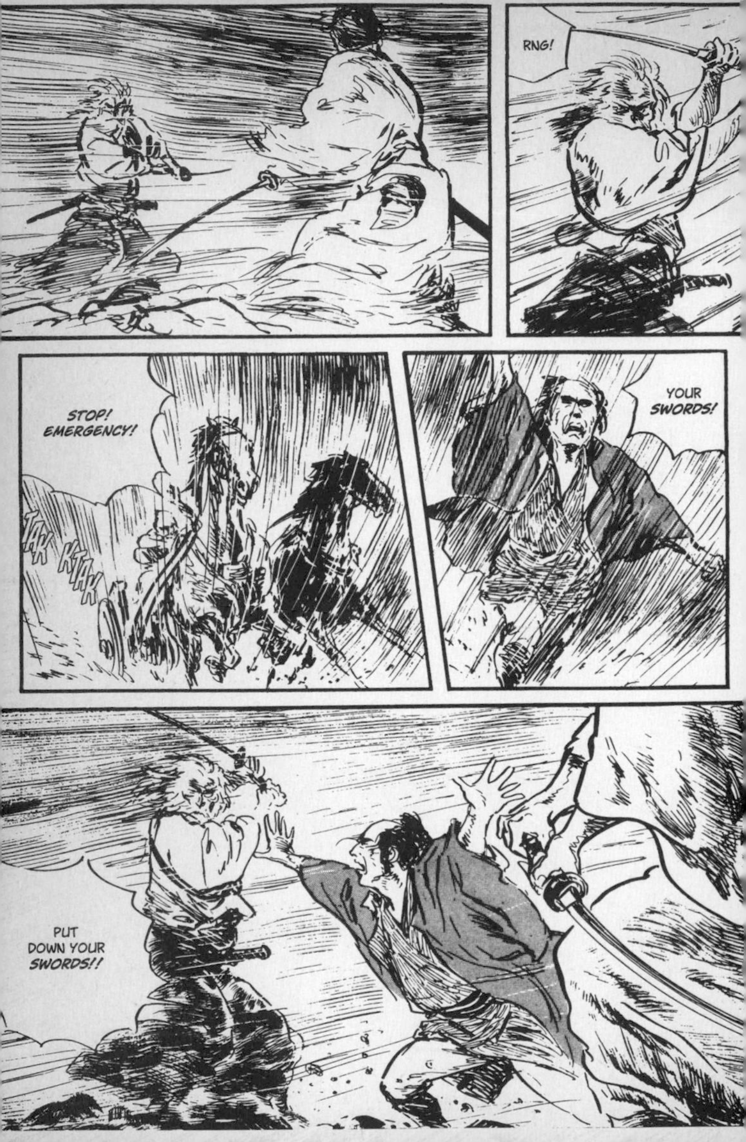
RNG!
YOUR SWORDS!
STOP! EMERGENCY!
TAK KTAK
PUT DOWN YOUR SWORDS!!

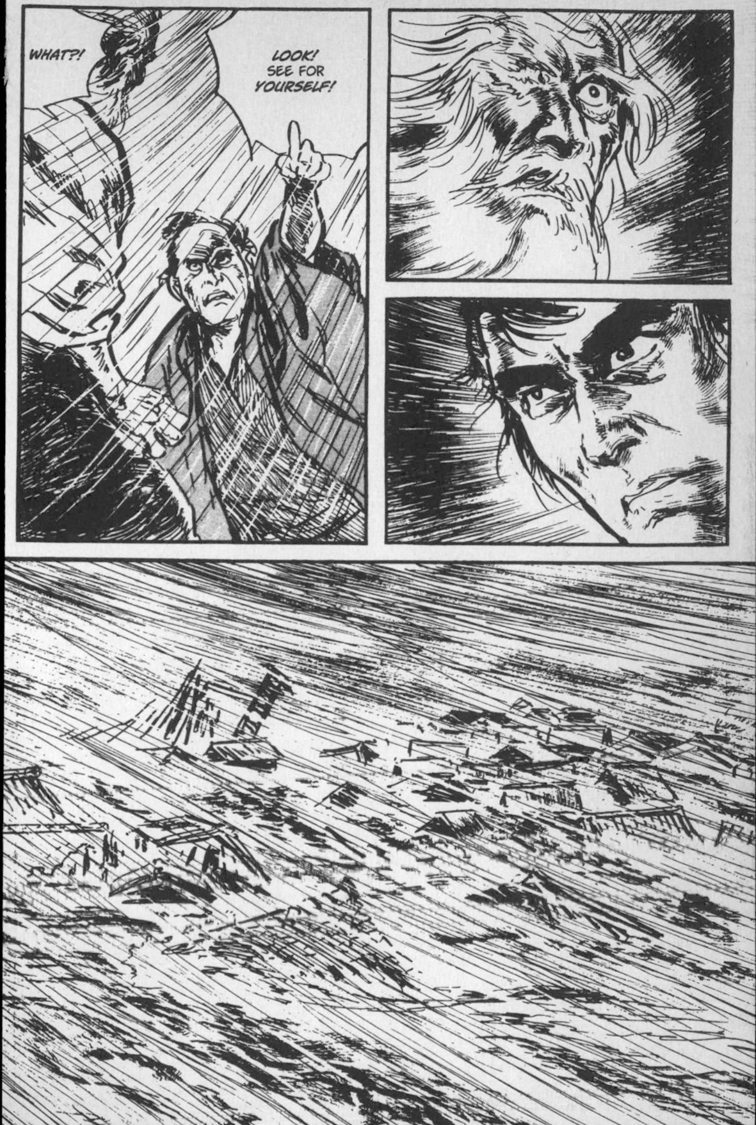
LOOK! SEE FOR YOURSELF!
WHAT?!

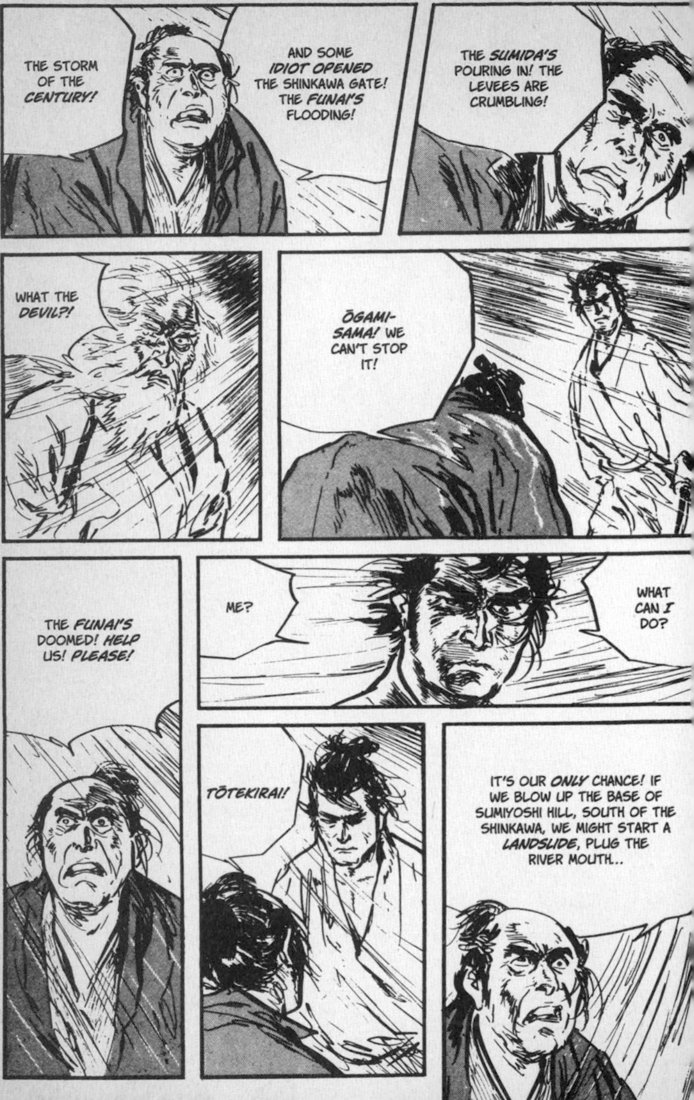
THE STORM OF THE CENTURY!
AND SOME IDIOT OPENED THE SHINKAWA GATE! THE FUNAI'S FLOODING!
THE SUMIDA'S POURING IN! THE LEVEES ARE CRUMBLING!
WHAT THE DEVIL?!
ŌGAMI-SAMA! WE CAN'T STOP IT!
THE FUNAI'S DOOMED! HELP US! PLEASE!
ME?
WHAT CAN I DO?
TŌTEKIRAI!
IT'S OUR ONLY CHANCE! IF WE BLOW UP THE BASE OF SUMIYOSHI HILL, SOUTH OF THE SHINKAWA, WE MIGHT START A LANDSLIDE, PLUG THE RIVER MOUTH...

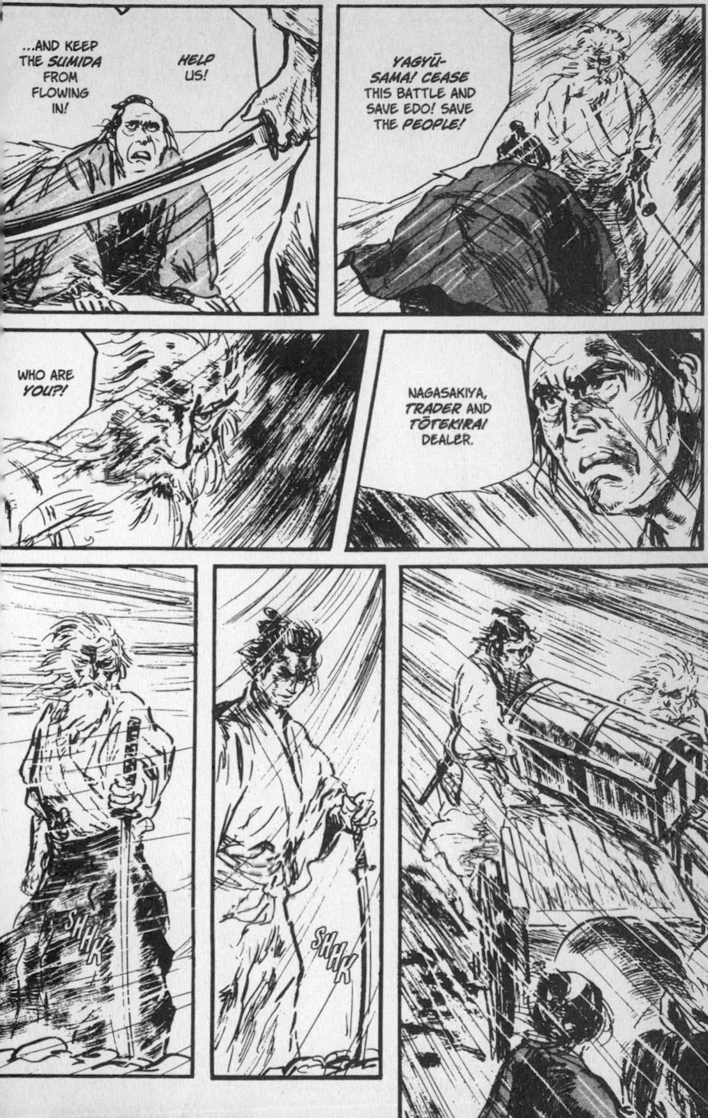
...AND KEEP THE *SUMIDA* FROM FLOWING IN!
HELP US!
YAGYŪ-SAMA! CEASE THIS BATTLE AND SAVE EDO! SAVE THE *PEOPLE!*
WHO ARE *YOU?!*
NAGASAKIYA, *TRADER* AND *TŌTEKIRAI* DEALER.
SHHK
SHHK

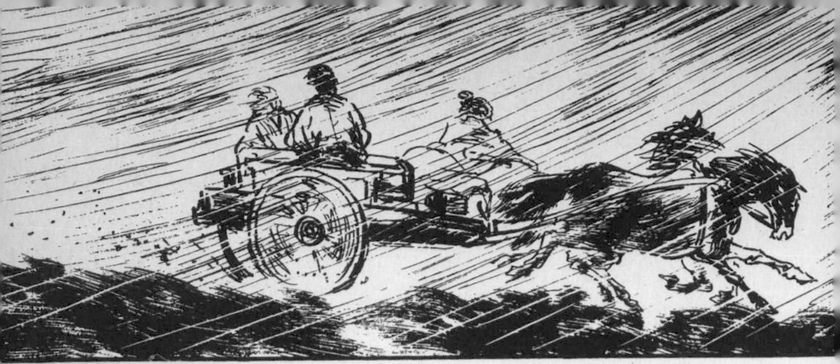

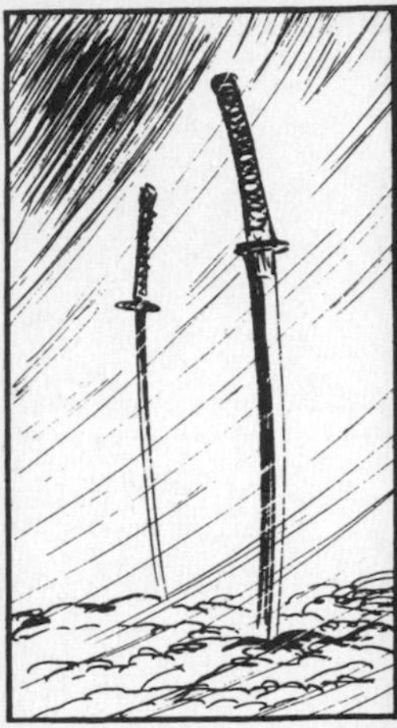

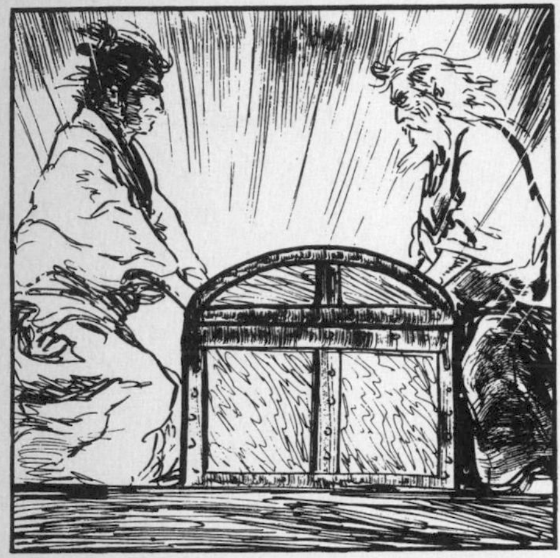

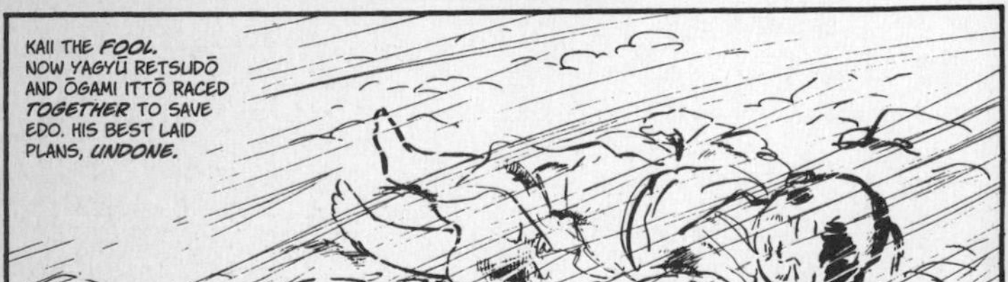
KAII THE *FOOL.* NOW YAGYŪ RETSUDŌ AND ŌGAMI ITTŌ RACED *TOGETHER* TO SAVE EDO. HIS BEST LAID PLANS, *UNDONE.*

the hundred and eleventh

Fire on the River of Blood

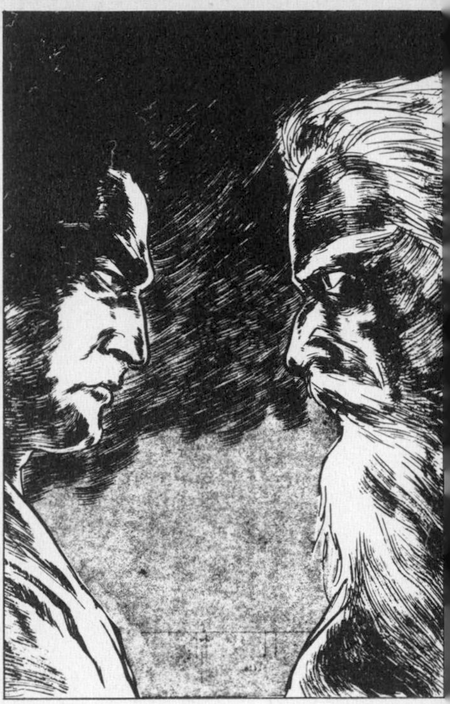

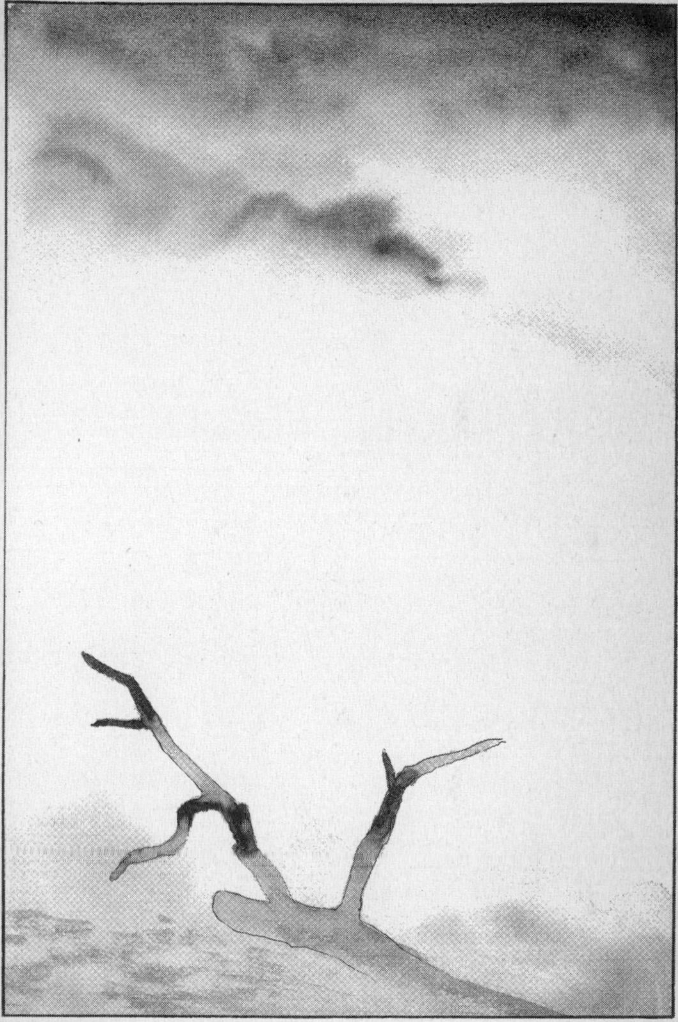

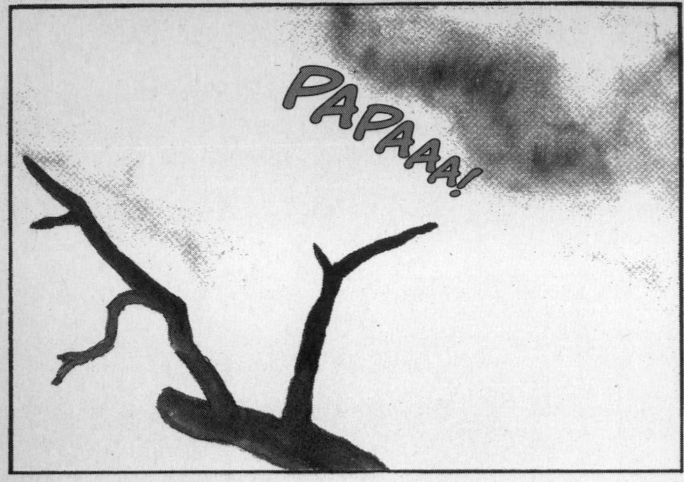
PAPAAA!
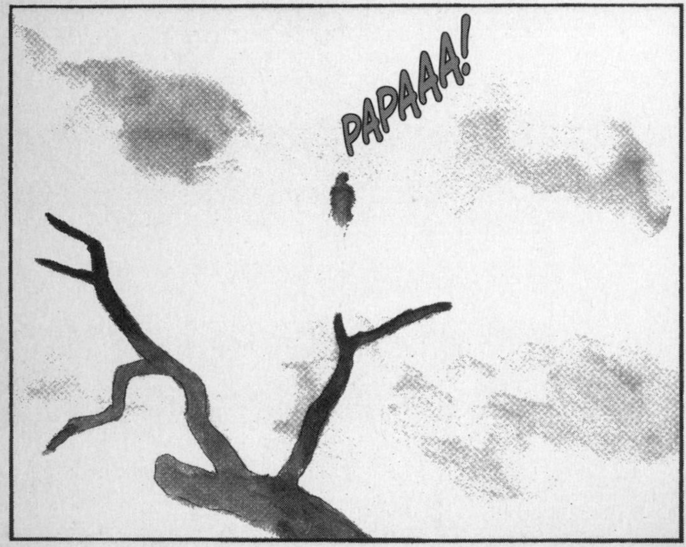
PAPAAA!

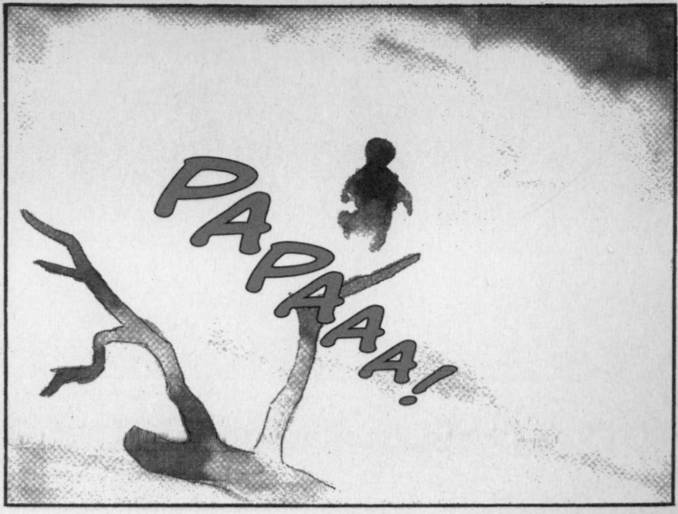
PAPAAA!
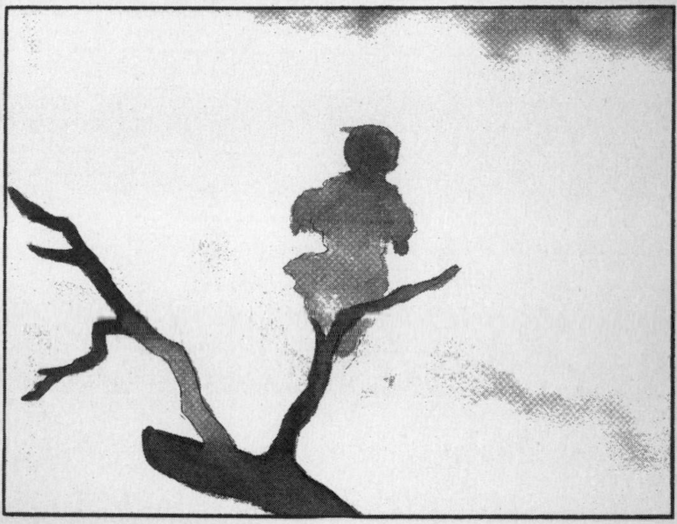

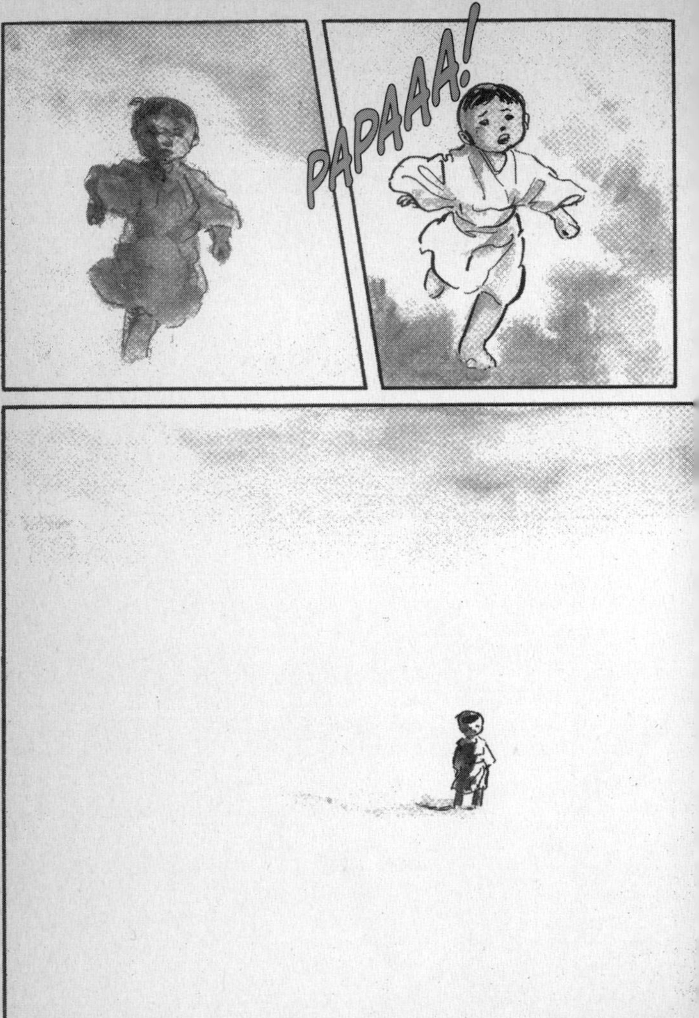
PAPAAA!

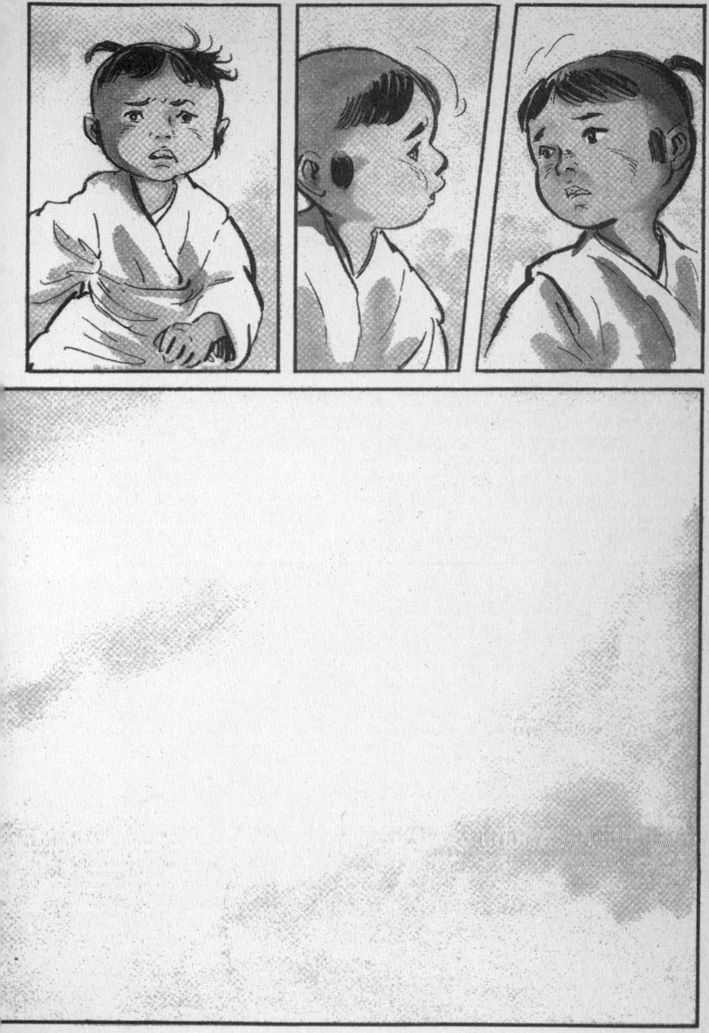

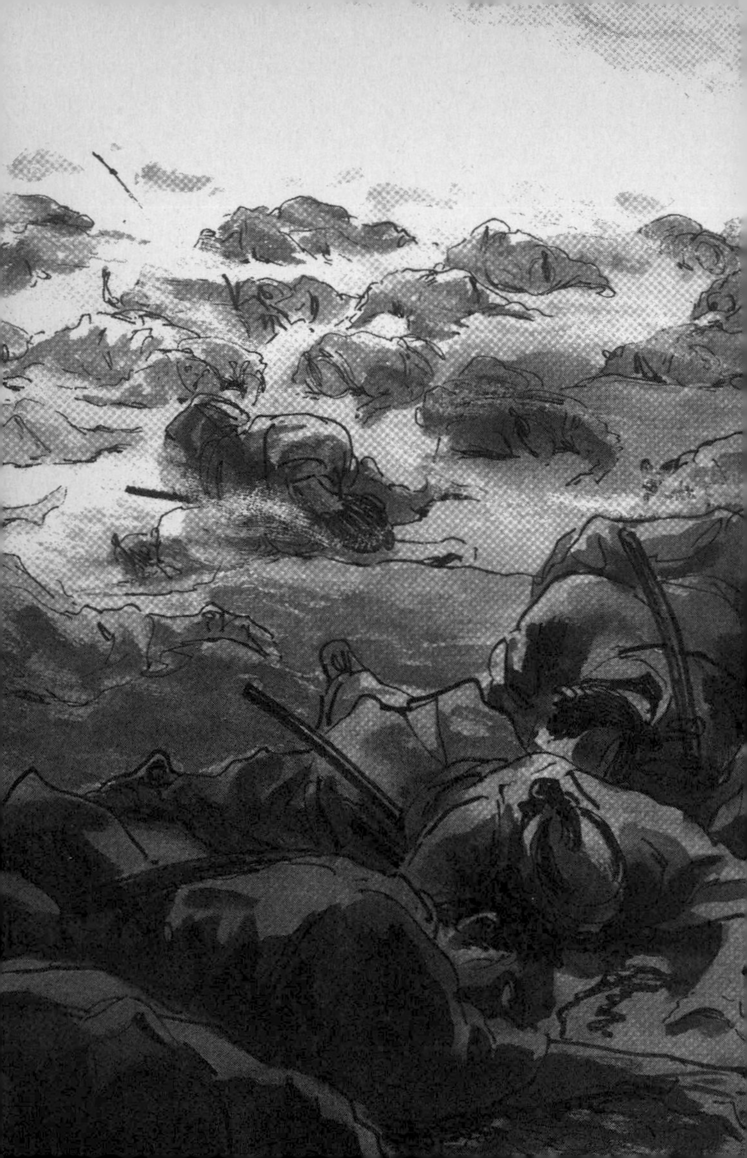

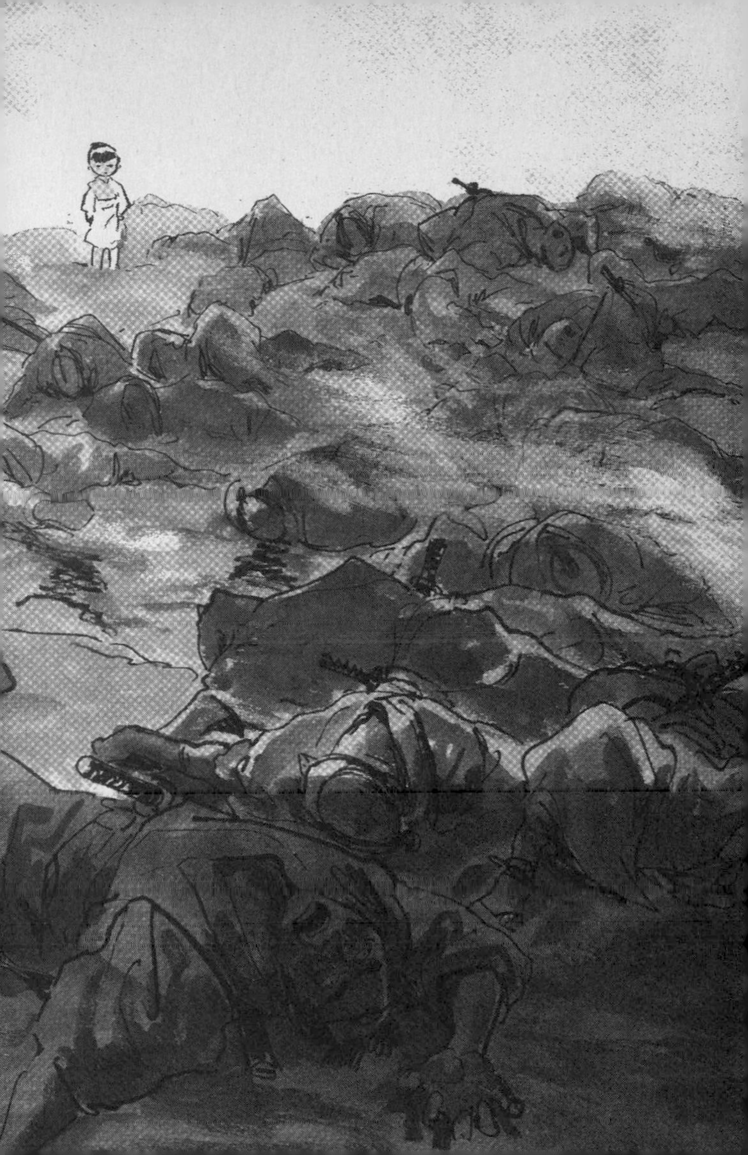

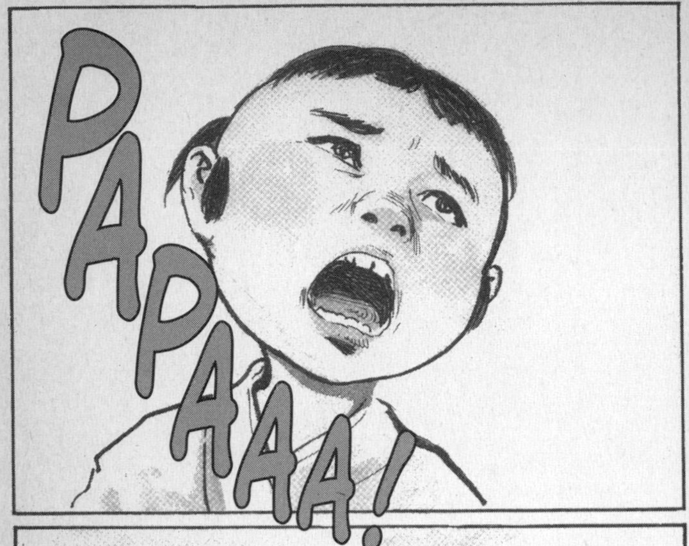
PAPAAA!
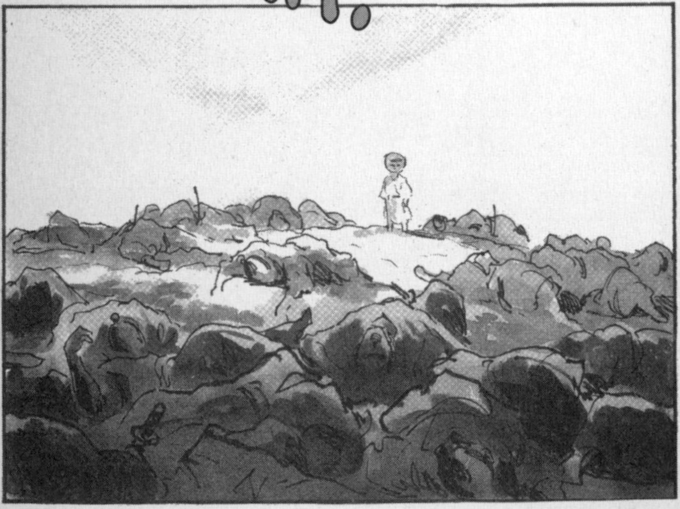

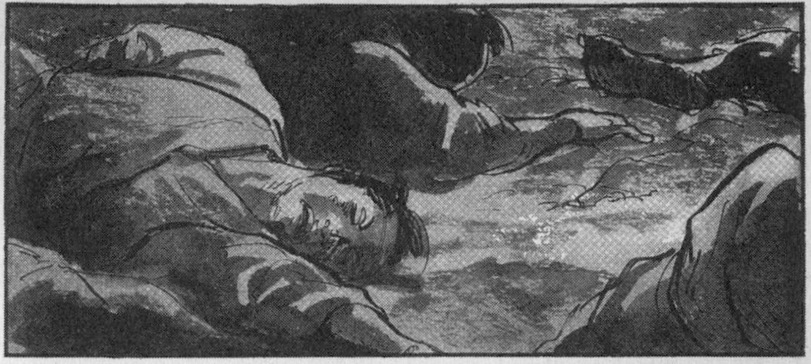
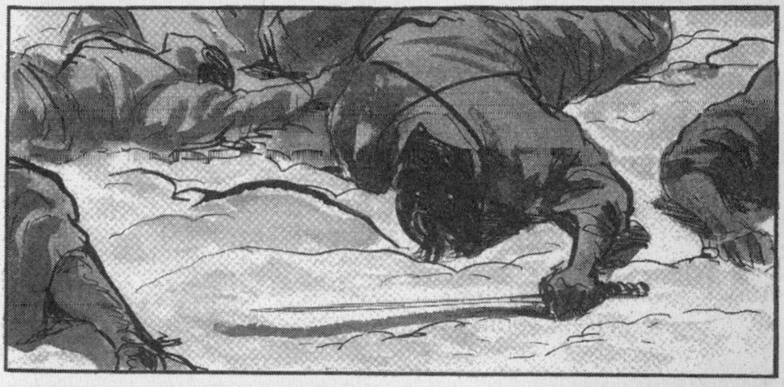
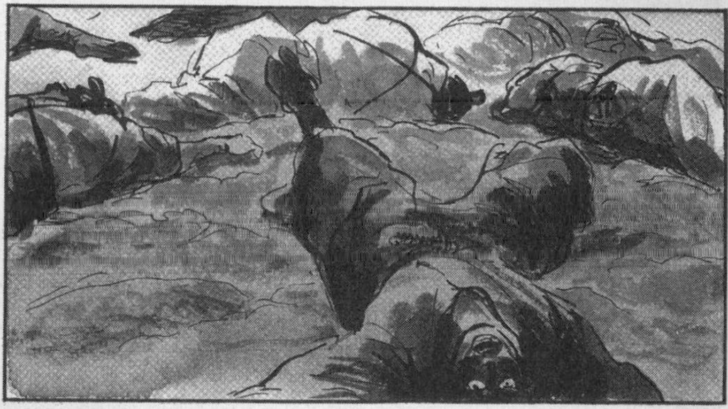

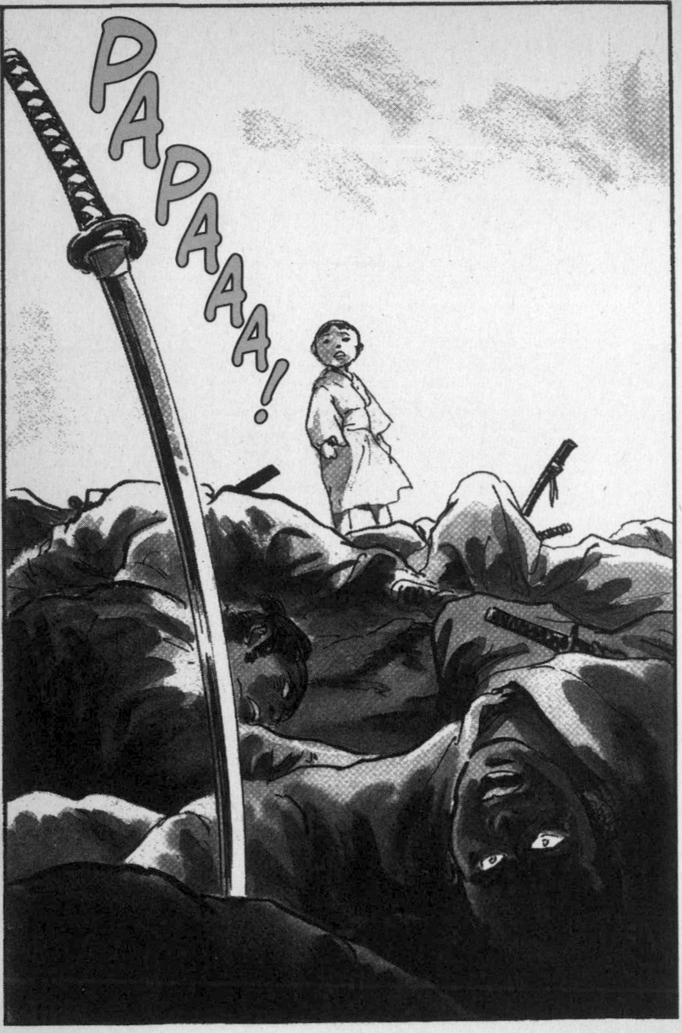
PAPAAAA!

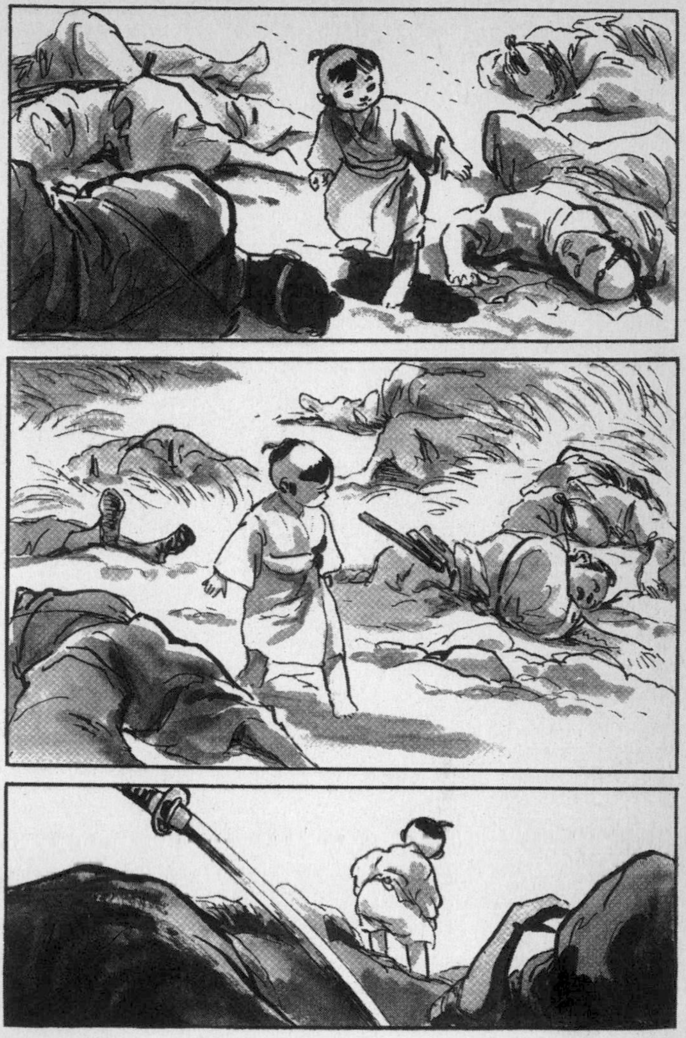

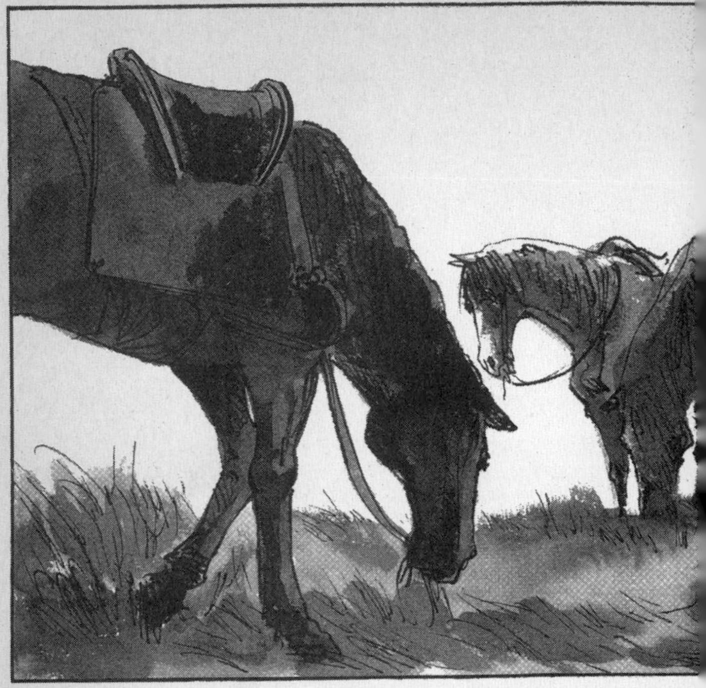
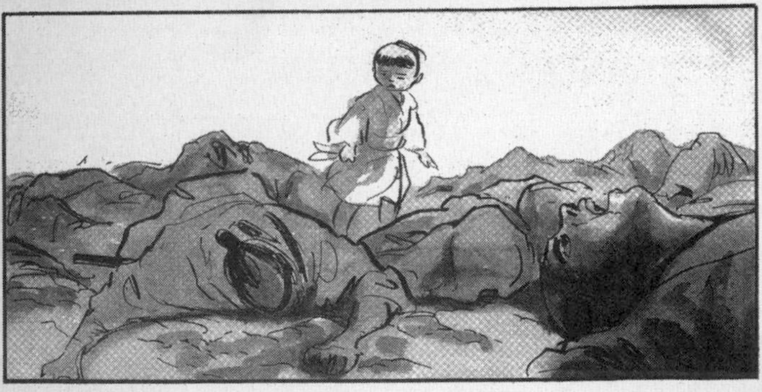

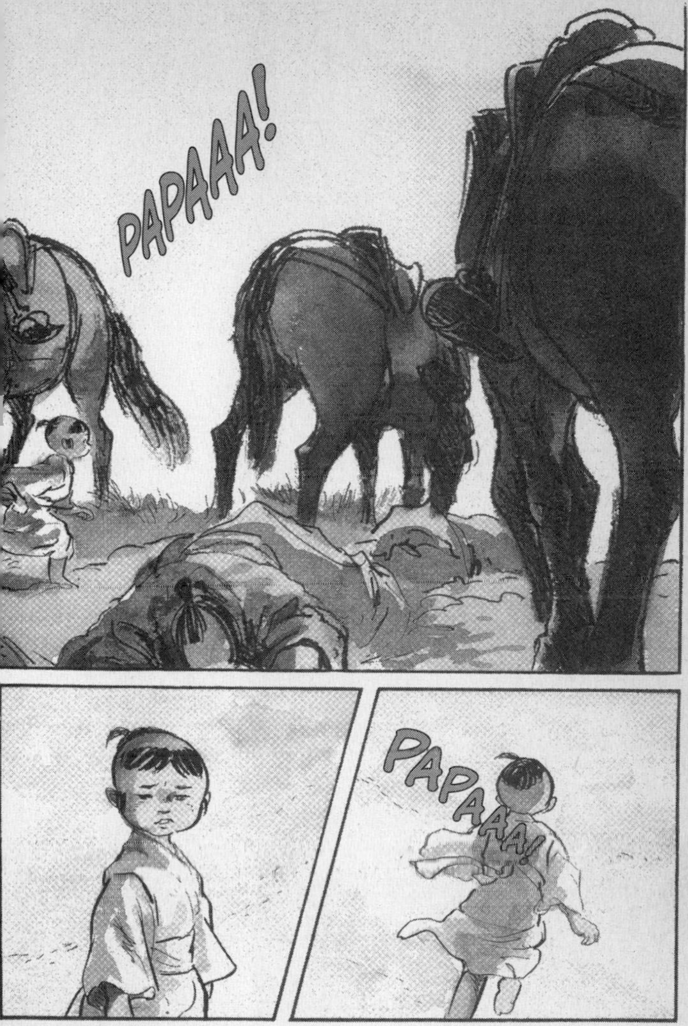
PAPAAA!
PAPAAA!

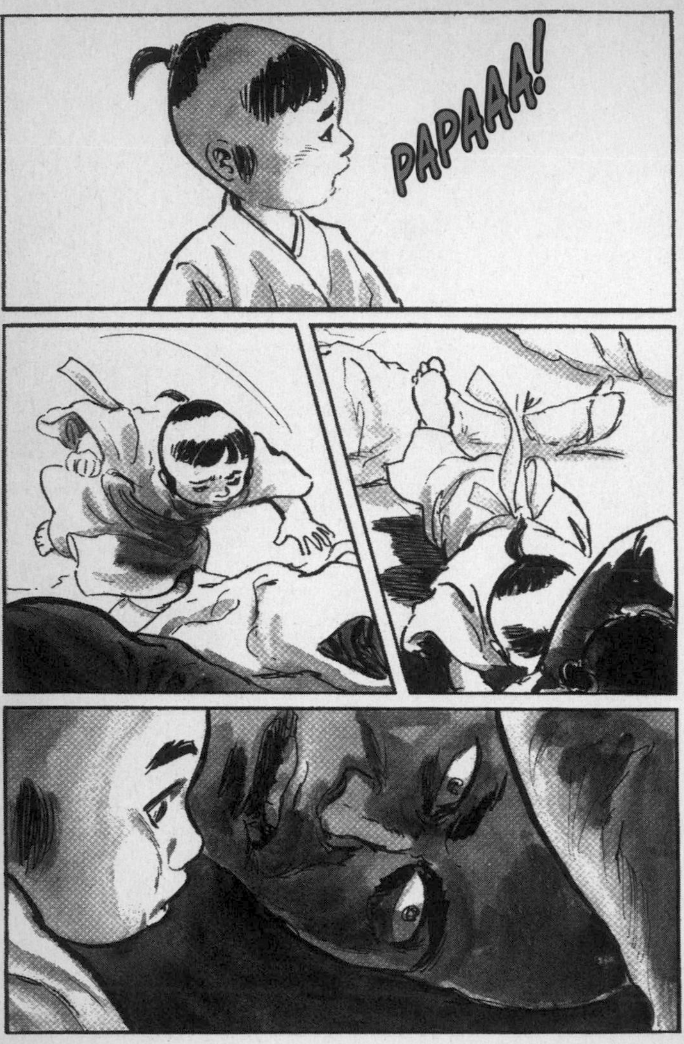
PAPAAA!

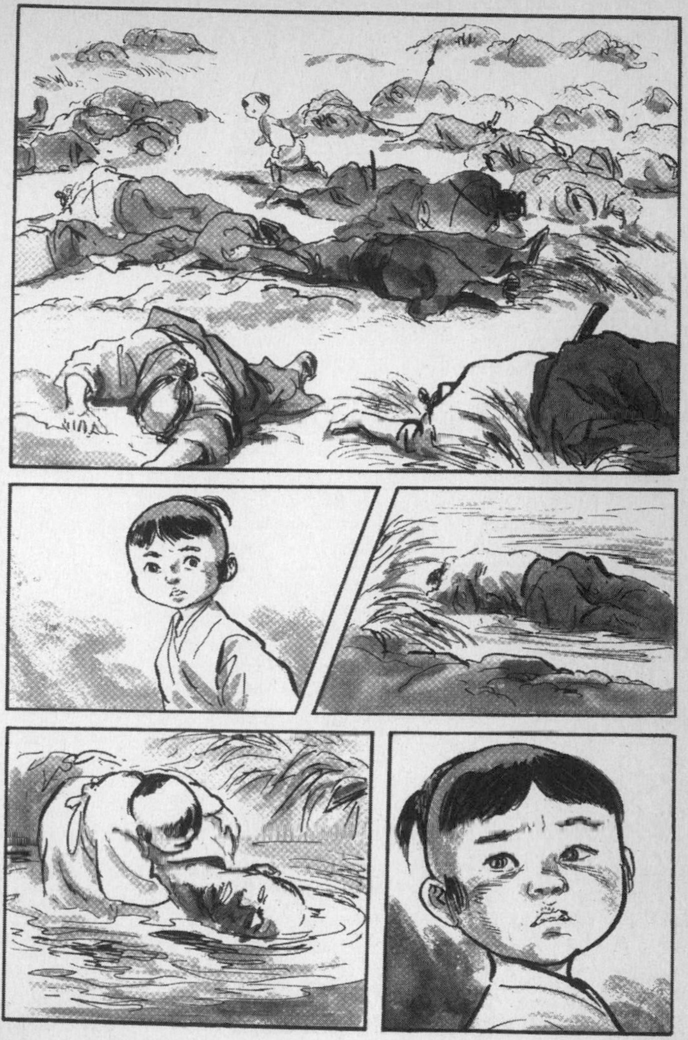

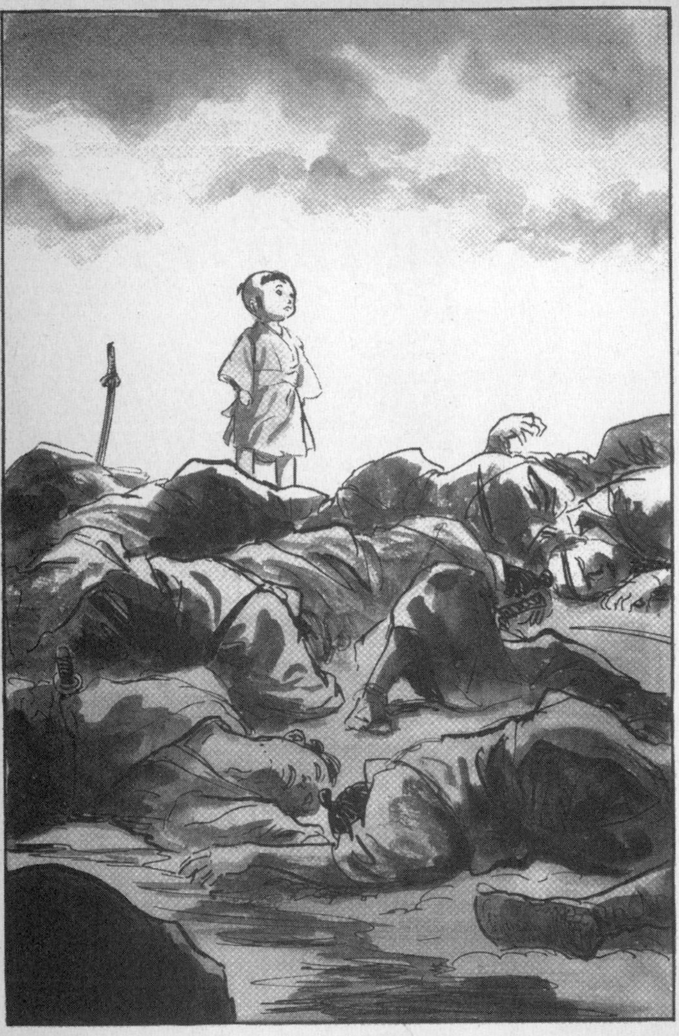

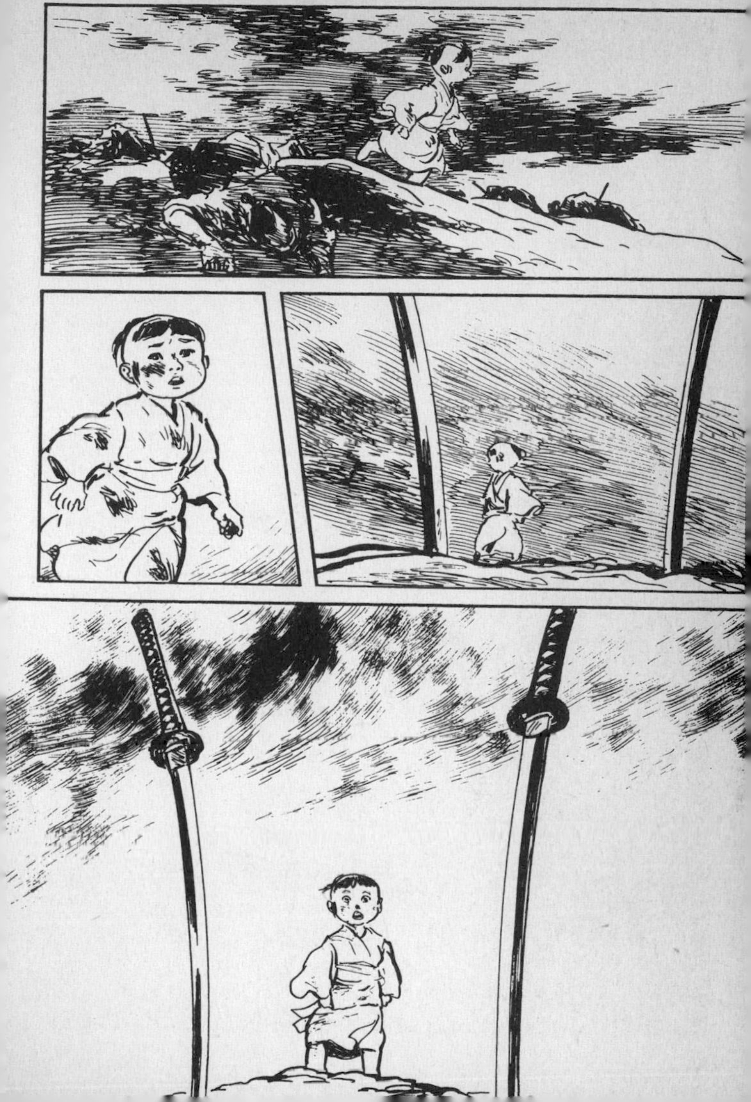

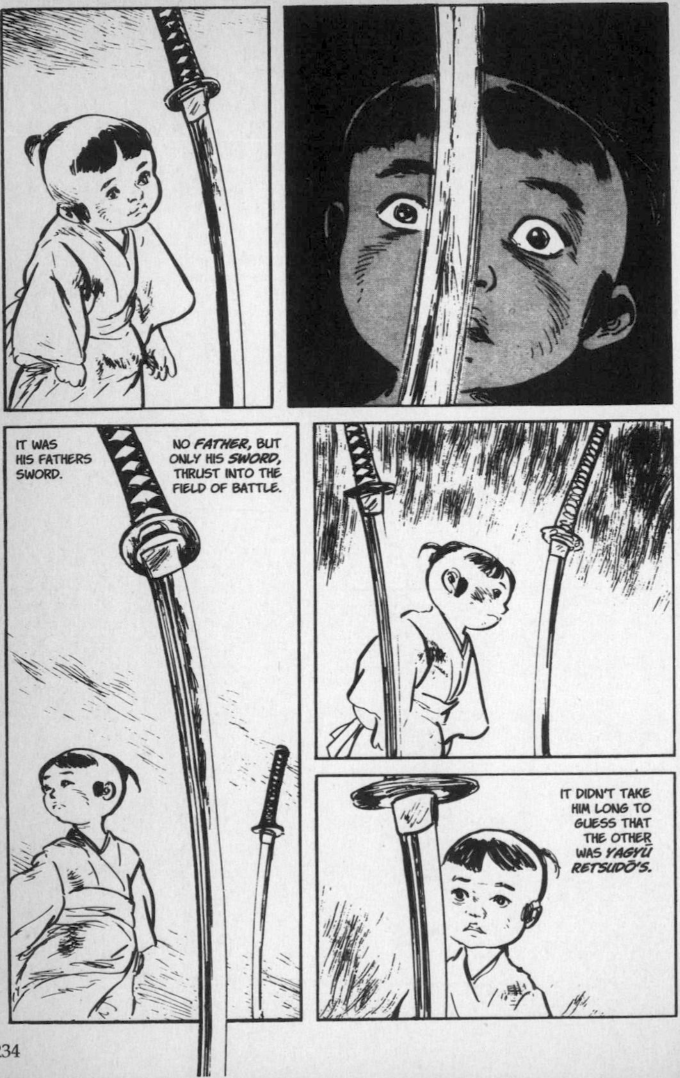
IT WAS HIS FATHERS SWORD.
NO *FATHER,* BUT ONLY HIS *SWORD,* THRUST INTO THE FIELD OF BATTLE.
IT DIDN'T TAKE HIM LONG TO GUESS THAT THE OTHER WAS *YAGYŪ RETSUDŌ'S.*

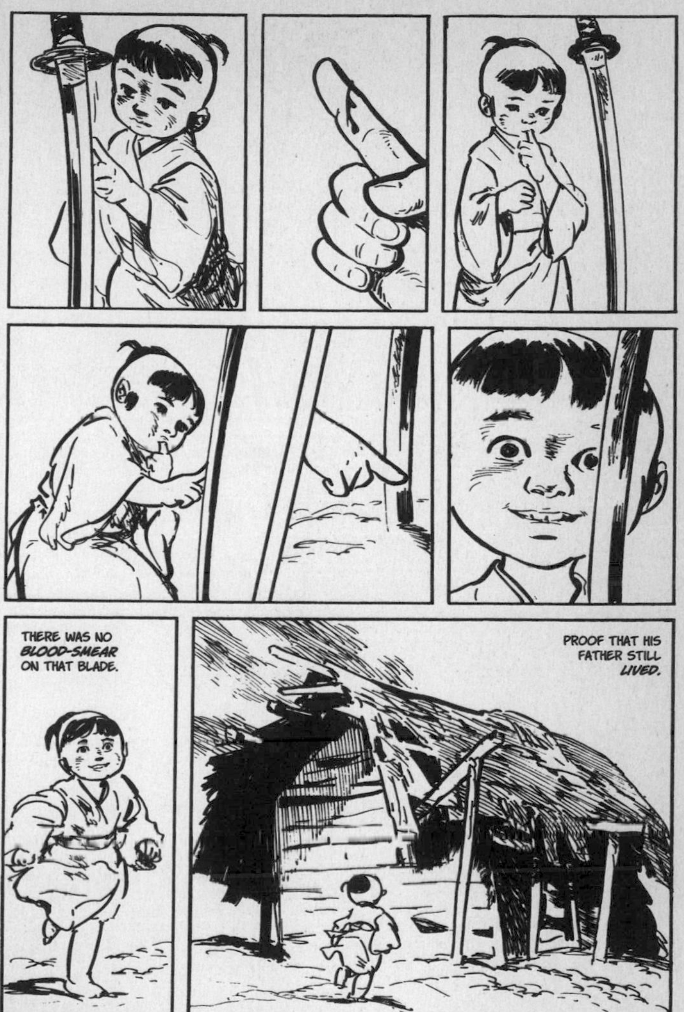
THERE WAS NO *BLOOD-SMEAR* ON THAT BLADE.
PROOF THAT HIS FATHER STILL *LIVED.*

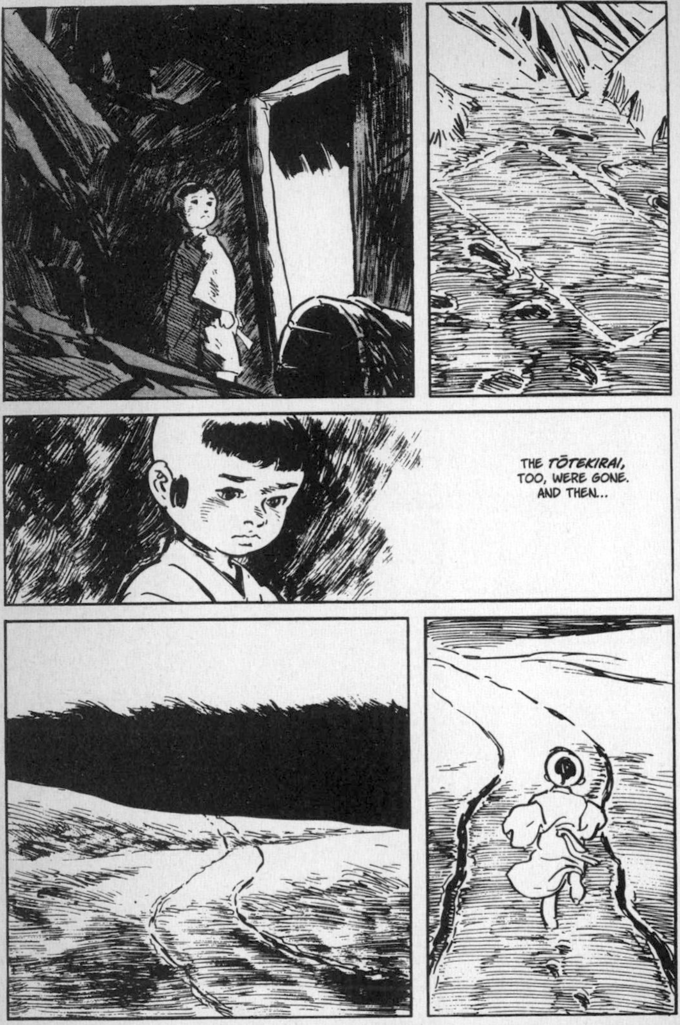
THE *TŌTEKIRAI,*
TOO, WERE GONE.
AND THEN...

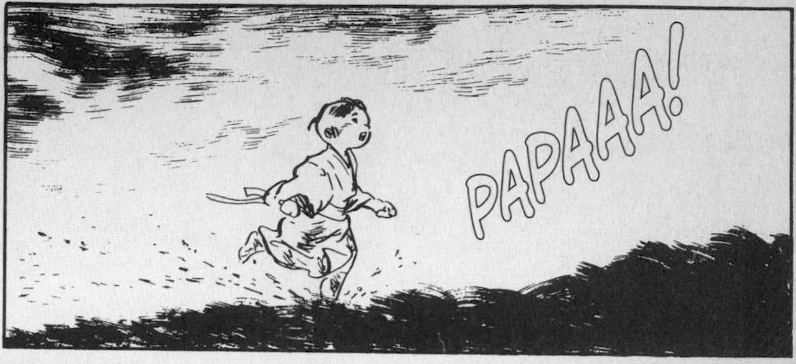
PAPAAA!

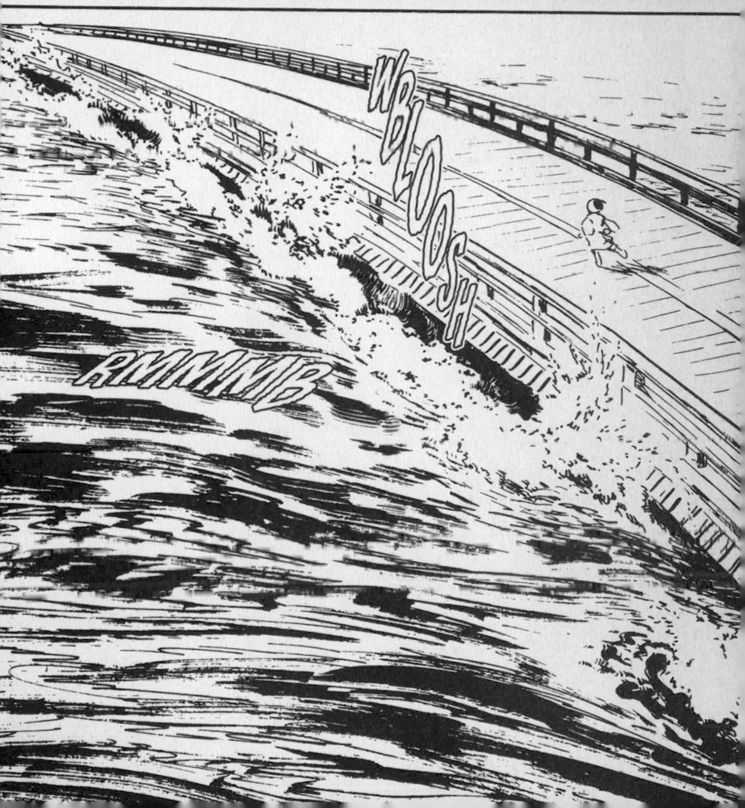
WBLOOSH
RMMMMB

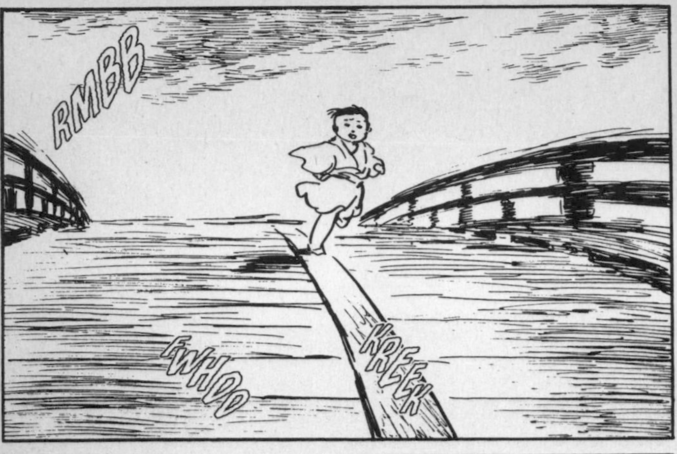
RMBB
KREEK
FWHOO

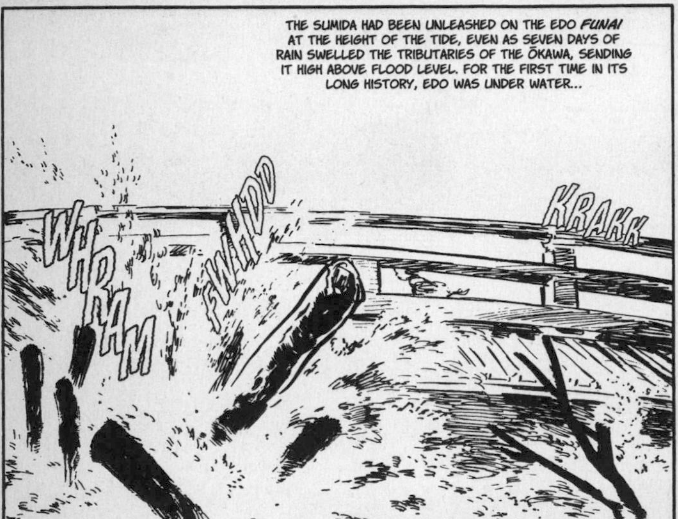
THE SUMIDA HAD BEEN UNLEASHED ON THE EDO *FUNAI* AT THE HEIGHT OF THE TIDE, EVEN AS SEVEN DAYS OF RAIN SWELLED THE TRIBUTARIES OF THE ŌKAWA, SENDING IT HIGH ABOVE FLOOD LEVEL. FOR THE FIRST TIME IN ITS LONG HISTORY, EDO WAS UNDER WATER...
KRAKK
FWHOO
WHRAM

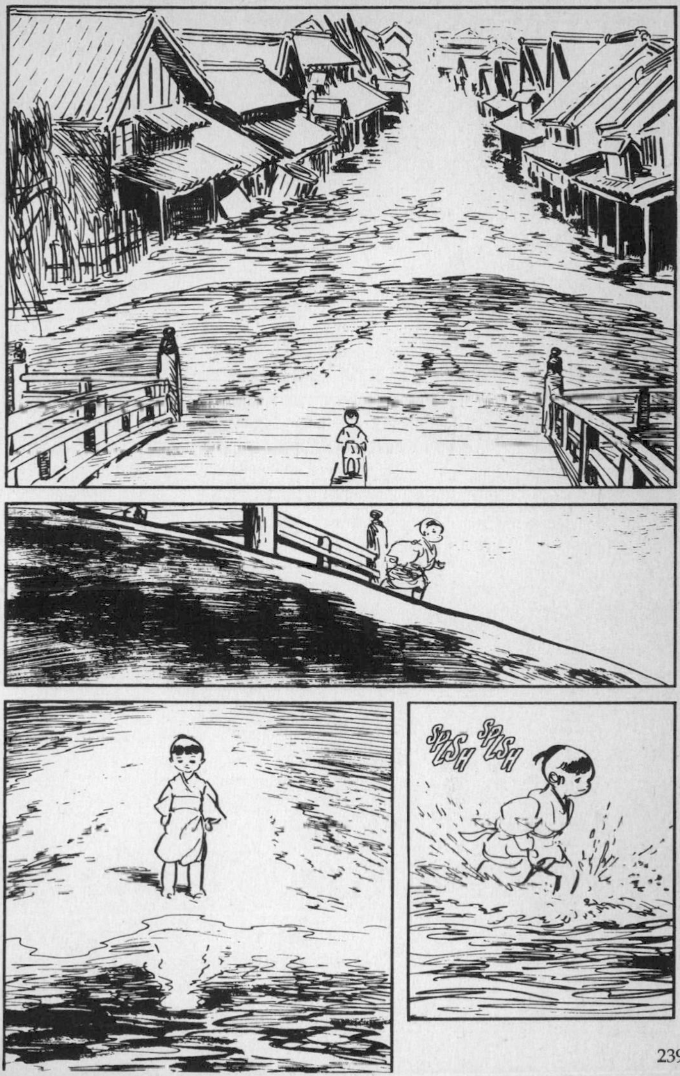
SPLSH SPLSH

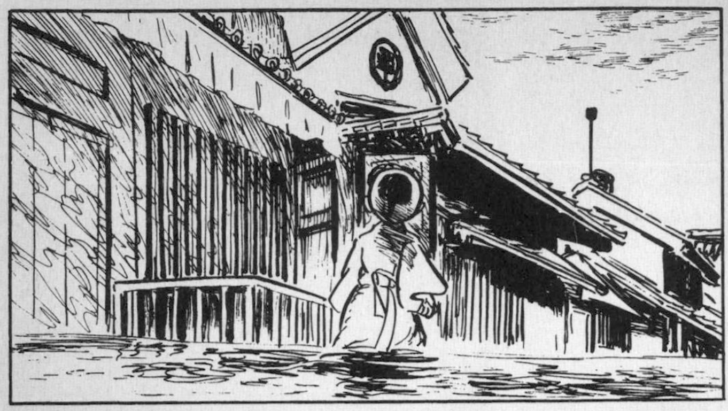

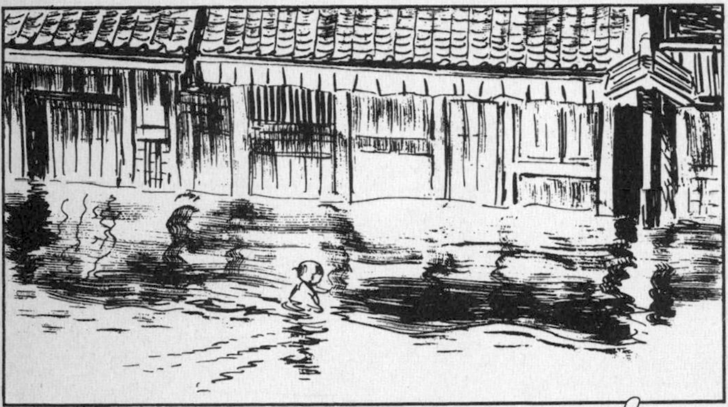

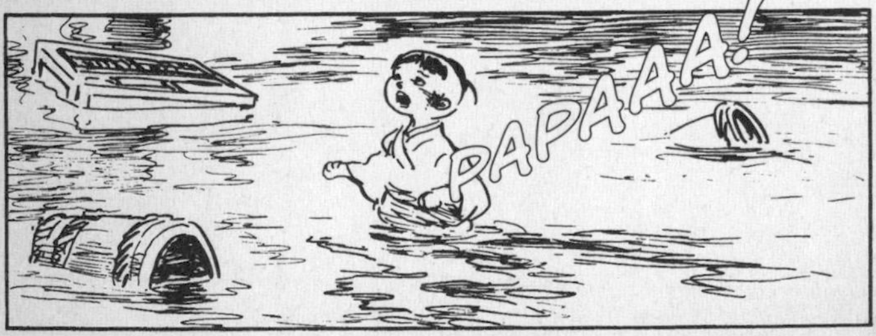
PAPAAA!

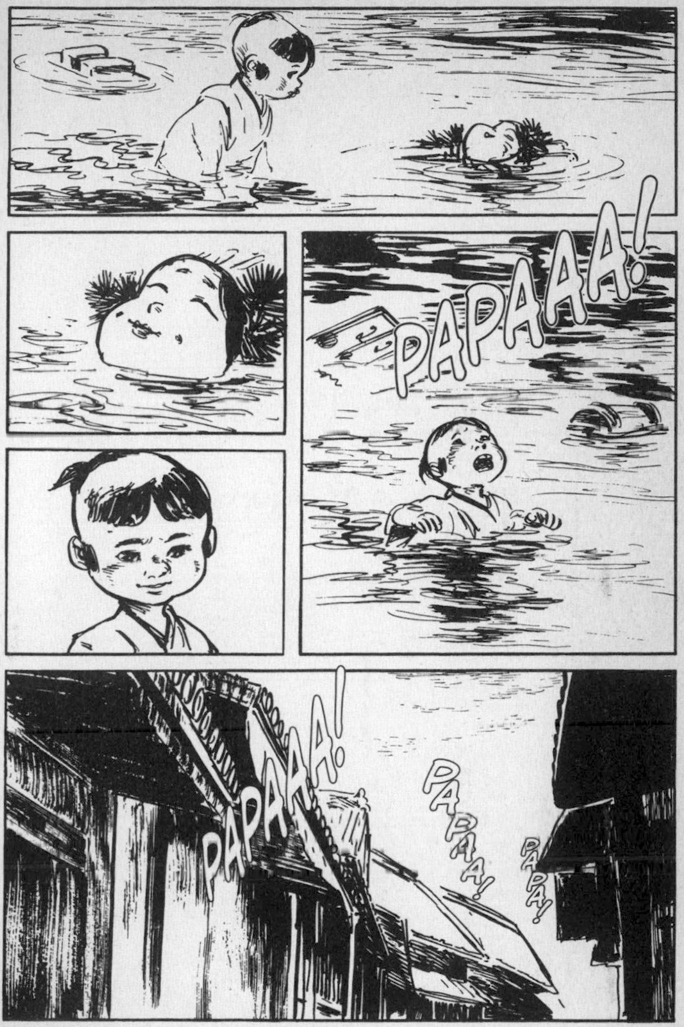
PAPAAA!
PAPAAA!
PAPAA!
PAPA!

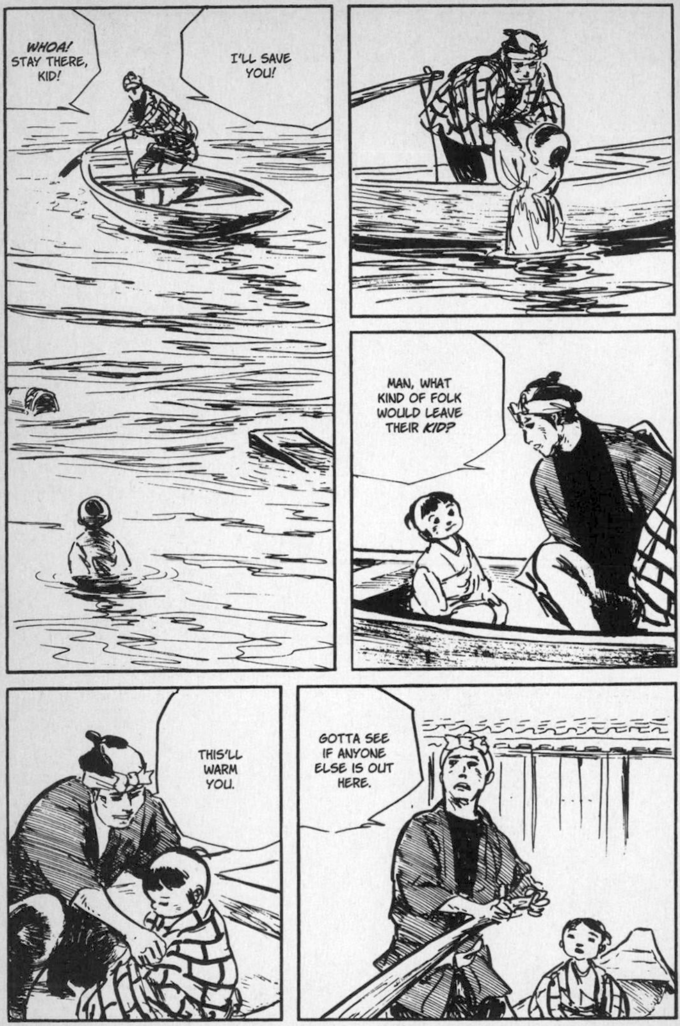
WHOA! STAY THERE, KID!
I'LL SAVE YOU!
MAN, WHAT KIND OF FOLK WOULD LEAVE THEIR KID?
THIS'LL WARM YOU.
GOTTA SEE IF ANYONE ELSE IS OUT HERE.

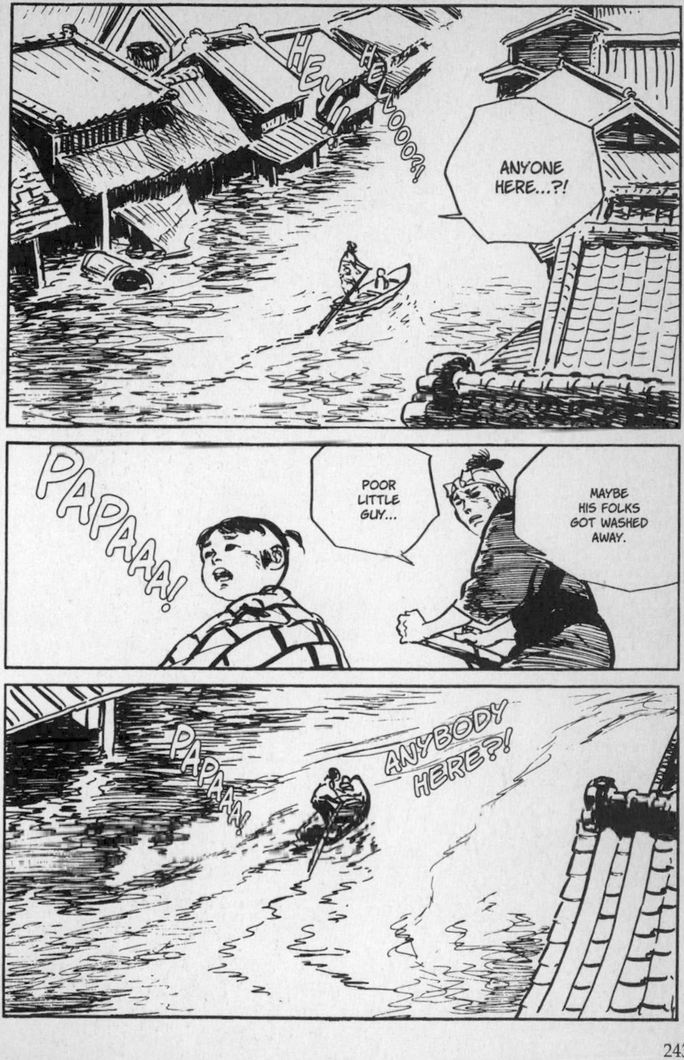
HEY!!
HELLOOO?!
ANYONE HERE...?!
PAPAAAA!
POOR LITTLE GUY...
MAYBE HIS FOLKS GOT WASHED AWAY.
PAPAAA!
ANYBODY HERE?!

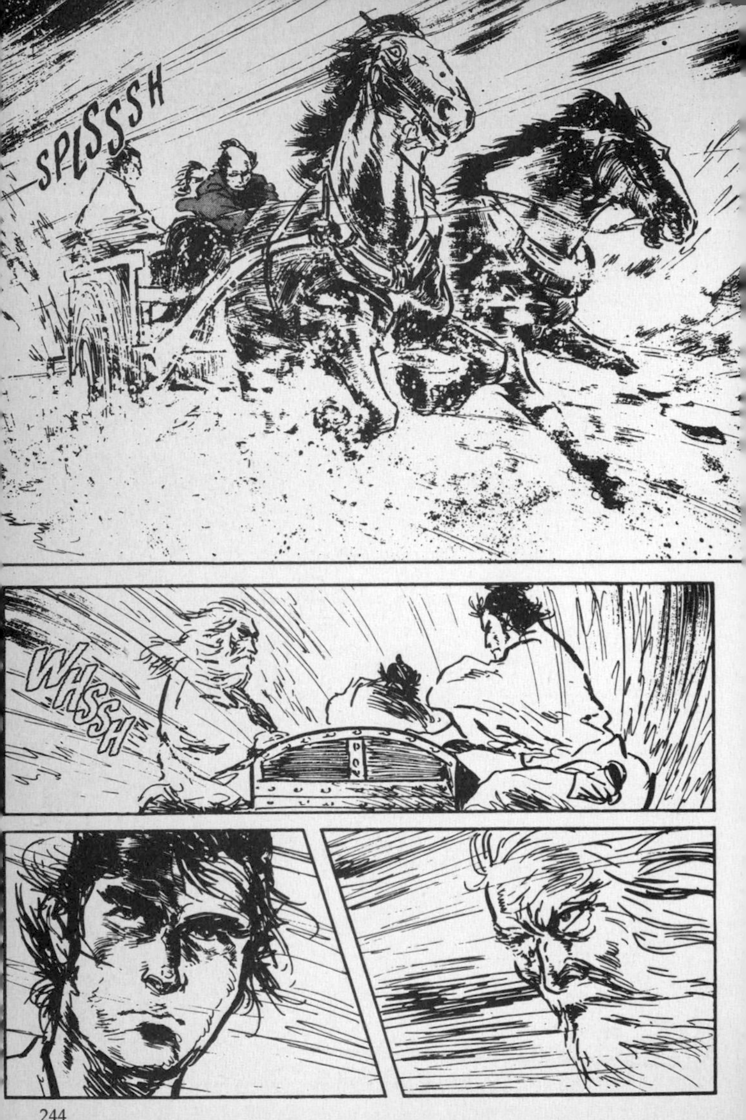
SPLSSSH
WHSSH

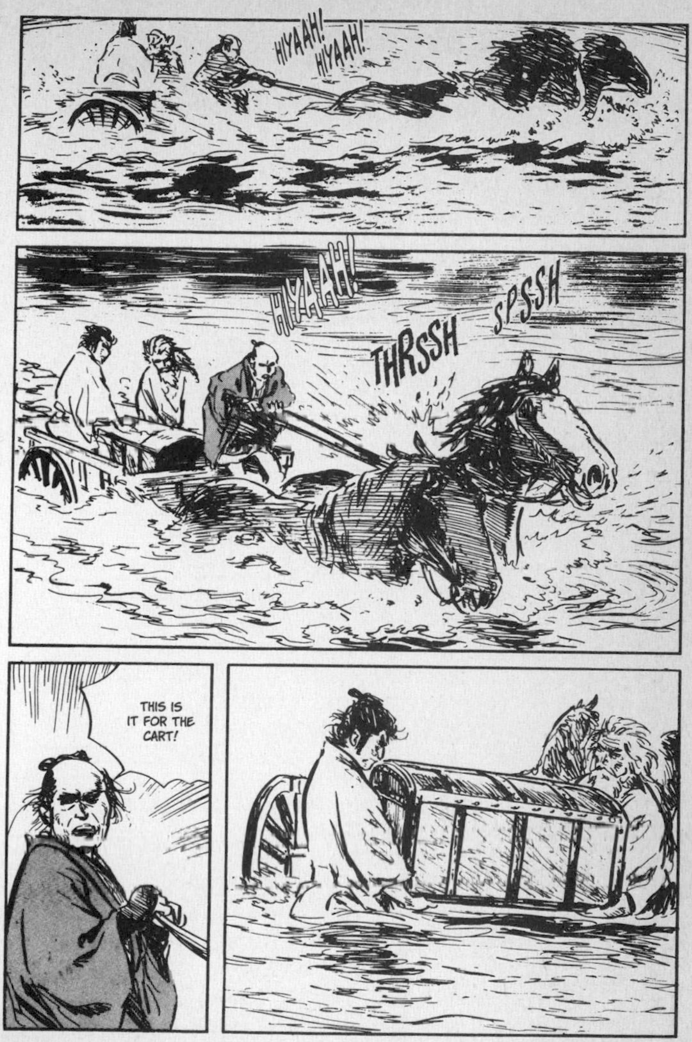
HIYAAH! HIYAAH!
S.P.SSH
HIYAAH!
THRSSH
THIS IS IT FOR THE CART!

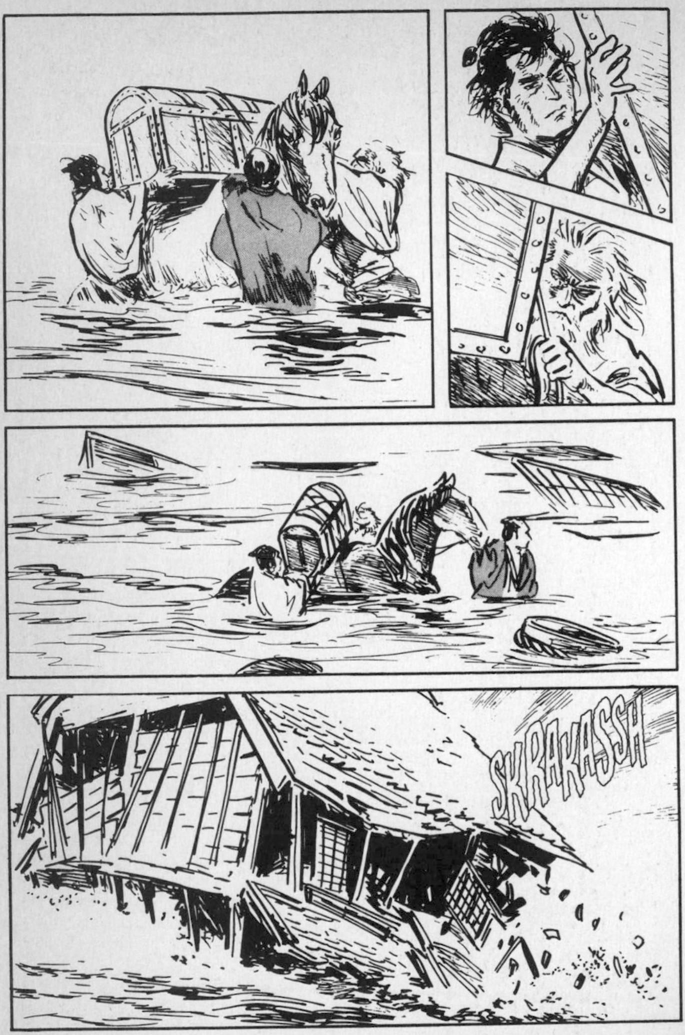
SKRAKASSH

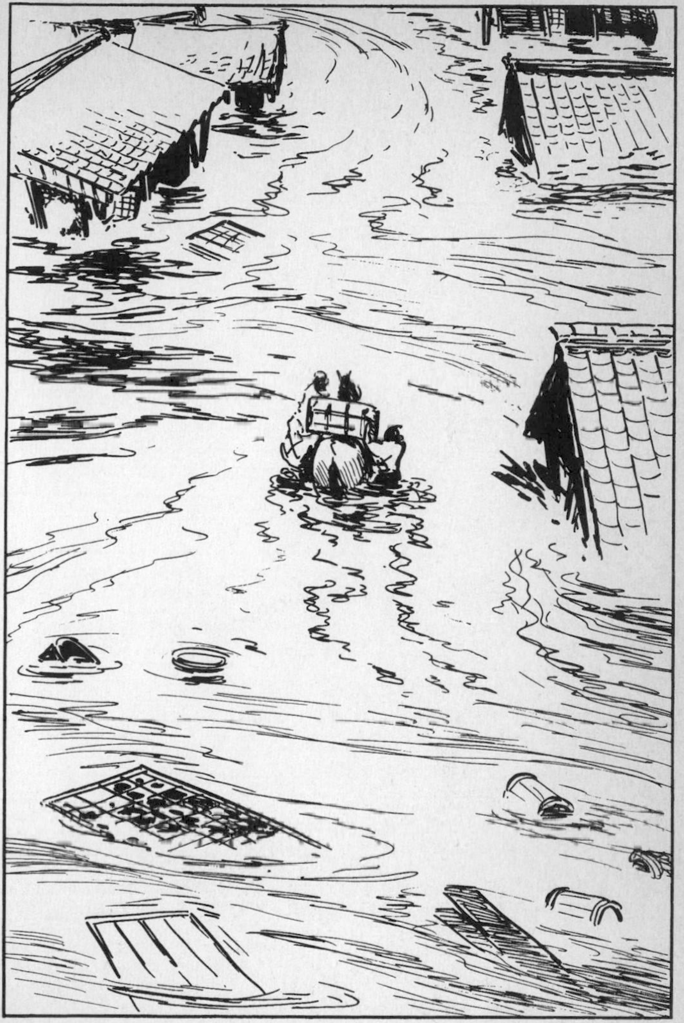

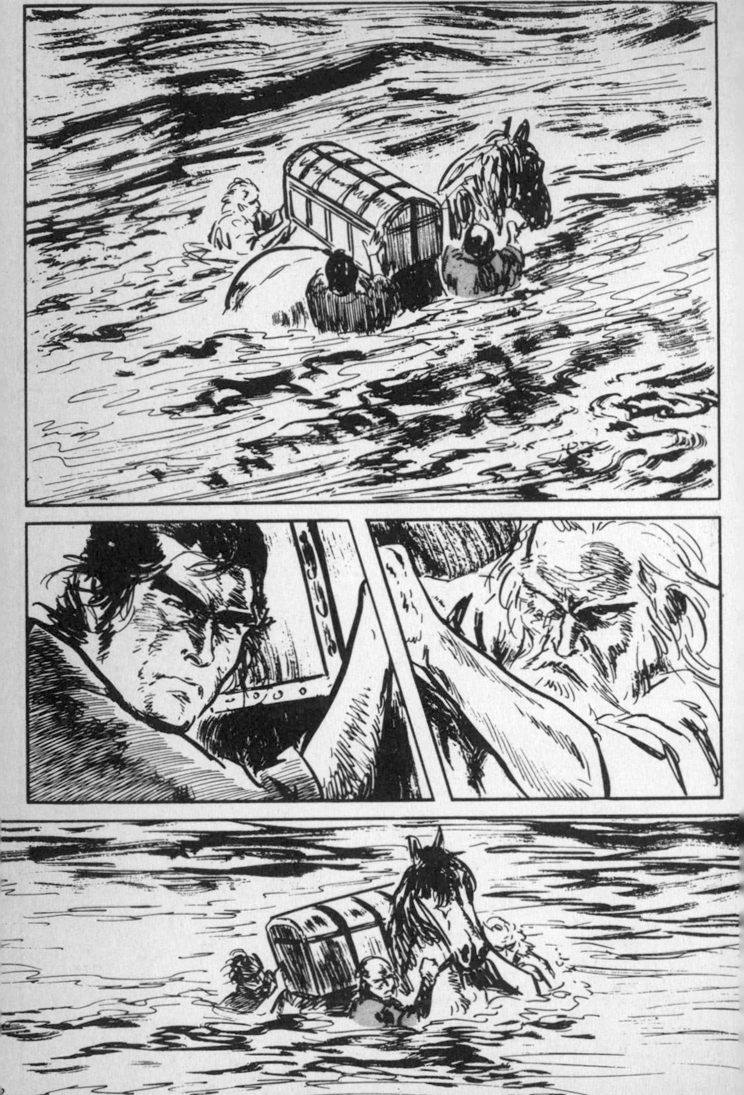

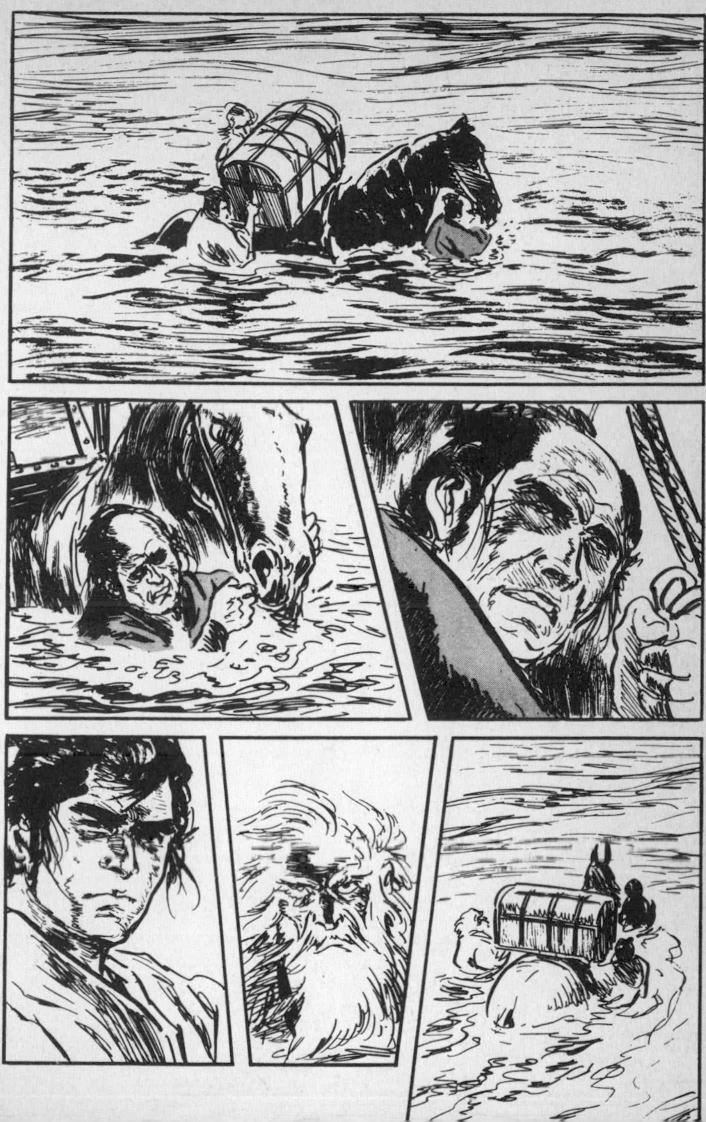

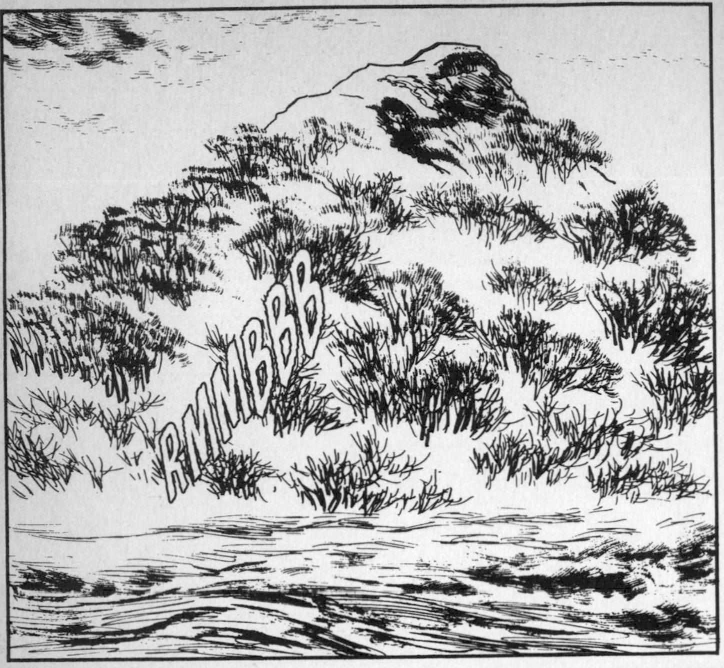
RMMBBB
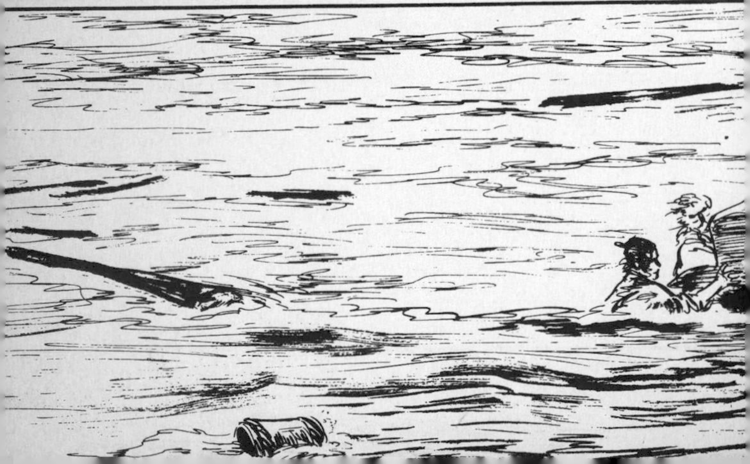

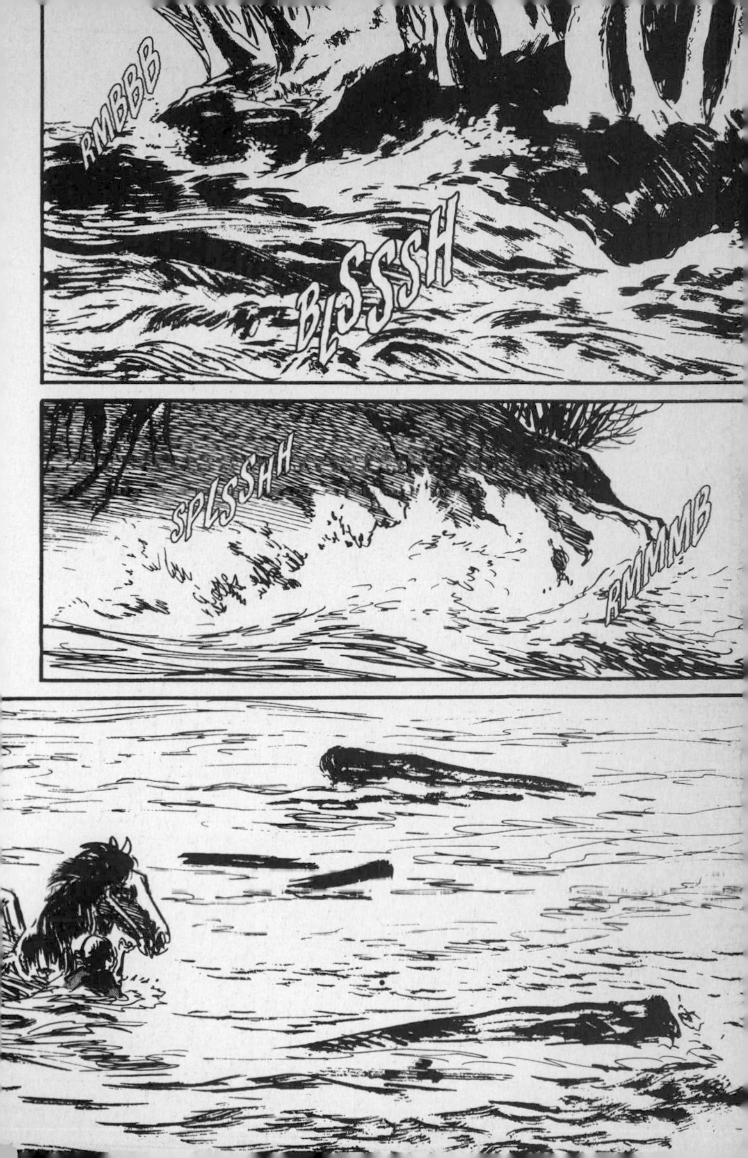
RMBBB
BLSSSH
RMMMB
SPLSSHH

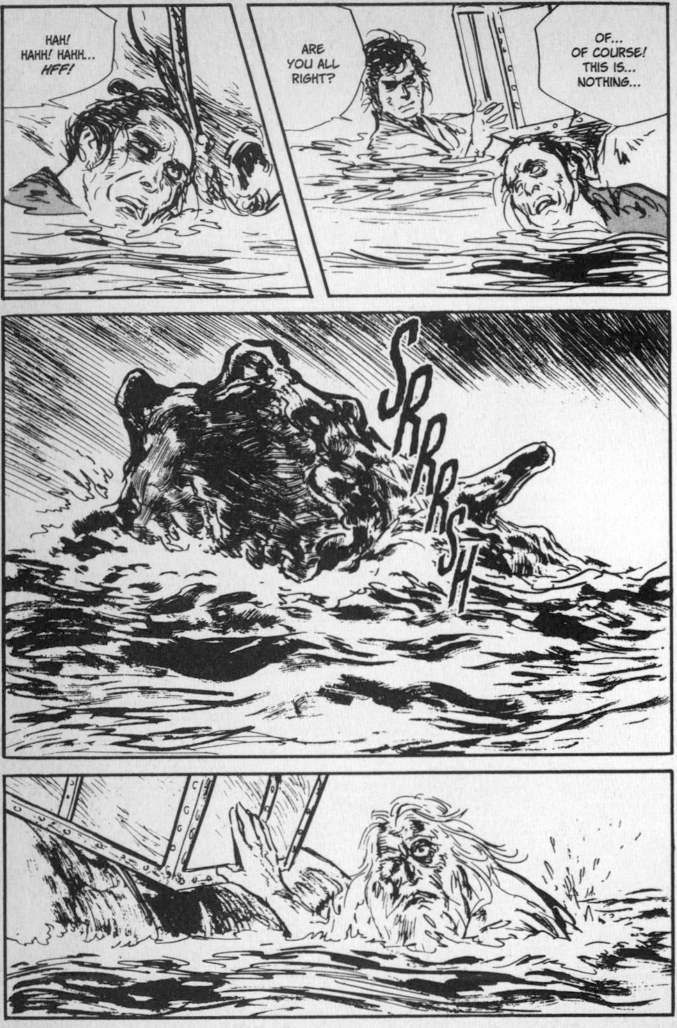
HAH! HAHH! HAHH... HFF!
ARE YOU ALL RIGHT?
OF... OF COURSE! THIS IS... NOTHING...
SRRRSH

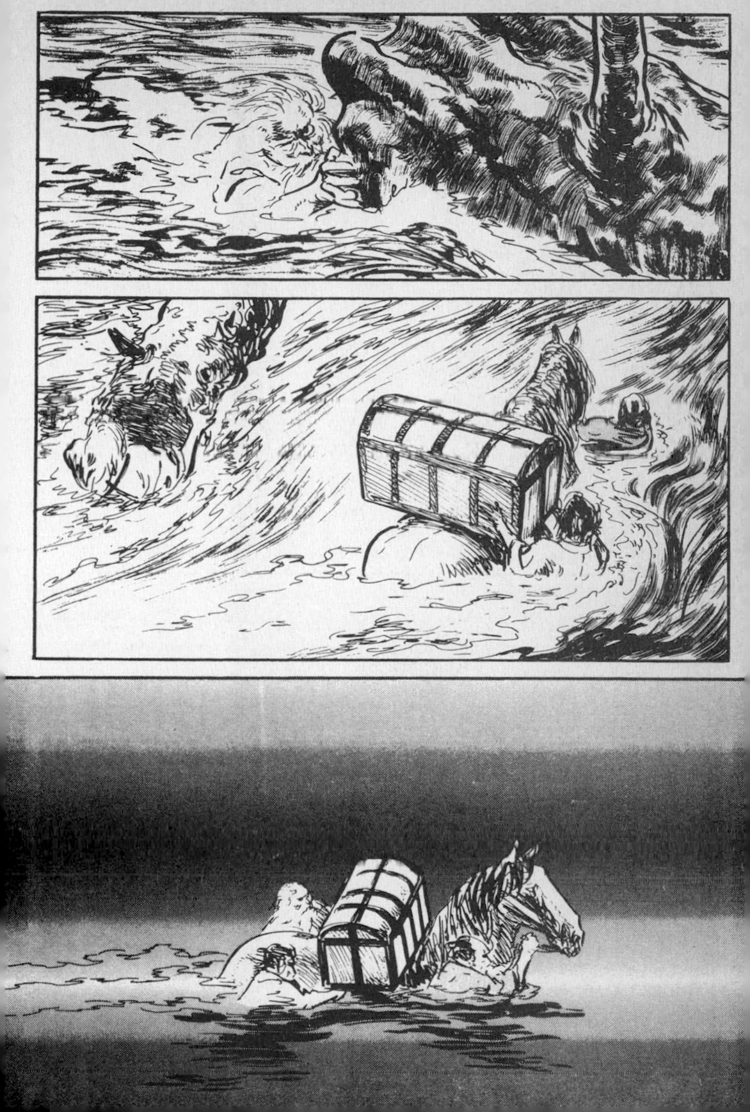

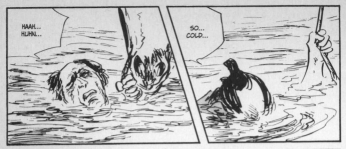

HAAH...
HUHN...

SO...
COLD...

NAGA-
SAKIYA!

C...
COLD...

RMMMMB

254

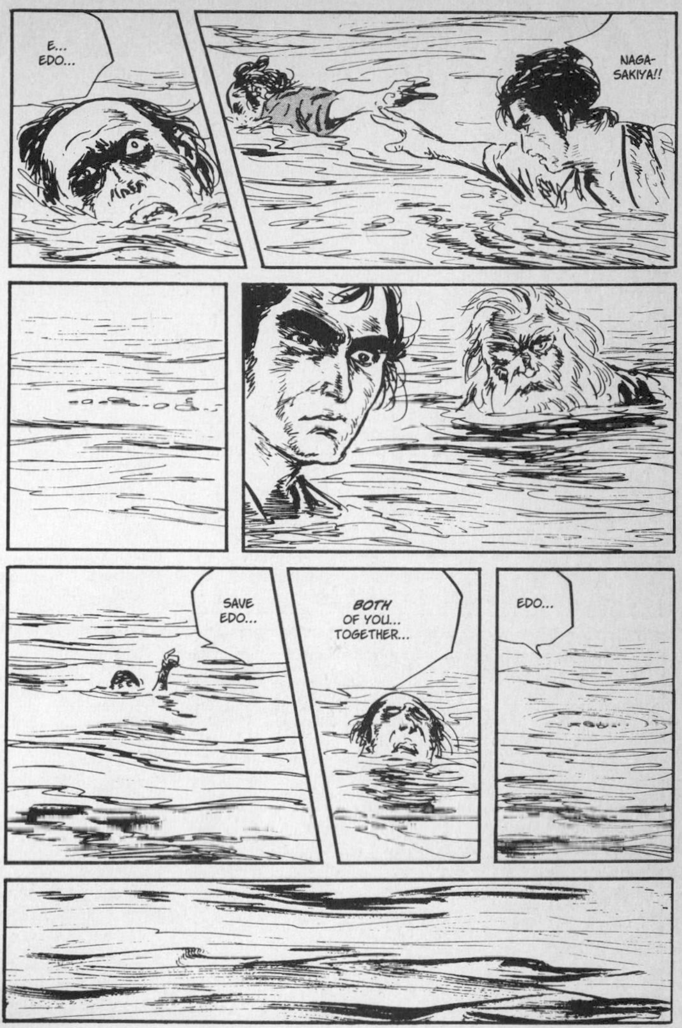
E...
EDO...
NAGA-
SAKIYA!!
SAVE
EDO...
BOTH
OF YOU...
TOGETHER...
EDO...

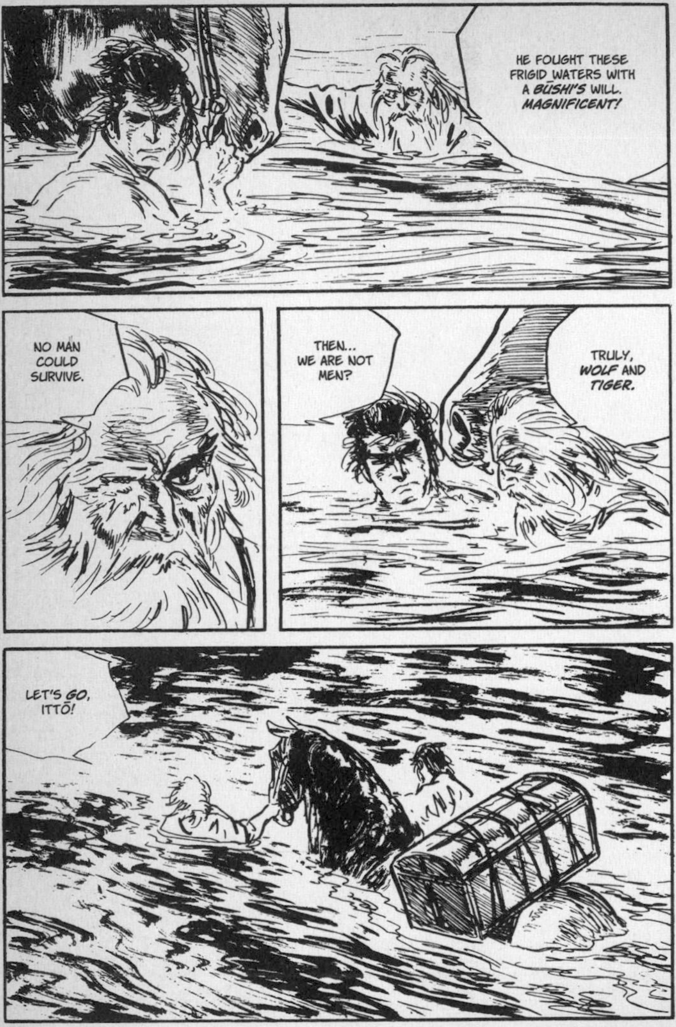
HE FOUGHT THESE FRIGID WATERS WITH A *BŪSHI'S* WILL. *MAGNIFICENT!*
NO MAN COULD SURVIVE.
THEN... WE ARE NOT MEN?
TRULY, *WOLF* AND *TIGER.*
LET'S *GO,* ITTŌ!

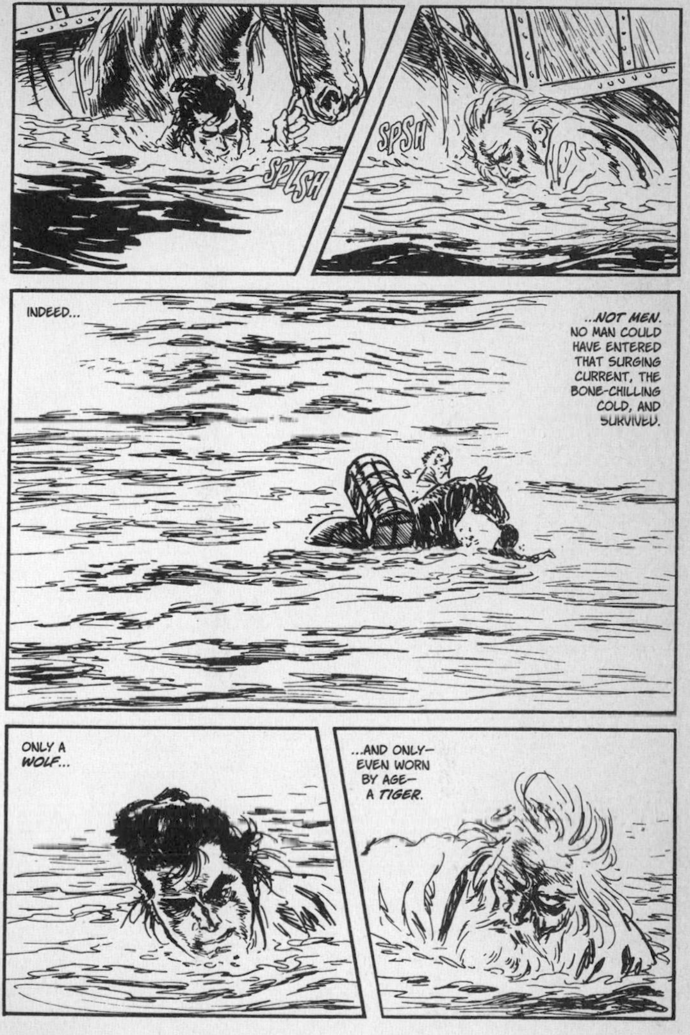
SPLSH
SPSH
INDEED...
...NOT MEN. NO MAN COULD HAVE ENTERED THAT SURGING CURRENT, THE BONE-CHILLING COLD, AND SURVIVED.
ONLY A WOLF...
...AND ONLY— EVEN WORN BY AGE— A TIGER.

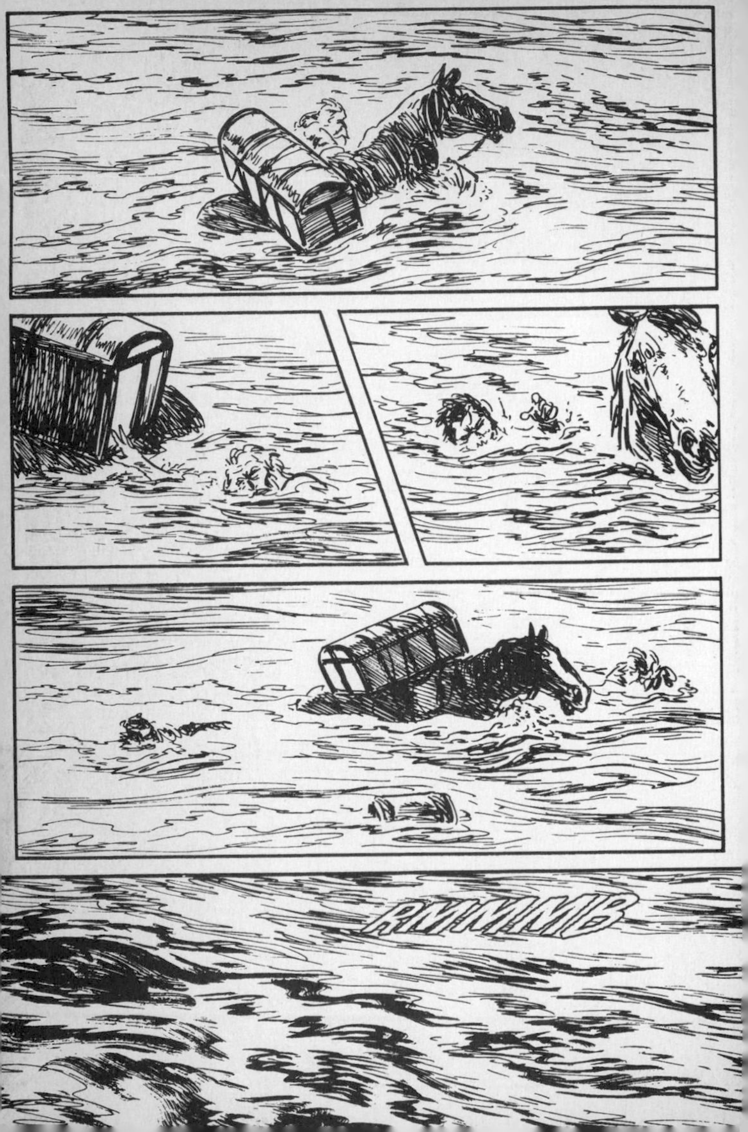
RMMMMB

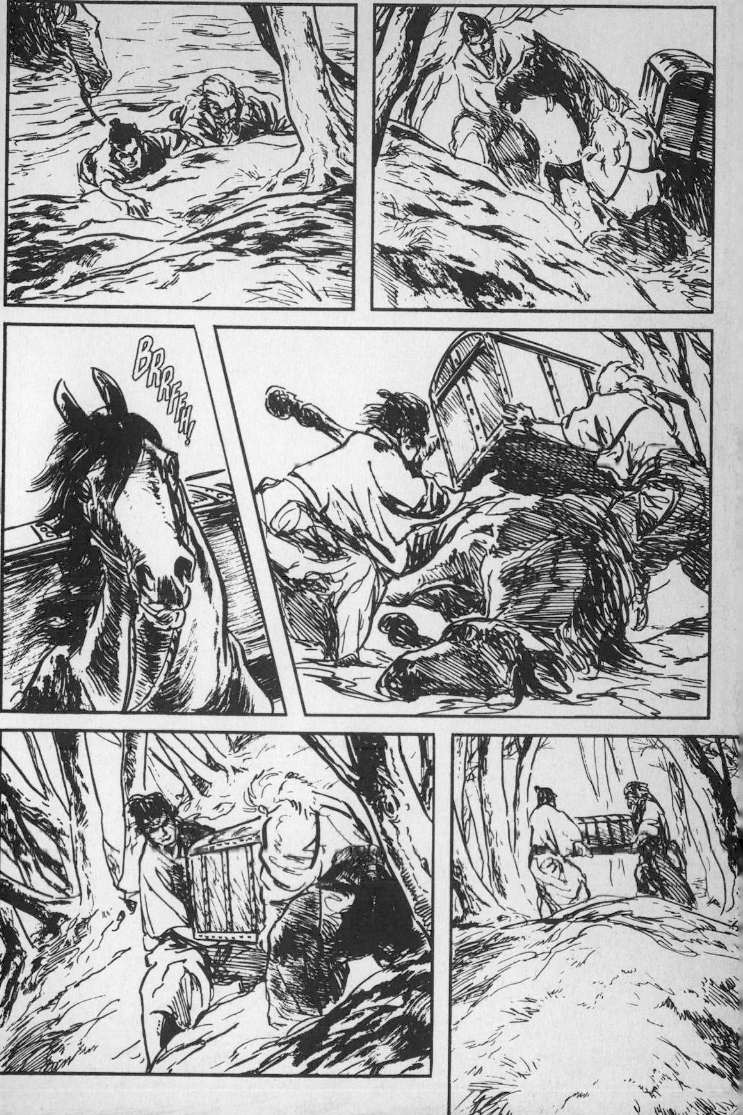
BRRFFH!

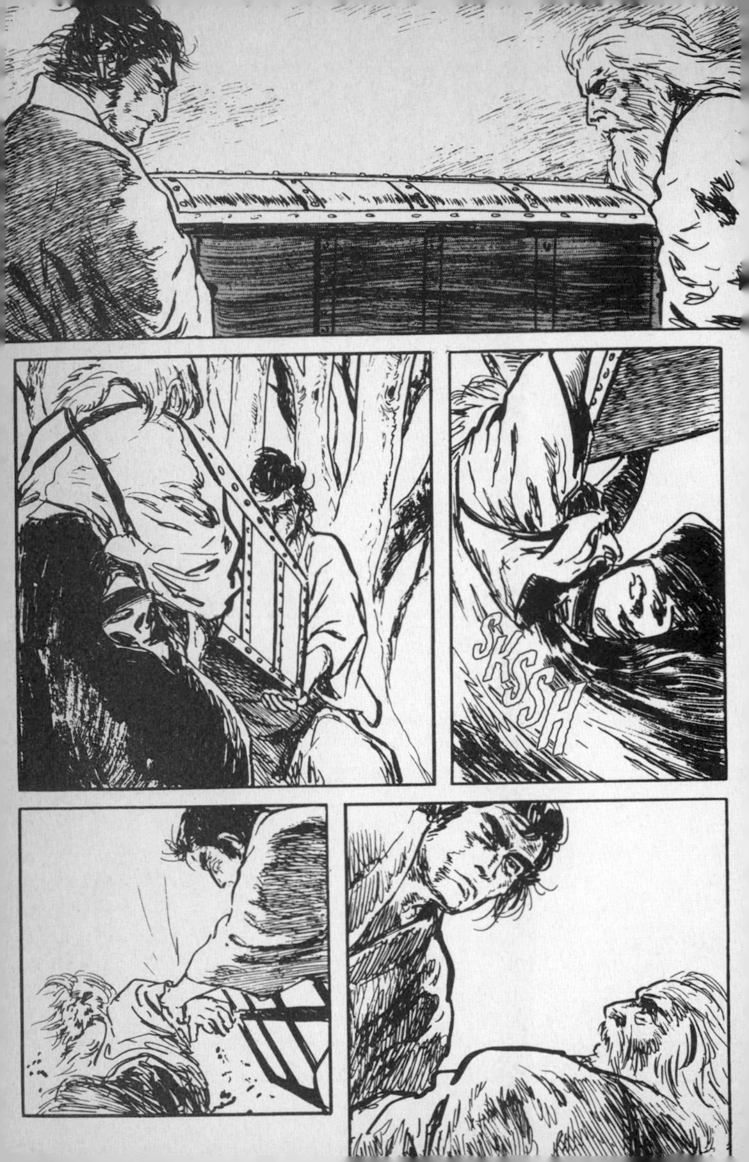
SKSSH

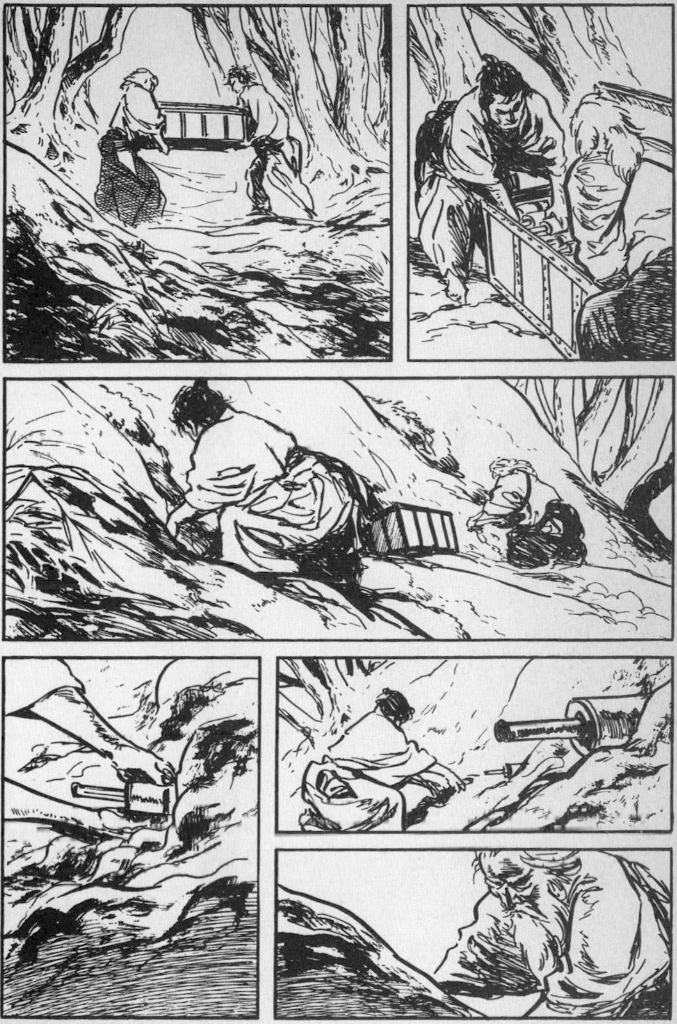

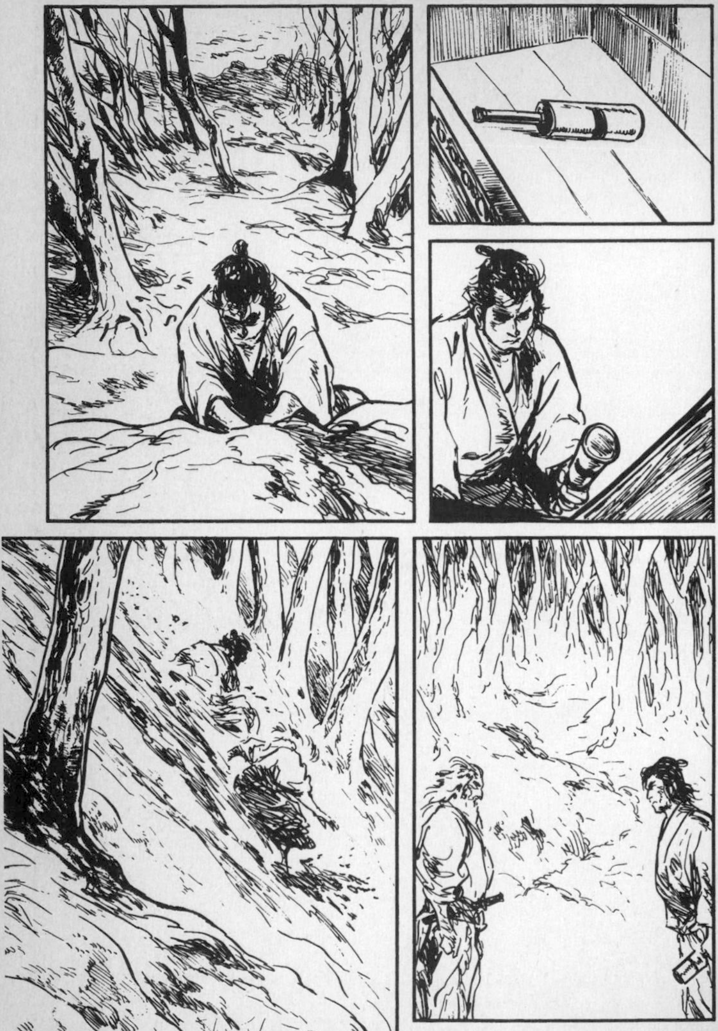

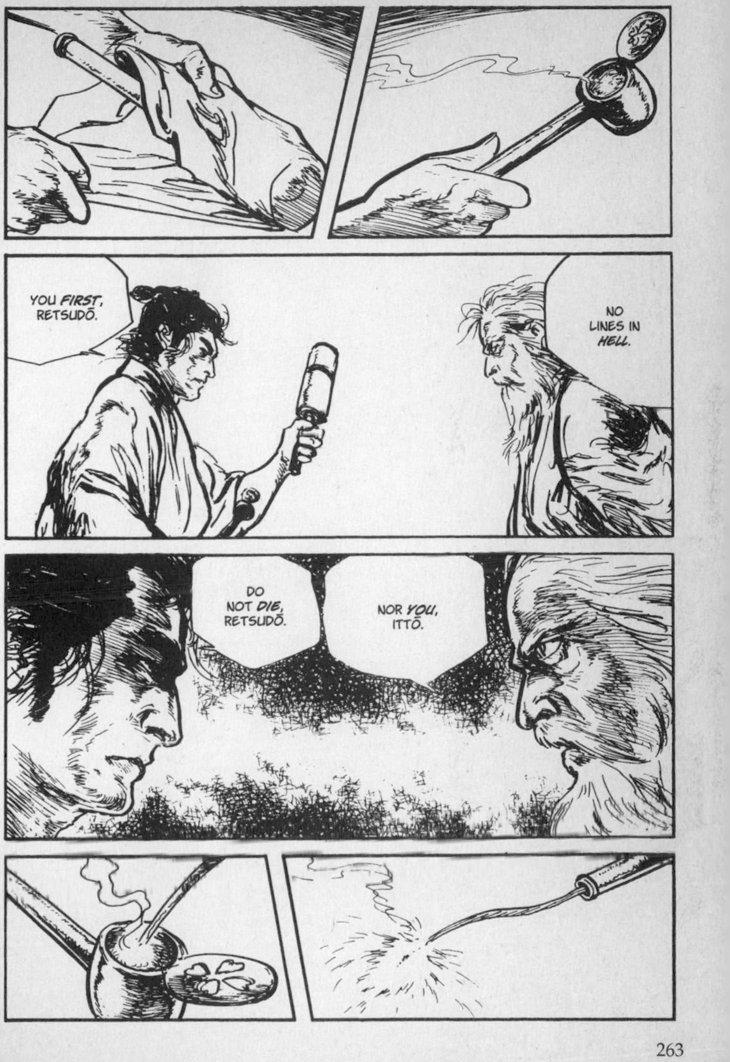
YOU FIRST, RETSUDŌ.
NO LINES IN HELL.
DO NOT DIE, RETSUDŌ.
NOR YOU, ITTŌ.

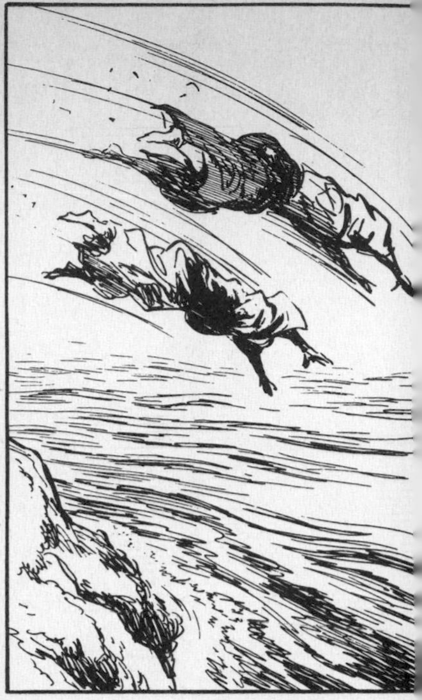
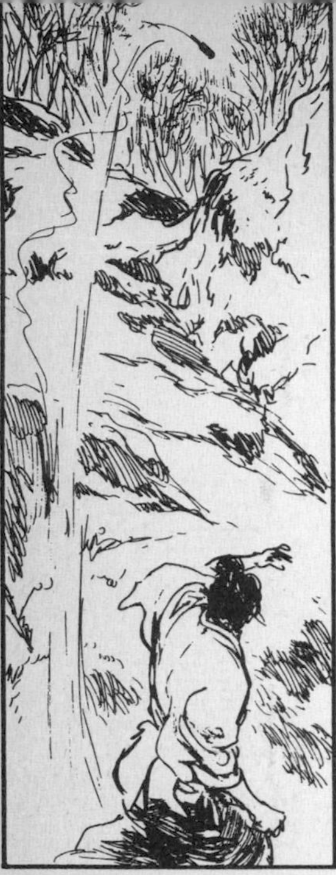
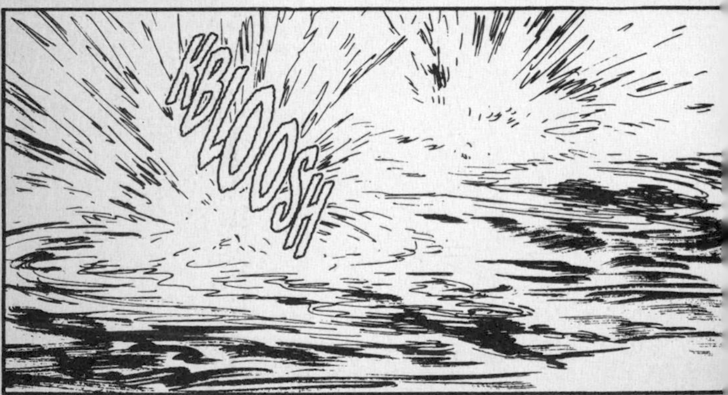
KBLOOSH

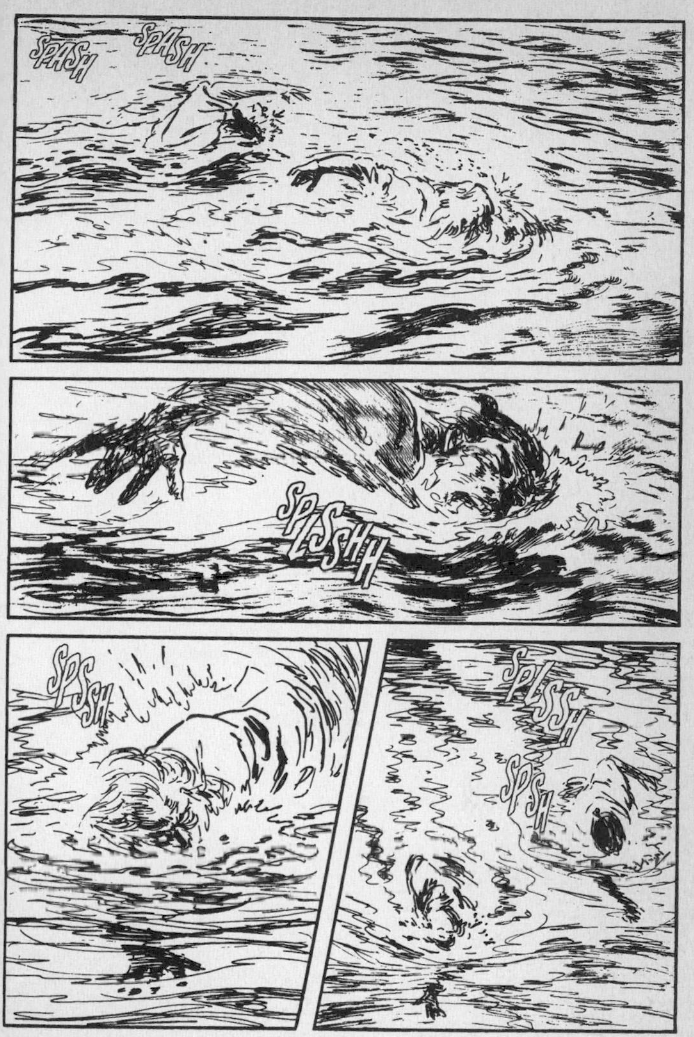
SPASH
SPASH
SPLSSHH
SPLSSH
SPSH
SPSSH

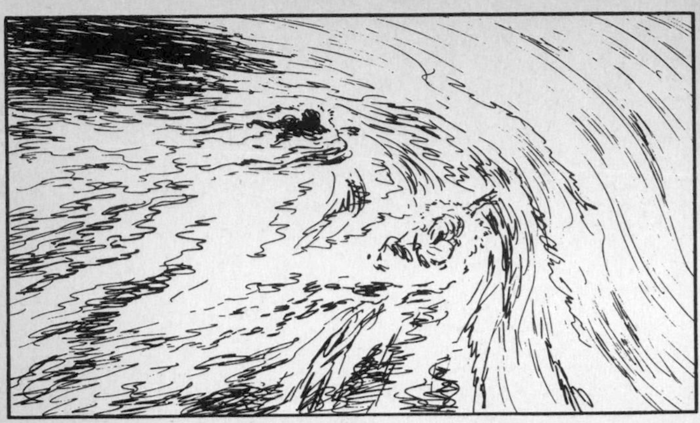

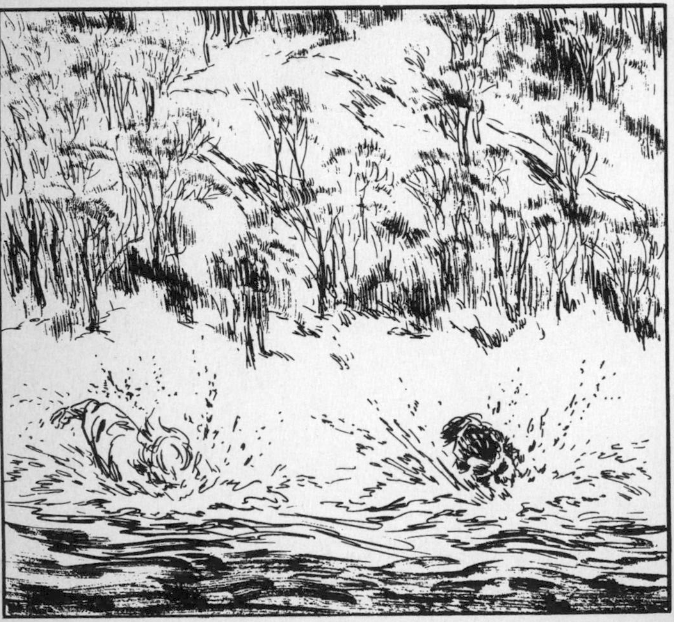

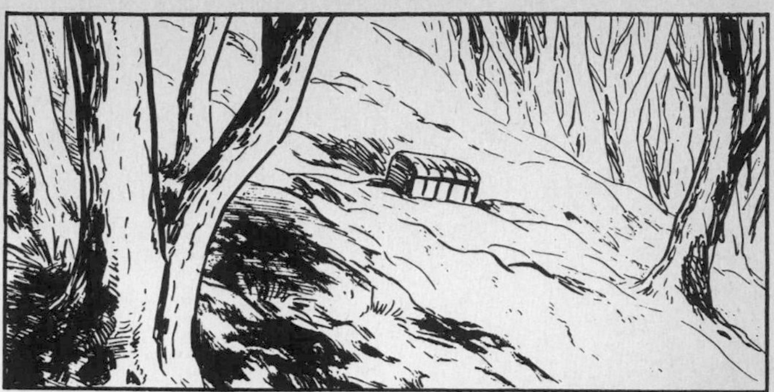

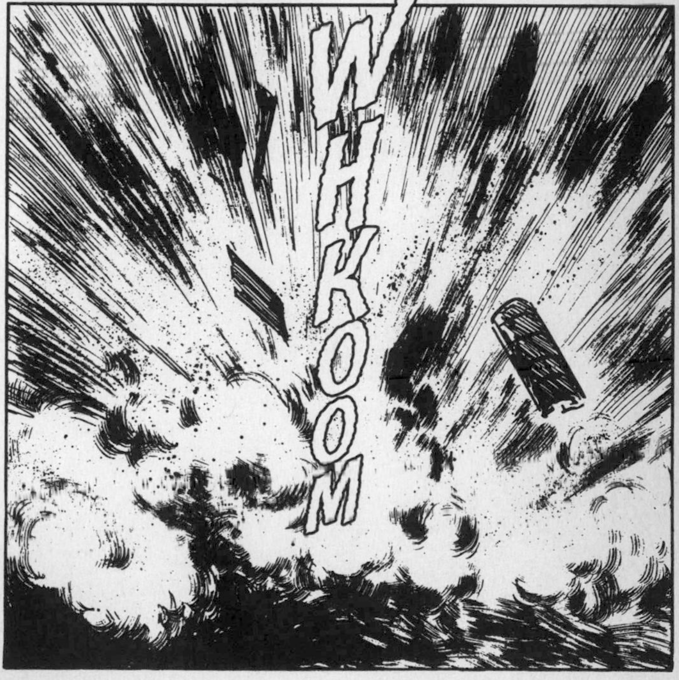
WHKOOM

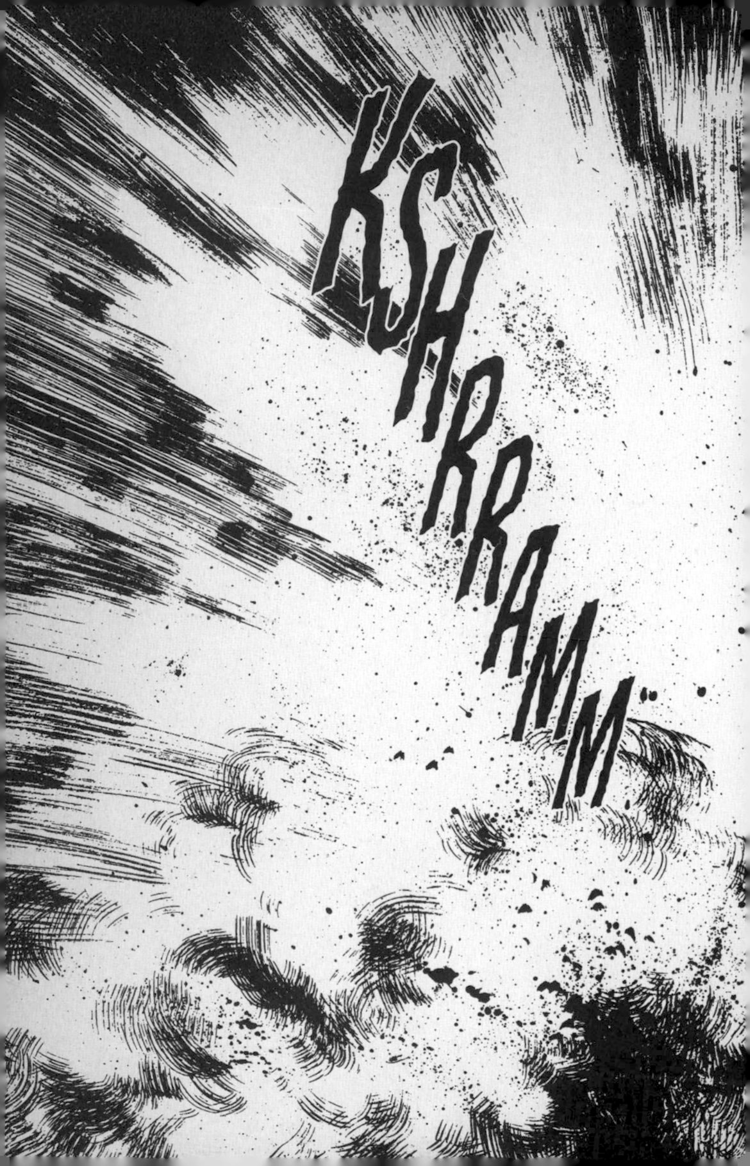
KSHRRAMM

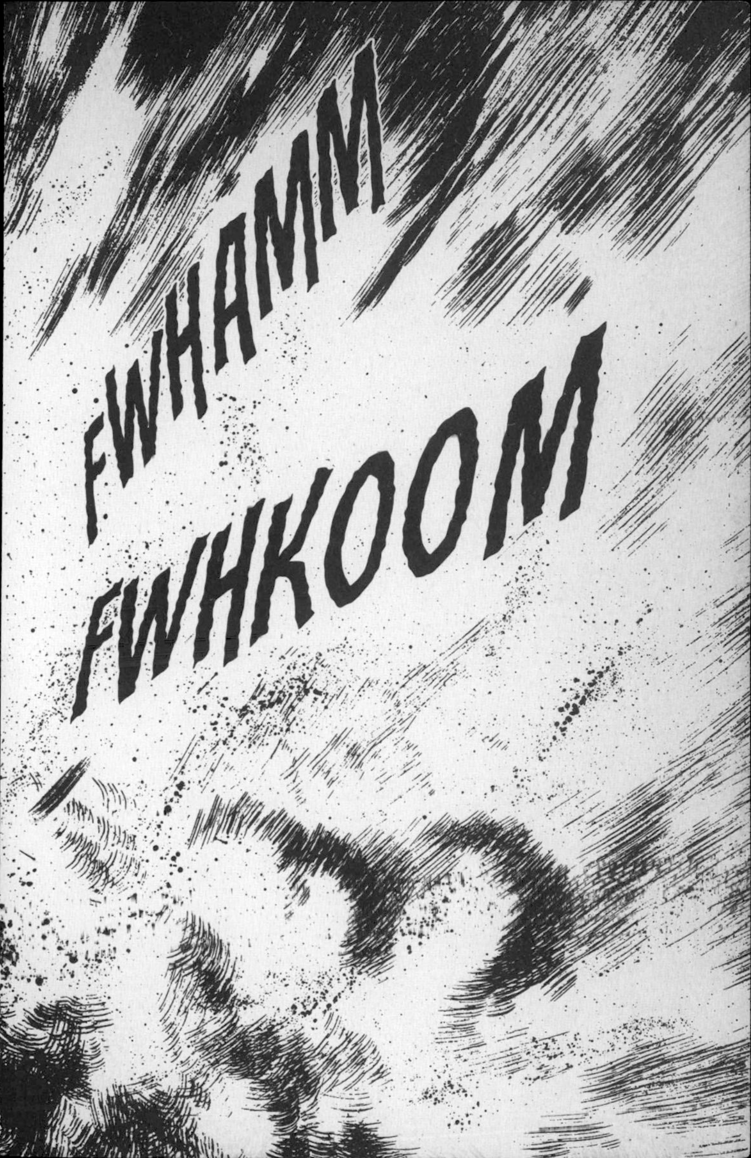
FWHAMM
FWHKOOM

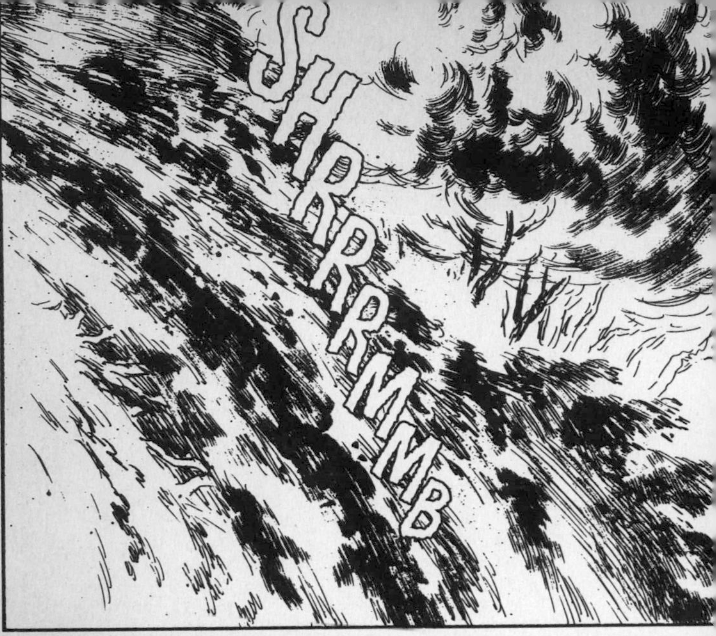
SHRRMMB
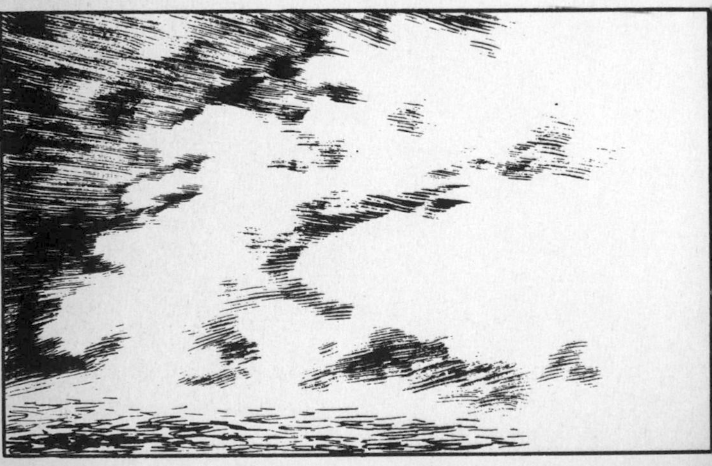

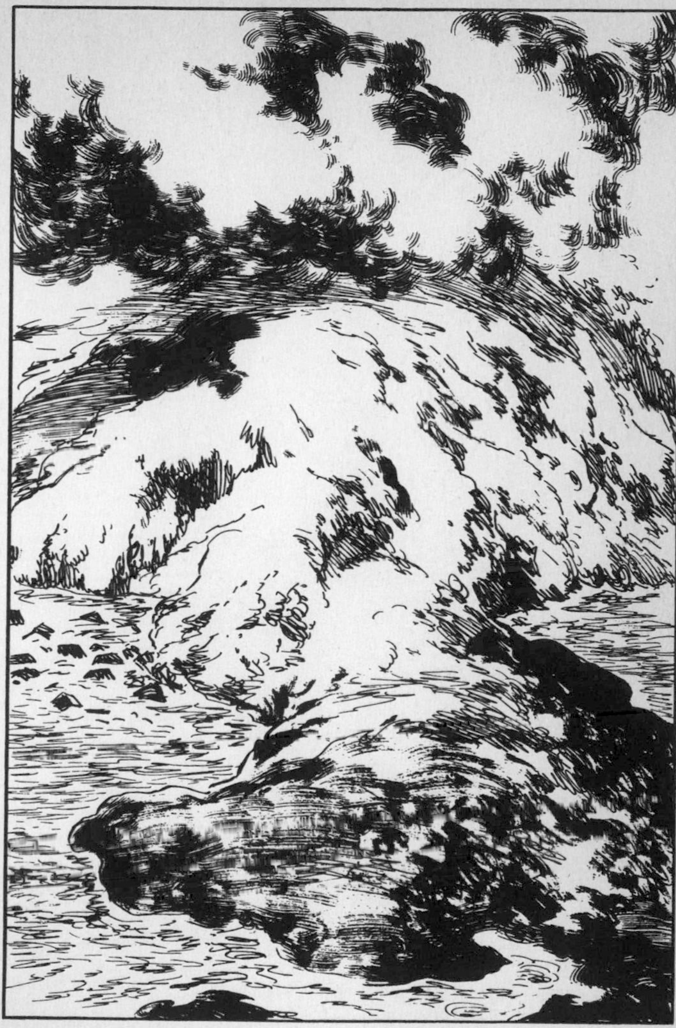

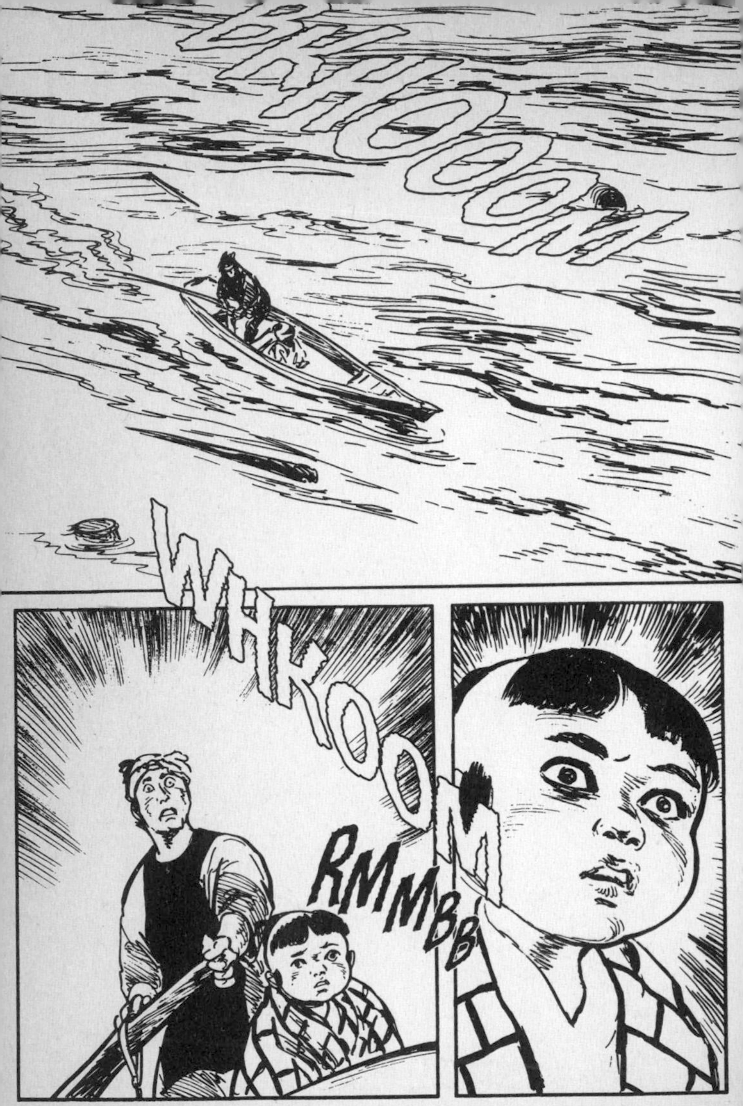
WHOOOM
RMMBB

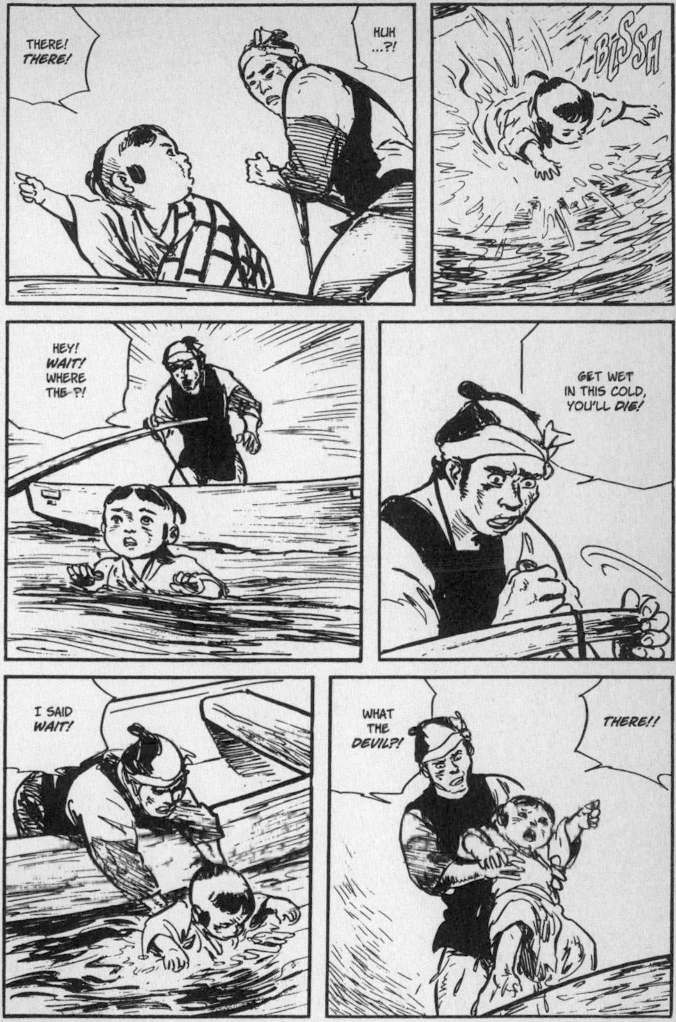
THERE! THERE!
HUH ...?!
BLSSH
HEY! WAIT! WHERE THE-?!
GET WET IN THIS COLD, YOU'LL DIE!
I SAID WAIT!
WHAT THE DEVIL?!
THERE!!

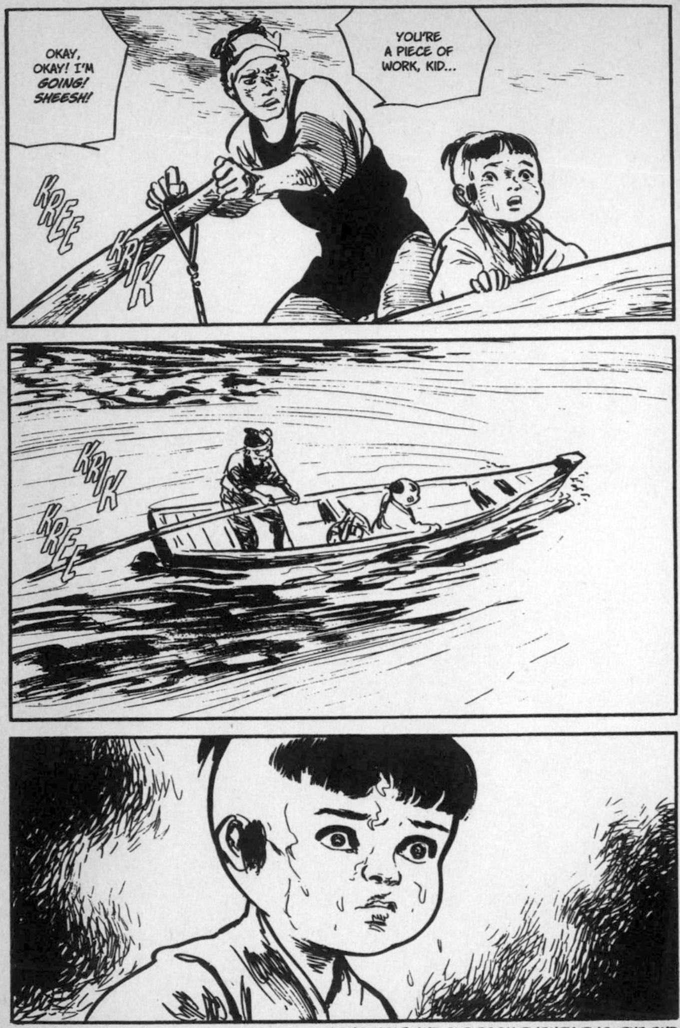
OKAY, OKAY! I'M GOING! SHEESH!
YOU'RE A PIECE OF WORK, KID...
KREE
KRIK
KRIK
KREE

LONE WOLF AND CUB BOOK TWENTY-TWO: THE END
TO BE CONTINUED

子連れ狼

GLOSSARY

buke
Samurai families.

bushi
A samurai. A member of the warrior class.

bushidō
The way of the warrior. Also known as *shidō*.

daimyō
A feudal lord.

daisuimon
One of the main water gates used to regulate tidal fluxes in Edo's rivers.

dōtanuki
A battle sword. Literally, "sword that cuts through torsos."

Edo
Edo was a castle town, that rose up around the moats and ramparts of Edo castle, the stronghold of the Tokugawa clan. The central core of the city, administered by the *machi-bugyō* city commissioner, who reported directly to the shōgun's senior councilors, and was demarcated on official maps by a black line, the *kurobiki*, and was called the *go-funai*.

enishi
A fateful, chance connection between two people.

funai
The central core of Edo (see *Edo*).

gozabune
A government official's ship.

honorifics
Japan is a class and status society, and proper forms of address are critical. Common markers of respect are the prefixes *o* and *go*, and a wide range of suffixes. Some of the suffixes you will encounter in *Lone Wolf and Cub*:
chan – for children, young women, and close friends
dono – archaic; used for higher-ranked or highly respected figures
san – the most common, used among equals or near-equals
sama – used for superiors
sensei – used for teachers, masters, respected entertainers, and politicians.

ki
Energy. The fundamental mind/body energy of Eastern medicine.

kuchiyaku
Kuchiyaku were the tasters for the

shōgun family. They were called kuchiyaku, or "official mouths," because they checked for poison with their own tongues.

machi-bugyō
The Edo city commissioner, combining the post of mayor and chief of police. A post held in monthly rotation by two senior Tokugawa vassals, in charge of administration, maintaining the peace, and enforcing the law in Edo. Their rule extended only to commoners; samurai in Edo were controlled by their own *daimyō* and his officers. The *machi-bugyō* had an administrative staff and a small force of armed policemen at his disposal.

measurements
bu – approximately 3 millimeters.
sun – approximately 3 centimeters.
shaku – ten *sun*, approximately 30 centimeters.
ri – approximately 4 kilometers (2.5 miles).

meifumadō
The Buddhist Hell. The way of demons and damnation.

ryū
Often translated as "school." The many variations of swordsmanship and other martial arts were passed down from generation to generation to the offspring of the originator of the technique or set of techniques, and to any *deishi* students that sought to learn from the master. The largest schools had their own *dōjō* training centers and scores of students. An effective swordsman had to study the different techniques of the various schools to know how to block them in combat. Many *ryū* also had a set of special, secret techniques that were only taught to school initiates.

the Shuu Jing
One of the Five Classics of early Chinese writing. Pronounced *shōkyo* in Japanese. The Classic of Documents, The Book of History.

tōtekirai
Hand-thrown explosives. A primitive hand grenade.

子連れ狼

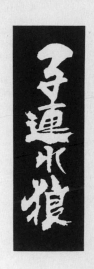

KAZUO KOIKE

Though widely respected as a powerful writer of graphic fiction, Kazuo Koike has spent a lifetime reaching beyond the bounds of the comics medium. Aside from co-creating and writing the successful *Lone Wolf and Cub* and *Crying Freeman* manga, Koike has hosted television programs; founded a golf magazine; produced movies; written popular fiction, poetry, and screenplays; and mentored some of Japan's best manga talent.

Lone Wolf and Cub was first serialized in Japan in 1970 (under the title *Kozure Okami*) in *Manga Action* magazine and continued its hugely popular run for many years, being collected as the stories were published, and reprinted worldwide. Koike collected numerous awards for his work on the series throughout the next decade. Starting in 1972, Koike adapted the popular manga into a series of six films, the *Baby Cart Assassin* saga, garnering widespread commercial success and critical acclaim for his screenwriting.

This wasn't Koike's only foray into film and video. In 1996, *Crying Freeman*, the manga Koike created with artist Ryoichi Ikegami, was produced in Hollywood and released to commercial success in Europe and is currently awaiting release in America.

And to give something back to the medium that gave him so much, Koike started the *Gekiga Sonjuku*, a college course aimed at helping talented writers and artists — such as *Ranma 1/2* creator Rumiko Takahashi — break into the comics field.

The driving focus of Koike's narrative is character development, and his commitment to character is clear: "Comics are carried by characters. If a character is well created, the comic becomes a hit." Kazuo Koike's continued success in comics and literature has proven this philosophy true.

GOSEKI KOJIMA

Goseki Kojima was born on November 3, 1928, the very same day as the godfather of Japanese comics, Osamu Tezuka. While just out of junior high school, the self-taught Kojima began painting advertising posters for movie theaters to pay his bills.

In 1950, Kojima moved to Tokyo, where the postwar devastation had given rise to special manga forms for audiences too poor to buy the new manga magazines. Kojima created art for *kami-shibai*, or "paper-play" narrators, who would use manga story sheets to present narrated street plays. Kojima moved on to creating works for the *kashi-bon* market, bookstores that rented out books, magazines, and manga to mostly low-income readers. He soon became highly popular among *kashi-bon* readers.

In 1967, Kojima broke into the magazine market with his series *Dojinki*. As the manga magazine market grew and diversified, he turned out a steady stream of popular series.

In 1970, in collaboration with Kazuo Koike, Kojima began the work that would seal his reputation, *Kozure Okami* (*Lone Wolf and Cub*). Before long the story had become a gigantic hit, eventually spinning off a television series, six motion pictures, and even theme song records. Koike and Kojima were soon dubbed the "golden duo" and produced success after success on their way to the pinnacle of the manga world.

When *Manga Japan* magazine was launched in 1994, Kojima was asked to serve as consultant, and he helped train the next generation of manga artists.

In his final years, Kojima turned to creating original graphic novels based on the movies of his favorite director, Akira Kurosawa. Kojima passed away on January 5, 2000 at the age of 71.

LONE WOLF AND CUB

子連れ狼

**VOLUME 1:
THE ASSASSIN'S ROAD
1-56971-502-5
$9.95 U.S., $14.95 Canada**

**VOLUME 2: THE GATELESS
BARRIER
1-56971-503-3
$9.95 U.S., $14.95 Canada**

**VOLUME 3: THE FLUTE OF
THE FALLEN TIGER
1-56971-504-1
$9.95 U.S., $14.95 Canada**

VOLUME 4:
THE BELL WARDEN
1-56971-505-X
$9.95 U.S., $14.95 Canada

VOLUME 5:
BLACK WIND
1-56971-506-8
$9.95 U.S., $14.95 Canada

VOLUME 6: LANTERNS FOR
THE DEAD
1-56971-507-6
$9.95 U.S., $14.95 Canada

VOLUME 7: CLOUD
DRAGON, WIND TIGER
1-56971-508-4
$9.95 U.S., $14.95 Canada

**VOLUME 8: CHAINS
OF DEATH**
1-56971-509-2
$9.95 U.S., $14.95 Canada

**VOLUME 9: ECHO OF
THE ASSASSIN**
1-56971-510-6
$9.95 U.S., $14.95 Canada

**VOLUME 10:
HOSTAGE CHILD**
1-56971-511-4
$9.95 U.S., $14.95 Canada

**VOLUME 11:
TALISMAN OF HADES**
1-56971-512-2
$9.95 U.S., $14.95 Canada

VOLUME 12:
SHATTERED STONES
1-56971-513-0
$9.95 U.S., $14.95 Canada

VOLUME 13: THE MOON IN THE
EAST, THE SUN IN THE WEST
1-56971-585-8
$9.95 U.S., $14.95 Canada

VOLUME 14: DAY OF
THE DEMONS
1-56971-586-6
$9.95 U.S., $14.95 Canada

VOLUME 15: BROTHERS
OF THE GRASS
1-56971-587-4
$9.95 U.S., $14.95 Canada

VOLUME 16:
GATEWAY INTO WINTER
1-56971-588-2
$9.95 U.S., $14.95 Canada

VOLUME 17:
THE WILL OF THE FANG
1-56971-589-0
$9.95 U.S., $14.95 Canada

VOLUME 18: TWILIGHT
OF THE KUROKUWA
1-56971-590-4
$9.95 U.S., $14.95 Canada

VOLUME 19: THE MOON
IN OUR HEARTS
1-56971-591-2
$9.95 U.S., $14.95 Canada

VOLUME 20:
A TASTE OF POISON
1-56971-592-0
$9.95 U.S., $14.95 Canada

VOLUME 21:
FRAGRANCE OF DEATH
1-56971-593-9
$9.95 U.S., $14.95 Canada

VOLUME 22:
HEAVEN AND EARTH
1-56971-594-7
$9.95 U.S., $14.95 Canada

VOLUME 23:
TEARS OF ICE
1-56971-595-5
$9.95 U.S., $14.95 Canada